2-50

A CENTURY OF
Cornhill
TESTS

A CENTURY OF
Cornhill
TESTS

BY KEN LAWRENCE
PHOTOGRAPHS BY PATRICK EAGAR
Foreword by David Gower

Patrick Stephens Limited

First published in 1995

British Library Cataloguing-in-
Publication Data:
A catalogue record for this book is
available from the British Library

ISBN: 1 85260 532 4

Library of Congress
catalog card no. 95 78116

Patrick Stephens Limited
is an imprint of Haynes Publishing,
Sparkford, Nr Yeovil, Somerset BA22 7JJ.

Designed and typeset by G&M,
Raunds, Northamptonshire
Printed in Britain by
Butler & Tanner Ltd,
London and Frome

Contents

Foreword

BY DAVID GOWER

Cornhill and I began our Test careers together on 1 June 1978. Not surprisingly, I remember it quite well, as most people making their international debut would, and not just because my first ball went crashing through square leg for four.

It was, as *Wisden* described it, 'an auspicious start'. Every time I look back on the hundred or so Tests I played after that, I thank my guardian angels that the man who delivered my first international long hop was only Liaqat Ali and not Imran Khan. It could have been worse: I could have been unlucky enough to make a debut a couple of years later against a West Indies attack that included Michael Holding, Andy Roberts, Joel Garner and Colin Croft – in *any* order – and I promise you that their long hops were a lot harder to deal with.

At least by coming into Mike Brearley's experienced side I could play myself in a little bit, learn from playing alongside some rather more seasoned pros, and take advantage of a below-strength Pakistan team to score some runs and build some confidence before taking on the best in the world.

As it happens, when that West Indies team played here in 1980, I did not play much of a part in the series at all, with just one appearance in the first Test and a summer spent rebuilding that early confidence before the tour to the Caribbean the following winter, where it all went a lot better for me.

So, in effect, Cornhill and I played ourselves in together. We were both just as green and wet behind the ears when it came to Test cricket, and whereas I could not claim to have been ever-present since that debut, they obviously have not missed a game.

If you cast your mind back to those days, you will remember that world cricket, not just English cricket, was under great pressure from the so-called Packer revolution. When Kerry Packer (KP to his mates, and Mr Packer to the rest of us) bought himself most of the top players in the world and set up his own competition in Australia and New Zealand in direct opposition to 'official' cricket, he actually did the whole cricketing world a huge favour by alerting the authorities world-wide to two things.

First, they had for far too long got away with blatant daylight robbery in not paying the players more than a pittance to represent their countries and, second, they had remained oblivious to the possibilities of marketing the game in any shape or form.

Packer's simple ploy of offering real money to his players was most appreciated by those concerned, and it paved the way for completely revised pay scales when the dust settled and cricket was handed back to the former governing bodies.

Which is where Cornhill came marching in for the season of 1978 and ever since, giving the TCCB the wherewithal to offer England players a 500% pay rise – well, at least to those who had played before – and a new incentive for people like me to make a living out of the game. Mind you, at 21, I would have played for nothing just for the privilege: and that is exactly what the problem had been – the authorities knew that men would play for their country and not argue the toss over finance.

Nowadays, everyone knows the real score. Cricket is big business, albeit still very minor compared to the genuinely global sports such as golf and tennis, and the game and the players are hugely grateful to sponsors all over the world.

Cornhill have long been established as the sponsors of English Test cricket, although it would seem that Cornhill's results have been a touch more consistent than England's over that period! It has been a wonderful relationship, with both sides deliriously happy with the benefits, and an outstanding feature of the deal has been the sheer friendliness of the relationship between the sponsors and the players.

For those of us who have been around since the beginning, a gentle stroll to the Cornhill marquee at the end of the day is like a trip to one's club, with a smiling welcome at the door and a glass of your favourite tipple automatically called for as you enter.

Cornhill's sponsorship of English Test cricket can be held high as a shining example of how well sport and business can mix. On behalf of all those many players who have been able to benefit as a result, here is a very big 'Thank you', and a toast to many more years of the same.

David Gower

David Gower is Cricket Consultant to National Westminster Bank, and Cricket Correspondent to the *Sunday Express*.

How it all began

At Old Trafford on 27 July 1995, whilst England were engaged in the Fourth Test match of the summer against the West Indies, Cornhill were celebrating a century – 100 Cornhill Test matches, not out. Here, for the first time, is the story of how, 18 years before, a virtually unknown insurance company gambled £1 million to become a household name and, by lifting cricket out of crisis, became a big name at Lord's.

It was a special year, 1977 – The Queen's Silver Jubilee. There had been a fairly quiet start to it. Red Rum had won the Grand National at Aintree for an historic third time and was fêted as a hero by the whole nation; Manchester United were warming up to win the FA Cup Final against Liverpool; and cricket was waiting, as it does with fresh floods of adrenalin every four years, for the arrival of the Australians. But, suddenly, cricket was thrown into deep crisis. When the 17 Aussie players had flown in to Heathrow, 13 of them had signed secret – and very lucrative – contracts to join a professional 'circus'. Kerry Packer, multi-millionaire head of a media chain, that included newspapers and TV, was hijacking the world's best players to play in matches to be televised on his Australian Channel 9. On 13 May he revealed that English players were also joining him – Tony Greig, John Snow, Derek Underwood and Alan Knott (later to be joined by Dennis Amiss; but not by Bob Woolmer, who had second thoughts). In England, the South African Tony Greig had been luring the English players to join Packer while on tour as England captain, and was immediately thrown out of the job, prompting the famous retort in *The Times* by John Woodcock: 'What has to be remembered is that he is not an Englishman by birth or upbringing but only by adoption. It is not the same thing as being English through and through.'

The piratical Packer was hugely rich; cricket was poor. The Test & County Cricket Board could not withstand his attack on their players any more than could Australia, the West Indies, India, Pakistan and South Africa. He was not a man to trifle with in business – and TV business was what this furore was all about. He wanted to show Australian Test cricket on his Channel 9, but the Australian Cricket Board refused to deal with him, sticking with Australia's version of the BBC. Infuriated, Packer decided to run his own teams and his own series. They would be playing under lights, with a white ball in garish clothing. Would the game, could the game, ever be the same again? Cricket boards held emergency meetings. At Lord's they knew their players should be paid more – but a Labour Government pay freeze restricted them. They even had meetings with the Chancellor, Denis Healey, to see how the situation could be resolved. There was, it seemed, just one way: find a sponsor who would insist that the players benefited. But where did the TCCB look for such a company?

Sponsors were not entirely new to cricket. The Gillette Cup was inaugurated back in 1963, then the John Player League and Benson & Hedges Cup. The World Cup had been sponsored by Prudential in 1975, and Peter Lush, then the Board's Promotions Manager, had negotiated a deal with Schweppes. However, slightly to everyone's surprise – if much to the Board's delight – they opted to attach their name not to the Test matches but to the County Championship. Lush remembers: 'While English cricket needed money badly for development of the game at grass roots [nothing changes, it seems!] it was also required to improve the salaries of players and umpires at Test level. Packer's arrival was earth shattering, totally unexpected and a real threat to the game internationally. Australia had to field a second team for quite a while, and people were pretty worried.'

As the days and weeks went by, with cricket getting more frantic and Packer ever more ruthless in his demands for co-operation over a TV deal, which the authorities saw as nothing but blackmail, meetings were continuing in the wood-panelled boardroom at 32 Cornhill, in the heart of the City of London. Cornhill were a well-established insurance company with a thriving motor insurance side. But, as their business was done through brokers, their name was far from well known. If they were to expand, they needed a higher profile – the only question for Cornhill was how this could be achieved. Cornhill General Manager, Cecil Burrows, his top Management team and Publicity advisers were looking at the traditional route of national advertising to raise awareness of the Cornhill name.

Packer's ravaging of English Test

cricket and Cornhill's quest for a high profile might have remained two separate events but for the fact that the Cornhill Publicity team took notice of news coverage of David Evans's attempt to halt the Packer bandwagon.

Ah! The Rt. Hon. David Evans. He is well known today: a colourful Member of Parliament, right-wing member of the 1922 Committee and one-time Chairman of Luton Town Football Club. If Kerry Packer was the catalyst of a revolution, the self-made Evans was the sort of man who led the way over the trenches. He may be a millionaire today, but he certainly was not in 1977, yet he put up his own money – £17,000 he thinks it was – to try to stop Packer. Evans was angered by Packer's intervention but, nonetheless, considering that Test players were being paid just £210 a match, felt it to be 'a good idea; but that we should have thought about it first.'

Evans took the brave step of offering to pay £1,000 per man for two Tests to stop more players joining Packer and, in the numerous press and television interviews that followed, appealed for a major sponsor to step forward and to offer long-term financial support to save the game he so loved.

Doug Insole, the former Essex and England batsman who was now Chairman of the TCCB, heard the one o'clock news on his car radio as he was driving to Trafalgar House in London's Berkeley Street. He had been ruminating on his journey at the plight of English cricket. The game had hardly been thriving during the seventies, but the 1975 World Cup had revitalised things a little, and grounds were full again. Then came Packer and, with him, a crisis. Now someone was offering to bail the game out – and he knew nothing about it. When he reached Trafalgar House his secretary rang to say that a whole posse of Pressmen was camped outside his office, and City Editors had been ringing him for a statement. 'It may all be rubbish – I know noth-

ing about it,' she was told, and Insole set about trying to reach Evans; but in vain. 'I simply couldn't get through to him. I didn't doubt that he was there, but he wasn't talking to me!'

Back at Cornhill, the Publicity team recognised the possibilities of both helping to preserve traditional Test cricket, part of England's heritage, and of doing something to solve their own company awareness problem. Ray Treen, now Cornhill's Chief Executive and then Cecil Burrow's deputy and part of the small Senior Management team involved, recalled: 'I don't think any of us knew that much about cricket, but we did know that there were tremendous possibilities, so we called the man we had seen on television and quoted in the newspapers – David Evans – who said that if we were serious about sponsoring the Tests, then we should speak to the TCCB and that we would have to act quickly.'

The Board Chairman now responded with alacrity. He organised a meeting and, together with Bernie

Coleman, the Board's Marketing Committee Chairman and a man to whom cricket owes a huge debt for his foresight and enterprise down the years, the Secretary to the Board, Donald 'DB' Carr, and Peter Lush went to Cornhill's head office. It was the meeting of the Cornhill grey suits and the Czars of Lord's that would ensure that cricket would never again be the poor relation of world sport. This was now the Tuesday of the week in August that England were due to play the Aussies in the final Test at The Oval. Cornhill made their offer and there was considerable debate. The Board wanted the money over a shorter period (£750,000 over three years) while Cornhill wanted a longer period. The company also wished to know what rights they could expect – matters like advertising boards, tickets, hospitality facilities and shirt advertising (the latter was refused, though Cornhill were promised first refusal in the future). And then Cornhill demanded that the whole deal was clinched in 48

hours. Doug Insole, taken aback, said that it was impossible, but Cornhill insisted that if it was not completed by the Friday they would withdraw.

Midway through the meeting a call was put through to the Boardroom. Everyone was staggered – it was a Press inquiry. Here they were in a secret meeting, yet a cricket writer, Brian Scovell of the *Daily Mail*, knew they were there. How? How does any big news story leak? No one knows. The TCCB wanted a three year deal, but Cornhill insisted on five – and on it being for a million pounds. The magic million, and all that. Cornhill then insisted that the announcement of their deal should be made on the Saturday, to make the Sunday newspapers. Lush, at the TCCB, remembers advising them to wait until the following Monday. 'I pointed out that, even if the Ashes had already been regained, the Sunday papers would be full of the match. The sponsorship deal would not get much space. But they were quite adamant, so I agreed – and they got lucky.' Rain

had affected the first two days and, with England 3-0 up in the series, it was all something of an anti-climax. Rain washed out most of Saturday, and Cornhill got all the publicity they could have wished. Cecil Burrows, 55 in 1977, had last played cricket at school. Now he was interviewed by Peter West on television and talked about 'cricket hitting a million' and his delight at helping to keep 'the great tradition of cricket alive.' And Doug Insole praised Cornhill for their 'magnificent support, based on all the right standards.' Thus the few lines that they might have received, had there been anything like a full day's play, became huge stories.

Throughout Friday – from early dawn until way past midnight – Cornhill's Publicity team toiled. They first planned how to tell every one of their 40 branches to ensure that the staff knew what was happening. Many seemed astonished that a company like theirs should be doing something so new, and that the boss was seen on

television. They produced a multi-page press release, and in the evening through until the small hours put the press pack together. There was time only for a drink and a sandwich at the pub next door, but it simply added to the excitement. The next morning, rain conveniently stopped play and the focus was on Cornhill at The Oval press conference, and then Cecil Burrows was interviewed on television.

Cornhill and David Evans treasure a copy of the cartoon that depicts quite brilliantly the summer-long fight for cricket's salvation in 1977. It shows a British bulldog seeing off an Australian mongrel trying to steal the ball and ruin the game. Between them they saved the game. As Peter Lush submits, 'Cornhill have been brilliant for cricket – immaculate sponsors. They certainly enabled players to be fairly rewarded for reaching the top of their tree.' But the Test & County Cricket Board played their part. They are not a body renowned for instantaneous action, let us say; their structure is built upon committees and, like Eartha Kitt's Englishmen, they always take their time. On this occasion, however, Insole ensured that no time was wasted. Each member of the Executive Committee was contacted as soon as the cricket contingent had reached Lord's after the meeting at 32 Cornhill. Then he, Carr and Lush

rang each of the 17 counties (Durham were not members in those far off days) to inform them of the action being taken, so that they would know before the press announcement. Insole recalls: 'Cornhill had made it clear they wanted a quick decision from us and a quick announcement. We had one or two other companies showing an interest, but Cornhill were quicker off the mark than them. Theirs was a reasonable offer, they were genuine, very earnest people and I felt we needed a swift decision.'

Then there were slight worries for Cornhill. Even for a company determined to promote itself, the expenditure of £1 million was a hard commercial decision. It was, though, only 0.2% of their premium income and was money that might well have been spent on national advertising. The stark fact was that only 2% of the population were aware of Cornhill, and the public were reluctant to insure with firms they had never heard of. So, having won the day as far as cricket was concerned, they now had to win the commercial war. It was their good fortune that Peter West was, apart from his television duties, a partner in West Nally, a sports promotion firm based in Berkeley Square, London. On the Monday morning after the sponsorship announcement, West Nally pre-

sented themselves on the doorstep of 32 Cornhill, offering their services. In the first place it was them – and, thereafter, Karen Earl who left West Nally to set up her own sports consultancy – who helped make it all work so brilliantly for Cornhill.

If any company wanted a textbook to see how sponsorship can work, or should work, they need only study the Cornhill experience. They developed a marketing mix which worked. There were advertising hoardings, banner boards and then their name on the scoreboard, which gave splendid exposure. There were Player of the Match and Player of the Series Awards and they looked after the Press, not simply with meals and drinks but with a whole host of statistics. The players were invited to the Cornhill hospitality tent at the end of each day's play – and they normally came. Crawford White, the ex-cricket writer for the *Daily Express*, was employed as a cricket adviser and press box liaison man. When 'Chalky' finally retired after doing a marvellous job for Cornhill, they appointed Bob Taylor, the former England wicketkeeper, as a cricket adviser. He even returned to Lord's after his retirement as a player to help England out of an injury crisis. He simply finished his glass of red wine in the Cornhill hospitality area, got his wicketkeeping gloves out of his car and rejoined his old colleagues in the dressing room and subsequently on the pitch! Overall, moreover, as Cornhill had no other major advertising they had a clear cut test. Explained Chief Executive Ray Treen: 'Our surveys showed just how successful we were. If we needed any more convincing, it came when we shared a marketing exercise with a major life assurance company through the AA. Cornhill received the greater response.'

One hundred Cornhill Test matches later, all concerned can look back and say, quite honestly, that the deal hammered out in 48 hours in 1977 was one in which everyone won – the game itself, the players, the umpires and an insurance company that is now very, very well known.

And in the beginning there was . . . a Press Conference. Flanked by Doug Insole (LEFT) and David Evans (RIGHT) Cecil Burrows tells the world of Cornhill's £1 million, five-year deal.

Introduction

I am very happy to have been part of the Cornhill management team that took the initiative, some 18 years ago, of becoming the sponsors of English Test cricket. Our objective was to gain the public awareness and prestige that such a sponsorship would bring, and we are very pleased that this aim has been successfully achieved.

Over these 18 years, Cornhill has worked very closely with the Test & County Cricket Board, starting with our negotiations in 1977 with Doug Insole, the then Chairman of the TCCB. Since that time, many other well-known figures have occupied that chair – Raman Subba Row, Charles Palmer, Frank Chamberlain and the current occupant, Dennis Silk.

Our long association has also enabled us at Cornhill to build many friendships in the world of cricket. Names like Alec and Eric Bedser, the later Peter May, Ted Dexter and Alan (AC) Smith, immediately spring to mind.

Test cricket is now one of the most high-profile sports in this country.

We are proud to have continued our support of English Test cricket for over 18 years, through both the ups and downs of England's results. This book relives the most exciting stories from this period and seeks to combine the cricket action of the first 100 Cornhill Tests with the performances of those who have so enriched the game. We hope you enjoy this book and its many memories.

Ray Treen
Chief Executive

1978

Had anyone known how the depressingly wet summer of 1978 was going to turn out, they would have played 'The Entry of the Gladiators' over the Tannoy system as the flags of England and Pakistan were unfurled above Edgbaston on 1 June. You could, I suppose, have argued that Cornhill Insurance were gladiators in their way – a little known insurance company who had 'invested' £1 million to sponsor Test match cricket. And, indeed, their golden hoardings were ringing this famous old cricket ground to commemorate what was for them, and for cricket, a momentous day; a debut of what, in 18 years, would become a glorious century. But it was the entry of the young gladiators, I.T. Botham and D.I. Gower, who lifted the gloom of the whole summer. If the rain had come to Cornhill's aid the previous August – when it stopped play at The Oval and they had announced their sponsorship deal to handsome headlines – it must have given them cause

David Gower announced his arrival on the Test match scene with a pull for four off the first ball he received. He was 21, in his first Test, and the nonchalance of the stroke left everyone at Edgbaston breathless with excitement. He continued, making a cultured 58, helping England to 452 for eight declared.

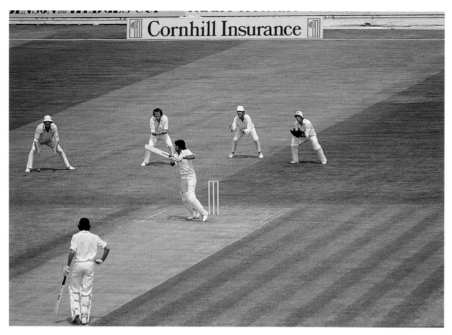

The first day at Edgbaston in June 1978. Javed Miandad is batting and Cornhill announce their arrival as Test match sponsors with the boundary advertising board.

to wonder whether they were doing quite the right thing. And when the Pakistan party arrived they were hardly echoing Browning's words: 'Oh, to be in England; Now that April's there . . .' April was pretty desperate and so was May, and so was June . . .

The Pakistan side lost 12 days of their 48-day programme, and another 13 were quite badly affected. Yet there were the new Cornhill banners, shining out like golden ingots, there was the new golden boy, David Gower, pulling his first ball in Test cricket for four. 'What a princely entrance,' murmured that prince of commentators, John Arlott. Then, as if in afterthought: 'My, this boy is good.' And there was Botham, a Botham so exciting that Wisden was announcing him as 'possibly our greatest find since Walter Hammond, 50 years ago.'

But, sadly, it was also a series of controversy as well as frustration. Pakistan – justifiably – omitted from their squad those who signed for Kerry Packer (those hilariously being dubbed in the market places of Lahore, Hyderabad and suchlike as 'the Packerstanis'). Thus weakened, England beat them comfortably, two-nil (both by an innings), with the last

Test damp, dreary and drawn. Indeed, the one and only player who left Leeds happy was Sadiq Mohammad, their opener, who hit 97 to claim the Player of the Match award – one of the bonuses introduced by Cornhill to reward underpaid cricketers.

But despite the goodwill being generated by the new sponsors, there

was an unpleasant taste to the whole series. For the first time in Test cricket in England, players were wearing helmets, both for batting and fielding. Eighteen years on there are those who still decry their arrival – but one incident at Edgbaston supported arguments in favour of the helmet. Following on on the Saturday, Pakistan sent in the left-handed tail-ender Iqbal Qasim as night-watchman in the penultimate over. On Monday, the fourth and final morning, Bob Willis hurled three bouncers at the non-batsman: nasty, lifting deliveries that flew just over his head. Unruffled – or apparently unruffled – Qasim defied England for 40 minutes before Willis, changing the angle of his attack, scorched a lifting ball into the batsman's face. Blood flowed, stitches were required; then complaints flowed and diplomacy was required. Pakistan manager Mahmood Hussain protested that Willis was unfair, bowling as he did at a 'non-recognised batsman'. Mike Brearley, England's captain, argued that Qasim looked a competent defensive batsman and would not accept that Willis bowled too many bumpers. He got little support from the Test and County Cricket Board, however. They said that they 'bitterly

Chris Old became only the second bowler in history to take four wickets in five balls, a performance that helped him to Cornhill's Player of the Match award at Edgbaston.

It's the age of the helmet, the first sign of self-preservation, as Bob Willis bowls to Sadiq Mohammad at Edgbaston.

regretted' the incident and 'reminded' their captain of his responsibilities.

Although there would be greater controversies in series with Pakistan in the years ahead, it was an unhappy affair. Rather than disputes in the headlines, the need was for on-field dramas to keep cricket interesting, and the new generation in David Gower and Ian Botham, and the slightly senior one in the shape of Chris Old, provided them. Gower, a blond-haired debutant of 21, struck his first ball in Test cricket for four; a nonchalant pull that marked him down as sheer class. Botham had already played in five Tests, but now gave notice that he, too, was going to be around a long time. He scored 100 precisely, striking the ball immensely hard. Clive Radley, today the senior MCC coach at Lord's, hit 106 but was out-paced by the ebullient Botham at Edgbaston. At Lord's in the second Test no one was to outshine him. After scoring a dazzling century he wound up the game with 8-34 – the best bowling by an Englishman since Jim Laker took 9 for 37 and 10 for 53 in that historic match against the Aussies at Old Trafford in 1956. Before he launched into the New Zealanders, 'Both' had taken 13 Pakistan wickets at 16.07, as well as topping the batting averages (212 runs in his three innings at 70.66).

Such deeds were enough to win him the Player of the Series award, but despite the fact that England's batsmen piled up 452-8 declared at Edgbaston, it was Chris Old, the Yorkshire swinger, who stole Cornhill's first Player of the Match award; he took four wickets in five balls (a quite unique performance, equalled only by M.J.C. Allom on his England debut against New Zealand in 1929/30, and by Wasim Akram in 1990/91) and finished with seven for 50. After the fired-up Willis had softened up the opposition, he had reduced Pakistan from 125-5 to 125-9 in just five deliveries. Moving the ball late on a pitch he appreciated,

The full power of Ian Botham's destructive stroke play is evident at Lord's as he has the close-in Pakistan fielder Javed Miandad leaping for safety.

Anxious fielders gather around tailender Qasim after he was hit in the mouth by a rising ball from Bob Willis (on the right), an incident which sparked fury and then an apology from the TCCB.

the scorebook recorded his over thus: 0 w w nb w w 1. He took 143 wickets in a 46-Test career, but this was always going to be the highlight. The gladiators would be testing their powers against sterner opposition in the years ahead, but New Zealand who followed Pakistan in this summer of '78 would not be providing it.

NEW ZEALAND TOUR

There was one statistic at the close of the 1978 season that haunted New Zealand's players to Hallowe'en and beyond. It was there in the first class batting averages. Right on top was C.E.B. Rice, Clive of South Africa, patron saint of Nottinghamshire cricket. Second was G.M. Turner of Worcestershire; Glenn Turner of New Zealand! His figures

would have left any batsman happy: 38 innings, seven times not out, 1,711 runs in the season, with a not out top score of 202 and an average of 55.19. They just made New Zealanders mad, for Turner opted to play for his English county during the summer that New Zealand were touring here, seeking their first victory in England. They struggled all summer, never getting enough runs, and they duly lost all three Tests. What might they have achieved had Turner been playing with them, rather than for Worcestershire in his benefit season? That is merely a rhetorical question; it serves to anger New Zealanders still and has no answer.

The fact of the matter is that Geoff Howarth batted manfully against high quality bowling from Bob Willis (according to Botham, the *only* world class English quickie during his years on the Test scene), 'Both' himself and

Phil Edmonds – Howarth averaged 74.00, scoring 296 runs, including the only Test century New Zealand managed; and John Wright was next to him in their averages with 116 runs at 29.00. They are telling figures and Turner would most certainly have fared better than Wright.

At The Oval, staging the first rather than last game of a series for once, Gower maintained his momentum, becoming the youngest since Peter May to score a century, and winning Trevor Bailey's vote as Player of the Match. He went through his whole range of shots before being run out for 111, always elegant, occasionally a little careless – a criticism that was to dog the rest of his career, of course. He and Botham were exciting, the one a right-handed bludgeon the other a left-handed rapier. Troubled at times by a shoulder injury, David showed this early that

David Gower pulls a four in the mid-wicket area at The Oval on his way to becoming the youngest English player since Peter May to score a Test century.

Geoff Boycott returned to the England side at Trent Bridge, scoring 131 in almost seven hours, and ensuring that England reached 429 for a victory by an innings

Robert Anderson can keep on running – straight back to the pavilion. David Gower's pinpoint throw has him run out for a duck at Trent Bridge.

RIGHT Geoff Howarth, batting here at Lord's where he scored 123 in the final Test, could have done with the solidity that Glenn Turner might have supplied in his often lone battle against high quality bowling.

his under-arm throw could be deadly; his running out of Robert Anderson in the second Test at Trent Bridge was superb. He swooped in from the covers, could see but one stump yet hit it. Botham had the added advantage of his bowling, which alone would have carried him into the Test side. At The Oval he took only four wickets. When they moved on to Trent Bridge he took nine in the match (for 93).

A familiar figure returned after missing four Tests – Geoffrey Boycott. He had suffered the ignominy back in February of captaining England to their first-ever defeat by New Zealand in Wellington. Now, on those huge acres in south-east London, he exacted some revenge, batting for five

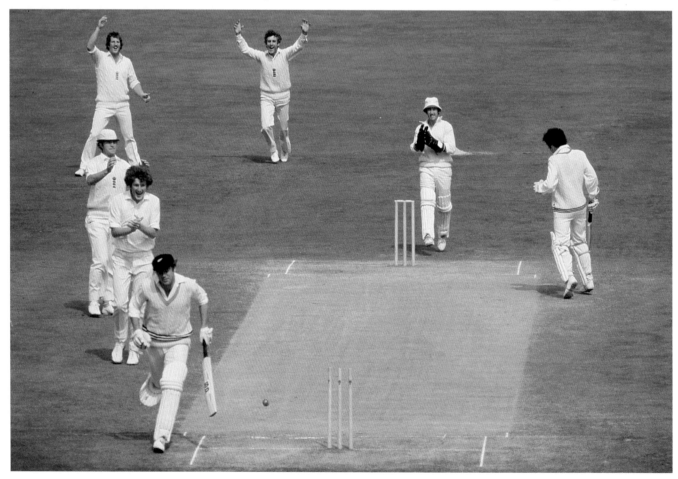

Is there no limit to the man's abilities? Not content with taking 11 wickets in the match at Lord's, Ian Botham brilliantly runs out Richard Hadlee.

minutes short of *seven hours*, in scoring 131. Had Botham or Gower batted for seven hours they might well have scored twice that figure, but this was Boycott – reliable, dependable and a trifle slow! His impact on the final Test at Lord's was negligible, however. After Howarth's gallant 123 (all the more meritorious for the fact that he had influenza and had one totally sleepless night), which helped New Zealand to their only first innings lead in the series, Willis and Botham destroyed them. Starting their second innings with a lead of 50, hopes of repeating their Wellington victory were high.

Botham, who had collected six first innings scalps, now hit the stumps three times as he claimed five more (match figures of 11 for 140). Willis had four (for 16) as New Zealand collapsed in 160 minutes for 67. England, requiring 118, had a rocky start, losing Boycott and Radley for only 14 to Hadlee, but it was totally appropriate that David Ivon Gower should make batting look simple on a most difficult track. He scored 46, and at 84-3, with Graham Gooch still standing firm, England were poised for a clean sweep.

Gower's first season in Test cricket thus concluded with 438 runs in the two series at almost 55. And Botham? He batted better against Pakistan, but bowled well all summer long. His 263 runs averaged around 44, and his 37 wickets cost him about 15 apiece. More important, perhaps, his final five wicket haul against the New Zealanders was his eighth such tally in 21 innings. There was majesty abroad. It was a modest season of cricket for Cornhill's debut, but two crown princes who might rule the kingdom for many seasons to come were being hailed.

1979

The Monument in the City of London is a towering 202-foot high, while Sunil Gavaskar is barely 5 ft. 5 in. in his boots. But the Indian opener must have seemed as dominating and as immovable as The Monument to England's bowlers during 1979.

The Indians began their tour in deep distress having lost all three of their games in the Prudential World Cup at the start of the summer (one, most humiliatingly, to Sri Lanka). And out of their 16 first class matches they won just one. In the four-game Test series they had moments of glory, but never seemed likely to overwhelm an England side in which Geoff Boycott, David Gower and – most particularly – the brilliant Ian Botham were at their peak. Until, that is, the final match at The Oval. There they shared in one of the most gripping Tests ever played. Had it been a boxing match it would have been said that they slugged it out, toe to toe, for 15 rounds.

The run machine from Fitzwilliam: Geoffrey Boycott scoring his first hundred of the 1979 summer at Edgbaston. Wicketkeeper Reddy can only ruefully admire.

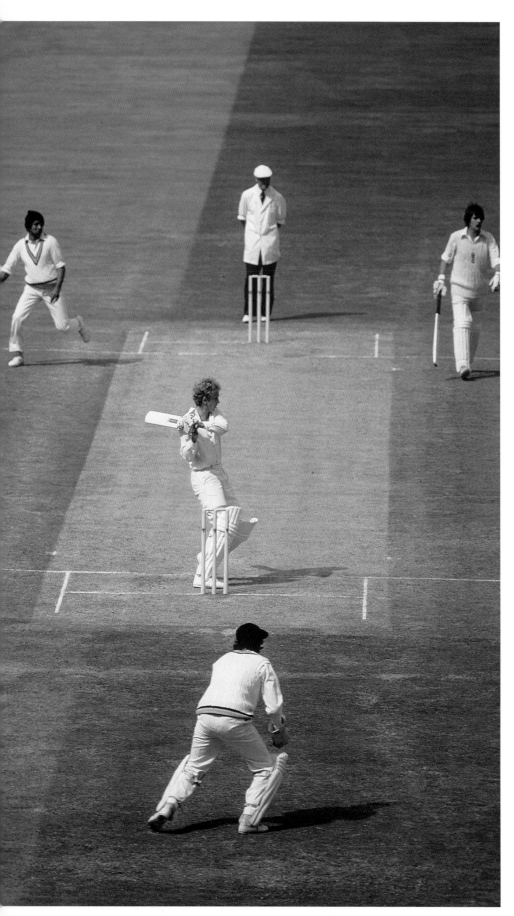

David Gower, in scintillating form at Edgbaston against India. An unbeaten 200 was just one reason he won his second Cornhill Player of the Match award.

Basically, they did.

Gavaskar began this final fray with a tally of runs and an average that underlined his consistency: 308 at a smidgen above 60. Now he would rewrite the record books and produce an epic that had even English fans feeling sympathy for a fight back that went without the reward of victory. With three balls left, any one of four results was still possible – an Indian win that would have levelled the series 1-1, a draw, a tie, or an England victory. But to start at the beginning, England batted, if without histrionics, for 305. Kapil Dev, a 20-year-old all-rounder who bore the brunt of the bowling throughout the tour (16 Test wickets from 173 overs), and the skipper, Venkataraghavan (today considered one of the world's top umpires), took three apiece, and the innings was notable for the fact that Botham, with the third of his 38 runs, became the fastest in history to reach 1,000 Test runs and 100 wickets. He then proceeded, with help from Willis and Hendrick, to despatch India for 202. Boycott, the run machine from Fitzwilliam, added a second hundred to the one he scored in the first Test at Edgbaston, and at 334-8 Mike Brearley declared.

India had 500 minutes to score 438, and they made a convincing start towards an improbable target. Gavaskar, known universally as Sunny, relished the fight. They knocked off 76 on the Monday and then went on during the final day at just under 50 an hour for three hours. After 5 hours 15 minutes batting, Chauhan nicked Willis to be caught by Botham: 213-l. Vengsarkar stepped up the pace, and tea arrived with India 304-l; and when the last 20 overs were due, India needed only 110 with nine wickets in hand. In seven-and-a-half hours England had missed nothing in the field, but now Botham dropped Vengsarkar on the long-off boundary off Willey. He quickly atoned – in Edmonds's next over Vengsarker dollied one to mid-wicket and Botham gobbled it: 366-2. Venkat then made the mistake that probably cost India the match. He changed the batting order. Instead of the experienced Viswanath, the big-hitting Kapil Dev entered – and immediately exited (caught Gooch, bowled Willey) – 367-3. Gavaskar and Sharma added 22, and with eight overs left Brearley brought back Botham, ever the man for the occasion. The wily Brearley, having slowed the over rate, then called for a drinks break – and concentration thus disturbed, after eight long hours and nine minutes, Gavaskar holed out to Gower. He had scored 221 chanceless runs in something over eight hours, with a summer's aggregate of 542 runs at an average of 77.42. Lacking their anchor man, India lost their momentum. Viswanath went to Willey and, having struck the critical blow by getting Gavaskar, Botham had Singh and Sharma leg-before in successive

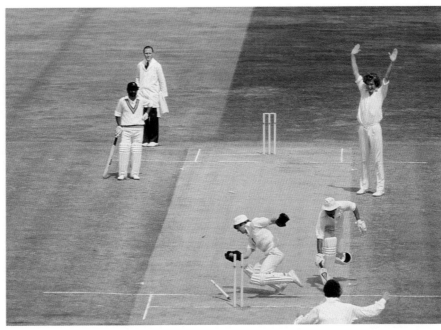

Bob Taylor was too quick for Gavaskar at Edgbaston, running him out for 61. But the little master had the final laugh – 542 Test runs, more than any other batsman in the series.

overs. Brearley's astuteness had paid off. Botham's last four overs had brought three wickets for 17 and India were struggling with a 15 run target from the final six balls. It was too much for them.

No picnics on the second day at Lord's. Rain meant no play, either.

LEFT *'The finest innings in 20 years'* – *Ian Botham on his way to 137 (out of England's 270) at Headingley.*

RIGHT *A typically peerless Gavaskar drive during his innings of 78 at Headingley.*

BELOW *Sunil Gavaskar was in his most supreme form at The Oval, scoring 221 and setting up a great finale to the 1979 series – any one of four results possible with three balls remaining. Here he is untroubled by the close attention of Botham, wicketkeeper David Bairstow and Mike Hendrick.*

An historic moment at Lord's; Ian Botham has Gavaskar caught to give him his 100th Test wicket. Then, at The Oval, he scored his 1000th run to become, at 23 and after 21 Tests, the fastest to complete the double.

England's series-winning victory had come in the first Test at Edgbaston where Boycott struck 155 and where the young Gower was in scintillating form. The left-hander was unbeaten with 200, that earned him Cornhill's Player of the Match award (his second – having been thus acclaimed in the first Test against New Zealand the previous summer). That they lost by only an innings and 83, India had Gavaskar (61 and 68) and Viswanath (78 and 51) to thank. If they wished to apportion blame, it would have been heaped on Botham (seven for 156 in the match), and

Mike Hendrick (six for 75). At Lord's, what seemed a comfortable England win was foiled by Vengsarkar (103) and Viswanath (113) after a five wicket haul by Botham had destroyed India in their first innings. In just 2 years and 19 days, and in only his 19th Test, 'Both' took his 100th wicket when Brearley quite brilliantly caught Gavaskar. Bowled out for 96, India faced a deficit of 323 as a Gower-inspired England piled up 419-9. But the two centurions stayed together for 210 runs in 5 hours 20 minutes to save the day.

Just as the second day at Lord's was washed out, so was Headingley again hit by bad weather – rain prevented play from Thursday afternoon to the Monday - but then the Yorkshire faithful were treated to what Jim Laker, the match adjudicator, called 'one of the finest innings in the past 20 years.' From whom? Ian Botham, of course! He at least proved he was human when he took the ball: 13 overs and not a single wicket!

1980

The West Indians were, of course, the main menu in 1980, but the Australians were also here, a sort of savoury after the main course, for the Cornhill sponsored Centenary Test. They had celebrated the very first meeting of the two countries at Melbourne in 1977; Lord's staged the 100th anniversary of the first match on English soil. That, as it happened, was not at Thomas Lord's green acres but across the river at The Oval. One hundred years on, the Kennington ground put on the hors-d'oeuvre – a 'wrinklies' match between Old England and Old Australia. (The Aussies won this one, also!)

One can only assume that the rain-maker somewhere up there was not in those days a cricket man. It rained. What should have been an all-time jamboree, finished like a fall-out between relatives. Some 200 or so former Aussie stars and a few English ones, like Lock, Loader and the immortally lionised Larwood (who had made their homes 'down under'), together with a veritable army of administrators, were flown in for the party. It has never been possible to walk all around Lord's without bumping into someone you know or some famous face or other. In 1980 you couldn't walk five yards without doing so. The Lord's Taverners suggested that Cornhill took over a

Kim Hughes delighted Lord's fans with a splendid century in the Centenary Test.

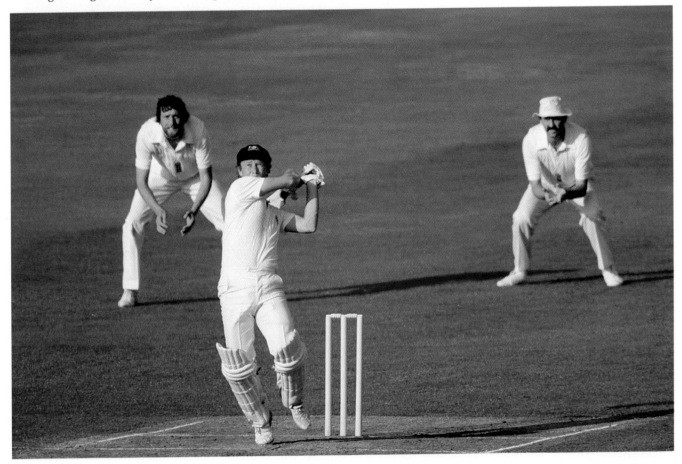

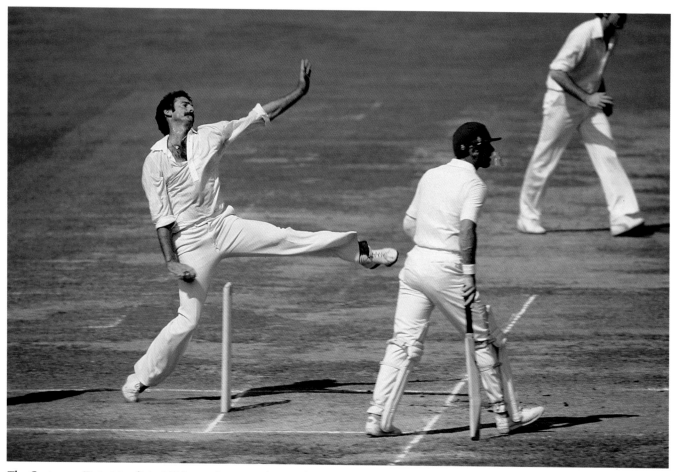

The Centenary Test at Lord's in 1980 was the excuse for 200 former England and Australian Test players to congregate at Lord's and for that greatest of fast bowlers, Dennis Lillee, to demonstrate his classic action in taking five wickets in the Cornhill Test.

London theatre for the night to entertain all the visitors, and that ensured the party was off to a good start. But the weather, coupled with a scene involving, believe it or not, two members of the MCC and the umpires and players on the steps of the pavilion on the Saturday, changed the tone considerably. Sadly, the incident was seen by TV viewers; MCC apologised to the umpires, Dickie Bird and David Constant, and took the 'necessary disciplinary action'.

It all stemmed from a reluctance on the part of the umpires to resume play when most people except the England captain and themselves felt play was possible after the fifth pitch inspection. For the first and only time, the President of the MCC, Mr S.C. 'Billy' Griffith, interfered, urging the umpires to get on with some cricket. They did, but when they passed through the Long Room to resume play, they had a police escort.

Kim Hughes scored 117 in the first innings (to push his claim to be captain of Australia after Greg Chappell) and 84 in the second, and Graeme Wood scored a dogged century as well. Set 370 to win at something over one run a minute, England ducked the challenge. Boycott played as he seemed to enjoy the most, grinding out another 100, taking his Test aggregate to 7,115 runs, thus overtaking Don Bradman and Len Hutton. It was his sixth century against the Aussies and his 19th in total, but do figures always tell the full story?

WEST INDIES TOUR

England faced the 1980 summer with a new captain – and an old problem. Mike Brearley had stepped down, and Alec Bedser, then chair-

man of the England selectors, took his advice and called in Ian Botham. At 24 he was a 'veteran' of 22 Test matches, but while a brilliant all-rounder he was an unknown quantity when it came to man-management and leadership. Well known was the problem that the West Indians brought with them: five high-quality fast bowlers and a slow over rate. Oh, yes: also perhaps the best batsman in the world – I.V.A. Richards, a friend of Botham's off the field. On it was another matter; as England would find out. Graham Gooch scored 394 runs in this series; Viv Richards totalled 379, but he collected his in only six innings, whereas Goochie batted 10 times.

That England lost only one Test with the rest drawn was entirely because of the weather. It was the wettest summer in 26 years. Eight hours were lost at Lord's, and more than 10 at Old Trafford. At The Oval

Viv Richards shared in a magnificent partnership of 223 with Haynes at Lord's, scoring 145 himself, of which 100 came in boundaries – and this was just one of them, off Botham.

a day went, but there was still an exciting finish; and at Leeds, where the fifth was played, two more days were rained off – making a grand total of seven.

Botham ruminates to this day on what might have been at Nottingham. As if to show that the cares of office were not going to bother him, he top scored with 57 out of England's modest 263. When Gordon Greenidge and Richards carried West Indies reply to 107-l, things looked ominous. Suddenly finding some of the assistance that Andy Roberts (5-72) and Joel Garner (3-44) had found in groundsman Ron Allsopp's pitch, Mike Hendrick had Greenidge caught behind by Alan Knott (the Packer 'rebels' were now acceptable to the England selectors). Faoud Bacchus posed a threat, but it was Willis who halted the flow and finally restricted West Indies to 308. A second innings of 252 gave England a lead of only 208, and even though Greenidge went early, a typical Richards innings, laced with eight boundaries, turned matters West Indies' way. Botham, though troubled by a niggling back (which caused him to wear a corset later in the summer) trapped him just before the fourth day's play ended for 48, but only 99 were required on the following morning.

Only! England fought them, tooth and claw. Desmond Haynes was dropped on 23, one of two chances that went astray in the slips. Willis was bowling superbly – and, despite Haynes, was making inroads. With 13 still required Andy Roberts heaved the ball towards cover, where David Gower, the safest of safe catchers, was waiting. The golden boy dropped it. It is the moment that still wakes Botham in a cold sweat, leaving him wondering what might have been. A match is won and lost by many factors, not a single dropped catch, but when one recalls that

Desmond Haynes highlighted the Lord's Test with a supreme innings of 184 which bettered Clyde Walcott's 168 in 1950, the previous best by a West Indian on the ground.

High, wide and handsome – Graham Gooch on his way to a rock-like 123 at Lord's.

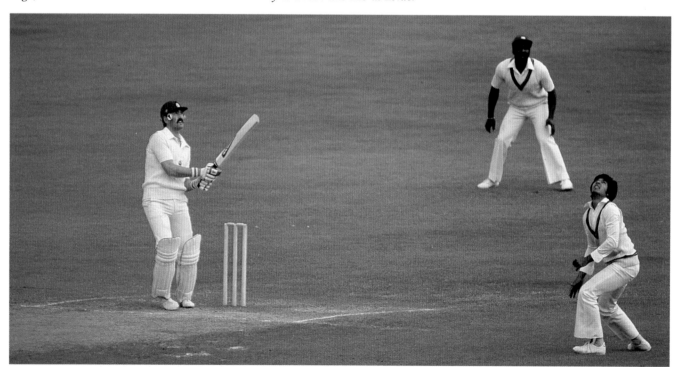

Clive Lloyd helped himself to his 13th Test hundred on the Old Trafford ground of his adopted county, Lancashire.

Haynes, who went on to make 62 after being dropped in the slips and was then brilliantly run out by Peter Willey, left the field in tears thinking that his dismissal would bring his side defeat, Botham is entitled to wonder how the course of history might have changed if Gower had clung on. Instead, the West Indies clung on for a two-wicket victory that would settle the series.

After losing his partner, Boycott, at 20, Gooch went on to make 123 in bad light at Lord's, but the highlight at headquarters was the partnership between Haynes and Richards. The former hit 184 before falling leg before to Botham (to his credit, the captain accepted the heaviest workload, bowling 37 overs), and Richards – with 100 in fours – scored a supreme 145. Not even the weather could stop Clive Lloyd, West Indies' skipper, from compiling his 13th hundred on his county ground, which won him the Cornhill Player of the Match award if not the spoils of victory at Old Trafford. He was denied a win at The Oval by Peter Willey's first Test match hundred (he hit a second on the winter tour to West Indies). England contrived to reach 92-9 in their second innings, a lead of only 197, but Willey and Willis (24 not out) carried England to safety at 209-9, at which point Botham declared and they all went home – England with a sense of considerable relief. One has to think that if the West Indies had bowled their overs quicker than 12 or so an hour they might have got a few more in and they might have got the result they were after. Well, it is just a thought.

1981

Mention the year 1981 in a room full of men, and one will immediately reply, 'Ah! Headingley.' Another is just as likely to add: 'And Botham,' for they are synonymous. You don't have one without the other, even to this day. Grandfathers will set grandsons on their knees and tell the tale of England's greatest cricketing days. I was there, they may say.

Really. Just as time lends enchantment to the memories, so it does to distances, for many of them were not within 100 miles of the famous old Yorkshire cricket ground on those July days when the nation came to a standstill. In High Streets up and down the land where Currys and other TV sales or rental stores attracted huge and enraptured groups, in

offices and on workshop floors everyone stopped to watch television sets or listen to the nearest radio. For this was the biggest upset since Goliath lost on a tko. Australia were in England attempting to regain the Ashes. England, in some crisis under Ian Botham's leadership, contrived to lose the first Test at Nottingham. Botham's own form was under scruti-

There were nine wickets for Terry Alderman at Trent Bridge. This is one of them – Paul Downton leg before for just three runs.

ny (as, indeed, was that of his fast bowler Bob Willis) and the Aussies turned the screw. The legendary Dennis Lillee (three wickets in England's first innings) and the studious new boy, Terry Alderman (four), speared England through the heart with five apiece in England's second knock, setting up their team's four-wicket win.

The selectors deliberated long and hard about Botham. That his form had deserted him was not in dispute; but the question was whether the burden of captaincy was to blame? They chose to allow him one more drink in the last chance saloon – at Lord's. The Australian captain, Kim Hughes, was less hospitable. He put England in (as he had at Trent Bridge) and 'Both' was leg before to Geoff Lawson for a duck in the first innings, bowled Ray Bright in the second for another. Head down all

the way, his despair was obvious as he walked back in – a fallen hero. Willis, affected by a viral infection, did not bowl well, dishing up 32 no-balls in the match and, once the weather ended the contest as a draw, Botham offered his resignation before the trap door was sprung. It was not the first case of cricket euthanasia – but it was possibly the one of most import. For Botham himself, it was 'like a huge weight being lifted.' He had never accepted that he couldn't handle the captaincy – he always believed his form would return. Not even he could have dreamed just how.

Mike Brearley was cajoled into a return. He had scored a hundred against the Aussies for Middlesex, but it was his inspirational leadership England needed now. Willis was left out of the Headingley squad, then reselected when he assured Alec

Bedser that he would be fit. To avoid unnecessary disappointment, an invitation that had in the meantime been sent to Mike Hendrick was quickly recalled. It was intercepted by his Derbyshire club and quietly destroyed before it reached its destination. Destiny was in the mixing bowl.

Australia again won the toss, but this time batted under a traditional grey Leeds sky. Dropped catches and a dogged maiden Test hundred from John Dyson saw Australia on 203-3 when rain ended play on the first day. It seemed the launch pad to a huge total as the Aussies advanced to 332-5. But suddenly, dramatically, Botham the lost cause became Botham the great white hope again. It was the psychology of Brearley that England had to thank for this, the first, breakthrough. Botham had been tinkering with his action, moving sideways

John Dyson hit a century in the first innings, but he is another Headingley victim for Willis in the second.

At full pace and in full flow – Leeds belonged to two men in 1981, Ian Botham and Bob Willis. Willis is at full pace on his way to eight wickets for 43 and Botham is in full flow on his way to 149.

before releasing the ball, to try to get more swing. Brearley told him to go back to his old ways, simply putting his back into it. He did, to some effect. At a cost of only 35 runs, he took the wickets of Hughes, Border, Yallop, Lawson and Marsh, giving him an analysis of 6-95. Some noticed that he had not performed like it since he had taken on the captaincy. No matter. There were problems ahead; more work to be done. Lillee, Alderman and Lawson had England on the run. Only Botham denied them, with a fiercely hit 50 (his first, incidentally, in 20 Test innings) before he became Rod Marsh's 264th victim, which allowed the Aussie 'keeper to overtake Alan Knott's record. England followed on, 227 behind. Before close of play Graham Gooch had fallen to Lillee, out – ignominiously – for the second time in the same day, having faced just four deliveries. If there was anything to mar the memory of the occa-

RIGHT Ian Botham in his glory game at Headingly in 1981. He could not recall one defensive shot!

Ian Botham acknowledges the applause from an enraptured Yorkshire crowd as he reaches three figures.

sion it was that – as at Lord's – there was a furore over the ending of play when the light was good enough to play on and make up for lost time; but a fatalistic feeling remained that a draw was inevitable. Certainly the bookmakers thought so. Ladbrokes man, Ron Pollard, posted his odds (500-1 an England victory), booked out of his hotel and went home to London. It wasn't very often Mr Pollard got it wrong, but this time he did. A couple of Aussie players had a small bet, but their hopes of a 'killing' were not high when Brearley, Gatting and Gower were out in little more than an hour on the Monday morning. England were 41-4. It was an improvement when Boycott and Willey (who, poignantly, had never been in a winning England side) promoted that to 105-5. Cue I.T. Botham.

When people talk about (or, for that matter, even write about) the theatre, the pure drama of the sportsman's stage, one thing can often be forgotten: the Bothams and the Gowers have no dress rehearsals. They go out and perform just the once. One mistake and – unless they are lucky – it's the final curtain. Nor are they totally in control of their fate. When 'Both' went in to join

Boycott, the Yorkshireman was on 40. He (Boycott) faced all but three balls of the next five overs. Then Boycott was out to Alderman. How might the game have changed had Botham faced that Alderman delivery. Fortunately, he did not and history was made.

First Botham and Dilley, then Botham and Old and finally Botham

and Willis forged partnerships that would carry England to an unbelievable 356. Botham scored the majority – but without the others he could not have done so. At the time he conceded, and still does today, that it was one mammoth fluke. Neither he nor Dilley, when they came together, considered a winning total. Players in the dressing room had showered, put away their whites and were ready to go home. Out in the middle, umpire Barrie Meyer, a former Gloucestershire player, was concentrating on the game, as these officials have to. 'We are aware of what is going on, but with so much else to think about we are not involved as if we were sitting in the stands among the crowd,' says Meyer. But he knew it was a crisis for England, and when Botham started to throw his bat at the ball as Dilley was doing with complete abandon, he gently chided the Somerset batsman as he tried to whack a couple out of the ground: 'Both; this is a bit of a crisis, don't you think you should play yourself in a bit?' 'What do you think I have done?' retorted Botham, carting the ninth ball he had faced for a second four! But, slowly the cavalier mood changed. Botham's style did not do so ('I don't remember a defensive shot,'

Wicketkeeper Rod Marsh wonders just how they stop Botham as yet another four powers towards the boundary.

His innings at Leeds may have been historic and spectacular, but Botham himself considers his second innings hundred at Old Trafford a far better performance – less a slog, ferocious yet pure.

he said later.) Mike Brearley called it 'village green slogging', and so it was. It could never be argued that it was a *great* Test match innings, but of its kind it was the finest ever. When he entered the fray the score was 105-5. He lost Boycott and Taylor fairly quickly, yet when he ran out of partners, on 149, the score was 356. Not necessarily a winning lead (129) but certainly something no one believed could have been achieved. Much ink and many yards of paper have been expended on Botham's histrionics that day. He put on 117 with Dilley in 80 minutes, and a further 67 with Chris Old. While Willis scored two, another 37 were put on for the last wicket – and still it was not over.

Mind you, it seemed that it was as Australia (many of them still in a state of shock) cleared 55 of the 130 they required for the loss of just one wicket. Then Brearley displayed the tactical skill for which he was famed – for which he had been recalled. He switched Bob Willis to the Kirkstall Lane end – to devastating effect. Willis bowled as though possessed by demons. He took eight wickets for 43 – his best Test performance, it hardly needs to be said – and, with Old a perfect foil at the other end, totally destroyed Australia. For only the second time in more than a century, a side following on had won.

When the tales of Headingley '81 are told, Botham's name is the foremost, but he would be the first to give the praise to others: to Brearley, for inspiring both him and Willis; to Willis, for his speed on the final day; to Dilley, for his long-handled support that encouraged him to join in; and, perhaps as important as anything, to the superb catching that brought the wickets on that breathless final day.

England won at Edgbaston and then at Manchester to win the series and the Ashes, and drew at the Oval. They were exciting, at times

LEFT *Allan Border, battling to a century at Old Trafford, striving as perhaps only he could to try to save his side from losing the Ashes.*

BELOW *Mike Brearley's return to captain England meant that England retained the Ashes.*

extraordinary, matches, yet they paled in comparison to Headingley. Botham's influence on the series was immense – England's leading run getter with 399, and leading wicket taker with 34. Willis took 29, and the next best was Dilley with 14. Australia were a mixture of good and bad, with Allan Border magnificent (533 runs at 59.22). They must have wondered what they had done to deserve their fate at Headingley – the Ashes seemingly theirs for the taking, and then meeting up with someone quite unique, a man who, as Viv Richards would put it, was 'one in a million' – Ian Terence 'Beefy' Botham.

1982

This was the year of the all-rounder. No, not Botham this time – though he had his moments. It was the year of Kapil Dev and Imran Khan, two outstanding players from the sub-continent who jousted royally with our own hero all summer long. First to arrive was India's Kapil for the three-Test series against an England side now deprived of 14 players who were banned for three years for touring South Africa. This was also the year when, despite small crowds for the County game, cricket proved that there was a vast interest in the game: 20,538,533 telephone calls were made for up-dated scores and when, at the age of 33, Bob Willis was appointed captain of his country. A successful captain at that – he won three of the summer's six Tests, and won both series. He even won his first toss (the first of four on the trot, in fact) which allowed England to bat against a side with only two threatening bowlers, Dilip Doshi, the ortho-dox left-arm spinner, and Kapil.

It was the opening bowler who drew first blood at Lord's: three early wickets reducing England to 37-3. But Gower and Botham (who else?), and then Botham and Derek Randall restored order with some fine bat-ting. Phil Edmonds was, like Randall, recalled to replace banned 'rebels', and he contributed his best Test score (64). Randall reached 126, and with Paul ('Walter') Allott (41 not out) and Willis (28) putting on 50 for the last wicket, England were well set

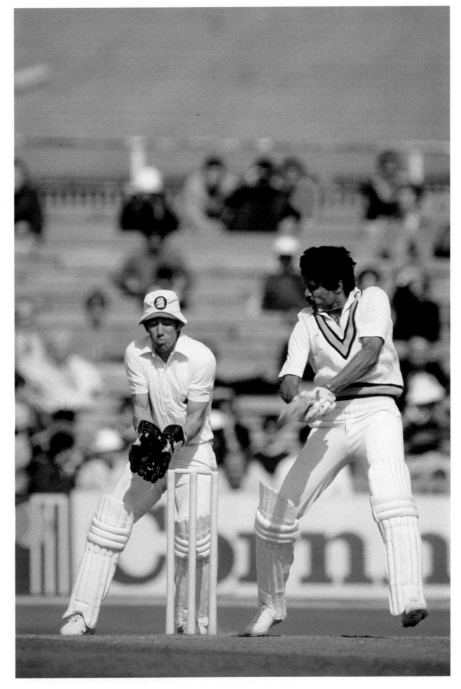

1982 was the year of the all-rounder, and the year of Kapil Dev in particular. At Old Trafford he scored 65 off 55 balls.

with 433. India collapsed to Botham and Willis, only Gavaskar and Kapil reaching double figures, and they followed on. Vengsarkar – stylish as ever, but powerful with it – spearheaded the rescue operation with 157, but as Willis suddenly decimated their middle order with four wickets, three of them in nine balls, India were threatened with an innings defeat once more. Kapil, a joyous player who enjoyed his cricket come what may, came in to thrash a devastating 89, which ensured England batted again. Kapil then proceeded to take three wickets before the close on the fourth evening, the figures 3-18 on the big Lord's scoreboard slightly embarrassing England. But despite Kapil's prodigious efforts (and 43 overs bowled in England's first

LEFT *Dilip Vengsarkar spearheaded a rescue operation at Lord's with a stylish 157. Here he pulls Derek Pringle for four.*

BELOW *A dramatic picture of England's close fielders waiting like hungry sharks for Ravi Shastri to edge a flat-out Botham, as India are made to follow on at Lord's.*

innings hinted at overwork) Allan Lamb polished things off quickly the following morning. India, one down, were already on the back foot.

Manchester, nine days later, lived up to its reputation. All five days were affected by the weather and it was individual achievements, rather than the meaningless draw, which rated the attention. Botham again revived a flagging England from 161 for 5 to 425 with a blistering century; he scored 128 off 169 balls, including two sixes and 19 fours. Doshi had a six-wicket haul, never wilting despite trundling for 47 overs. When India's sixth wicket fell, to allow Kapil to stride in swinging his bat, they could boast only 173 runs and required a further 52 to avoid the follow on. They took no time at all. Kapil

RIGHT Ian Botham, in cheeky mood at Old Trafford, tries a reverse sweep on his way to a century.

BELOW Ian Botham – again! – overshadowed everyone at The Oval. Here, Sunil Gavaskar cannot avoid a fierce shot from him, and suffers a broken bone in his leg.

launched into everyone, scoring 65
(off 55 balls) in a partnership with
Patil worth 96. When he lost his
dominating partner, Patil himself
declared war, with Willis his chief
adversary. As he sped to an unbeaten
129, he showed little respect for
either the new ball or the England captain, hammering six fours from one
seven-ball over. The fifth of them carried him to his hundred, and his second 50 had arrived from only 51 balls.
But, we had seen nothing yet . . .

The Oval has generally been a
good batting track (unless, that is,
Lock and Laker were bowling in tan-
dem on it), and the July sunshine
ensured there would be a feast for
someone. Indeed, even though
Gavaskar could not bat because of a
broken bone in his leg, 1,306 runs
were scored, England piling up 785
of them, and only 26 wickets fell.
The story of the match was – again! –
Botham, but leaving the best until
last, let it be recorded that Allan
Lamb (a South African *playing* for
England while Englishmen were
banned for playing in his country!)
turned in his maiden Test century,
Randall hit 95, Chris Tavaré was
unbeaten with 75 in his second
knock and Kapil Dev crashed 97 off
92 balls when his side still required
plenty to make England bat again.
But 'Both' overshadowed them all. He
was like some primeval destroyer; a
colossus; a man apart. Few, if any,
had seen his like before. There are, in
fact, those who feel that not even his
pyrotechnics against Australia 12
months before exceeded his great-
ness on this day.

The stark facts are that in 268 minutes he scored 200 runs of savage
beauty off 220 balls, an achievement
only ever bettered by Walter
Hammond and Denis Compton. He
finished, out to a reverse sweep, on
208, *en route* to which he had driven
a ball from Shastri with such power
that he broke a bone in Gavaskar's
left leg, and one six with such feroci-
ty that it holed the pavilion roof.
There were three other sixes and 19
fours. Despite it all, he was not
selected as Cornhill's Player of the
Series. That honour went to Kapil

Dev. His Test analyses that summer were: 292 runs from four innings, with a top score of 97 and an average of 73. He bowled 133 overs, taking 10 wickets at 43.90 apiece. Botham's figures, in contrast, were: 403 runs from three innings, with a highest score of 208, and an average of 134.33. He bowled 93.3 overs and took six wickets at 43.50. Of one thing we can all be certain: It was not a bowler's summer.

ENGLAND V PAKISTAN

One saw the best and the worst of Pakistan cricket in 1982. There was a glorious double-century from Mohsin at Lord's, the mystery of Abdul Qadir their leg-spin magician and there were the two sides of Imran Khan. Like Kapil in the preceding weeks he was the Player of the Series, as well as winning two of the Cornhill Player of the Match awards (and they both joined Wisden's gallery of Cricketers of the Year when the season was done and dusted). That the cultured, intelligent and affluent Imran was a great cricketer was never in doubt. While he was not as good a batsman as Botham, his bowling was better (Mike Brearley rated him the world's Number 1 at one stage). Yet he had a propensity to complain. It has seemed down the years, playing cricket against the Pakistanis, that they have something approaching a persecution complex. When things went wrong, or against Pakistan, it was someone else's fault – generally, in 1982, the umpires! That said, and despite Zaheer's surprising lack of form (they might well have expected twice as many as his 131 Test runs, considering how well he

LEFT *First blood at Edgbaston. Ian Botham looks round ruefully to find Imran has bowled him for a modest two runs in the first Test.*

RIGHT *Imran Khan was the Player of the Series, emphasising that he was a truly great all-rounder during 1982. Derek Randall falls victim to him at Edgbaston – though not before he had scored 105.*

Mudassar Nazar is congratulated as he bowls Randall at Lord's, the first of his six wickets, which helped Pakistan to victory by 10 wickets.

knew English wickets), Pakistan were tougher opposition than India, and with a twist or two of better fortune they might have sneaked a series victory.

They lost at Edgbaston by 113 runs, yet it could have gone either way. England mustered 272 and 291, with Randall getting a second innings hundred. Then, needing 313 to succeed, Pakistan pushed the self-destruct button. Botham took two wickets in his first over, and he and Willis took six for 77 in 22 overs as ill-disciplined batting let Pakistan down. Imran alone stayed calm for 65, but defeat in the end was comprehensive. Willis, who had damaged his neck avoiding an Imran bouncer, had not recovered in time for Lord's, leaving Gower to skipper a losing

side. Although getting two lives, Mohsin Khan scored a double-century to the delight of the Lord's hordes. Other, bigger names would add to the record, but this was only the second time since the war that the feat had been achieved in a Test (Martin Donnelly of New Zealand did so in 1949). England's batsmen seemed mystified by Qadir (tossing a coin might have been the better way of deciding which was his googly and which his leg break!) in their first innings and, forced to follow on, fell foul of Mudassar's innocuous medium-pacers. He took 6 for 32, sending Chris Tavaré into a trance almost. When one remembers (or tries to forget, perhaps) long and painful innings, Trevor Bailey's 68 in 458 stupefying minutes at Brisbane in 1958

comes to mind. At Lord's, Tavaré batted 67 minutes without scoring, and then eked out 82 in 6 hours 47 minutes in a successful effort to stave off an innings defeat, if not the inevitable 10 wicket margin that Pakistan were to record.

The umpires (who would be an umpire?) were castigated by Imran again in the deciding match at Headingley. A vociferous appeal (something the Pakistanis were adept at) for a catch behind the wicket when Gower may or may not have tickled one from Qadir, when he had scored only seven in his first innings, was turned down. Imran argued that this decision cost his side the series, the England batsman going on to score 74. Sikander was clearly shown on TV replays to be

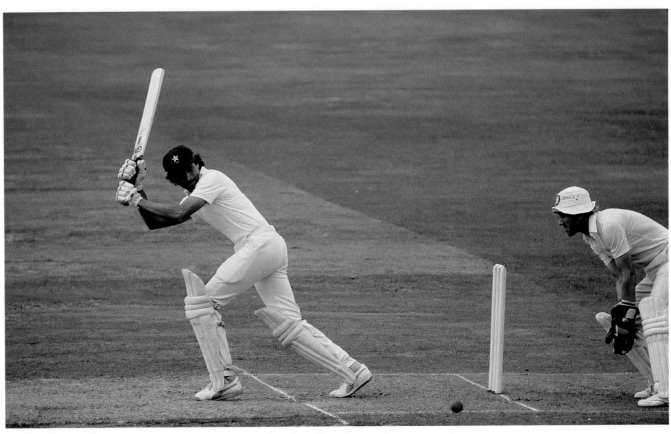

Mohsin Khan scored a glorious double century at Lord's – the only Pakistan player ever to do so.

Derek Randall is run out for eight at Headingley by Sikander Bakht.

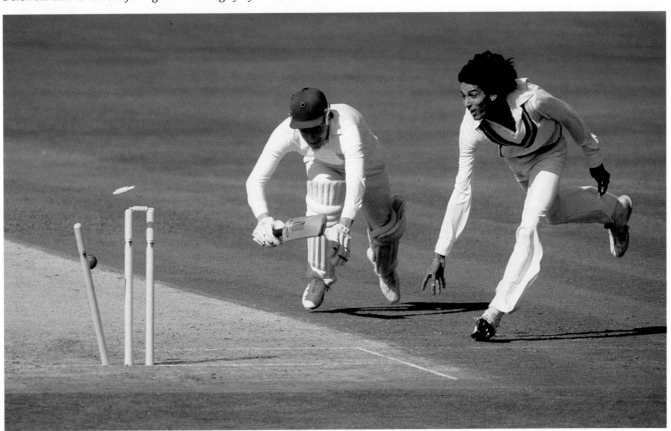

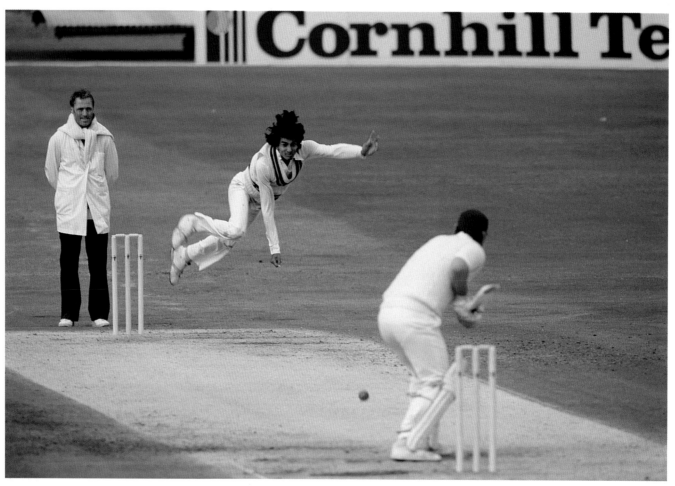

Sikander is airborne as he tries for extra pace at Headingley.

not out when given out in Pakistan's second innings, but it was the visitors' own lack of self-discipline, of not knowing when to attack and when to defend, that really contributed to their tally of 199. England looked to have an easy task – 219 to win – and with Tavaré and 'Foxy' Fowler putting on 103 and the score reaching 168 before a second wicket fell, they seemed home and dry. But suddenly there was panic; five went for 21, England having refused two offers for bad light, aware of a poor weather forecast for the final day. When Botham came in and hastened to accept the next offer for the light, England had time to breathe again. 'Both' departed when play resumed, but Vic Marks and Taylor knocked off the 20 required without further drama. Willis and Botham shared 15 wickets between them, and if it is the bowlers who win matches, then they get the credit for Leeds. No one, however, would deny that, in Imran, Pakistan had one of the giants of the game, one who warranted his Player of the Series award.

1983

It was enough to make the egg and tomato tie of MCC members curl at the edges when, in 1983, it was suggested that some of the famed oil paintings housed at Lord's were 'fakes'. These, though, were not alone in having their authenticity doubted – summer, for example, was decidedly dubious, since in June grounds were still like duck ponds. Gloucestershire had not had a full day's play by the first week of June, and Lord's lost 89 hours of cricket in five weeks. By the end of the second Test at Headingley against New Zealand there were those who were wondering whether, after all, some of the England team were not fakes as well. For 52 years, and in 28 matches, our friends from the southern hemisphere had been second best: 17 defeats and 11 draws. In the World Cup which preceded the Test series, England had qualified for the semi-finals, whereas New Zealand had not. Yet at Headingley, on the first day of August, they beat England by five wickets and with a day to spare. While MCC withdrew 14 of their 120-year-old paintings and the damp start to summer gave way to sunny conditions, England took the last two Tests to win the series 3-1.

New Zealand's all-rounder Richard Hadlee showed again that he was the genuine article. He had always been ranked alongside the giants of his era – Botham, Imran and Kapil – and it would be a brave man indeed who

A rare picture of failure. Ian Botham is bowled at The Oval for a mere 15 runs by Richard Hadlee, on his way to his 200th Test wicket.

ABOVE *Geoff Howarth captained New Zealand to an epic first victory over England at Headingley, despite being victim of a bad call by John Wright which led to Allan Lamb running him out for 13.*

LEFT *His middle stump gone, the others askew, Jeff Crowe does not have to turn round to know that he has become Bob Willis's 300th Test victim at Headingley in 1983.*

said one was much better than the rest. Now, at 33, the Kiwi was bowling off a shortened run, but he was still good enough to become Cornhill's Player of the Series. He took 21 wickets (at 26.61) and scored 301 runs at an average of over 50, and he became the first New Zealander to take 200 Test wickets. Headingley was memorable, as far as England were concerned, for Willis reaching his 300th Test victim and Gower stroking another 100 in his own, inimitable style.

It was not Hadlee but Lance Cairns who destroyed England, who were

ABOVE *David Gower is brilliantly caught by Martin Crowe at Lord's to give Evan Gray his first Test scalp.*

RIGHT *A familiar picture of Ian Botham, clubbing his way to 103 at Trent Bridge.*

put in on a pitch that favoured movement rather than sheer pace. He took seven wickets (and 10 in the match for the first time) and England were put out for 225. New Zealand responded with 377, which could have been more but for two bad run outs. They were not decisive, however; England were dismissed for 252, Ewen Chatfield this time finding the late swing to collect five wickets, and Gower alone standing defiant, reaching his first three-figure total in a home Test for four years. New Zealand hearts were beating ever faster as, seeking only 101, they lost five wickets (all to Willis) for 35 before Coney and Hadlee won the most glorious day in their cricket history. That they lost the other matches

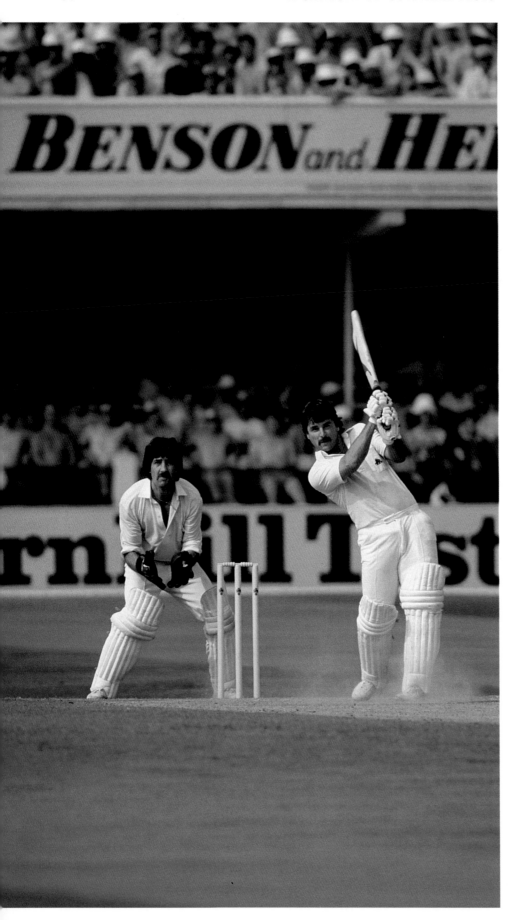

Allan Lamb on his way to an unbeaten 137 in the second innings at Trent Bridge, helping England to a 165-run victory and a 3-1 win in the series.

pretty badly was not something they could be proud of, but the one win atoned for a great deal. At The Oval, Fowler, Tavaré and Lamb got hundreds, while Marks and Edmonds spun England to victory. At Lord's Gower helped himself to another hundred. Nick Cook, a late call-up, had a 'five for' and Hadlee claimed his second such five-wicket haul of the series. Botham took a hundred off loose bowling at Trent Bridge, while Cook, continuing to exploit guile, flight and spin, took five more. Hadlee ended the tour in personal triumph – 92 not out – but the 165 run defeat left New Zealand with only memories of Leeds to console them.

1984

A new word was introduced into the sporting dictionary in 1984 – 'Blackwash'. Clive Lloyd's West Indians came to England with three of the world's most menacing fast bowlers, and they saw with disdain a side under-powered in virtually all areas, and they conquered by five Tests to none – a blackwash. Too often, however, they appeared to target the batsman rather than the stumps, and the ugliness reached a peak at The Oval. The series was already won and lost. Lost, in fact, by England on almost humiliating terms: one by an innings and 180 runs, another by an innings and 64, the other two by nine and by eight wickets. What happened at The Oval was unnecessary. It was unprincipled. It was unedifying. Perhaps the fact that England's bowlers had actually given them a hard time for once, dismissing them for 190, led to Malcolm Marshall's bowling late on the first day. Joel Garner had dismissed Chris Broad, and England

In glorious black and white, England get the message at The Oval. BLACKWASH. Jubilant West Indian fans had come prepared to see their team win the final Test by 172 runs and the series by five matches to nil.

sent in Pat Pocock, an off-spinner and very much a non-batsman at almost any level. (His Test career was 25 matches, 206 runs at an average of 6.24.) Yet Malcolm Marshall, a truly great fast bowler, summoned all his speed and delivered vicious, short-pitched deliveries at Pocock. Worse, he was allowed to do so by the umpires, David Constant and Barrie Meyer.

John Woodcock, *The Times* Cricket Correspondent and Editor of Wisden in 1985, led the assault on these formidable West Indians. 'Their presence has brought a new and, dare I say it, chilling dimension to the game. Batsmen, however protected, face them at their peril.' Surrey's Pat

LEFT Andy Lloyd, winning his first cap, lasted seven overs at Edgbaston before being felled by Marshall and ending up in hospital for 10 days with blurred vision.

BELOW Lord's in all its former glory – the old Tavern stand and scoreboard lit up by the June sunshine in 1984

RIGHT Allan Lamb was the mainstay of England's batting in 1984. He scored hundreds at Lord's, Leeds and Old Trafford.

Gordon Greenidge in awesome form at Old Trafford, where he scored a magnificent 223.

Pocock will endorse those sentiments. Marshall had him caught by Gordon Greenidge the next morning; Michael Holding caught and bowled him in the second innings. The scorer was not troubled on either occasion. Nor was he, for that matter, in Pocock's only other two innings that summer. He was not a threat to West Indies. Marshall was too good a player to resort to such an attack, and the umpires should have stopped it.

That said, England, under the new leadership of David Gower, were totally outgunned all summer through. West Indies had the heavy artillery; England had snipers with rifles which the visitors' final victory in the fifth Test by 172 runs merely underlined. Botham had sniped effectively, with 19 wickets in the series and 347 runs (at an average of 34.70). He scored 64 at Edgbaston and 81 at Lord's but Allan Lamb, with hundreds at Lord's, Leeds and Old Trafford, was the mainstay of the batting, with Fowler chipping in with 106 at Lord's. Lamb owed much to the courage of Paul Terry for his three figures at Old Trafford. Terry became the second England batsman to suffer a bad injury (Andy Lloyd spent 10 days in hospital after a ball from Marshall smashed into his helmet in the first Test) when his left arm was broken by one from Winston Davis, which did not rise as he expected. Terry batted with his arm plastered, allowing Lamb to get the two runs he required for precisely 100. At The Oval, Botham took three early wickets which reduced the West Indies to 70-6, perhaps inflaming tempers a little in the process, and he became the third (behind Willis and Fred Trueman) to take 300 Test wickets. He also took five in an innings for the 23rd time in 73 Tests. What a debt English cricket owed this buccaneer. Little wonder that wherever he played he was the one man guaranteed to empty just about every bar in the ground when he took to pillaging the opposition.

ABOVE *Paul Terry, broken arm in plaster, bravely went out to bat, enabling Allan Lamb to score the two runs he needed for a century at Old Trafford. But when he faced Joel Garner, he lasted just two balls before losing his off stump.*

LEFT *Cricket's new 'chilling dimension' – Pat Pocock trying to avoid a ferocious bouncer from Malcolm Marshall at The Oval in 1984. It was, he said later: 'Truly terrifying speed, with intimidation a way of life even for tailenders.'*

Gordon Greenidge was in quite awesome form all summer. He scored over 1,000 first class runs, 572 in Tests, with double hundreds at Manchester and at a packed Lord's where only Bradman and Hammond had scored more than him. But perhaps the over-riding message of the year came from the Archbishop of Canterbury, a devotee of cricket. It was, he said, a game to be played, not a battle to be won. There was a message there for someone but I am not sure anyone was listening.

SRI LANKA V ENGLAND

If England thought that a depressing run without a single victory would be concluded when they played Sri Lanka in a Cornhill-spon-

The Sri Lankans brought enjoyable batting and a lot of colour to their first Test match at Lord's.

sored one-off Test match, they were due for disappointment. Sri Lanka, far from being over-awed by either a debut Test or a Lord's appearance, excelled themselves. They had the crowd cheering their attractive batting. It was remarkably different from the cricket played by the West Indians, with their unrelenting pace and bludgeoning batting. The Sri Lankans batted as they were taught – as our Test match graduates from public school and university yester-year were taught. And they certainly put England to the sword, with Sidath Wettimuny scoring 190, and the skipper, Duleep Mendis, failing by only six runs to score two separate hundreds. Where they won the plaudits, Broad and Tavaré got the bird for their dreadfully slow batting (a combination of eyes on tour places and bad form), and Sri Lanka left Lord's with the better of the draw and more to remember than England, who had now gone 12 games without a win.

1985

Losing to the West Indians is one thing, but losing an Ashes series against the Australians is altogether another. Thus, a 3-1 Ashes-regaining win in 1985 made it a vintage year for English cricket. That the Aussies may have been a pretty moderate bunch mattered not at all. There are few warmer moments in sport than to be at The Oval on the final day of an Australian tour as the hordes gather in their thousands in front of the old pavilion to see England's captain accept the accolades and the replica of the famous urn. To David Gower went the honour, on 2 September, in this momentous year. All six grounds staged a match, with England winning at Headingley; Australia drawing level, thanks to Allan Border's enormous display, at Lord's; a couple shared; and finally two crushing England victories at Edgbaston and The Oval.

Those are merely bare facts; but an Ashes year never fails to produce many moments of drama. The tour began with one, in fact. Australia returned immediately to the scene of the 1981 crime – Headingley. Andrew Hilditch scored 119 for the Australians, and another 80 in his second knock, but England were clear winners by five wickets. Tim Robinson emerged as an opener, experiments with Randall being ditched, and he looked good with 175 in his first home match. Botham reminded everyone of his '81 exploits

Reigning supreme at Lord's – Allan Border, who scored 196 runs in his first innings (plus a further 41 second time out) to ensure that his side won at least one Test during the series.

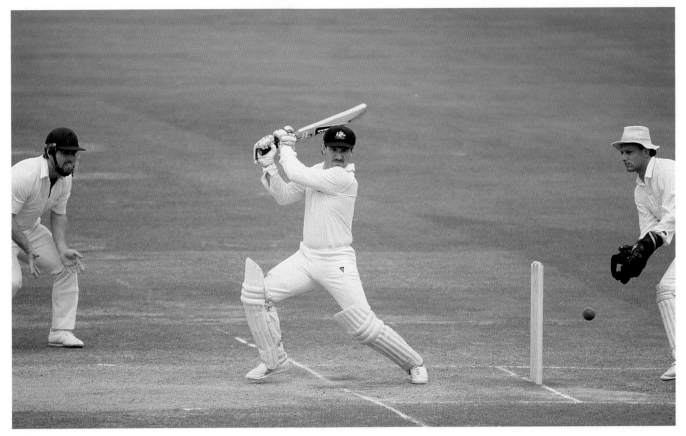

Mike Gatting, driving fiercely on his way to 160, a first Test century at home, at Old Trafford. Aussie wicketkeeper Wayne Phillips can only look on in admiration – and despair.

with a crash-bang-wallop 60 during which he mauled the Aussie new boy, Craig McDermott, quite fearfully. McDermott would later become the scourge of English batsmen, but here he was on a learning curve. He took four wickets but went for 134. Indeed, throughout the tour he and Lawson bore a heavy workload and took heavy punishment: they bowled 480 overs between them, and their 52 wickets cost over 1,700 runs. At Lord's, Border reigned supreme. He was four short of a double century as Australia piled up 425, and added another 41 when his side were wobbling slightly, to steer them to victory in the fourth innings. Botham simply refused to be overshadowed; he took seven Aussie wickets in the match, including his 326th victim, which made him England's top wicket-taker.

Geoff Lawson, who was affected by bronchial problems much of the tour, took five wickets at Trent Bridge, where a really fine hundred by Gower was the basis for a 456 total. Wood and Ritchie countered with centuries, helping the Australians to an 83 run lead, but with drizzle and bad light the event just fizzled out. There was a similar result at Old Trafford, but here the Aussies had their backs to the wall almost the entire game. One had seen worse sponges at a WI stall than the one the groundsman produced for a Test wicket, and Gower inserted Australia. Edmonds and Botham took four apiece, and Australia were well short of a driving-seat total. McDermott, learning and improving all the while, had his finest Test match, taking eight English wickets. Mike Gatting, who shared a splendid 156 stand with Lamb, was finally caught behind by Phillips for 160. The wicketkeeper then supported Border valiantly as Australia battled to get their draw. The captain was unbeaten with 146, while Phillips,

who spent 50 vital minutes waiting to break his duck, was 39 when play concluded. It was an honourable draw for Border.

There was no such fighting spirit at Edgbaston or The Oval, however. It was rain that posed the biggest threat to England's victory in Birmingham by an innings and 118, holding off just long enough for Botham and Richard Ellison (whose match total of 10 for 79 won him the Player of the Match award) to bowl them out. England had a ball when they batted – Robinson scored 148, Gower 215 and Gatting was 100 not out when Gower declared at 595-5. Botham had gone in with the scoreboard reading 572-4 and hit his first ball into the pavilion for six, his second for four and the fourth for another six! The bowler? McDermott. Thomson took just one wicket (Gooch) and that gave him his 200th in Tests, and his 100th against England. As Australia battled in their second innings Phillips was controversially caught. An angry Border argued that there was enough doubt for the batsman to have had the benefit, and felt that the disputed catch cost them the match. Phillips, who had battled with real guts for 59, had struck a ball from Edmonds which hit Lamb on the instep at silly point and dollied up to Gower. Unsighted, umpire David Shepherd sought

Phil Edmonds, who held eight catches as well as taking 15 wickets, is razor sharp as he catches Graeme Wood off Botham at Edgbaston.

Controversy at Edgbaston! Phillips, on 59 and batting well, slashes at Edmonds. The ball flies up off Lamb's boot as he takes avoiding action, and dollies to Gower. Out, rule the umpires. Unfair, argues Border. There was enough doubt for a 'Not out' decision. As the man said: Read the scorebook – 'Phillips c Gower, b Edmonds 59'.

Graham Gooch, who shared in a 351-run partnership with David Gower at The Oval, clips away one of his 27 fours in his innings of 196.

David Constant's opinion, which was that the catch was good. England won the final match by an innings and 94 – but the Ashes were gone as far as Australia were concerned within the first two hours. David Gower won the toss, batted, saw Robinson an early victim (yorked by McDermott for three) and then enjoyed three lives as he set out on a huge partnership with Gooch. Both scored big hundreds, Gooch only four short of a double; what might have been England 29 for two became 371 for two. Australian heads went down and they were finally routed. Allan Border, one of the world's great patriots, was left pondering whether his side had forgotten both why they were playing Test cricket and that feeling of national pride. England simply enjoyed the moment; they didn't even think about the winter tour to come – to the Caribbean.

RIGHT Skipper David Gower opens the champagne, Ian Botham pours the beer as England celebrate an Ashes victory at The Oval in 1985.

1986

Was it the ultimate nadir? England's cricket had, down the years, suffered slings and arrows of outrageous fortune greater by far than any envisaged by Mr William Shakespeare. But 1986 took some beating. England lost to India. They lost to New Zealand. They lost their key all-rounder. And they lost a captain. Was it, one wondered in hindsight, only 12 months before that the wonderful David Gower had regained the Ashes? Yes, it was – but in the meantime he had lost 5-nil in the West Indies and contrived to lose, not marginally but quite comprehensively, a Test at Lord's against India. People like Mr Frederick Sewards Trueman OBE did not believe England should lose to such nations. England's selectors agreed with him, and Peter May, the chairman, relieved the ex-public school leader of his duties and gave the job to a more pugnacious working class lad called Mike Gatting. The move hardly worked. Despite Gatting's own form, England lost their first Test under him to India and thus the three-match series, and then lost to New

It was a serial of successes for India in 1986, and no one did better than Dilip Vengsarkar. His unbeaten 126 made him the first overseas player to score three centuries at Lord's.

Zealand. By this time, of course, as *Test Match Special* listeners will recall, Mr Trueman was rendered speechless. The matter of the missing all-rounder was different. Ian Botham had 'brought the game into disrepute' by admitting to smoking pot, and was banned from 29 May to 31 July. The powers that be knew what they were doing; in punishing the naughty boy they were punishing their national team. To their credit they took the action needed – but, by golly, 'Both' was missed.

The match, his 21st as India's captain, was a personal triumph at Lord's for Kapil Dev. His first win! He also broke the back of England's second innings, dismissing Gooch, Robinson and Gower for one run in 19 balls, and then climaxed victory with 18 runs off one Edmonds over – three fours plus a six which won the game. England had a Gooch century to cheer them, and a first Test 50 from Derek Pringle. Vengsarkar made history, scoring an unbeaten 126 to become the first overseas player to clock up three Lord's hundreds. England made life easier for the spinner, Maninder Singh, at 20 a veteran of 15 Tests, by allowing him to maintain his rhythm rather than attacking him; thus he moved in after Kapil's assault with three wickets for only nine runs from 21 overs.

When this writer was a boy and the town's silver band used to play at football matches, the wits of the crowd had a saying when the locals were off-colour that 'only the band played well'. Wisden quite wondrously dug up this old adage after the Headingley defeat. The Hammond Sauce Works Band, it recorded, was 'the indisputable success for England'. England lost by 279 runs, with Botham missing and Gower out (a damaged shoulder to go with a damaged ego). It was not the best of Headingley pitches and India mustered 272, batting first. Roger Binny was their executioner (with 5-40) as England toppled to 102. Vengsarkar compiled a studied 102, and the tail wagged so well that England needed 408 to win. They managed 128 and lost, with Peter

Well played, lads! The band, that is. England contrived to lose to India at Headingley by 279 runs, but the Hammond Sauce Works players were 'an indisputable success'.

May's words ringing in their ears: 'We were outplayed in every department.' He didn't mention the band. Gatting seemed to take his words seriously, scoring an unbeaten 183, but the only real debate about the final Test was whether, in the 48 minutes lost to the weather on the last afternoon,

Timber! Chris Smith hears it crashing as he is bowled by Madan Lal at Headingley.

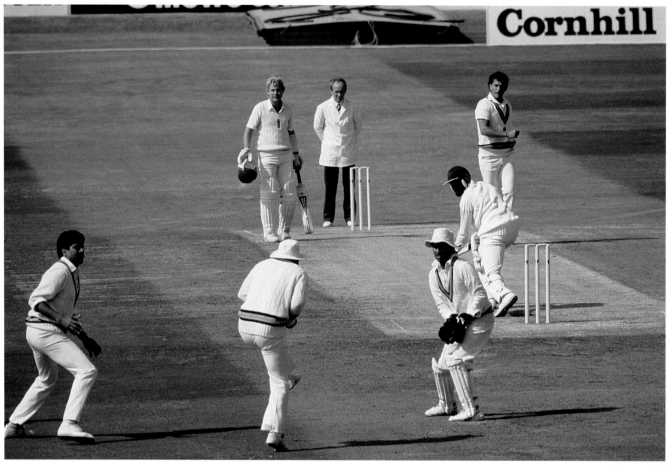

Wilf Slack becomes one of Roger Binny's seven victims as he is caught by Gavaskar at Headingley.

India might have got another 62 runs (Azharuddin was giving a foretaste of what we would see in seasons ahead and Kapil was still to bat) or whether England would have taken five wickets. One suspects neither.

NEW ZEALAND TOUR

If Godfrey Evans, a veteran of 91 Test matches, felt that the New Zealand series of 1986 was a trifle monotonous, well – he was entitled to his opinion. But when he adds that the highlight of the whole summer was the remarkable reappearance of a 45-year-old wicketkeeper, then everyone has to sit up and take notice, for the be-whiskered Mr Evans knows a thing or two about those with gloves on who stand behind the stumps. As far as he is concerned, Bob Taylor was 'a genius in his footwork, his handling and his

concentration' and to see him 'keeping at Lord's on a July day when he was supposed to be supping wine with Cornhill clients in their hospitality tent was a joy. To the rest of us it was more a matter of some amusement when they sounded an SOS for Taylor to help England out in a crisis, even though – it must be said – he kept impeccably. It was just as though he had not been retired for a couple of years.

Bob, who had played 57 Tests dating from 1970 to 1983, was appointed Cornhill's 'special ambassador', the sponsor's link with the dressing room, the Press box and the brokers who were entertained during Test matches. He was fulfilling his duties quite admirably on Friday 25 July 1986 – glass of red wine, a typical cricket lunch and a reminiscence or three with the Cornhill guests. All was well with his world. It was not all well with England's wicketkeeper Bruce French, however. A Hadlee

bouncer had struck him on the back of the head, he needed three stitches in the wound and time to recuperate. When New Zealand began their innings, having bowled England out for 307, Gloucestershire's Bill Athey put on the gloves for two overs while officials hunted down Taylor. When he realised it was not a joke, Bob collected his own gloves from his car ('Well, you never know when I might need them,' he would laugh), borrowed some gear and trotted out to an enormous welcome from a crowd who, like Godfrey Evans, knew a genius when they saw one. For 74 overs, with the kind (or over-generous as some critics would put it) permission of the New Zealand captain, Jeremy Coney, he made not a mistake. He had an excellent view of Martin Crowe's hundred as New Zealand responded with 342, but when Bobby Parks, a younger player but one of less stature arrived, he then returned to his duties as

Moment of crisis. Bruce French is hit on the back of the head. He needed stitches and England needed a substitute wicketkeeper.

Just like old times – and what a lot of pleasure it gave many people to see Bob Taylor, a venerable 45, back behind the stumps helping England out of an injury crisis at Lord's in 1986.

LEFT *Richard Hadlee, in superb form at Trent Bridge, where he took 10 wickets in the match, winning the Player of the Match award and helping New Zealand to win the Second Test.*

ABOVE *An aggressive Martin Crowe at Lord's. He scored 106, and shared a record stand of 210 with Bruce Edgar (83).*

Cornhill host while Graham Gooch scored a masterly 183. The awful Lord's weather prevented any sort of a climax, but did allow New Zealand opener John Wright to bag a 'pair', twice a Dilley victim.

The tourists won the series at Trent Bridge with a victory (by eight wickets) marked by Hadlee, at 35 still a truly magnificent performer, taking 10 wickets in a Test for the seventh time, and yet another astonishing controversy. With Martin Crowe on 44 and New Zealand needing just one run, Gatting tossed the ball to Gower and invited him to bowl. Gower, now revealed as a latent 'chucker', threw it

Ian Botham claimed better scalps than Jeff Crowe's, but no other gave him greater satisfaction. With it he broke Dennis Lillee's record of 355 Test wickets, at The Oval in 1986.

– a no-ball, conceding one run. Crowe hit it for four runs, however, and the argument began as to whether or not they counted. Ultimately, the umpires agreed that they did, and Wisden recorded Crowe with 48 not out. It was that sort of a series, really. Wright atoned for his 'pair' at Lord's with 119 at The Oval; Gower (131) and Gatting (121) shared a stand of 223 and Ian Botham, in a ferocious return from his ban, scored 59 from 36 balls. He then took a wicket with his first ball, and in his second over became leading Test wicket taker with his 356th victim. If England thought losing the series was agony, it was nothing to the anguish of New Zealand opener Trevor Franklin. He broke a thumb at Nottingham, missed the Tests, and then suffered multiple fractures to a leg from a luggage trolley at Gatwick airport. Apart from that, it was a good tour!

1987

One day, perhaps, there will be a Test series between England and Pakistan that is all sweetness and joy rather than malevolence, recrimination and bitterness. But don't bet on it – a 20-year form guide suggests that the year of 1987 is about par for the course. Suggestions of cheating, allegations of deliberate time-wasting and abuse of substitutes all made headlines during a summer when too often cricket was washed out leaving huge empty spaces on the back pages that needed to be filled. If one wondered what on earth there was left to pollute a series between these two nations, the answer came in December. The Cornhill series won by Pakistan, England travelled to Asia for a return contest, and we were treated to the unedifying spectacle of an England captain and a Pakistan umpire nose to nose in argument. But that unsavoury Shakoor Rana affair was still to come as Pakistan arrived here to a cold, wet and windy welcome. Worst hit were the first two Tests, at Manchester and Lord's. At Old Trafford an injured Imran batted but could not bowl, and Pakistan played for time. Eleven overs in an hour was, not unreasonably, condemned. Micky Stewart, installed as England team manager, called for a

LEFT *A cheerless match at Old Trafford, half the match lost to the weather – but David Gower managed a bright 22 before top-edging a catch to wicketkeeper Yousuf, off Wasim Akram.*

RIGHT *Old Trafford, where else? Dickie Bird and Barrie Meyer take shelter from the rain which wiped out more than half of the first Test.*

tightening up of what constituted 'genuine injury'. Imran countered with a call for neutral umpires, and objected to 'us being slagged off and called cheats.' It was revealed that Pakistan had not wished for either David Constant ('A disgraceful man,' said their manager Haseeb Ahsan with no tongue apparent in his cheek) or Ken Palmer to be on the umpire's panel. The TCCB quite rightly backed their men and both stood.

At Manchester, Pakistan batted for only 64 overs; at Lord's they didn't bat at all, and it was not until July and Headingley that meaningful cricket was under way. There, they were only required to bat once – England were beaten by an innings in little more than three days. They

LEFT *Salim Malik's eyes send a message to Neil Foster's back. He scored 99 at Headingley, but Foster was in superb form, taking eight wickets for 107. Malik clearly didn't like this one at all.*

BELOW *Jack Richards becomes Imran's 300th Test victim at Headingley, caught at forward short leg.*

were undone by the brilliance of Imran, backed by Wasim, who took England's top five for 31 in an hour on the first morning. Bowled out for 136, England compounded their situation by dropping four catches, three of them off the luckless Foster, who took eight for 107 but deserved even better figures. He moved the ball both ways and his accuracy demanded that the batsmen had to play every ball. Aided by these reprieves, the composure of Salim Malik and the long handle of Wasim Akram, Pakistan reached 353. Malik, very straight (he cut out the hook and the cut early on in his career) scored 99, and Wasim 43 off 41 balls. Going in again, England lost Broad (very dubiously, to a catch behind by Yousuf) and Robinson in Imran's first two overs. Botham showed his anger

RIGHT *Not, perhaps, for the first time in his life, Ian Botham over-reaches himself!*

BELOW *Let off in the deep when only nine, Javed Miandad went on to score 260 at The Oval, passing 6,000 Test runs on the way. Here he hits John Emburey high and handsomely.*

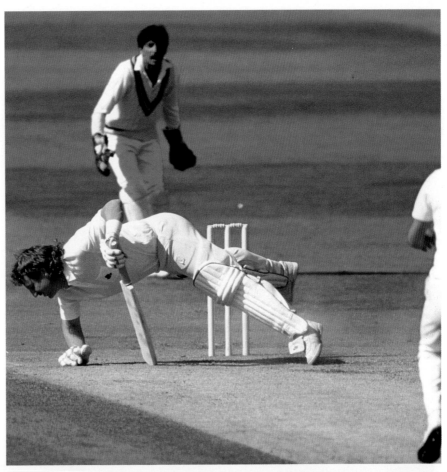

Whether batting (at The Oval, where he scored 118), bowling (at Headingley, where he took 3-37 and 7-4) or simply captaining the side (in discussion with umpires Palmer and Shepherd regarding the condition of the ball) no man did more than Imran Khan to ensure a first ever series win in England in 1987.

when the wicketkeeper dropped, retrieved and then claimed a 'catch' – an action which brought Yousuf a prompt rebuke from his captain. Overall, however, England were pretty well outplayed; Imran finishing with seven wickets, his fifth putting him alongside the elite who have taken 300 Test wickets. England lost by an innings and 18 runs.

England went surprisingly close to winning at Edgbaston after two big first innings. Pakistan had scored 439 and 205. England had opened with 521, Gatting scoring 124 and Imran, with 6-129, recording his 21st five or better Test tally. Needing 124 from 18 overs, England should have got them comfortably, but Athey, involved in three run-outs, then performed a fair imitation of Boycott, scoring only 14 runs in seven overs. England finished on 107-9, and Athey finished out of the side for The Oval. By scoring a mammoth 708 in this south-east corner of London Pakistan ensured that they would not lose their grip on the series. Javed, passing 6,000 Test runs on the way, hit 260, Salim Malik 102 and Imran 118. He raced from 57 to three figures while Javed added not even a single to his score. Dilley claimed six wickets for 154, but Botham's figures were horrific – he conceded 217 runs in his 52 overs for three wickets. Qadir took 11 wickets in the series – 10 of them in this match. Taking 7-92 in the first innings, he reduced England to 232, and it was left to Gatting (150 and his ninth Test hundred) and Botham (51) to salvage a draw for England when they followed on.

1988

Rather like day lilies or Morning Glory flowers, English captains were blooming one day and withering the next throughout the summer of 1988. England chose 23 players in all against the West Indies (and this, let it be remembered, for a five-match series, not six) and managed almost a captain a game. Four held the honour – Mike Gatting at Trent Bridge, John Emburey at Lord's and Old Trafford, Chris Cowdrey (potential officer material even if he was barely Test standard) at Headingley for his one and only game as skipper, and Graham Gooch (more a budding sergeant major with an immense potential for runs) at The Oval. Despite his experience as captain in 1986, his 51 consecutive games from 1981–86, his 100 Test matches (to that time) and 7,000 runs (not to mention a stunning catch at Lord's to dismiss Curtly Ambrose for a duck) it appeared that D.I. Gower was not considered the right man for the job – and, indeed, he was left out of the fifth and final Test at The Oval. Strange days and stranger coves, those selectors!

Graham Gooch was one of only two batsmen to make an England hundred: here he tucks Ambrose away during his 146 at Trent Bridge.

There were plenty of 'high fives' during this summer as West Indies won four Tests and drew the other.

Victory in the three one-day Internationals was nothing but fool's gold for England. Regardless of the changes of captain and the lack of any consistency or settled team, West Indies were the better side by far – there were plenty of 'high fives' this summer. There was no one to compare with Malcolm Marshall, a supreme fast bowler and a far from useless No. 8. His six-laden knock of 72 at Trent Bridge was joyous; his 35 wickets at 12.65 left England a poor second. England's best days were at Trent Bridge where Gooch (146) and Gower (88 not out) excelled in the second innings and Broad and Gooch began the summer's business with their only three-figure opening stand. (The aggregate of the next half dozen first wicket partnerships didn't add up to their 125.) Gooch passed 4,000 Test runs, but was first to go, bowled by Marshall, to start a mini collapse. The top five batsmen then came and went for just 61 runs, and from 125 without loss they tumbled to 186-5. They were bowled out for 245 – the tone and the pace for the summer had been set. Carl Hooper, a 21-year-old newcomer, with a classical innings of 84 showed the quality that was to both delight English eyes at times and destroy too often their hopes over the next seven years. Ambrose lashed 43, Marshall his 72, and Emburey went for 62 off his first seven overs and 95 off 16 in all. England needed 203 to avoid an innings defeat – and knew they were in for a tough summer. The draw they achieved was honourable enough (and the only one they were to get) but trouble was brewing, on and off the field.

To say that Gatting was the best County captain around, and the gutsiest, would not have got anyone into a fight, but now – in an hour of need – England were about to sack him. Newspaper stories suggesting that instead of going straight to bed following the coffee and the After Eights, Gatting had celebrated his

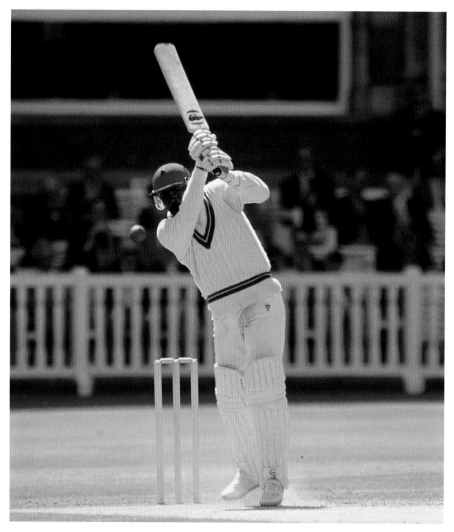

31st birthday by giving a barmaid a drink in his room. England accepted that there was no sexual impropriety but thought it improper behaviour and replaced him with Emburey. At Lord's the bowlers did a job for him (Dilley had 5-55 and our guests were bowled out for 209) but the batsmen, Gooch and Gower excepted, did not. Marshall, after 6-69 at Nottingham, now took another six (for only 32). Gordon Greenidge, with stands worth 83 with Richardson and an ever more confident captain in Viv Richards, scored 100 to carry West Indies out of England's reach. England needed to bat for 172 overs or score 441 to avoid defeat. Despite

LEFT *Gordon Greenidge scored the only West Indian century during the 1988 tour – 103 at Lord's – a majestic innings which brought him his 15th Test hundred.*

BELOW *It was the picture that spawned a dozen clichés. He leapt like a swallow! He dived like a salmon! In fact, David Gower took off like a Tiger Moth to make this stupendous catch at Lord's: Curtly Ambrose, c Gower b Small 0.*

RIGHT *The magnificent new Mound Stand at Lord's, packed for the 1988 Test match, which drew almost 78,000 people who paid a £1 million 'gate' for the first time in England.*

Lamb, who came in at 31-3 and did not depart until the score was 254-9, it was beyond England. Marshall had another four wickets, and the only riches to exceed his at Lord's were those of the TCCB. Takings for the game exceeded £1 million for the first time.

At Old Trafford England lost by an innings and 156. It lasted into a fifth day only because of the weather. Marshall, as in the first Test (and as might well have been in the second), was voted Player of the Match. 'Young Charlie' Childs, the Essex left-arm spinner, made his debut here a few days short of his 37th birthday. He must have wondered what it was all about. England were 55-4 at lunch on Day One, and out for 135. His new skipper, an off-spinner, then took the ball. His

LEFT *Malcolm Marshall was lethal all summer long – a record 35 wickets in the series, and 10 at Lord's. Here he runs in while taking 6-35 in England's first innings.*

BELOW *Christopher Cowdrey was England's third captain in four Tests but he went for a duck in the first innings at Headingley and here is bowled by Walsh in the second for five.*

team mates put down two costly chances, and every West Indian batsman then helped himself to a few. Weighing the weather against the opposition's chances of survival, Richards paid too much respect to England. Marshall unzipped them with seven wickets for just 22 and England were put out, humiliatingly, for 93.

It was slightly different at Leeds. But only slightly. England *thought* they could scent a long overdue home victory, but it was fool's gold again. With only Tim Curtis (in for Broad) gone in their second innings, they were six runs ahead. Inside two hours, nine more had gone for 58. At The Oval the West Indian bowlers shared the wickets as England fell for 205, Robin Smith in his second Test being the only one past 50. Neil Foster lifted drooping English heads and hearts with some gilt-edged fast

RIGHT *England's new work force – Graham Gooch is installed as captain for The Oval match, joining forces with team manager Micky Stewart.*

BELOW *Neil Foster took 5-64 at The Oval, but this ball to Gordon Greenidge was smashed for four.*

bowling in which he claimed their top five batsmen and helped England to a tiny, yet psychologically important, first innings lead. Gooch duly played a typical cliché-writer's innings (that of a captain) while all around him fell before there was time to panic. At 55-3 Foster, hardly a Botham, came in at five as night-watchman instead of 10, and with 34 hard-earned runs helped his County colleague carry the score to 108 before he fell to Benjamin. Despite Gooch, all steel and grim determination, England were out for 202, of which the new leader hit 84. He was named Cornhill's England Player of the Series and Marshall, inevitably, was the West Indian choice. As the presentations were made, the flag of the Cross of St George fluttering high above The Oval pavilion was seen to be at half mast. By accident or design, it mattered not. It summed up English cricket, which had now seen the national team go 18 games without a win.

SRI LANKA IN ENGLAND

The problem of being Sri Lankan is three-fold. To start with, people cannot even spell, let alone pronounce your name correctly. If Viv Richards, Richie Richardson, Malcolm Marshall and Curtly Ambrose are playing down the road, they tend to hog the headlines. And, as Sri Lanka did in 1988, to take on England at Lord's with such limited experience is inhibiting to say the least. Sri Lanka, so keen to learn, played nine first class games in 1988, drew eight and lost the Cornhill Test. Better players than theirs had been intimidated by the long walk down the stairs from the Lord's dressing room, through the Long Room and across the grass to the wicket; so far, so much time to think about getting an unplayable first ball. Little surprise then, when Gooch had won the toss and inserted them, that Sri Lanka found themselves 63 for six before lunch. They recovered, to 194, England scored 429 and the visitors had an uphill task to avoid defeat. But they tried – tried mightily. The lessons of the first morning were heeded, and second time around England found wickets less easy to collect. Sri Lanka reached 331, Ranatunga, the vice captain hitting 10 fours in a splendid 78. Samarakekera and Mendis batted well, reaching half centuries as Sri Lanka won the hearts of the Lord's crowd. Their lead was never enough, and they duly lost by seven wickets, but they suggested that when they began to bowl half as well as they batted, Sri Lanka would start to win Test matches. England had won their first after a trot of 18 without a win, and their first at Lord's for five years, without suggesting they were now about to go five years or even 18 matches without losing.

1989

It was a summer of black despair, 1989. It wasn't simply that the Australians were the better players. They seemed superior in every way – their attitude, their professionalism and their sense of purpose. It was Allan Border's fourth tour to England, his second as captain, and there was no more dedicated player to a cause than 'AB'. England had Ted

Dexter as chairman of the new England Committee which was – among other things – to pick the team. And David Gower was back as captain. But nothing went right all summer. Twelve Aussies precisely appeared in the six Test matches (of which they won four, decisively not narrowly, and drew two). Twenty-nine players were chosen for an

England team in total disarray. They were hit by injuries, appallingly so – but they have a greater depth than any other nation from which to select. They found 16 of their top players heading for a rebel tour of South Africa mid-way through. And they finished with a captain under pressure – one who had walked out of a Press conference, angered at the

There is no mistaking this umpire, even from the rear. It is David Shepherd dealing with a tricky situation at Leeds in 1989.

LEFT Steve Waugh scored one of the finest centuries ever seen at Headingley – 172 (not out) of Australia's huge total.

RIGHT Avoiding action by Robin Smith at Lord's as Merv Hughes tests him with a bouncer.

hostility of questioning about his tactics. Questioning, let it be remembered, from former team-mates turned journalists, a breed beginning to inflame ill-feeling among those still playing. To add to England's own shortcomings, Mark Taylor scored more runs (839) than any tourist except Don Bradman, and Terry Alderman, whose medium-fast swing bowling was designed for English wickets, claimed a record 41 Test victims.

It was quickly evident that, despite a new management team, England's problems were the old ones. At Headingley they really suffered; they went in without a spinner, won the toss and put Australia in, lost Gatting and Botham before the start to injury. Taylor provided the foundation with 136 as Australia built a massive total. Steve Waugh scored one of the finest centuries the Yorkshire ground had witnessed – 172 not out when Border declared at 601. Robin Smith, his South African compatriot, Allan Lamb, and Kim Barnett batted well to ensure that England avoided the follow-on. Border made his batsmen hustle along at four an over (another 60, ominously to Taylor) enabling him to declare at 230-3. He had 83 overs to bowl England out, but with Alderman taking his second 'five-for' in the match, needed only 56 of them. Alderman, with his 10-151, was the Cornhill Player of the Match, and all the honours went to his side. As, sadly, they were destined to do in the weeks ahead.

At Lord's England met their usual fate. Another defeat, this time by six wickets. Six years later, at a Cornhill Player of the Year lunch, I would listen as a former MCC President and the chairman of the TCCB, Dennis Silk, said (not quite in these words, but the gist of it was the same) that it was time England rid themselves of their 'Lord's disease' and won a match

England were grateful for the first day flooding at Edgbaston. The Aussies didn't have enough time for anything but batting practice.

there. Nothing much changes! In '89 Australia won by six wickets, but England did make a fight of it in the later stages. Gower, who had made 57 of their first innings 286, departed, less than gruntled, the Saturday night press conference saying he was off to the theatre (the subsequent publicity delighting the box office, where there was an upsurge in ticket sales!). His team had conceded a 242-run lead, with Steve Waugh cracking a second unbeaten century (152) and sharing a ninth wicket stand of 130 in 108 minutes with Lawson (74). They then lost three wickets before the close – none of which was guaranteed to put any

No one did more than Terry Alderman, here having Tim Curtis caught by David Boon at Old Trafford, to win the Ashes. He took 41 Test wickets: a record.

ABOVE *The continual sniping during 1989 left David Gower so disenchanted that after walking out of the Press conference at Lord's he walked out of the captaincy at Old Trafford. He, Micky Stewart and Ted Dexter explain his departure.*

RIGHT *England had a long record of wicket-keepers who could bat a bit, and the dogged Jack Russell was determined to be amongst them. He scored his maiden Test century at Old Trafford.*

captain in good humour. But Gower appreciated the error of his ways, apologised to the Press and then on the Monday turned in his best innings for a long while, a determined rather than elegant hundred. The players met the Queen, but she would have had to set the Buckingham Palace corgis on to the Aussies to prevent their winning.

The Birmingham weather helped England to a draw at Edgbaston. Waugh managed only 43, but Dean Jones contributed 157 and the Aussies totalled 424. They dismissed England for 242 but contented themselves with batting practice in the time remaining. The big news at Old Trafford was not that a disenchanted Gower was quitting, but that an equally disenchanted Gatting (who, it transpired, had been first choice as

LEFT *Mark Taylor, seen walking off to generous applause at Trent Bridge with opening partner Geoff Marsh after they had batted throughout the day. Only Don Bradman had ever scored more runs than Taylor in a series.*

BELOW LEFT *It was Allan Border's fourth tour of England, and Australia's 'Captain Grumpy' seemed at peace with the world as he collected the replica of the Ashes at The Oval.*

England captain before Gower, but had been vetoed by Ossie Wheatley, chairman of the TCCB Cricket Committee) was leading a 16-strong team to South Africa. Despite Smith (143) and a maiden Test century by wicketkeeper Jack Russell (128 not out in the second innings), first Lawson with six wickets, then Alderman with five delivered another easy Australian victory. It was even easier at Trent Bridge. The insatiable Taylor and his opening partner Marsh batted all of Thursday and until after noon on Friday to break just about every record with a stand of 329. Taylor hit a career best 219, Marsh 136, and England's new boys, Michael Atherton and Devon Malcolm received an early taste of the grimness of an Ashes series. Robin Smith collected another hundred, but England took a horrible beating. Dean Jones stole the Aussie limelight at The Oval, hitting an attractive hundred before being caught superbly by Gower. Gower, in England's first innings (79) and essentially Smith in the second with an unbeaten 77, ensured a second drawn game in a depressing (for England) series.

1990

To say that it was a lack-lustre series when Richard Hadlee was bowling, and one of the world's best off-spinners in John Bracewell was in action, might sound a trifle churlish. But it is not. Despite a glorious summer of high temperatures and higher scoring, the New Zealand half was hit by some bad weather and never really got off the ground. Soccer's World Cup was competing for attention, successfully so with England reaching a semi-final, and of the three Cornhill Test matches, the first two were drawn and the last – Hadlee's last – was lost. Trevor Franklin had a good summer to erase memories of his previous banana-skin visit; he topped their batting averages and scored their only century, at Lord's. There were rich moments, too, for Hadlee, though Trent Bridge was hardly one of them. Here on the Nottingham ground where he played from 1978 to 1987 and was revered by local supporters, he was bowled by DeFreitas for a duck. Though England ran up 345-9 declared, with Mike Atherton scoring 151, no one collared Hadlee. He took four wickets for 89. Lord's was no doubt the warmest memory for Richard John Hadlee, now Sir Richard, having been knighted in the Queen's Birthday Honours. The scorecard for this, the second Test, named him as Sir R. Hadlee, a delightful touch, and he led the New Zealanders down the steps through the applauding Members. He took three wickets only as England, put in, scored 334, but then

Mike Atherton scored a fine century at Trent Bridge.

he rescued his side with the bat. Although Franklin had reached 101, New Zealand lost four middle-order wickets (Jones, Franklin, Crowe and Rutherford) for only seven runs and, as Hadlee walked in for his final Lord's innings, his side was in some crisis at 285-5. Hadlee had been around too long to be fazed by this: Hemmings' second ball towered away for six and, shortly after, Small went in similar fashion. Hadlee reached 50 from 42 deliveries and went on to 86 before, seeking a 13th four to go with the two sixes, he swung once too often at Hemmings and was bowled.

LEFT *Farewell to a giant. Richard Hadlee, one of the truly great all-rounders, leads New Zealand off the field at Trent Bridge, a ground where he had been revered when he played for Nottinghamshire.*

BELOW *Devon Malcolm, Player of the Match at Edgbaston, receives his cheque and champagne from Cornhill's Bryan Schofield.*

RIGHT *The giant electronic scoreboard acknowledges cricket's newest knight at Lord's, where he scored 86 in his final Test on the ground.*

TOTAL 69 for 1 Wkts
GA Gooch 35
#AT Stewart 14

Last wicket 3
MA Atherton 0
b Morrison
Overs 23 Extras 20

N *MC Snedden
P Sir R Hadlee

72 Overs

It was spectacular stuff – but the rest was tame. England batted out time after Wright had declared, and Hadlee, as was becoming for a national hero a few days short of his 39th birthday, rested a hamstring and viewed from the dressing room balcony.

Hopes of a winning farewell to Test cricket were dashed for cricket's newest knight at Edgbaston. John Wright boobed badly – and admitted so – by putting England in when he won the toss, and the home side won, to their intense relief. Other than what most considered an insignificant victory over Sri Lanka, it had been five years since they had won a home Test. Now, with Devon Malcolm taking his second successive five-in-an-innings return (5-46, which won the Cornhill Player of the Match award), Gooch (154) and Atherton (82) giving England an opening stand of 170, and the walrus-like Eddie Hemmings bowling superbly, England were to win by 114 runs. Hemmings was, at 41, older even than Hadlee. The off-spinner had taken only 19 wickets in his previous eight Tests; now he took six for 33 in two hours to scupper New Zealand's first innings. Malcolm was the man who then denied New Zealand any reward from the match. He included Sir Richard among his victims, but Hadlee was named Player of the Series (Atherton was the England nominee) having also grabbed (for the 36th time no less) five wickets in his final bowling session. With his very last ball he had Malcolm leg before, giving him a record-breaking 431st wicket. Hadlee had thus averaged five wickets per Test over 86 Tests – truly a player of many series.

INDIA IN ENGLAND

India must have felt at home. Unrelenting sunshine, hard-baked pitches, bowlers toiling for little reward. Yes, 1990 was a batsman's paradise and, while there were 15 centuries scored in the three Test

Graham Gooch scored 752 runs against the Indians, 333 of them in one innings at Lord's. Here he pulls Shastri during that monumental knock.

The Grandstand scoreboard at Lord's records the famous Gooch innings. The No. 5? Robin Smith who, like Allan Lamb, also scored a hundred.

matches, one man was the overriding master – Graham Gooch. Like Michael Atherton when he assumed the captaincy three years later, Gooch was one of those whom the role inspired to greater deeds. When, in 1989, he had a bad trot, particularly against Terry Alderman who nailed him four times in five Tests, and his average of 20.33 was enough to give lesser mortals a nervous breakdown, Gooch went off and worked at his game. Later his work ethic would be much criticised, but there is no denying that it paid handsome dividends for him. Against the New Zealanders he had scored 306 runs, at an average

RIGHT *India's batting contributed to a memorable summer with their captain Azharuddin scoring a sensational 179 at Old Trafford.*

BELOW *The bold, majestic Kapil Dev saved the follow on at Lord's by hitting Hemmings for four successive sixes. This was the fourth.*

Allan Lamb hit a superb 109 against India, which looked like a match-winning innings at Old Trafford until India were saved by Sachin Tendulkar, a cricketing babe who played like a veteran.

of 61.20. That was just for starters. The Indians took the full face of his broad bat. He scored a total of 752 against them, at an average of 125.33, and with his other first class runs for Essex he harvested 2,746 and averaged just over 100. If any one doubted that he was a great batsman before this Cornhill series began they would have been forced to accept the fact after the first Test at Lord's. He scored 333 runs in the first innings and added 123 more in the second. It was a monumental performance, a magnificent one by any standard. He batted the better part of two days (627 minutes), faced 485 balls, hit three of them for six and 43 for four. Lamb and Smith seemed bit players, yet both scored hundreds. Weary, but still defiant, India replied to England's 653-4 declared with 454. When it seemed, with the last wicket pair at the crease, that they would have to follow on, it was saved in majestic manner by Kapil Dev. He knew Hirwani was unlikely to sur-

vive an over, so he took matters into his own hands: the third, fourth, fifth and sixth balls of Hemmings's 20th over went, driven straight, for enormous sixes. The follow on was saved by one run – and Hirwani was out next ball without scoring! England then set the Indians 472 to win in seven hours, and they actually played as if they intended doing so. Two wickets down for only 23 did not deter the stroke making, but it was an impossible task on a worsening pitch. England won by 247 runs. Despite that margin, it was an absorbing game in which Azharuddin, in particular, Shastri and Kapil played full parts. A 60-year Lord's record was broken with 1,603 runs in total, and there were six centuries from five players. Who would have wished to be a bowler?

There were another half dozen centuries in the drawn affair at Old Trafford. Gooch and Atherton were going from strength to strength as a partnership; 204 at Lord's was fol-

lowed with 225 on Atherton's home ground (and, indeed, there was a 176 stand at The Oval to come). Both hit hundreds, as did Robin Smith, fast proving himself one of the 10 best players in world cricket. Before Lamb scored his second successive ton, Azharuddin compiled a sensational 179, which included 100 between lunch and tea. Yet they were all to be upstaged by the boy prodigy, Sachin Tendulkar, who followed 68 in the first innings with an unbeaten 119 for a maiden Test hundred. At 17 years and 112 days, he played with an immense maturity and a talent that matched it. He had all the strokes, being particularly strong off the back foot, and was not afraid to use them. He was put down at 10, was not disturbed and instead made England pay for the mistake. Some likened him to Gavaskar, and

RIGHT Just 17, Sachin Tendulkar up-staged all the big names with a maiden Test century of immense quality at Old Trafford.

David Gower's batting was at its sweetest at The Oval, where he plundered an unbeaten 157 to ensure England saved the match and the series.

Tendulkar actually played in his hero's pads. With the sides sharing 1,614 runs, it was no surprise the match was drawn, leaving India needing to win at The Oval to square the series. That they did not do so, they had to blame Gower. India did all that was necessary with the bat: 606 for nine declared, with a superb 187 from Shastri and a rather more measured 110 than might have been expected from Kapil. England got nowhere near the follow-on figure (bowled out for 340, Prabhakar taking 4-74) and Gooch and Atherton set about the task of scoring 267 to make India bat again. They posted another three figure partnership, but in the final analysis it was David Gower, the much-maligned left-hander, who salvaged a draw and thus the series. His tour was under threat, according to informed speculation, and he answered that with one of his finest knocks. Not taking a semblance of a risk, he carried his bat,

booked his visit to Australia and ended a run-drenched summer with 157. The individual figures (above) for the leading batsmen make fascinating reading.

It would be unkind to reproduce the bowling figures. Suffice it to mention that Hirwani was India's top wicket-taker (9), he conceded 586

runs for an average of 65.11, while Shastri's two wickets cost him 341 runs. Angus Fraser, in comparison, was positively miserly, for England: 16 wickets, 460 runs and an average of 28.75!

	I	N.O.	Runs	Hundreds	Avge
England					
R.A. Smith	6	4	361	2	180.50
G.A. Gooch	6	0	752	3	125.33
D.I. Gower	6	2	291	1	72.75
M.A. Atherton	6	0	378	1	63.00
A.J. Lamb	6	0	364	2	60.06
India					
M. Azharuddin	5	0	426	2	85.20
R.J. Shastri	5	0	336	2	67.20
S.R. Tendulkar	5	1	245	1	61.25
Kapil Dev	5	1	220	1	55.00
S.V. Manjrekar	5	0	216	0	43.20

1991

From the first ball at Headingley in June to the last one at The Oval in August it was a wonderful series for England. They had lost another Ashes tour, badly, in the winter and faced a West Indian side supposedly 'in transition'. There seemed nothing terribly transitory about Richardson, Haynes, Hooper, Ambrose, Marshall and Patterson, and England did well to square the series 2-2 in an enthralling finale. They had the rock-like, battle-hardened Gooch and the fiercely aggressive Smith in supreme form. Both scored just about twice as many runs as any of their team-mates, and Gooch carried his bat at Leeds – the first opener to do so in 10 years – ensuring our first home win over West Indies in over 20 years. Graeme Hick, the most talked about young batsman in the country, unfairly labelled the 'new Bradman' for the weight of his runs in County cricket, made his debut here after a seven year wait to play for England. Curtly Ambrose ensured that he did not complete the series. The 6 foot 7 inch Leeward Islander sent him packing six times out of the seven he

The Saturday of a Lord's Test is always special, but in 1991 Robin Smith made it spectacular with a quite devastating knock (148 not out) which included 20 boundaries.

ABOVE Rain prevented any play on the fourth day of the Lord's Test.

LEFT Graeme Hick was an Ambrose victim six times, and at Trent Bridge he was twice struck on the helmet by the West Indian.

batted. Hick scored 73 runs (at 10.42) and the first of many arguments that he could not deal with fast, short-pitched bowling arose. Ambrose had played only 25 Tests as he reached Headingley, but he was clearly world class. Hostile and fast, with both the yorker and bouncer in his armoury, he still had splendid control. And when Hick entered he always seemed to find that extra nip and just the right line to embarrass him. The 'L' in his initials (C.E.L.) stands for Lynwall. His parents must have known something 27 years earlier, and while he was too gangling to have Ray Lindwall's style, he had pace enough to take 28 English wickets at 20 apiece. Indeed, had he been fully fit on the last day of the series, when England were chasing 143 and losing wickets, there might well have been a different ending.

Thanks principally to Gooch, and to DeFreitas who took eight wickets in the match, England had the thrill of immediately being one-up in the series. And it stayed that way after Lord's where Smith hit a devastating hundred, Hooper had his first century against England, Pringle took five wickets and rain took two days out. Thus, a draw. West Indies squared things at Nottingham where Gooch and Atherton produced another three-figure opening stand, but Ambrose (eight in the match) was too fiery for all the others bar Smith, who never flinched. He batted well against the pace men; brought up on hard, fast wickets in South Africa, he relished taking the ball on the up,

RIGHT *Graham Gooch was always the player the opposition most wanted to remove – hence the joy as Ambrose bowls him for 13 at Trent Bridge.*

BELOW *A sign of the times. Edgbaston in 1991, and a sponsor's logo adorns the outfield. It sparked angry debate but quickly became an accepted part of the cricket scene.*

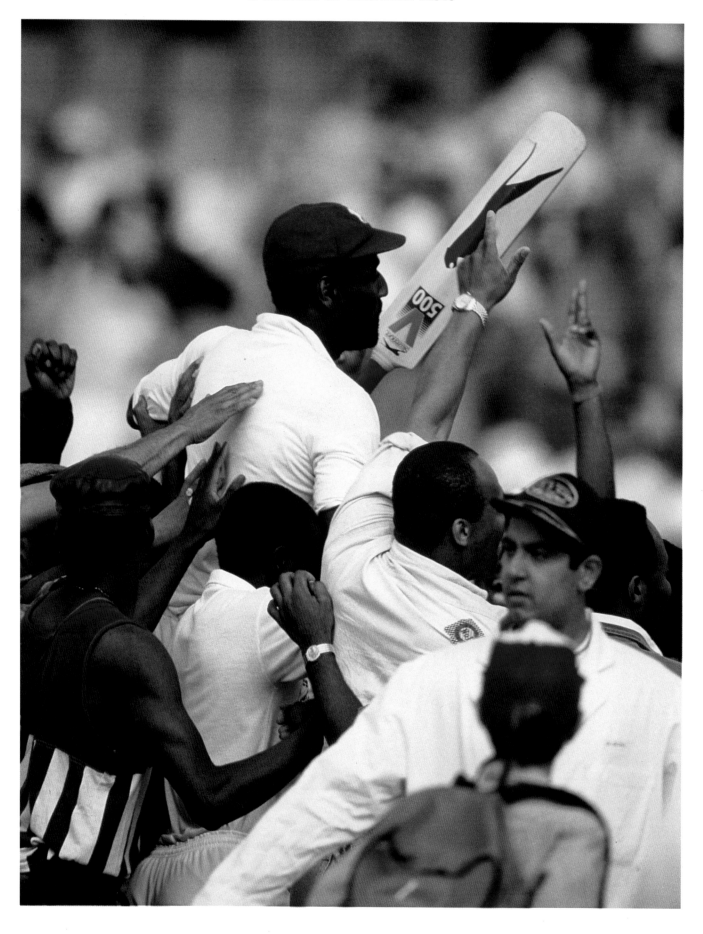

pulling ferociously, or spectacularly driving it square. An injured finger side-lined him at Edgbaston, and his aggression was sorely missed. England were never comfortable and lost by seven wickets. Richie Richardson registered his 13th Test hundred, and his first against England, on an Edgbaston pitch that no one could trust. It was an innings that marked him down as another for the future; he was renowned for his hard-wicket batting, but now he proved he could play on English ones as well. If you did not recognise him from his speciality, the square drive, you could not miss the man with the maroon sun hat (he despised a helmet, never bothering with one).

And so it was on to The Oval. Viv Richards's 121st and final Test; his 50th as captain. He scored a wondrous second innings 60, applauded all the way to the wicket and all the way back, but he lost the toss and with it almost certainly the match. England had to battle for their runs against bowlers relishing a wicket with pace and bounce. After a century opening stand, this time from Gooch and Hugh Morris, they were 120-3 when Smith went in. First with Ramprakash, then Stewart and finally with Botham (recalled for his 98th appearance), he saw the score to 336 before being leg before to Marshall. England finished on 419 and West Indies then collapsed in astonishing fashion. Phil Tufnell (also recalled but for only his fifth Test) with a brilliant display of left arm spin took six wickets for 25 and, despite a defiant Haynes who carried his bat for 75, West Indies had to follow on. They did so in the grandest style. Richardson hit another hundred, Hooper scored 60, including three sixes (two off 'Tuffers', one off 'Syd'

LEFT *Phil Tufnell bowled beautifully at The Oval, taking 6-25. Patterson, caught by Botham, is his sixth scalp.*

BELOW *Ian Botham, attempting to hook Ambrose at The Oval, over balances and nudges his own wicket.*

Lawrence) in 20 minutes before the arrears were cleared! Lawrence, with 5-106, was the destroyer this time. West Indies were out for 385 and it was left to Botham to face one delivery which he struck for four to win the match by five wickets and square the series. There is, in fact, a small postscript to this series. The West Indies brought with them a 22-year-old left-handed batsman who played eight first class matches, but not a Test, in which he scored 341 runs with a top score of 93 and an average of 28.41. His name? Brian Lara.

SRI LANKA IN ENGLAND

The Sri Lankans, appearing in their second one-off Test match in four years at Lord's, played cricket that was enjoyable to watch. It was not, however, winning cricket. They badly needed experience to toughen

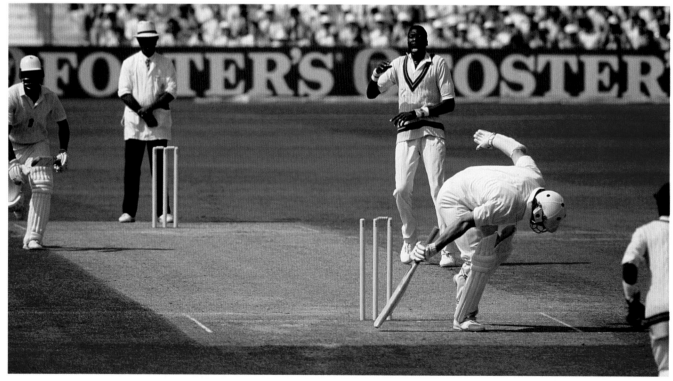

Rumesh Ratnayake was deceptively quick at Lord's in their single Test match, and he was rewarded with five wickets there.

them for Test matches (which would, hopefully, spill over into their domestic game) but the Test playing countries like England who wished to help them become a force were not able to afford even a three-Test tour. Selling tickets had become important. But my own memories of their 1991 visit are fond. As ever, their batting was resplendent, particularly against bowling that was less than the highest order and on easy-paced wickets. But their bowling, if tidy, was not penetrative enough. Yet my lasting memory is of Rumesh Ratnayake, their 27-year-old all-rounder, bowling well for five wickets at Lord's (that could have been six had century-maker Stewart not been dropped on 24), and then batting extravagantly for 52 off 51 balls. They lost, of course, by 137 runs, but one day, hopefully not too distant, a single Cornhill Test match will be a series.

1992

Not exactly the most peaceful year of the century, 1992. It produced a deal of exciting cricket, but also some quite deplorable incidents. Allegations of cheating (e.g. ball tampering), biased umpiring, delusions of racism and insults, and upsets with match referees. There were some appalling over rates, and a problem with paying customers in Birmingham; two balls bowled on the second day meant that the Edgbaston crowd had no money returned under TCCB regulations, and they were pretty miffed about it. Having just been recruited by the TCCB to be their media manager, I was at the centre of each and every rumpus. I was used to problems – for 35 years I had been involved in the production of Fleet Street newspapers, a stressful enough occupation. But I had never endured anything like this. For those who hope now to read all about those four months – sorry, chaps! I was in the dressing rooms, the umpires' rooms, match referee's room when the disagreements were at full spate, but my view then remains today; that I was in a privileged position and the secrets should remain secret. Anyway, this is a book to celebrate 100 Cornhill Test matches, not an exposé. Nevertheless, the series was plagued with incidents almost daily, and it is impossible to ignore them.

At Edgbaston, for instance. The teams had three days batting practice: Miandad scored 153 and Salim Malik 165, Stewart responding with

A brilliant batsman when in the mood, Javed Miandad scored an unbeaten 153 at Edgbaston – and shows his delight about it.

ABOVE Sunday, 21 June 1992 provided one of the most gripping days in Test match history. And when Ian Salisbury, in a quality spell of leg spin, bowled Aamir Sohail at Lord's, reducing Pakistan to 68-6, England smelled victory – yet in the end they lost by two wickets.

RIGHT Waqar helps Pakistan to win the Lord's Test as a batsman, scoring 20 not out, including this mighty four off Malcolm.

190 and Smith with 127. It was the furore over the two balls that was remembered, with the matter ending in court. Suggestions that the cricket authorities wanted two balls bowled merely to ensure that they did not have to pay back a second day's takings (the first day had been washed out and ticket money refunded) were ludicrous. Those who felt that should have listened in as senior administrators (frequently interrupted by police pressurising for an early abandonment) agonised for two hours about how to overcome the problem. To put the record straight, the Board was in effect a secretariat to 18 counties; the money actually belonged to those counties – it was not within the TCCB's remit to give

it away as the rules then stood.

So, with the sounds of the fans' fury still echoing the teams tried again at Lord's. The result was a two wicket win for Pakistan in an epic Sunday finale. Seventeen wickets fell during the day (though not Stewart's, who batted through England's second knock). With Pakistan facing defeat at 95-8, two feared competitors with the ball, Wasim and Waqar, stole victory *with the bat*, defying England for an hour while scoring 46 runs. With one ball left of this fourth day, Pakistan needed one run to win.

LEFT *The moment so many had waited for – in his 115th Test David Gower cover drives Aqib to pass Geoff Boycott's England record of 8,114 Test runs.*

RIGHT *Devon Malcolm is hit by a ball from Aqib that led to his being warned for intimidatory bowling.*

BELOW *Confrontation! It was a tough match for umpires David Shepherd and Roy Palmer at Old Trafford, with Pakistan constantly disputing decisions.*

The umpires are required to inspect the ball regularly, but it is not always thrown to them with good grace

England needed two wickets, and in the MCC Committee Room they were again agonising: Surely they wouldn't have to return the next morning for *one* run? Wasim ended the dilemma with a sweet cover drive that won the match. It was one of the greatest day's cricket anyone could recall, and totally appropriate that Cornhill should announce a £3.2 million two-year renewal of their sponsorship.

I am not quite sure now what my true love gave me on the fourth day of Christmas, but on the fourth day of the Old Trafford match David Gower gave us the most exquisite cover drive for four, which carried him past Geoffrey Boycott's record of 8,114 Test runs. Aamir Sohail's batting was just as expansive as Gower's and even more productive. He scored 205, and he and Ramiz Raja blazed away with a 115 opening stand before Ramiz was given out by Roy Palmer, umpiring his first Test, to a rather 'iffy' catch. This was without doubt the spark to the inflammatory scenes that were to follow. Aqib bounced Devon Malcolm, undisputed as the world's worst No. 11, and was warned for intimidatory bowling. Aqib threw a childlike display of petulance, his captain supporting rather than cooling him. Aqib, Miandad and Intikhab Alam, the manager, then accused Palmer of throwing his sweater back at the bowler rather than handing it to him. Thanks to the patience of the BBC's cricket producer, Keith Mackenzie, and his technicians, film was found for Conrad Hunte (a two-day stand-in for Clyde Walcott, the match Referee) which clearly showed this not to be the case. Aqib was fined and the manager warned, but the whole incident tainted the match. It was no better at Headingley, where England were to win by six wickets, a victory based on a first innings century from Graham Gooch and a reprieve for the captain in a tense second innings. Gooch, clearly run out by feet perhaps rather than inches when he was on 14 was given not out by Kenny Palmer, Roy's elder brother. Had he been trying to favour the home side, as the deeply suspicious visitors believed, Palmer could have found closer incidents than this one. He was himself horrified by what he saw on TV later, but the explanation was simple: he had watched to see if the wicketkeeper took the ball cleanly, and erred – honestly, but unfortunately. Clyde Walcott, back as match Referee, fined the substitute, Rashid Latif, for his outrageous dissent when an appeal for a catch by the

RIGHT *Aqib, feeling that umpire Roy Palmer, threw rather than passed his sweater to hum, refuses to hand it to the umpire for his following over. Miandad intervenes.*

BELOW *Stand-in Match Referee Conrad Hunte is leading Miandad, Bob Bennett, the Lancashire chairman, and Pakistan manager Khalid Mahmood back to the pavilion after a special viewing of the sweater-throwing incident from various angles on BBC TV recordings.*

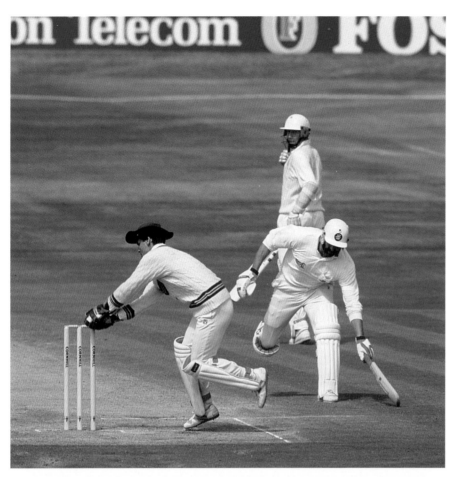

The flashpoints which helped to sour the Headingley Test. Graham Gooch was given not out (LEFT) when clearly short of the crease as England were fighting to score the 99 they required for victory and (BELOW) David Gower survives a frenzied appeal for lbw against Mushtaq.

RIGHT There was no argument at The Oval, however, where Waqar bowls Gower for a single.

wicketkeeper was turned down (when he might well have suspended him thus costing him his first cap at The Oval) and again a Test match had an unnecessary sour taste. Neil Mallender, playing the first of his two Tests, distinguished himself with eight wickets; Salim Malik was twice not out with 82 and 84; and, for two hours in which he scored 31, Gower, aided by the young Ramprakash, fought doggedly against the heavy artillery of Wasim and Waqar and the wiles of Mushtaq. They came together at 65-4, with the England dressing room in a state of tension, and battled through to 99 and a hard won triumph. How it might have gone had Gooch been given out at 14 is a

No two players did more to win the Cornhill Trophy for Pakistan than Waqar and Wasim . . . 15 wickets at The Oval and 43 between them in the series.

matter for conjecture. Wasim and Waqar left no room for conjecture at The Oval, however. They took 15 wickets between them (Wasim had equalled Imran's record of 21 wickets in a series, Waqar broke it in this match) and only Atherton in the first and Smith in the second innings mastered them. From being 182-3 after opting to bat first, England collapsed to 207 out (Wasim 6-67). Pakistan took a 173 run lead, Latif looking a quality player in his first Test with 50, and Malcolm taking five wickets. Waqar then took centre stage. He reduced England to 59-4, finished with 5-52 and – a little like the Lord Mayor's Show – Ramprakash was required to bowl one ball to allow Pakistan victory by 10 wickets.

Sadly, the ball tampering business which had begun during the one-day Texaco International at Lord's back in May, roared into new life at the final press conference, with Micky Stewart mischievously saying he knew how Pakistan doctored the ball, but was not saying more. That Pakistan had mastered a method of making an old ball, rather than a new one, swing violently was obvious. All this was outside the Laws and the spirit of the game. Ball tampering, lifting the seam or keeping a shine with the help of facial cream or, primarily, hair grease, was nothing new. It could also be done by adding to the scuffing on one side while keeping the other as pristine as possible. A sight of finger nails being utilised brought the famous saying 'Whoa, steady on!' from the BBC commentator and ex-Australian captain, Richie Benaud, followed by an involuntary 'Jesus'. There was much splendid cricket played in 1992; it was a shame that ball tampering occupied so many headlines.

1993

Wrist spinners had been about as thick on English cricket grounds as the elm tree after Dutch Elm disease struck. They were a relic of the past – until 1993, that is. Then one arrived looking all he was cracked up to be: a beach boy with dyed blond hair, a rather aggressive nature with a reluctance to accept discipline and war-paint all over his face. The war-paint was not out of keeping: Shane Warne, 23, and a leg spinner, won most of his battles against the English batsmen, and most certainly the war. England lost a 6-Test series comprehensively; they were second best until they scored a surprise victory at The Oval, but the Ashes were long gone (four matches lost, one drawn) by then and Warne had taken 34 wickets (at 25.79 apiece). Nor were they the tail-enders. England utilised 10 batsmen in the top six of the order and, with the exception of Hick (ticketed 'Reserved' for big Merv Hughes) every one of them was 'Warned'.

One of the most significant balls ever bowled in Test cricket. Shane Warne's first in an Ashes Test, at Old Trafford. Mike Gatting was stunned by a ball the bowler later conceded 'was a fluke – I was just hoping to get it on the square.' It bowled Gatting and influenced a whole Ashes series.

LEFT *A bizarre moment at the start of a bizarre summer for Gooch. Instinctively he flicks the ball away as it was falling on his stumps and is given out, handled the ball, under Law 33. He had scored 133 and England's hopes of saving the first Test went with him.*

BELOW *Allan Border catches Peter Such off Hughes to conclude the first Test in Australia's favour at Old Trafford.*

RIGHT *At Lord's where he was once an office boy, Michael Slater scored a maiden Test century, excelling with attacking shots like this in his 152.*

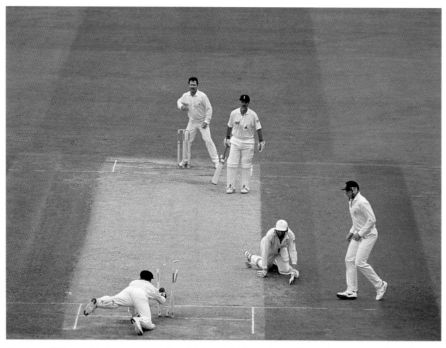

Setting off for a third run at Lord's which would have brought up his 100, Mike Atherton turned, slipped and was run out for 99.

Gooch was nailed by him five times. Atherton, Smith and Stewart four times each. Gatting was twice Warne's scalp – the first time memorably and stunningly. I doubt if any single ball bowled in cricket history had quite the effect of his first one in an Ashes Test. No one who was at Old Trafford on Friday 4 June 1993 (second day of the first Cornhill Test match) will ever forget what they saw. Certainly Mike Gatting won't. Peter Such, making his England debut, had taken six for 67, and despite a century from Mark Taylor, Australia were restricted to 289. There were no alarm bells. Gooch and Atherton put on 71 before the Lancashire man was out, caught behind by the ever-alert, ever-aggressive Ian Healy.

Enter Gatting – and enter Warne. 'Gatt' was the best player of spin bowling in England. But he had not seen Warne – Australia had not played him in their match against Middlesex. Now, in the 28th over of England's innings, our best and the man Martin Crowe had described as 'the world's best', were face to face. Warne ambled in, the ball snaked from the back of his hand and pitched 18 full inches outside leg

stump. Gatting, believing – having every right to believe – that the ball was safe, played no shot. As the ball suddenly turned viciously there was a silence that was deafening as it then took the top of the off-stump. Gatting seemed paralysed. He stared in stunned disbelief before, with a

shake of the head, he departed. From that moment, England were losers. Warne was always the threat, the one to keep batsmen awake at night. He was never mastered, conceding less than two runs in each of his 440 overs. Defeat, then, by 179 runs at Manchester and humiliation to come at Lord's. Here Taylor helped himself to another hundred, while Michael Slater, as charming a young cricketer as you could ever wish to meet, and the perfect attacking foil to Taylor, scored 152 at the ground where but a short time before he had been working in the MCC office. Boon hit 164, Mark Waugh 99, Border 77 and Australia declared at 632-4. That was 62 more than England could manage in two attempts. Even with McDermott unable to bowl (he was taken to hospital with a twisted bowel that put him out of the tour) Australia dismissed England twice. Atherton scored 80, Smith was given out (stumped) by a third umpire watching TV high up in the pavilion – an unwanted first – and the first knock mustered just 205. Atherton was again the stumbling block until he slipped when sent back by Gatting and was run out for 99. A spinners' Test: Warne collected eight wickets,

Merv Hughes snares an intruder at Trent Bridge just as he snared Graeme Hick in the first two Tests – quite emphatically!

Graham Thorpe became the first England batsman in 20 years to score a Test hundred on his debut. Here at Trent Bridge he is congratulated by Nasser Hussain.

Tim May (under-valued as Warne's partner) six, and Border one – a little souvenir of his final visit to Lord's.

At Trent Bridge, match referee Clive Lloyd warned the Aussies about their sledging. England actually scored over 400, allowing them to declare with Graham Thorpe becoming the first Englishman in 20 years to score a Test debut hundred. England could not bowl them out, neither could the Aussies get 371 to win. Stalemate, for once. Not so at Leeds, or at Birmingham. England lost both – and at Headingley they lost their captain, at Birmingham Ted Dexter. I think Graham Gooch decided to quit on the Saturday night at Headingley. On the Sunday he was in jovial, buoyant mood. He was never the dreary 'Essex man' as he was so often perceived. He has a real sense of humour, but it was clear that the cares of leading a losing team had grown too much. Ian Chappell, a former Aussie captain, reckoned that Gooch 'froze, like a rabbit caught in the headlights. It was obvious he wasn't the man to lead England to an Ashes victory.' Goochie subscribed to that view by declaring that the team would benefit from 'new ideas, a new approach and someone else to look up to.' That man would be Michael Atherton. He was the right choice, a man in decent form, but defeat at Edgbaston was as emphatic as at Leeds. This time the resignation was Ted Dexter's. The much-maligned chairman of the England Committee had intimated that he would not be seeking re-election, but cricket could not wait and Ted was forced into quitting. He had done much good, with the 'A' and Under-19 teams particularly, and in the welfare of county players. He must have had some grim satisfaction when his final selection as chairman won at The Oval by 161 runs. Whether the Aussies were tired, disinterested by this stage or beaten by a better side is

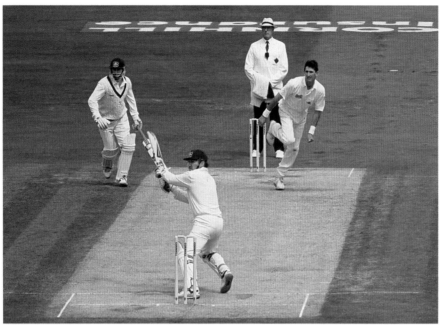

Allan Border ground England down at Leeds with his first double century against them. This was the shot which brought 200 up, enabling him to declare at 653-4.

hard to say, but as England had not won against Australia since Melbourne in December 1986 it was an auspicious occasion and a joyful one for Atherton. Devon Malcolm and Angus Fraser, who enjoy part-nering one another, were restored, and with England having scored 380 put Australia out for 302. Fraser took five wickets, Malcolm three, and there was an air of confidence around the England team suddenly. Ramprakash, a last-minute call up for the injured Thorpe, batted beautifully for 64 in the second innings, and Australia were set 390. Two or three decisions went badly for Australia, particularly one against Slater who was clearly caught off his arm guard, and they folded for 229. Fraser was Cornhill's Player of the Match, Gooch (who top-scored in the series with 673 runs and became England's leading run-getter) was the home side's Player of the Series, and Keith Fletcher nominated Shane Warne – who else? – as Australia's Player of the Series.

Graham Gooch drives Paul Reiffel for four at The Oval to pass David Gower's record as the leading English run-getter.

1994

The question was pointed but very fair as the New Zealanders arrived for the 12th tour of England: *Was there life after Richard Hadlee?* The answer is that there was, but it was a very much tougher life than when the colossus from Christchurch strode the cricket scene for 86 Tests, taking 431 wickets and scoring 3,124 runs. Chris Cairns, the nearest they had to an all-rounder to take over from Sir Richard, was injured and didn't even arrive, and the key fast bowler, Danny Morrison, was also injured and played no part in the tour. So the emergence of Adam Parore as a wicketkeeper who could more than hold his end up, and Dion Nash as an all-rounder, were a bonus to a party that lost the Test series and won only one of their 12 first class games. With 213 runs, Parore had the second best aggregate, scoring useful runs in the three Tests. He did

One of the world's most majestic batsmen, Martin Crowe passed 5,000 Test runs at Lord's where he scored 142.

not concede a bye in a long stint at Trent Bridge, and he took seven catches. Nash had a sensational Lord's: 11 wickets for 169 in the match (17 in the series) and a lusty 56 which probably had much to do with Middlesex then signing him as their overseas player for 1995.

England won the opener at Trent Bridge by an innings and 90 – a match marked by Steve Bucknor becoming the first overseas umpire to officiate in England under the newly instituted ICC International Panel. DeFreitas took nine, including his 100th Test wicket, while Atherton (with 101) and Gooch (with 210 – to which he added only 13 runs in three more innings) were England's chief run-getters. It was a different story at Lord's where Martin Crowe (passing 5,000 Test runs) scored 142 of the highest quality, and Bryan Young contributed 94 to ensure New Zealand had a total big enough to embarrass England. With greater penetration, the tourists might well have won this Test. England needed 407, and while Stewart scored 119 it was never on. With an hour left, England had only three wickets standing, but one of them was the stubborn Rhodes, and he saw England through to the close safely, adding 24 more to his unbeaten 32 in the first innings. Gough and DeFreitas shared in the first of their two wonderful partnerships of the summer, with an exhibition of free hitting which brought them 130 at Old Trafford. Atherton, seemingly thriving on the responsibility of cap-taincy, scored his seventh Test hun-dred as England powered their way to 382. None of those expected to contribute hugely did so, and the 69 from DeFreitas and Gough's 65 were badly needed in more ways than one. They then took seven wickets between them to put New Zealand out for 151. Yet another supreme century from Martin Crowe, his 17th in total and fifth against England,

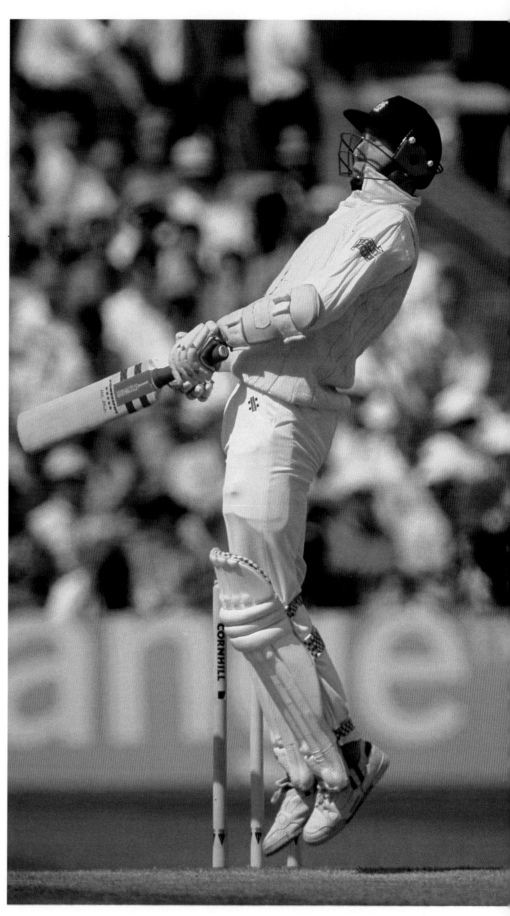

Michael Atherton thrived on the captaincy, scoring 273 runs against New Zealand, but here he has to take evasive action at Old Trafford before completing a battling 111.

ABOVE Dion Nash proved there was life after Richard Hadlee. He had a sensational match at Lord's, taking 11 wickets, with Graham Gooch twice a victim lbw.

LEFT New boy on the block. Darren Gough made his Test debut at Old Trafford, survived Adam Parore's appeal for a stumping, and proceeded to make 65. Then, with pace, aggression and a Waqar-like yorker, he went on to take six New Zealand wickets.

plus Parore's best innings of the tour, salvaged matters for New Zealand. It was Crowe's farewell to England, and despite knee problems that limited his mobility, he scored 380 runs (at 63.33) taking his Test aggregate to 5,230 runs. While the Old Trafford crowd may have been disgruntled at the weather, which held England up, they most certainly didn't begrudge this most dignified and likeable cricketer a single run.

SOUTH AFRICA

They had been away a long time these Springboks, and didn't the

Lord's crowd let them know just how much they had been missed. As Andrew Hudson and Gary Kirsten followed England out on this July Thursday in 1994, the Members rose as one man to applaud them, and within moments the whole ground had erupted in a tumultuous roar of welcome. The emotion was so thick it could have been spooned up like golden syrup. If any sport is going to provide fairy tale endings, I suppose it is cricket – and a fairy-tale ending there was to this first visit in 29 years for the South Africans who, in this politically correct age, were now being called The Proteas. Not that it mattered what they were called. There may have been no Graeme Pollock or Barry Richards, but here at cricket's HQ the new tourists were just as resolute and had quite the same fighting spirit. And they won; won overwhelmingly by 356 runs. Sadly, this historic victory – and those words do not overstate the moment – was almost totally consumed by the headlines of the England captain's dust. A five-hour century from Kepler Wessels and a five-figure return for that flaxen-haired thoroughbred Allan Donald were the stuff of headlines back in Cape Town, but even Darren Gough's eight-wicket haul in the match took a distant second place to the dirty story of what was in Michael Atherton's pocket. Donald and his manager Mike Procter felt cheated at the way their triumph in bowling out England – seeking 456 to win the game – for a mere 99 was so diminished. They felt Atherton's contretemps with match Referee Peter Burge of considerably less significance – but, as is the way of these things, the Press did not. A handful of dust, with which he dried his hands on a steamy day, and whether it was being used for illegal reasons (i.e. to dry one side of the ball) stole all the South Africans' glory. To any-

An historic and highly emotional moment at Lord's as Andrew Hudson and Gary Kirsten walk out to open the South African innings after an absence of 29 years. It was a tumultuous welcome.

Kepler Wessels was a grimly determined captain for South Africa, and at Lord's he batted for almost five hours in scoring his 105.

one who knows Atherton, to suggest he was either a liar or a cheat would be insulting. But Ray Illingworth, new bossman of the England set-up, quickly fined him £2,000, taking the heat from the situation as far as the match Referee was concerned (although Mr Burge did fine Atherton later for a show of dissent that few others could discern.) But there had to be sympathy for South Africa, for there would be few such moments of glory for them as England re-grouped to draw at Leeds and to level the series with a Devon Malcolm-inspired performance at The Oval. Lord's was the high spot; they were unsettled on faster wickets and their top batsmen did not deliver as Wessels might have hoped.

Surrey's Graham Thorpe won an overdue recall at Headingley and showed the folly of his omission with knocks of 72 and 73. Atherton, for the second time in little more than a year, was out on 99 and, with Stewart contributing 89, England declared at a healthy 477-9. At one stage, the tourists seemed certain to follow on, but Peter Kirsten, elder brother of the opener and in his 40th year, resisted with a brave maiden century. Quite deservedly, he was named Cornhill's Player of the Match for it. Hick,

showing signs of finally delivering what he had promised for so long, scored 110 – his first Test century at home – as England set South Africa 298 to win. A dogged 65 from Gary Kirsten ended English hopes, and thus Leeds produced its first draw in 14 years on a most unlikely Headingley pitch which did not for

once help the swing and seam bowlers.

It was a different matter at The Oval. There they found a typically true and fast pitch which produced a finish no one who was there on the Saturday and Sunday will ever forget. If the bowlers were prepared to put their backs into it, they got some assistance – no one more so than Devon Malcolm whose 9-57 put him right up there in the top half dozen best Test bowling performances. There had been little to suggest such dramatic happenings in the earlier stages. An heroic Brian McMillan, who held the South African's first innings together with 93, had been struck by a quick one from Malcolm, as was Jonty Rhodes. Jonty, who had come with the reputation of a new Colin Bland, had been exciting in the field, but here he was architect to his own misfortune, ducking low down to a ball from which Malcolm might well have won an lbw appeal. The batsman was taken to hospital and stayed overnight, but returned when

Brian McMillan topped both the South African batting and bowling and took sensational catches, like this one which dismissed Graeme Hick for 25 at Headingley.

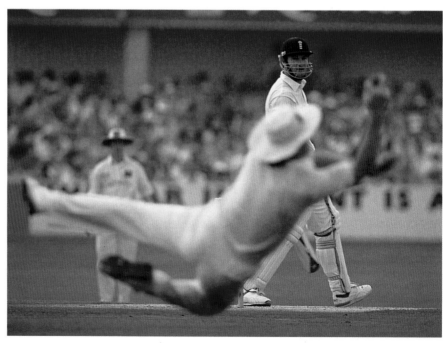

None of the South Africans really relished Devon Malcolm's pace at The Oval: Peter Kirsten's leg stump takes off like Concorde.

his side was in trouble in their second innings on the Sunday.

At the half-way point, just before the close on Friday, it was evenly balanced: South Africa 332, England 222-7. Then DeFreitas and Gough put on a 30-minute spectacular that would have graced the closing stages of a one-day final. Putting bat to ball in glorious fashion, they scored 59 from 50 balls and changed the whole pattern of the match. If England were not imbued with new spirit from this pair's pyrotechnics, then Devon Malcolm was on the Sunday morning. Fanie De Villiers, who took 12 wickets in the series, then made possibly his biggest mistake in life; he bounced – and hit – Malcolm. The big man from Kingston, normally so placid and affable, was unhurt but enraged. 'You guys are history,' he snapped at De Villiers, and so they were. And so was he, for that matter: In 16 overs and three balls he took nine wickets. In all my years of watching big sport, whether at Wembley or Twickenham, Lord's or Longchamp I had never been so enthralled. As prayers were being said in churches up and down the country, the South Africans, batting again with a 28-run lead, could themselves have done with some help from on high. Devon, whose radar has often been turned off, was fully tuned in. And he was frighteningly fast. He simply scythed through them. One wicket for no runs, two down and still not a run scored, and then, in just nine balls, it was three for one. Malcolm had gripped the crowd by the throat. Grown men were in ecstacy and behaving like schoolboys. Cullinan was a man apart, and looking a Test batsman to keep an eye on, and only he plus the dogged courage of Wessels and McMillan enabled South

The final, history-making ball. Malcolm delivers it, Allan Donald – who has bowled a few rockets in his time – is out without scoring, and Malcolm has taken his ninth wicket for 57 runs.

Devon Malcolm, bounced and struck by Fanie de Villiers at The Oval, glowers down the pitch at the bowler and warns him 'You guys are history.' They were; and so was he.

Africa to reach the heights of 175. The remainder were simply decimated. Each wicket brought forth greater cheers, and it was only Thorpe and Gough, who combined to dismiss the valiant Cullinan, that prevented Malcolm from taking all 10. He was nominated as Player of the Match and England's Player of the Series (McMillan took the Cornhill cash as the key South African). It had been a troubled summer for England, and particularly their young captain, but as England knocked off the runs before lunch and the crowd swarmed to picnic on the outfield, his world must have suddenly seemed a much happier place.

1995

Glory be! God is an English gentleman after all – and, no doubt, a member of MCC. How else can one explain a match at Lord's that was made in Heaven and another at Old Trafford of such titanic proportions? Had Cornhill written a script for the summer of 1995 they could not have bettered the reality of their 18th season of cricket sponsorship and their 100th Test match. In bare detail, England were thoroughly humiliated at Headingley in the opening Test, played champagne cricket to level matters at Lord's in a quite memorable match, and were incinerated by the West Indians' scorched-earth bowling on an Edgbaston pitch tailor-made for Ian Bishop, Curtly Ambrose and Courtney Walsh. Thus it was that England turned up with a revamped side (only five survived for one reason or another) for Cornhill's 100th in Manchester. It was a game England simply had to win . . . and they did so, thrillingly and quite magnificently in one of the toughest Test matches ever played.

The warmth of the Yorkshire club's hospitality never seems to be matched by their weather. Ray Illingworth was in a new sheepskin, the West Indians had three or four sweaters apiece to keep them from freezing, and had the Committee room been full of Eskimos it would have been no surprise. The first Test was that sort of a match. It began with a real 'silly season' story of Brian

Carl Hooper lashed four sixes as he hurried West Indies to a 9-wicket victory at Headingley. This one came off Richard Illingworth.

Lara being subject to a voodoo on him (the result of some land deal back in Trinidad). There was more likely a voodoo curse on England. They chose to open with Robin Smith and play Alec Stewart as wicketkeeper and No. 5 to universal disapproval, lost the toss, had to re-start seven times on Day One and then lost Mike Atherton to the last ball of the day for 81. He had by now developed into a player of immense stature. He was also beginning to handle the Press well. 'I would rather have 80 than nought,' he answered to those who wondered why he didn't continue and get a hundred. It was virtually half England's total, thanks to some pretty slipshod batting by others. Nor was the bowling much better. Angus Fraser had been omitted in favour of Devon Malcolm – a decision which probably not even the captain totally approved ('Angus is one I'll always rate,' he said three Tests later), Darren Gough broke down, and while he batted he could not bowl, and it was more the rush of blood West Indian batsmen suffer all too often these days that prevented them from getting more than 282. Graham Thorpe, who so reminds one of the late Kenny Barrington with a Union Jack where his heart should be, who, with a defiant 61, steered England to a 125 run lead, but it was never enough to trouble the West Indians. Carl Hooper (74), who failed first time around with a duck, and Brian Lara (48), who was thought to have also failed by making only 53 instead of his usual few hundred, saw them to a nine wicket win. Chairman Illy was unbowed: 'We can do better than that,' he asserted. And, by golly, they could.

As demoralising and dreadful as they were at Headingley, England finally redeemed themselves at Headquarters. Heroes were thick upon the ground. Fraser, properly restored, was all heart and commitment; his unremitting accuracy must have been like Chinese water torture. Thorpe was all guts; Smith, playing for his Test future, all courage and grim determination for eight hours; Stewart had one moment of sheer

The moment that turned a Test match. Lara was batting brilliantly at Lord's with 54 runs from 62 balls when, trying to cover drive Gough, he got a touch. The ball was falling short of first slip, but Stewart dived to take a catch of the highest quality and put England on the way to a famous victory.

If ever a man deserved a hundred it was Sherwin Campbell at Lord's battling valiantly in a losing cause for over five hours, but it was not to be . . . he fell seven short.

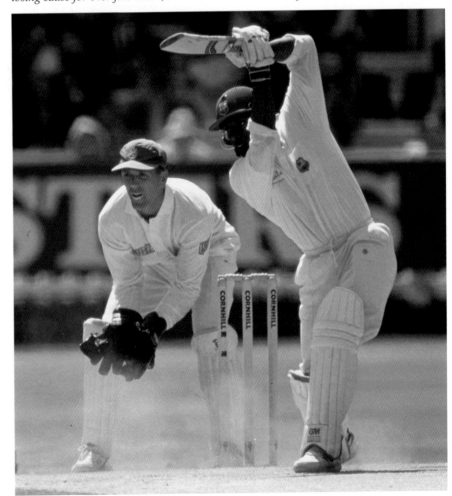

England's new man of the moment, Dominic Cork, to his immense joy, finally lures Sherwin Campbell into giving a catch to the wicket-keeper. Campbell was dismissed for 93 and Cork had his fifth of seven wickets for 43 – two supreme performances.

genius that further vindicated his dual role. Dominic Cork, after eight one-day Internationals, had a dream debut with seven match-winning wickets in the second innings (plus 53 runs in total), and Chairman Illy had a smile of satisfaction at the end. At the outset, mind, he had a deal of stick. Having selected Steve Rhodes and insisted he would play, he then sent the downcast wicketkeeper back to Worcester, and retained Stewart. It was a brilliant catch that Alec took to dismiss Lara, just as the young man from Trinidad was swinging the game away from England, that justified Illy's judgement. At 54, the score at 99-1 and a partnership with Sherwin Campbell worth 84, Lara followed a ball from Gough that was going away from him and got an edge. It was never going to reach first slip but, like an osprey swooping for breakfast, Stewart launched himself and

held a devastating catch, left-handed. It was the turning point.

England's first innings total had been at least a hundred less than Atherton had hoped for. He himself was out to a wicked yorker from Ambrose, and after Smith and Thorpe had shared a stand of 111, wickets went to poor batsmanship. Mark Ramprakash, nervous and desperately needing confidence, collected the first of his two ducks, which would cost him his place, and just about the only satisfaction was the Bothamesque spirit, that England so miss, displayed by Cork, who cut his first ball in Test cricket for four and scored 30.

Lara, the first of Fraser's five wickets (his second such tally in a Lord's Test) was also his hundredth, in his 25th Test, and Angus made a nonsense of the statement by Andy Roberts, the West Indian coach, that

their game plan was to score 500 and bat just the once for victory. Mind you, when his side were being bowled out well short of that total he also expressed the opinion that it was the worst Test pitch he had ever seen in England, but perhaps he sensed that his charges were already on a slippery slope. When England batted a second time, Smith showed his quality and courage with 90 splendid runs. But it was no one-man show: Stewart, restored to the front line, Hick with his best knock against opponents who consider him a bunny, Thorpe (concussed by a Walsh beamer and in hospital overnight for X-rays and a head scan), Cork and Gough all did their bit to set the tourists a 296 target. Thus was the scene set for the most gripping finale to a great Test match.

Campbell and the sublime Lara, 38 not out overnight, marched out to

ABOVE *He ducked and he weaved but he never once flinched. Robin Smith gets another short one from Ian Bishop at Edgbaston during a non-stop attack on his body. His brave 41 out of England's 89 was, said Mike Atherton, 'worth a century'.*

RIGHT *England were on their knees, but Bishop and Jimmy Adams fall to theirs in joyful embrace when Smith's resistance is finally ended.*

battle towards the 228 they still required, with only Hooper out. Lara, with rich artistry, cover drove Gough for his 50, did the same two balls later and then, in a single heart-stopping moment, he erred and Stewart was diving to make that sensational catch. It was 99-2, the odds suddenly in England's favour, and Atherton tossed the ball to Cork. The 23-year-old from Derbyshire was about to create his own bit of history. He first had Adams caught by Hick. In his next over Richardson was leg before without scoring. Immediately after lunch, in his ninth over, he had

Sherwin Campbell will for ever know he was caught behind, bowled Fraser, in Cornhill's 100th Test match at Old Trafford. The bowler's appeal and the boundary board are all the evidence he needs.

Arthurton caught by substitute Paul Weekes. Weekes then took a really stunning catch off Gough to send Murray packing, and despite the disciplined Campbell, the writing was etched large on the big scoreboard: 177-6. First Gibson fell to Cork, then Campbell – seven short of a richly-deserved hundred – and Ambrose and Walsh became victims six and seven for Cork. His seven for 43 was the second best return ever by an English debutant, and he darted for a souvenir stump like one of the missiles he had been throwing at West Indies bats all afternoon.

The series was squared. It was a first victory over the West Indians at Lord's since 1957, and English hopes of a series win were high. 'Roll on Edgbaston,' said a jubilant England captain. Andy Roberts had derided the Lord's wicket, but his was a modest criticism compared to what England's dressing room felt about Birmingham's brown and green strip. As the first ball of the match from Ambrose reared higher and higher from short of a length, searing over and ever wider of the wicketkeeper's hands some 30 yards behind the stumps, Tom Graveney muttered: 'That will wake a few of them up in our dressing room!' Didn't it just. Wes Hall, the visitors' manager, had commented after Lord's that they would play England on any pitch, or on a car park if they wanted. Now he and his team had a pitch that was just what Doctors Ambrose, Bishop and Walsh might have prescribed. Atherton, now appointed captain for the series, was out third ball without scoring; Hick was not the man for this sort of crisis and went for three. Thorpe batted supremely for his 30 runs, and received a totally unplayable ball, right up at his throat, from Ambrose. Smith and Stewart showed fight, but the fact was that many batsmen got out to poor shots. Steve Rouse, former left-

RIGHT When luck is with you, make the most of it. Cork did. No-one noticed that he had dislodged a bail; there was no appeal and he batted on . . . to make an unbeaten 56!

BELOW RIGHT Brian Lara was on a different plane from everyone as he scored 145 in his bid to salvage something for the West Indies from Cornhill's 100th Test.

arm Warwickshire bowler who is now the groundsman, was outspoken: 'Atherton played a poor shot, Hick got opened up and was playing towards mid-on, Stewart went back instead of forward, Smith hit a long hop to cover and Gough had a slog.' Phew! Tough words – but no one can argue that there was not the same venom in the pitch when England bowled as there was when they were batting. Nor that all the hard work at Lord's had been wasted. Fingers were battered (Jason Gallian, replacement for Ramprakash, collected seven runs and a broken digit) but, more important, minds were battered. West Indies totalled 300 and then ran through England in just 30 overs for 89. One man rose to the occasion with one of the bravest innings ever seen on a cricket field: Robin Smith. Hit time and again by Walsh and Bishop (Ambrose damaged a groin and these two bowled 51 of the 74 overs England survived in total), the Hampshire man refused to show he had been hurt. As the ball hurtled into his arms or his ribs, he never once rubbed the spot, never once conceded he was in pain. It was a heroic performance, and anyone who ever doubted that the South African had anything but an English heart pounding away inside him now knew differently. Atherton called the pitch a disgrace, but – more important – he called for the performance to be forgotten as they went into the fourth Test of the summer – Cornhill's Century.

The champagne flowed even before the game in Manchester – a bizarre affair where brilliant sunshine stopped play, where Cork knocked a bail off but got away with it because no one noticed until too late and no one appealed, when West Indies bowled 34 no balls and gave away 64

In only his third Test match Dominic Cork joins the history-makers. He bowls Richardson off bat and pad (left) with the fourth ball of his first over on the Sunday morning; traps a disgruntled Murray leg before with his next ball (below left) and then on his knees, arms raised in jubilation has Hooper also leg before wicket for a hat-trick, only the 22nd in Test history (bottom).

extras in all in England's first innings, and bowled without a single slip, let alone a battalion of them, in the second. And it was at Old Trafford where England threw away their flaccid clothing and adorned themselves in their fighting outfits. Cornhill had a celebration party at an old country hotel 16 miles distant from Old Trafford for the 30 or so involved in the beginning of their sponsorship. That some of them reached the ground late the next day was because of snarled up traffic, which caused that 16 miles to take two hours, and was nothing at all to do with popping corks. Nor was champers the reason Michael Holding – yesteryear's great bowler, who knew his way to the wicket better than most, and now a journalist – was also slightly delayed. Not sure of the one mile from hotel to ground, he followed an England player's car. Unfortunately it was Graeme Hick's, and he was heading towards the M6 and the M5 on his way back to Worcester, having been omitted by England!

Holding's successors also lost their way. On a wicket expected to take spin, it was the seamers, Fraser and Cork, who took four apiece putting out the West Indians for 216 – a moderate total that still owed much to Lara. Because he was not scoring 375 each time he batted, there was criticism of Lara; but watching him here, he was still batting on a different plane from everyone else. West Indian spinners having gone out of fashion since Ramadhin and Valentine and Lance Gibbs, it was Walsh who gave his side hope on the first evening, bowling new boy Nick Knight and the restored John Crawley who was in obvious distress at shouldering arms to the third ball of the last over and losing his off stump. The next day, in an effort to retrieve matters, the West Indians bowled some pretty torrid stuff. Dickie Bird (showing more courage than most umpires) finally warned Walsh for intimidation – a long over-due step. Thorpe and Smith still needed a little luck and a lot of grit as they fought to give England a win-ning lead. Like street fighters, their team-mates all battled, but their 104 stand was the crucial one. England leading by 221 were surely about to celebrate along with the sponsors. In scoring 149 in their second innings overnight, West Indies were still 62 runs behind and with only seven wickets left. Now Dominic Cork, Player of the Match at Lord's, stamped his indelible authority on this match. With his fourth ball of the morning Richie Richardson played on: Cork was a little lucky, the batsman a trifle unlucky. As he came forward and slightly across his wick-et, the ball clipped Richardson's pad, ricocheted on to the bat and into his stumps. Murray entered, shuffled across and was plumb leg before; the injured Hooper came out to join a stunned Lara, helpless at the other end as the carnage continued. A no-ball meant a seventh ball in Cork's over. Again it was absolutely straight, again the batsman missed it and again umpire Cyril Midgley's finger went up. The first English hat-trick since Peter Loader, also against the West Indies but at Leeds in 1957 and only the 22nd such feat in the histo-ry of Test cricket. And in only his third Test!

While Lara was at the crease, all was not lost for the West Indians. He passed the three figure mark – Cornhill's apart, the first century of the series – and protecting his tail-end partners, farming the bowling, clipping the fours and generally per-forming like the giant he is, scored 145 and gave West Indies a 93 run lead. If England ignored the psycho-logical problem, they were home and

The tension mounts as Atherton awaits the verdict of the third umpire, Chris Baldertone. It went against him – run out for 22.

'Forget Edgbaston,' ordered Mike Atherton; and one of the biggest smiles of the summer shows that his next order will be to 'Remember Old Trafford.'

dry. But, had they not been bowled out for 46 not that long ago? Had West Indies not scattered them for 89 in only the last match? In short, England worried, could they do it again? Briefly, it seemed they might.

Atherton was senselessly run out; 1-39, and a sudden decline. Knight went; 2-41. Still no *real* danger, but Thorpe succumbed within six balls. Three down for 45 – and ostensibly for four as Smith played a ball from the outstanding Bishop into his face. He retired, was ordered to hospital even though he wished to stay and fight on if needed, and X-rays showed a fractured cheekbone. Jack and John, Russell the much maligned wicketkeeper, and Crawley, a Lancashire man full of talent, saw them safely home by six wickets.

The hundredth Cornhill Test was over. There could have been no finer match, no finer result for such an occasion. The celebrations had a real meaning. England had squared the series once more. It was on to Trent Bridge and then The Oval with God in his Heavenly pavilion and all well with English cricket again. In the four Tests thus far, much had been learned. Perhaps the most important was that in 1995 we had been reminded just how much we had missed the brilliance of Ian Botham. Dominic Cork was no Beefy, but he had the man's essential qualities; he relished the battle, he was determined and, like Botham, displayed the knack of making things happen. He has a long way to go, but had already won two Player of the Match awards in his first three Test matches.

However, reflecting on the past 18 years, I have no hesitation in stating that during that time I.T. Botham was a man apart –*The Player of a Century of Cornhill Tests.*

England's Captains

JOHN MICHAEL BREARLEY

Captained England 31 times (between 1977 and 1981).
He won 18, lost 4 and drew 9. Total number of Tests played: 39. He scored 1442 runs at 22.88.

IAN TERENCE BOTHAM
Captained England 12 times (1980–81). He lost 4 and drew 8. Total number of Tests played: 102.
He scored 5200 runs at 33.54, with 14 centuries, and took 383 wickets at 24.80.

ROBERT GEORGE DYLAN WILLIS

Captained England 18 times (between 1977 and 1981). He won 7, lost 5 and drew 6.
Total number of Tests played: 90. He took 325 wickets at 25.20 and scored 840 runs at 11.50.

DAVID IVON GOWER

Captained England 32 times (between 1984 and 1989). He won 5, lost 18 and drew 9.
Total number of Tests played: 117. He scored 8231 runs at 43.49, with 18 centuries.

MICHAEL WILLIAM GATTING

Captained England 23 times (between 1986 and 1988). He won 2, lost 5 and drew 16.
Total number of Tests played: 79. He scored 4409 runs at 35.55, with 10 centuries.

JOHN ERNEST EMBUREY

Captained England twice (1988). He lost both.
Total number of Tests played: 64. He has taken 147 wickets at 38.40 and scored 1713 runs at 22.53.

CHRISTOPHER STUART COWDREY

Captained England in one Test only (in 1988). He lost it.
Total Tests played: 6. He scored 101 runs at 14.42 and took 4 wickets at 77.25.

GRAHAM ALAN GOOCH

Captained England 34 times (between 1988 and 1993). He won 10, lost 12 and drew 12.
Total number of Tests played: 118. He scored 8900 runs at 42.58, with 20 centuries.

MICHAEL ANDREW ATHERTON

Captained England 22 times (since 1993). He has won 7, lost 10 and drawn 5.
Total number of Tests played: 49. He has scored 3525 runs at 38.73, with 7 centuries.

Players of the Series

1978	Pakistan	I.T. Botham (E)	
	New Zealand	R.W. Taylor (E)	
1979	India	I.T. Botham (E)	
1980	West Indies	J. Garner (WI)	
	Australia	K.J. Hughes (A)	
1981	Australia	I.T. Botham (E)	
1982	India	Kapil Dev (I)	
	Pakistan	Imran Khan (P)	
1983	New Zealand	R.J. Hadlee (NZ)	
1984	West Indies	C.G. Greenidge (WI)	
	Sri Lanka	S. Wettimuny (SL)	
1985	Australia	D.I. Gower (E)	
1986	India	M.W. Gatting (E)	D.B. Vengsarkar (I)
	New Zealand	D.I. Gower (E)	R.J. Hadlee (NZ)
1987	Pakistan	M.W. Gatting (E)	Imran Khan (P)
1988	West Indies	G.A. Gooch (E)	M.D. Marshall (WI)
1989	Australia	R.C. Russell (E)	T.M. Alderman (A)
1990	New Zealand	M.A. Atherton (E)	Sir Richard Hadlee(NZ)
	India	G.A. Gooch (E)	M. Azharuddin (I)
1991	West Indies	G.A. Gooch (E)	C.E.L. Ambrose (WI)
	Sir Lanka	A.J. Stewart (E)	R.J. Ratnayake (SL)
1992	Pakistan	G.A. Gooch (E)	Wasim Akram & Waqar Younis (P)
1993	Australia	G.A. Gooch (E)	S.K. Warne (A)
1994	New Zealand	P.A.J. DeFreitas (E)	D.J. Nash (NZ)
	South Africa	D.E. Malcolm (E)	B.M. McMillan (SA)

DAVID GOWER

Player of the Match

1978 1st Test v New Zealand at The Oval (111)
1979 1st Test v India at Edgbaston (200*)
1983 3rd Test v New Zealand at Lord's (108) (34)
1985 3rd Test v Australia at Trent Bridge (Capt.) (166) (17)

Player of the Series

1985 Australia – 732 runs – a record against Australia in a Test series in England.
1986 New Zealand – 293 – three Tests (passed 6,000 Test runs during series).

* = not out

Statistics
CORNHILL INSURANCE TEST MATCHES

HUNDREDS – MATCH BY MATCH

Name	Score	For	Against	Venue	Date
C.T.Radley	106	England	Pakistan	Edgbaston	01/06/78
I.T.Botham	100	England	Pakistan	Edgbaston	01/06/78
I.T.Botham	108	England	Pakistan	Lord's	15/06/78
D.I.Gower	111	England	New Zealand	The Oval	27/07/78
G.Boycott	131	England	New Zealand	Trent Bridge	10/08/78
G.P.Howarth	123	New Zealand	England	Lord's	24/08/78
G.Boycott	155	England	India	Edgbaston	12/07/79
D.I.Gower	200*	England	India	Edgbaston	12/07/79
D.B.Vengsarkar	103	India	England	Lord's	02/08/79
G.R.Viswanath	113	India	England	Lord's	02/08/79
I.T.Botham	137	England	India	Headingley	16/08/79
G.Boycott	125	England	India	The Oval	30/08/79
S.M.Gavaskar	221	India	England	The Oval	30/08/79
G.A.Gooch	123	England	West Indies	Lord's	19/06/80
D.L.Haynes	184	West Indies	England	Lord's	19/06/80
I.V.A.Richards	145	West Indies	England	Lord's	19/06/80
C.H.Lloyd	101	West Indies	England	Old Trafford	10/07/80
P.Willey	100*	England	West Indies	The Oval	24/07/80
G.Boycott	128*	England	Australia	Lord's	28/08/80
G.M.Wood	112	Australia	England	Lord's	28/08/80
K.J.Hughes	117	Australia	England	Lord's	28/08/80
I.T.Botham	149*	England	Australia	Headingley	16/07/81
J.Dyson	102	Australia	England	Headingley	16/07/81
I.T.Botham	118	England	Australia	Old Trafford	13/08/81
G.N.Yallop	114	Australia	England	Old Trafford	13/08/81
A.R.Border	123*	Australia	England	Old Trafford	13/08/81
G.Boycott	137	England	Australia	The Oval	27/08/81
A.R.Border	106*	Australia	England	The Oval	27/08/81
D.M.Wellham	103	Australia	England	The Oval	27/08/81
D.W.Randall	126	England	India	Lord's	10/06/82
D.B.Vengsarkar	157	India	England	Lord's	10/06/82
I.T.Botham	128	England	India	Old Trafford	24/06/82
S.M.Patil	129*	India	England	Old Trafford	24/06/82
A.J.Lamb	107	England	India	The Oval	08/07/82
I.T.Botham	208	England	India	The Oval	08/07/82
D.W.Randall	105	England	Pakistan	Edgbaston	29/07/82
Mohsin Khan	200	Pakistan	England	Lord's	12/08/82
G.Fowler	105	England	New Zealand	The Oval	14/07/83
C.J.Tavaré	109	England	New Zealand	The Oval	14/07/83
A.J.Lamb	102*	England	New Zealand	The Oval	14/07/83
D.I.Gower	112*	England	New Zealand	Headingley	28/07/83
D.I.Gower	108	England	New Zealand	Lord's	11/08/83
A.J.Lamb	137*	England	New Zealand	Trent Bridge	25/08/83
I.T.Botham	103	England	New Zealand	Trent Bridge	25/08/83
H.A.Gomes	143	West Indies	England	Edgbaston	14/06/84
I.V.A.Richards	117	West Indies	England	Edgbaston	14/06/84
G.Fowler	106	England	West Indies	Lord's	28/06/84
A.J.Lamb	110	England	West Indies	Lord's	28/06/84
C.G.Greenidge	214*	West Indies	England	Lord's	28/06/84
A.J.Lamb	100	England	West Indies	Headingley	12/07/84
H.A.Gomes	104*	West Indies	England	Headingley	12/07/84
A.J.Lamb	100*	England	West Indies	Old Trafford	26/07/84
C.G.Greenidge	223	West Indies	England	Old Trafford	26/07/84
P.J.L.Dujon	101	West Indies	England	Old Trafford	26/07/84
D.L.Haynes	125	West Indies	England	The Oval	09/08/84
A.J.Lamb	107	England	Sri Lanka	Lord's	23/08/84
S.Wettimuny	190	Sri Lanka	England	Lord's	23/08/84
S.A.R.Silva	102*	Sri Lanka	England	Lord's	23/08/84
L.R.D.Mendis	111	Sri Lanka	England	Lord's	23/08/84
R.T.Robinson	175	England	Australia	Headingley	13/06/85
A.M.J.Hilditch	119	Australia	England	Headingley	13/06/85
D.I.Gower	166	England	Australia	Trent Bridge	11/07/85
G.M.Wood	172	Australia	England	Trent Bridge	11/07/85
G.M.Ritchie	146	Australia	England	Trent Bridge	11/07/85
M.W.Gatting	160	England	Australia	Old Trafford	01/08/85
A.R.Border	146*	Australia	England	Old Trafford	01/08/85
A.R.Border	196	Australia	England	Lord's	27/06/85
R.T.Robinson	148	England	Australia	Edgbaston	15/08/85
D.I.Gower	215	England	Australia	Edgbaston	15/08/85
M.W.Gatting	100*	England	Australia	Edgbaston	15/08/85
G.A.Gooch	196	England	Australia	The Oval	29/08/85
D.I.Gower	157	England	Australia	The Oval	29/08/85
G.A.Gooch	114	England	India	Lord's	05/06/86
D.B.Vengsarkar	126*	India	England	Lord's	05/06/86
D.B.Vengsarkar	102*	India	England	Headingley	19/06/86
M.W.Gatting	183*	England	India	Edgbaston	03/07/86
G.A.Gooch	183	England	New Zealand	Lord's	24/07/86
M.D.Crowe	106	New Zealand	England	Lord's	24/07/86
J.G.Bracewell	110	New Zealand	England	Trent Bridge	07/08/86
D.I.Gower	131	England	New Zealand	The Oval	21/08/86
M.W.Gatting	121	England	New Zealand	The Oval	21/08/86
J.G.Wright	119	New Zealand	England	The Oval	21/08/86
R.T.Robinson	166	England	Pakistan	Old Trafford	04/06/87
C.W.J.Athey	123	England	Pakistan	Lord's	18/06/87
M.W.Gatting	124	England	Pakistan	Edgbaston	23/07/87
Mudassar Nazar	124	Pakistan	England	Edgbaston	23/07/87
M.W.Gatting	150*	England	Pakistan	The Oval	06/08/87
Javed Miandad	260	Pakistan	England	The Oval	06/08/87
Salim Malik	102	Pakistan	England	The Oval	06/08/87
Imran Khan	118	Pakistan	England	The Oval	06/08/87
G.A.Gooch	146	England	West Indies	Trent Bridge	02/06/88
A.J.Lamb	113	England	West Indies	Lord's	16/06/88
C.G.Greenidge	103	West Indies	England	Lord's	16/06/88
A.J.Lamb	125	England	Australia	Headingley	08/06/89
M.A.Taylor	136	Australia	England	Headingley	08/06/89
S.R.Waugh	177*	Australia	England	Headingley	08/06/89
D.I.Gower	106	England	Australia	Lord's	22/06/89
S.R.Waugh	152*	Australia	England	Lord's	22/06/89
D.M.Jones	157	Australia	England	Edgbaston	06/07/89
R.A.Smith	143	England	Australia	Old Trafford	27/07/89
R.C.Russell	128*	England	Australia	Old Trafford	27/07/89
R.A.Smith	101	England	Australia	Trent Bridge	10/08/89
G.R.Marsh	138	Australia	England	Trent Bridge	10/08/89
M.A.Taylor	219	Australia	England	Trent Bridge	10/08/89
D.M.Jones	122	Australia	England	The Oval	24/08/89
T.J.Franklin	101	New Zealand	England	Lord's	21/06/90
M.A.Atherton	151	England	New Zealand	Trent Bridge	07/06/90
G.A.Gooch	154	England	New Zealand	Edgbaston	05/07/90
G.A.Gooch	333	England	India	Lord's	26/07/90

G.A.Gooch	123	England	India	Lord's	26/07/90
A.J.Lamb	139	England	India	Lord's	26/07/90
R.A.Smith	100*	England	India	Lord's	26/07/90
R.J.Shastri	100	India	England	Lord's	26/07/90
M.Azharuddin	121	India	England	Lord's	26/07/90
G.A.Gooch	116	England	India	Old Trafford	09/08/90
M.A.Atherton	131	England	India	Old Trafford	09/08/90
A.J.Lamb	109	England	India	Old Trafford	09/08/90
R.A.Smith	121*	England	India	Old Trafford	09/08/90
M.Azharuddin	179	India	England	Old Trafford	09/08/90
S.R.Tendulkar	119*	India	England	Old Trafford	09/08/90
D.I.Gower	157*	England	India	The Oval	23/08/90
R.J.Shastri	187	India	England	The Oval	23/08/90
Kapil Dev	110	India	England	The Oval	23/08/90
G.A.Gooch	154*	England	West Indies	Headingley	06/06/91
R.A.Smith	148*	England	West Indies	Lord's	20/06/91
C.L.Hooper	111	West Indies	England	Lord's	20/06/91
R.B.Richardson	104	West Indies	England	Edgbaston	25/07/91
R.A.Smith	109	England	West Indies	The Oval	08/08/91
R.B.Richardson	121	West Indies	England	The Oval	08/08/91
G.A.Gooch	174	England	Sri Lanka	Lord's	22/08/91
A.J.Stewart	113*	England	Sri Lanka	Lord's	22/08/91
A.J.Stewart	190	England	Pakistan	Edgbaston	04/06/92
R.A.Smith	127	England	Pakistan	Edgbaston	04/06/92
Javed Miandad	153*	Pakistan	England	Edgbaston	04/06/92
Salim Malik	165	Pakistan	England	Edgbaston	04/06/92
Aamir Sohail	205	Pakistan	England	Old Trafford	02/07/92
G.A.Gooch	135	England	Pakistan	Headingley	23/07/92
G.A.Gooch	133	England	Australia	Old Trafford	03/06/93
M.A.Taylor	124	Australia	England	Old Trafford	03/06/93
I.A.Healy	102*	Australia	England	Old Trafford	03/06/93
M.A.Taylor	111	Australia	England	Lord's	17/06/93
M.J.Slater	152	Australia	England	Lord's	17/06/93
D.C.Boon	164*	Australia	England	Lord's	17/06/93
D.C.Boon	107	Australia	England	Headingley	22/07/93
A.R.Border	200*	Australia	England	Headingley	22/07/93
S.R.Waugh	157*	Australia	England	Headingley	22/07/93
M.E.Waugh	137	Australia	England	Edgbaston	05/08/93
G.A.Gooch	120	England	Australia	Trent Bridge	01/07/93
G.P.Thorpe	114*	England	Australia	Trent Bridge	01/07/93
D.C.Boon	101	Australia	England	Trent Bridge	01/07/93
M.A.Atherton	101	England	New Zealand	Trent Bridge	02/06/94
G.A.Gooch	210	England	New Zealand	Trent Bridge	02/06/94
A.J.Stewart	119	England	New Zealand	Lord's	16/06/94
M.D.Crowe	142	New Zealand	England	Lord's	16/06/94
M.A.Atherton	111	England	New Zealand	Old Trafford	30/06/94
M.D.Crowe	115	New Zealand	England	Old Trafford	30/06/94
K.C.Wessels	105	South Africa	England	Lord's	21/07/94
G.A.Hick	110	England	South Africa	Headingley	04/08/94
P.N.Kirsten	104	South Africa	England	Headingley	04/08/94
B.C. Lara	145	West Indies	England	Old Trafford	27/07/95

TEN WICKETS IN A MATCH — MATCH BY MATCH

NAME	FIGURES	FOR	AGAINST	VENUE	DATE
I.T.Botham	11-140	England	New Zealand	Lord's	24/08/78
I.T.Botham	10-253	England	Australia	The Oval	27/08/81
D.K.Lillee	11-159	Australia	England	The Oval	27/08/81
B.L.Cairns	10-144	New Zealand	England	Headingley	28/07/83
R.M.Ellison	10-104	England	Australia	Edgbaston	15/08/85
C.Sharma	10-188	India	England	Edgbaston	03/07/86
R.J.Hadlee	10-140	New Zealand	England	Trent Bridge	07/08/86
Abdul Qadir	10-211	Pakistan	England	The Oval	06/08/87
Imran Khan	10-77	Pakistan	England	Headingley	02/07/87
M.D.Marshall	10-92	West Indies	England	Lord's	16/06/88
T.M.Alderman	10-151	Australia	England	Headingley	08/06/89
D.J.Nash	11-169	New Zealand	England	Lord's	16/06/94
D.E.Malcolm	10-138	England	South Africa	The Oval	18/08/94

FIVE WICKETS IN AN INNINGS — MATCH BY MATCH

NAME	FIGURES	FOR	AGAINST	VENUE	DATE
C.M.Old	7-50	England	Pakistan	Edgbaston	01/06/78
I.T.Botham	8-34	England	Pakistan	Lord's	15/06/78
R.G.D.Willis	5-47	England	Pakistan	Lord's	15/06/78
Sarfraz Nawaz	5-39	Pakistan	England	Headingley	29/06/78
R.G.D.Willis	5-42	England	New Zealand	The Oval	27/07/78
I.T.Botham	6-34	England	New Zealand	Trent Bridge	10/08/78
I.T.Botham	6-101	England	New Zealand	Lord's	24/08/78
I.T.Botham	5-39	England	New Zealand	Lord's	24/08/78
R.J.Hadlee	5-84	New Zealand	England	Lord's	24/08/78
I.T.Botham	5-70	England	India	Edgbaston	12/07/79
Kapil Dev	5-146	India	England	Edgbaston	12/07/79
I.T.Botham	5-35	England	India	Lord's	02/08/79
R.G.D.Willis	5-65	England	West Indies	Trent Bridge	05/06/80
A.M.E.Roberts	5-72	West Indies	England	Trent Bridge	05/06/80
M.A.Holding	6-67	West Indies	England	Lord's	19/06/80
L.S.Pascoe	5-59	Australia	England	Lord's	28/08/80
D.K.Lillee	5-46	Australia	England	Trent Bridge	18/06/81
T.M.Alderman	5-62	Australia	England	Trent Bridge	18/06/81
G.F.Lawson	7-81	Australia	England	Lord's	02/07/81
I.T.Botham	6-95	England	Australia	Headingley	16/07/81
R.G.D.Willis	8-43	England	Australia	Headingley	16/07/81
T.M.Alderman	6-135	Australia	England	Headingley	16/07/81
I.T.Botham	5-11	England	Australia	Edgbaston	30/07/81
R.J.Bright	5-68	Australia	England	Edgbaston	30/07/81
T.M.Alderman	5-42	Australia	England	Edgbaston	30/07/81
T.M.Alderman	5-109	Australia	England	Old Trafford	13/08/81
I.T.Botham	6-125	England	Australia	The Oval	27/08/81
D.K.Lillee	7-89	Australia	England	The Oval	27/08/81
I.T.Botham	5-46	England	India	Lord's	10/06/82
R.G.D.Willis	6-101	England	India	Lord's	10/06/82
Kapil Dev	5-125	India	England	Lord's	10/06/82
D.R.Doshi	6-102	India	England	Old Trafford	24/06/82
Tahir Naqqash	5-40	Pakistan	England	Edgbaston	29/07/82
Imran Khan	7-52	Pakistan	England	Edgbaston	29/07/82
Mudassar Nazar	6-32	Pakistan	England	Lord's	12/08/82
I.T.Botham	5-74	England	Pakistan	Headingley	26/08/82
Imran Khan	5-49	Pakistan	England	Headingley	26/08/82
R.J.Hadlee	6-53	New Zealand	England	The Oval	14/07/83
R.G.D.Willis	5-35	England	New Zealand	Headingley	28/07/83
B.L.Cairns	7-74	New Zealand	England	Headingley	28/07/83
E.J.Chatfield	5-95	New Zealand	England	Headingley	28/07/83
N.G.B.Cook	5-35	England	New Zealand	Lord's	11/08/83
R.J.Hadlee	5-93	New Zealand	England	Lord's	11/08/83
N.G.B.Cook	5-63	England	New Zealand	Trent Bridge	25/08/83
D.R.Pringle	5-108	England	West Indies	Edgbaston	14/06/84
J.Garner	5-55	West Indies	England	Edgbaston	14/06/84
I.T.Botham	8-103	England	West Indies	Lord's	28/06/84
M.D.Marshall	6-85	West Indies	England	Lord's	28/06/84
P.J.W.Allott	6-61	England	West Indies	Headingley	12/07/84
M.D.Marshall	7-53	West Indies	England	Headingley	12/07/84
R.A.Harper	6-57	West Indies	England	Old Trafford	26/07/84
I.T.Botham	5-72	England	West Indies	The Oval	09/08/84
M.D.Marshall	5-35	West Indies	England	The Oval	09/08/84
M.A.Holding	5-43	West Indies	England	The Oval	09/08/84
I.T.Botham	6-90	England	Sri Lanka	Lord's	23/08/84
J.E.Emburey	5-82	England	Australia	Headingley	13/06/85
G.F.Lawson	5-103	Australia	England	Trent Bridge	11/07/85
C.J.McDermott	8-141	Australia	England	Old Trafford	01/08/85
I.T.Botham	5-109	England	Australia	Lord's	27/06/85
C.J.McDermott	6-70	Australia	England	Lord's	27/06/85
R.G.Holland	5-68	Australia	England	Lord's	27/06/85
R.M.Ellison	6-77	England	Australia	Edgbaston	15/08/85
R.M.Ellison	5-46	England	Australia	The Oval	29/08/85
C.Sharma	5-64	India	England	Lord's	05/06/86
R.M.H.Binny	5-40	India	England	Headingley	19/06/86
C.Sharma	6-58	India	England	Edgbaston	03/07/86
R.J.Hadlee	6-80	New Zealand	England	Lord's	24/07/86
R.J.Hadlee	6-80	New Zealand	England	Trent Bridge	07/08/86
G.R.Dilley	5-92	England	Pakistan	Edgbaston	23/07/87

Imran Khan	6-129	Pakistan	England	Edgbaston	23/07/87
G.R.Dilley	6-154	England	Pakistan	The Oval	06/08/87
Abdul Qadir	7-96	Pakistan	England	The Oval	06/08/87
N.A.Foster	8-107	England	Pakistan	Headingley	02/07/87
Imran Khan	7-40	Pakistan	England	Headingley	02/07/87
M.D.Marshall	6-69	West Indies	England	Trent Bridge	02/06/88
G.R.Dilley	5-55	England	West Indies	Lord's	16/06/88
M.D.Marshall	6-32	West Indies	England	Lord's	16/06/88
M.D.Marshall	7-22	West Indies	England	Old Trafford	30/06/88
D.R.Pringle	5-95	England	West Indies	Headingley	21/07/88
N.A.Foster	5-64	England	West Indies	The Oval	04/08/88
T.M.Alderman	5-107	Australia	England	Headingley	08/06/89
T.M.Alderman	5-44	Australia	England	Headingley	08/06/89
T.M.Alderman	6-128	Australia	England	Lord's	22/06/89
G.F.Lawson	6-72	Australia	England	Old Trafford	27/07/89
T.M.Alderman	5-66	Australia	England	Old Trafford	27/07/89
T.M.Alderman	5-69	Australia	England	Trent Bridge	10/08/89
T.M.Alderman	5-66	Australia	England	The Oval	24/08/89
D.E.Malcolm	5-94	England	New Zealand	Lord's	21/06/90
P.A.J.DeFreitas	5-53	England	New Zealand	Trent Bridge	07/06/90
E.E.Hemmings	6-58	England	New Zealand	Edgbaston	05/07/90
D.E.Malcolm	5-46	England	New Zealand	Edgbaston	05/07/90
R.J.Hadlee	5-53	New Zealand	England	Edgbaston	05/07/90
A.R.C.Fraser	5-104	England	India	Lord's	26/07/90
A.R.C.Fraser	5-124	England	India	Old Trafford	09/08/90
C.E.L.Ambrose	6-52	West Indies	England	Headingley	06/06/91
D.R.Pringle	5-100	England	West Indies	Lord's	20/06/91
C.E.L.Ambrose	5-74	West Indies	England	Trent Bridge	04/07/91
C.C.Lewis	6-111	England	West Indies	Edgbaston	25/07/91
B.P.Patterson	5-81	West Indies	England	Edgbaston	25/07/91
D.V.Lawrence	5-106	England	West Indies	The Oval	08/08/91
P.C.R.Tufnell	6-25	England	West Indies	The Oval	08/08/91
P.A.J.DeFreitas	7-70	England	Sri Lanka	Lord's	22/08/91
P.C.R.Tufnell	5-94	England	Sri Lanka	Lord's	22/08/91
R.J.Ratnayake	5-69	Sri Lanka	England	Lord's	22/08/91
Waqar Younis	5-91	Pakistan	England	Lord's	18/06/92
Wasim Akram	5-128	Pakistan	England	Old Trafford	02/07/92
N.A.Mallender	5-50	England	Pakistan	Headingley	23/07/92
Waqar Younis	5-117	Pakistan	England	Headingley	23/07/92
D.E.Malcolm	5-94	England	Pakistan	The Oval	06/08/92
Wasim Akram	6-67	Pakistan	England	The Oval	06/08/92
Waqar Younis	5-52	Pakistan	England	The Oval	06/08/92
P.M.Such	6-67	England	Australia	Old Trafford	03/06/93
P.R.Reiffel	5-65	Australia	England	Headingley	22/07/93
P.R.Reiffel	6-71	Australia	England	Edgbaston	05/08/93
S.K.Warne	5-82	Australia	England	Edgbaston	05/08/93
T.B.A.May	5-89	Australia	England	Edgbaston	05/08/93
A.R.C.Fraser	5-87	England	Australia	The Oval	19/08/93
M.G.Hughes	5-92	Australia	England	Trent Bridge	01/07/93
P.A.J.DeFreitas	5-71	England	New Zealand	Trent Bridge	02/06/94
D.J.Nash	6-76	New Zealand	England	Lord's	16/06/94
D.J.Nash	5-93	New Zealand	England	Lord's	16/06/94
A.A.Donald	5-74	South Africa	England	Lord's	21/07/94
D.E.Malcolm	9-57	England	South Africa	The Oval	18/08/94
I.R.Bishop	5-32	West Indies	England	Headingley	08/06/95
A.R.C.Fraser	5-66	England	West Indies	Lord's	22/06/95
D.G.Cork	7-43	England	West Indies	Lord's	22/06/95
C.A.Walsh	5-45	West Indies	England`	Edgbaston	06/07/95

HAT-TRICK

NAME		FOR	AGAINST	VENUE	DATE
D.G.Cork		England	West Indies	Old Trafford	27/07/95

BEST PERFORMANCES

HIGHEST SCORES

NAME	SCORE	FOR	AGAINST	VENUE	DATE
G.A.Gooch	333	England	India	Lord's	26/07/90
Javed Miandad	260	Pakistan	England	The Oval	06/08/87
C.G.Greenidge	223	West Indies	England	Old Trafford	26/07/84
S.M.Gavaskar	221	India	England	The Oval	30/08/79
M.A.Taylor	219	Australia	England	Trent Bridge	10/08/89
D.I.Gower	215	England	Australia	Edgbaston	15/08/85
C.G.Greenidge	214*	West Indies	England	Lord's	28/06/84
G.A.Gooch	210	England	New Zealand	Trent Bridge	02/06/94
I.T.Botham	208	England	India	The Oval	08/07/82
Aamir Sohail	205	Pakistan	England	Old Trafford	02/07/92
D.I.Gower	200*	England	India	Edgbaston	12/07/79
A.R.Border	200*	Australia	England	Headingley	22/07/93
Mohsin Khan	200	Pakistan	England	Lord's	12/08/82
A.R.Border	196	Australia	England	Lord's	27/06/85
G.A.Gooch	196	England	Australia	The Oval	29/08/85
S.Wettimuny	190	Sri Lanka	England	Lord's	23/08/84
A.J.Stewart	190	England	Pakistan	Edgbaston	04/06/92
R.J.Shastri	187	India	England	The Oval	23/08/90
D.L.Haynes	184	West Indies	England	Lord's	19/06/80
M.W.Gatting	183*	England	India	Edgbaston	03/07/86
G.A.Gooch	183	England	New Zealand	Lord's	24/07/86
M.Azharuddin	179	India	England	Old Trafford	09/08/90
S.R.Waugh	177*	Australia	England	Headingley	08/06/89
R.T.Robinson	175	England	Australia	Headingley	13/06/85
G.A.Gooch	174	England	Sri Lanka	Lord's	22/08/91
G.M.Wood	172	Australia	England	Trent Bridge	11/07/85
D.I.Gower	166	England	Australia	Trent Bridge	11/07/85
R.T.Robinson	166	England	Pakistan	Old Trafford	04/06/87
Salim Malik	165	Pakistan	England	Edgbaston	04/06/92
D.C.Boon	164*	Australia	England	Lord's	17/06/93
M.W.Gatting	160	England	Australia	Old Trafford	01/08/85
D.I.Gower	157*	England	India	The Oval	23/08/90
S.R.Waugh	157*	Australia	England	Headingley	22/07/93
D.B.Vengsarkar	157	India	England	Lord's	10/06/82
D.I.Gower	157	England	Australia	The Oval	29/08/85
D.M.Jones	157	Australia	England	Edgbaston	06/07/89
G.Boycott	155	England	India	Edgbaston	12/07/79
G.A.Gooch	154*	England	West Indies	Headingley	06/06/91
G.A.Gooch	154	England	New Zealand	Edgbaston	05/07/90
Javed Miandad	153*	Pakistan	England	Edgbaston	04/06/92
S.R.Waugh	152*	Australia	England	Lord's	22/06/89
M.J.Slater	152	Australia	England	Lord's	17/06/93
M.A.Atherton	151	England	New Zealand	Trent Bridge	07/06/90
M.W.Gatting	150*	England	Pakistan	The Oval	06/08/87

BEST INNINGS FIGURES

NAME	FIGURES	FOR	AGAINST	VENUE	DATE
D.E.Malcolm	9-57	England	South Africa	The Oval	18/08/94
I.T.Botham	8-34	England	Pakistan	Lord's	15/06/78
R.G.D.Willis	8-43	England	Australia	Headingley	16/07/81
I.T.Botham	8-103	England	West Indies	Lord's	28/06/84
N.A.Foster	8-107	England	Pakistan	Headingley	02/07/87
C.J.McDermott	8-141	Australia	England	Old Trafford	01/08/85
M.D.Marshall	7-22	West Indies	England	Old Trafford	30/06/88
Imran Khan	7-40	Pakistan	England	Headingley	02/07/87
D.G.Cork	7-43	England	West Indies	Lord's	22/06/95
C.M.Old	7-50	England	Pakistan	Edgbaston	01/06/78
Imran Khan	7-52	Pakistan	England	Edgbaston	29/07/82
M.D.Marshall	7-53	West Indies	England	Headingley	12/07/84
P.A.J.DeFreitas	7-70	England	Sri Lanka	Lord's	22/08/91
B.L.Cairns	7-74	New Zealand	England	Headingley	28/07/83
G.F.Lawson	7-81	Australia	England	Lord's	02/07/81
D.K.Lillee	7-89	Australia	England	The Oval	27/08/81
Abdul Qadir	7-96	Pakistan	England	The Oval	06/08/87
P.C.R.Tufnell	6-25	England	West Indies	The Oval	08/08/91
Mudassar Nazar	6-32	Pakistan	England	Lord's	12/08/82
M.D.Marshall	6-32	West Indies	England	Lord's	16/06/88
I.T.Botham	6-34	England	New Zealand	Trent Bridge	10/08/78

C.E.L.Ambrose	6-52	West Indies	England	Headingley	06/06/91
R.J.Hadlee	6-53	New Zealand	England	The Oval	14/07/83
R.A.Harper	6-57	West Indies	England	Old Trafford	26/07/84
C.Sharma	6-58	India	England	Edgbaston	03/07/86
E.E.Hemmings	6-58	England	New Zealand	Edgbaston	05/07/90
P.J.W.Allott	6-61	England	West Indies	Headingley	12/07/84
M.A.Holding	6-67	West Indies	England	Lord's	19/06/80
Wasim Akram	6-67	Pakistan	England	The Oval	06/08/92
P.M.Such	6-67	England	Australia	Old Trafford	03/06/93
M.D.Marshall	6-69	West Indies	England	Trent Bridge	02/06/88
C.J.McDermott	6-70	Australia	England	Lord's	27/06/85
P.R.Reiffel	6-71	Australia	England	Edgbaston	05/08/93
G.F.Lawson	6-72	Australia	England	Old Trafford	27/07/89
D.J.Nash	6-76	New Zealand	England	Lord's	16/06/94
R.M.Ellison	6-77	England	Australia	Edgbaston	15/08/85
R.J.Hadlee	6-80	New Zealand	England	Lord's	24/07/86
R.J.Hadlee	6-80	New Zealand	England	Trent Bridge	07/08/86
M.D.Marshall	6-85	West Indies	England	Lord's	28/06/84
I.T.Botham	6-90	England	Sri Lanka	Lord's	23/08/84
I.T.Botham	6-95	England	Australia	Headingley	16/07/81
I.T.Botham	6-101	England	New Zealand	Lord's	24/08/78
R.G.D.Willis	6-101	England	India	Lord's	10/06/82
D.R.Doshi	6-102	India	England	Old Trafford	24/06/82
C.C.Lewis	6-111	England	West Indies	Edgbaston	25/07/91
I.T.Botham	6-125	England	Australia	The Oval	27/08/81
T.M.Alderman	6-128	Australia	England	Lord's	22/06/89
Imran Khan	6-129	Pakistan	England	Edgbaston	23/07/87
T.M.Alderman	6-135	Australia	England	Headingley	16/07/81
G.R.Dilley	6-154	England	Pakistan	The Oval	06/08/87

BEST MATCH FIGURES

NAME	FIGURES	FOR	AGAINST	VENUE	DATE
I.T.Botham	11-140	England	New Zealand	Lord's	24/08/78
D.K.Lillee	11-159	Australia	England	The Oval	27/08/81
D.J.Nash	11-169	New Zealand	England	Lord's	16/06/94
Imran Khan	10-77	Pakistan	England	Headingley	02/07/87
M.D.Marshall	10-92	West Indies	England	Lord's	16/06/88
R.M.Ellison	10-104	England	Australia	Edgbaston	15/08/85
D.E.Malcolm	10-138	England	South Africa	The Oval	18/08/94
R.J.Hadlee	10-140	New Zealand	England	Trent Bridge	07/08/86
B.L.Cairns	10-144	New Zealand	England	Headingley	28/07/83
T.M.Alderman	10-151	Australia	England	Headingley	08/06/89
C.Sharma	10-188	India	England	Edgbaston	03/07/86
Abdul Qadir	10-211	Pakistan	England	The Oval	06/08/87
I.T.Botham	10-253	England	Australia	The Oval	27/08/81
M.D.Marshall	9-41	West Indies	England	Old Trafford	30/06/88
R.G.D.Willis	9-92	England	New Zealand	Headingley	28/07/83
I.T.Botham	9-93	England	New Zealand	Trent Bridge	10/08/78
Wasim Akram	9-103	Pakistan	England	The Oval	06/08/92
J.Garner	9-108	West Indies	England	Edgbaston	14/06/84
G.R.Dilley	9-128	England	West Indies	Lord's	16/06/88
T.M.Alderman	9-130	Australia	England	Trent Bridge	18/06/81
Imran Khan	9-136	Pakistan	England	Edgbaston	29/07/82
R.G.D.Willis	9-142	England	India	Lord's	10/06/82
I.T.Botham	9-144	England	Pakistan	Headingley	26/08/82
R.G.D.Willis	9-147	England	West Indies	Trent Bridge	05/06/80
N.G.B.Cook	9-150	England	New Zealand	Trent Bridge	25/08/83
G.F.Lawson	9-153	Australia	England	Old Trafford	27/07/89
P.A.J.DeFreitas	9-165	England	New Zealand	Trent Bridge	02/06/94
T.M.Alderman	9-188	Australia	England	Lord's	22/06/89
T.M.Alderman	9-194	Australia	England	Headingley	16/07/81
T.M.Alderman	9-197	Australia	England	Old Trafford	13/08/81
I.T.Botham	8-51	England	Pakistan	Lord's	15/06/78
D.K.Lillee	8-80	Australia	England	Trent Bridge	18/06/81
C.M.Old	8-88	England	Pakistan	Edgbaston	01/06/78
P.A.J.DeFreitas	8-93	England	West Indies	Headingley	06/06/91
C.A.Walsh	8-99	West Indies	England	Edgbaston	06/07/95

MOST RUNS

NAME	RUNS	MATCHES
G.A.Gooch	5880	72
D.I.Gower	4454	65
I.T.Botham	2944	57
R.A.Smith	2716	36
A.J.Lamb	2550	43
M.W.Gatting	2453	39
M.A.Atherton	2266	32
A.R.Border	2082	25
A.J.Stewart	1682	25
G.Boycott	1487	18
M.A.Taylor	1267	12
I.V.A.Richards	1228	20
D.C.Boon	1121	16
D.L.Haynes	1101	19
C.J.Tavaré	1049	17
G.A.Hick	997	20
Javed Miandad	979	16
C.G.Greenidge	978	14
J.E.Emburey	944	33
S.R.Waugh	922	12
R.T.Robinson	900	14
M.D.Crowe	845	13
S.M.Gavaskar	791	10
R.C.Russell	775	22
G.P.Thorpe	768	9
Salim Malik	736	10
J.G.Wright	714	11
R.B.Richardson	708	12
G.M.Wood	690	12

MOST WICKETS

NAME	WKTS	MATCHES
I.T.Botham	216	57
R.G.D.Willis	129	31
M.D.Marshall	94	18
P.A.J.DeFreitas	84	23
T.M.Alderman	83	12
G.R.Dilley	78	21
R.J.Hadlee	69	13
P.H.Edmonds	68	30
C.E.L.Ambrose	64	13
G.F.Lawson	63	15
J.E.Emburey	63	33
D.R.Pringle	61	25
A.R.C.Fraser	60	15
D.E.Malcolm	59	16
J.Garner	55	10
M.G.Hughes	50	12
C.A.Walsh	49	14
N.A.Foster	48	17
D.K.Lillee	44	7
Kapil Dev	43	13
Imran Khan	42	8
Wasim Akram	37	9
M.A.Holding	35	9
S.K.Warne	34	6
C.C.Lewis	31	13
C.J.McDermott	30	8
J.G.Bracewell	28	10
N.G.B.Cook	27	8
C.M.Old	27	8
P.J.W.Allott	26	11

MOST MATCHES

NAME	MATCHES		NAME	MATCHES
G.A.Gooch	72		G.R.Dilley	21
D.I.Gower	65		I.V.A.Richards	20
I.T.Botham	57		G.A.Hick	20
A.J.Lamb	43		D.L.Haynes	19
M.W.Gatting	39		G.Boycott	18
R.A.Smith	36		M.D.Marshall	18
J.E.Emburey	33		P.R.Downton	17
M.A.Atherton	32		N.A.Foster	17
R.G.D.Willis	31		C.J.Tavaré	17
P.H.Edmonds	30		D.C.Boon	16
A.J.Stewart	25		Javed Miandad	16
D.R.Pringle	25		D.E.Malcolm	16
A.R.Border	25		G.F.Lawson	15
P.A.J.DeFreitas	23		P.J.L.Dujon	15
R.W.Taylor	22		A.R.C.Fraser	15
R.C.Russell	22			

Averages
CORNHILL INSURANCE TEST MATCHES

ENGLAND

BATTING AVERAGES – INCLUDING FIELDING

Name	Matches	Inns	NO	Runs	HS	Avge	100s	50s	Ct	St
J.P.Agnew	3	4	3	10	5	10.00	–	–	–	–
P.J.W.Allott	11	16	3	204	52*	15.69	–	1	4	–
M.A.Atherton	32	59	0	2266	151	38.40	4	17	20	–
C.W.J.Athey	11	19	1	439	123	24.38	1	1	6	–
R.J.Bailey	1	2	0	46	43	23.00	–	–	–	–
D.L.Bairstow	3	5	1	123	59	30.75	–	1	7	1
K.J.Barnett	4	7	0	207	80	29.57	–	2	1	–
J.E.Benjamin	1	1	0	0	0	0.00	–	–	–	–
M.R.Benson	1	2	0	51	30	25.50	–	–	–	–
M.P.Bicknell	2	4	0	26	14	6.50	–	–	–	–
I.T.Botham	57	87	4	2944	208	35.46	8	13	61	–
G.Boycott	18	32	2	1487	155	49.56	5	5	3	–
J.M.Brearley	14	21	1	381	51	19.05	–	2	22	–
B.C.Broad	13	24	0	627	86	26.12	–	5	3	–
A.R.Butcher	1	2	0	34	20	17.00	–	–	–	–
A.R.Caddick	4	8	1	101	25	14.42	–	–	2	–
D.J.Capel	4	8	0	131	53	16.37	–	1	1	–
J.H.Childs	2	4	4	2	2*	–	–	–	1	–
G.Cook	3	5	0	138	66	27.60	–	2	5	–
N.G.B.Cook	8	15	3	121	31	10.08	–	–	4	–
D.G.Cork	3	5	1	129	56*	32.25	–	1	1	–
N.G.Cowans	6	10	2	58	22*	7.25	–	–	1	–
C.S.Cowdrey	1	2	0	5	5	2.50	–	–	–	–
J.P.Crawley	4	7	1	82	38	13.66	–	–	6	–
T.S.Curtis	5	9	0	140	41	15.55	–	–	3	–
P.A.J.DeFreitas	23	33	2	502	69	16.19	–	3	7	–
G.R.Dilley	21	32	7	322	56	12.88	–	1	7	–
P.R.Downton	17	27	3	463	56	19.29	–	2	44	1
P.H.Edmonds	30	37	11	504	64	19.38	–	1	23	–
R.M.Ellison	5	6	1	108	41	21.60	–	–	2	–
J.E.Emburey	33	48	10	944	75	24.84	–	6	19	–
N.H.Fairbrother	4	6	1	59	33*	11.80	–	–	–	–
N.A.Foster	17	28	5	316	39	13.73	–	–	4	–
G.Fowler	9	17	0	514	106	30.23	2	2	6	–
A.R.C.Fraser	15	21	3	137	29	7.61	–	–	3	–
B.N.French	9	12	3	158	59	17.55	–	1	16	–
J.E.R.Gallian	1	2	0	7	7	3.50	–	–	–	–
M.W.Gatting	39	71	8	2453	183*	38.93	6	12	29	–
G.A.Gooch	72	127	3	5880	333	47.41	15	26	64	–
D.Gough	7	11	2	219	65	24.33	–	1	2	–
D.I.Gower	65	113	9	4454	215	42.82	10	19	40	–
I.A.Greig	2	4	0	26	14	6.50	–	–	–	–
E.E.Hemmings	9	12	1	217	51	19.72	–	1	2	–
M.Hendrick	11	11	6	49	12	9.80	–	–	6	–
G.A.Hick	20	34	1	997	110	30.21	1	6	31	–
N.Hussain	4	8	2	184	71	30.66	–	1	2	–
A.P.Igglesden	1	1	1	2	2*	–	–	–	–	–
R.K.Illingworth	5	10	5	78	17*	15.60	–	–	3	–
M.C.Ilott	3	5	1	28	15	7.00	–	–	–	–
R.D.Jackman	2	3	0	28	17	9.33	–	–	–	–
P.W.Jarvis	4	6	1	75	29*	15.00	–	–	–	–
N.V.Knight	1	2	0	30	17	15.00	–	–	4	–
A.P.E.Knott	6	11	1	214	70*	21.40	–	2	17	–
A.J.Lamb	43	76	8	2550	139	37.50	11	6	36	–
W.Larkins	4	8	0	148	34	18.50	–	–	2	–
M.N.Lathwell	2	4	0	78	33	19.50	–	–	–	–
D.V.Lawrence	4	5	0	54	34	10.80	–	–	–	–
J.K.Lever	3	5	2	25	15	8.33	–	–	1	–
C.C.Lewis	13	18	1	338	65	19.88	–	2	13	–
T.A.Lloyd	1	1	1	10	10*	–	–	–	–	–
D.E.Malcolm	16	21	6	70	15*	4.66	–	–	3	–
N.A.Mallender	2	3	0	8	4	2.66	–	–	–	–
V.J.Marks	2	4	1	25	12*	8.33	–	–	–	–
P.J.Martin	3	6	0	52	29	8.66	–	–	4	–
M.P.Maynard	3	6	0	52	20	8.66	–	–	2	–
M.J.McCague	2	3	0	20	11	6.66	–	–	1	–
G.Miller	12	15	2	414	98	31.84	–	3	6	–
H.Morris	3	6	0	115	44	19.16	–	–	3	–
J.E.Morris	3	5	2	71	32	23.66	–	–	3	–
M.D.Moxon	6	12	0	207	74	17.25	–	1	5	–
T.A.Munton	2	2	1	25	25*	25.00	–	–	–	–
P.J.Newport	2	3	0	70	36	23.33	–	–	1	–
C.M.Old	8	9	2	114	29	16.28	–	–	1	–
P.W.G.Parker	1	2	0	13	13	6.50	–	–	–	–
P.I.Pocock	3	5	0	2	2	0.40	–	–	–	–
D.R.Pringle	25	41	2	534	63	13.69	–	1	8	–
N.V.Radford	2	3	1	13	12*	6.50	–	–	–	–
C.T.Radley	6	8	0	308	106	38.50	1	2	4	–
M.R.Ramprakash	12	21	1	333	64	16.65	–	1	8	–
D.W.Randall	13	20	1	667	126	35.10	2	4	12	–
S.J.Rhodes	6	8	4	222	65*	55.50	–	1	26	2
C.J.Richards	3	6	0	21	8	3.50	–	–	5	–
R.T.Robinson	14	23	2	900	175	42.85	3	2	6	–
G.R.J.Roope	4	5	1	136	69	34.00	–	1	6	–
B.C.Rose	3	6	1	243	70	48.60	–	2	2	–
R.C.Russell	22	34	8	775	128*	29.80	1	2	52	6
I.D.K.Salisbury	3	5	1	72	50	18.00	–	1	1	–
A.Sidebottom	1	1	0	2	2	2.00	–	–	–	–
W.N.Slack	2	4	0	19	19	9.50	–	–	2	–
G.C.Small	7	9	4	169	59	33.80	–	1	1	–
C.L.Smith	3	6	0	112	43	18.66	–	–	2	–
R.A.Smith	36	66	11	2716	148*	49.38	7	17	21	–
J.P.Stephenson	1	2	0	36	25	18.00	–	–	–	–
A.J.Stewart	25	43	4	1682	190	43.12	3	8	42	2
P.M.Such	8	11	4	65	14*	9.28	–	–	2	–
C.J.Tavare	17	31	1	1049	109	34.96	1	8	12	–
J.P.Taylor	1	2	1	0	0*	0.00	–	–	–	–
L.B.Taylor	2	1	1	1	1*	–	–	–	1	–
R.W.Taylor	22	30	4	338	64	13.00	–	2	70	1
V.P.Terry	2	3	0	16	8	5.33	–	–	2	–
J.G.Thomas	1	2	0	38	28	19.00	–	–	–	–
G.P.Thorpe	9	18	2	768	114*	48.00	1	7	9	–
P.C.R.Tufnell	6	8	3	5	2*	1.00	–	–	4	–
D.L.Underwood	1	1	0	3	3	3.00	–	–	–	–
S.L.Watkin	3	5	0	25	13	5.00	–	–	–	–
M.Watkinson	1	1	0	37	37	37.00	–	–	–	–
C.White	5	8	0	155	51	19.37	–	1	3	–

P.Willey	13	24	3	654	100*	31.14	1	3	1	–
N.F.Williams	1	1	0	38	38	38.00	–	–	–	–
R.G.D.Willis	31	40	19	321	28*	15.28	–	–	11	–
B.Wood	1	1	0	14	14	14.00	–	–	–	–
R.A.Woolmer	4	8	1	139	46	19.85	–	–	2	–

BOWLING AVERAGES

Name	Overs	Mdns	Runs	Wkts	Avge	Best	5wI	10wM
J.P.Agnew	92	12	373	4	93.25	2-51	–	–
P.J.W.Allott	326.5	68	905	26	34.80	6-61	1	–
M.A.Atherton	46	9	212	1	212.00	1-60	–	–
K.J.Barnett	6	0	32	0	–	–	–	–
J.E.Benjamin	28	3	80	4	20.00	4-42	–	–
M.P.Bicknell	87	17	263	4	65.75	3-99	–	–
I.T.Botham	1967.3	459	6024	216	27.88	8-34	15	2
G.Boycott	17	7	21	0	–	–	–	–
A.R.Butcher	2	0	9	0	–	–	–	–
A.R.Caddick	153	28	488	5	97.60	3-32	–	–
D.J.Capel	64	5	244	3	81.33	1-35	–	–
J.H.Childs	86	29	183	3	61.00	1-13	–	–
G.Cook	1	0	4	0	–	–	–	–
N.G.B.Cook	334.1	94	854	27	31.62	5-35	2	–
D.G.Cork	107.2	17	381	20	19.05	7-43	1	–
N.G.Cowans	177	33	651	14	46.50	3-74	–	–
C.S.Cowdrey	5.3	0	21	0	–	–	–	–
T.S.Curtis	3	0	7	0	–	–	–	–
P.A.J.DeFreitas	851	185	2481	84	29.53	7-70	3	–
G.R.Dilley	706.3	148	2097	78	26.88	6-154	3	–
P.H.Edmonds	1027.5	347	2203	68	32.39	4-6	–	–
R.M.Ellison	189.5	47	465	24	19.37	6-77	2	1
J.E.Emburey	1142.5	334	2549	63	40.46	5-82	1	–
N.A.Foster	621.4	140	1703	48	35.47	8-107	2	–
G.Fowler	1	0	8	0	–	–	–	–
A.R.C.Fraser	685.3	175	1769	60	29.48	5-66	4	–
M.W.Gatting	49	12	113	0	–	–	–	–
G.A.Gooch	307.2	87	728	15	48.53	3-39	–	–
D.Gough	240.2	34	821	23	35.69	4-46	–	–
D.I.Gower	1	0	5	0	–	–	–	–
I.A.Greig	31.2	6	114	4	28.50	4-53	–	–
E.E.Hemmings	334	91	899	24	37.45	6-58	1	–
M.Hendrick	381.4	130	787	24	32.79	4-45	–	–
G.A.Hick	137	46	344	6	57.33	2-77	–	–
A.P.Igglesden	37	3	146	3	48.66	2-91	–	–
R.K.Illingworth	105.4	29	332	6	55.33	3-110	–	–
M.C.Ilott	129	28	412	8	51.50	3-108	–	–
R.D.Jackman	105	30	247	8	30.87	4-110	–	–
P.W.Jarvis	126.3	14	507	8	63.37	4-107	–	–
A.J.Lamb	2	0	16	0	–	–	–	–
D.V.Lawrence	152.2	25	605	17	35.58	5-106	1	–
J.K.Lever	114.5	23	365	9	40.55	4-64	–	–
C.C.Lewis	459	102	1451	31	46.80	6-111	1	–
D.E.Malcolm	544.4	95	1883	59	31.91	9-57	4	1
N.A.Mallender	74.5	20	215	10	21.50	5-50	1	–
V.J.Marks	50	21	109	4	27.25	3-78	–	–
P.J.Martin	84	21	241	5	48.20	2-65	–	–
M.J.McCague	79.3	13	294	4	73.50	4-121	–	–
G.Miller	223.4	73	494	12	41.16	2-19	–	–
M.D.Moxon	6	2	27	0	–	–	–	–
T.A.Munton	67.3	15	200	4	50.00	2-22	–	–
P.J.Newport	91.3	18	339	9	37.66	4-87	–	–
C.M.Old	307.1	107	624	27	23.11	7-50	1	–
P.I.Pocock	123.3	44	298	7	42.57	4-121	–	–
D.R.Pringle	749.2	164	2142	61	35.11	5-95	3	–
N.V.Radford	63	7	219	3	73.00	2-131	–	–
M.R.Ramprakash	1.1	0	8	0	–	–	–	–
I.D.K.Salisbury	114.1	9	427	6	71.16	3-49	–	–
A.Sidebottom	18.4	3	65	1	65.00	1-65	–	–
G.C.Small	265.5	65	762	17	44.82	4-64	–	–
C.L.Smith	12	2	31	2	15.50	2-31	–	–
P.M.Such	362.5	100	805	22	36.59	6-67	1	–
C.J.Tavare	3	3	0	0	–	–	–	–
J.P.Taylor	26	6	82	2	41.00	1-18	–	–
L.B.Taylor	63.3	11	178	4	44.50	2-34	–	–

J.G.Thomas	43	5	140	2	70.00	2-124	–	–
G.P.Thorpe	6	1	14	0	–	–	–	–
P.C.R.Tufnell	295	67	810	22	36.81	6-25	2	–
D.L.Underwood	29.2	7	108	1	108.00	1-108	–	–
S.L.Watkin	89	17	305	11	27.72	4-65	–	–
M.Watkinson	32	6	92	5	18.40	3-64	–	–
C.White	89.1	17	304	8	38.00	3-18	–	–
P.Willey	107.5	35	259	5	51.80	2-73	–	–
N.F.Williams	41	5	148	2	74.00	2-148	–	–
R.G.D.Willis	1023.2	233	3025	129	23.44	8-43	6	–
B.Wood	3	2	2	0	–	–	–	–

AUSTRALIA

BATTING AVERAGES – INCLUDING FIELDING

Name	Matches	Inns	NO	Runs	HS	Avge	100s	50s	Ct	St
T.M.Alderman	12	13	8	42	12*	8.40	–	–	10	–
M.J.Bennett	1	2	0	23	12	11.50	–	–	1	–
D.C.Boon	16	28	5	1121	164*	48.73	3	5	18	–
A.R.Border	25	43	11	2082	200*	65.06	5	12	37	–
R.J.Bright	6	9	0	127	33	14.11	–	–	5	–
G.D.Campbell	1	0	0	0	0	–	–	–	–	–
G.S.Chappell	1	2	0	106	59	53.00	–	1	–	–
T.M.Chappell	3	6	1	79	27	15.80	–	–	2	–
J.Dyson	5	10	0	206	102	20.60	1	–	2	–
D.R.Gilbert	1	2	1	1	1	1.00	–	–	–	–
I.A.Healy	12	14	3	399	102*	36.27	1	2	35	5
A.M.J.Hilditch	6	11	0	424	119	38.54	1	1	3	–
R.M.Hogg	2	3	1	0	0*	0.00	–	–	1	–
T.V.Hohns	5	5	1	127	40	31.75	–	–	3	–
R.G.Holland	4	5	1	15	10	3.75	–	–	1	–
K.J.Hughes	7	14	0	501	117	35.78	1	2	3	–
M.G.Hughes	12	10	0	203	71	20.30	–	1	–	–
D.M.Jones	6	9	1	566	157	70.75	2	3	4	–
B.P.Julian	2	3	1	61	56*	30.50	–	1	2	–
M.F.Kent	3	6	0	171	54	28.50	–	2	6	–
B.M.Laird	1	2	0	30	24	15.00	–	–	1	–
G.F.Lawson	15	19	3	272	74	17.00	–	2	–	–
D.K.Lillee	7	10	3	153	40*	21.85	–	–	1	–
A.A.Mallett	1	0	0	0	0	–	–	–	–	–
G.R.Marsh	6	11	0	347	138	31.54	1	–	5	–
R.W.Marsh	7	12	1	232	52	21.09	–	1	24	–
G.R.J.Matthews	1	2	0	21	17	10.50	–	–	–	–
T.B.A.May	5	4	2	23	15	11.50	–	–	2	–
C.J.McDermott	8	10	1	111	35	12.33	–	–	2	–
S.P.O'Donnell	5	8	1	184	48	26.28	–	–	3	–
L.S.Pascoe	1	0	0	0	0	–	–	–	–	–
W.B.Phillips	6	11	1	350	91	35.00	–	2	11	–
P.R.Reiffel	3	3	0	62	42	20.66	–	–	1	–
G.M.Ritchie	6	11	1	422	146	42.20	1	2	3	–
M.J.Slater	6	10	0	416	152	41.60	1	2	2	–
M.A.Taylor	12	21	1	1267	219	63.35	4	6	16	–
J.R.Thomson	2	4	4	38	28*	–	–	–	1	–
S.K.Warne	6	5	2	113	37	37.66	–	–	4	–
M.E.Waugh	6	10	1	550	137	61.11	1	5	9	–
S.R.Waugh	12	17	8	922	177*	102.44	3	3	9	–
D.M.Wellham	2	4	0	145	103	36.25	1	–	1	–
K.C.Wessels	6	11	0	368	83	33.45	–	3	3	–
M.R.Whitney	2	4	0	4	4	1.00	–	–	–	–
G.M.Wood	12	23	1	690	172	31.36	2	2	6	–
G.N.Yallop	7	13	0	318	114	24.46	1	1	7	–

BOWLING AVERAGES

Name	Overs	Mdns	Runs	Wkts	Avge	Best	5wI	10wM
T.M.Alderman	594.2	144	1605	83	19.33	6-128	10	1
M.J.Bennett	32	8	111	1	111.00	1-111	–	–
A.R.Border	62	21	116	1	116.00	1-16	–	–
R.J.Bright	237.4	97	484	12	40.33	5-68	1	–
G.D.Campbell	24	0	124	1	124.00	1-82	–	–
G.S.Chappell	2	0	2	0	–	–	–	–
D.R.Gilbert	21	2	96	1	96.00	1-96	–	–
R.M.Hogg	40.4	8	123	4	30.75	3-47		

T.V.Hohns	134	53	300	11	27.27	3-59	–	–
R.G.Holland	172	41	465	6	77.50	5-68	1	–
M.G.Hughes	485.4	117	1460	50	29.20	5-92	1	–
B.P.Julian	82	16	291	5	58.20	2-30	–	–
G.F.Lawson	629.2	136	1906	63	30.25	7-81	3	–
D.K.Lillee	345.4	90	966	44	21.95	7-89	2	1
A.A.Mallett	28.2	5	86	2	43.00	1-25	–	–
G.R.J.Matthews	9	2	21	0	–	–	–	–
T.B.A.May	278	90	592	21	28.19	5-89	1	–
C.J.McDermott	282.2	32	1027	30	34.23	8-141	2	–
S.P.O'Donnell	145.4	31	487	6	81.16	3-37	–	–
L.S.Pascoe	35	6	132	6	22.00	5-59	1	–
P.R.Reiffel	140.4	31	396	19	20.84	6-71	2	–
G.M.Ritchie	1	0	10	0	–	–	–	–
J.R.Thomson	56	4	275	3	91.66	2-166	–	–
S.K.Warne	439.5	178	877	34	25.79	5-82	1	–
M.E.Waugh	56	17	161	1	161.00	1-43	–	–
S.R.Waugh	89	24	290	4	72.50	2-45	–	–
K.C.Wessels	6	2	18	0	–	–	–	–
M.R.Whitney	78	16	246	5	49.20	2-50	–	–
G.N.Yallop	8	2	17	0	–	–	–	–
K.C.G.Benjamin	71.5	12	251	10	25.10	4-60	–	–
W.K.M.Benjamin	67	17	151	12	12.58	4-52	–	–
I.R.Bishop	134.2	26	370	21	17.61	5-32	1	–
C.E.H.Croft	104	25	306	9	34.00	3-35	–	–
W.W.Davis	23	3	77	2	38.50	2-71	–	–
J.Garner	430.3	133	911	55	16.56	5-55	1	–
O.D.Gibson	34	3	132	2	66.00	2-81	–	–
C.G.Greenidge	3	2	4	0	–	–	–	–
R.A.Harper	157.4	58	339	18	18.83	6-57	1	–
D.L.Haynes	1	0	2	0	–	–	–	–
M.A.Holding	353.1	80	975	35	27.85	6-67	2	–
C.L.Hooper	111	20	261	4	65.25	2-36	–	–
A.I.Kallicharran	7	1	24	0	–	–	–	–
C.L.King	12	3	32	0	–	–	–	–
C.B.Lambert	0.4	0	4	1	4.00	1-4	–	–
C.H.Lloyd	1	0	1	0	–	–	–	–
M.D.Marshall	715.3	177	1758	94	18.70	7-22	6	1
B.P.Patterson	192.2	33	659	17	38.76	5-81	1	–
I.V.A.Richards	52	14	121	0	–	–	–	–
A.M.E.Roberts	105.2	24	262	11	23.81	5-72	1	–
P.V.Simmons	3	0	7	0	–	–	–	–
M.A.Small	21	2	78	3	26.00	3-40	–	–
C.A.Walsh	505.2	115	1364	49	27.83	5-45	1	–

WEST INDIES

BATTING AVERAGES – INCLUDING FIELDING

Name	Matches	Inns	NO	Runs	HS	Avge	100s	50s	Ct	St
J.C.Adams	4	6	0	160	58	26.66	–	2	1	–
I.B.A.Allen	2	2	2	5	4*	–	–	–	1	–
C.E.L.Ambrose	14	19	5	184	43	13.14	–	–	2	–
K.L.T.Arthurton	5	7	0	186	75	26.57	–	1	5	–
S.F.A.F.Bacchus	5	6	0	121	61	20.16	–	1	1	–
E.A.E.Baptiste	5	6	1	174	87*	34.80	–	1	1	–
K.C.G.Benjamin	3	4	1	40	15	13.33	–	–	1	–
W.K.M.Benjamin	3	2	0	9	9	4.50	–	–	1	–
I.R.Bishop	4	6	1	57	16	11.40	–	–	–	–
S.L.Campbell	4	7	0	302	93	43.14	–	3	7	–
C.E.H.Croft	3	3	2	1	1*	1.00	–	–	–	–
W.W.Davis	1	1	0	77	77	77.00	–	1	–	–
P.J.L.Dujon	15	20	1	604	101	31.78	1	4	53	–
J.Garner	10	11	1	92	46	9.20	–	–	7	–
O.D.Gibson	1	2	0	43	29	21.50	–	–	–	–
H.A.Gomes	5	8	3	400	143	80.00	2	1	1	–
C.G.Greenidge	14	20	1	978	223	51.47	3	2	10	–
R.A.Harper	8	9	1	243	74	30.37	–	2	13	–
D.L.Haynes	19	31	5	1101	184	42.34	2	7	8	–
M.A.Holding	9	11	4	219	69	31.28	–	2	3	–
C.L.Hooper	14	23	3	620	111	31.00	1	4	15	–
A.I.Kallicharran	5	6	0	102	37	17.00	–	–	6	–
C.L.King	1	1	0	12	12	12.00	–	–	–	–
C.B.Lambert	1	2	0	53	39	26.50	–	–	2	–
B.C.Lara	4	7	1	414	145	69.00	1	3	3	–
C.H.Lloyd	9	10	1	424	101	47.11	1	3	11	–
A.L.Logie	9	12	2	484	95*	48.40	–	3	10	–
M.D.Marshall	18	23	2	388	72	18.47	–	2	5	–
D.L.Murray	5	6	0	145	64	24.16	–	1	14	–
J.R.Murray	4	6	0	84	26	14.00	–	–	14	–
B.P.Patterson	5	7	3	13	5*	3.25	–	–	1	–
I.V.A.Richards	20	27	2	1228	145	49.12	2	10	18	–
R.B.Richardson	12	20	1	708	121	37.26	2	4	11	–
A.M.E.Roberts	3	4	1	78	24	26.00	–	–	–	–
P.V.Simmons	5	10	0	181	38	18.10	–	–	4	–
M.A.Small	1	1	1	3	3*	–	–	–	–	–
C.A.Walsh	14	18	4	134	18	9.57	–	–	1	–

BOWLING AVERAGES

Name	Overs	Mdns	Runs	Wkts	Avge	Best	5wI	10wM
J.C.Adams	12	1	32	0	–	–	–	–
I.B.A.Allen	47	4	180	5	36.00	2-69	–	–
C.E.L.Ambrose	576.2	149	1380	64	21.56	6-52	2	–
K.L.T.Arthurton	11.5	3	23	0	–	–	–	–
S.F.A.F.Bacchus	1	0	3	0	–	–	–	–
E.A.E.Baptiste	125	39	265	8	33.12	3-31	–	–

NEW ZEALAND

BATTING AVERAGES – INCLUDING FIELDING

Name	Matches	Inns	NO	Runs	HS	Avge	100s	50s	Ct	St
R.W.Anderson	3	6	0	42	19	7.00	–	–	–	–
T.E.Blain	1	1	0	37	37	37.00	–	–	–	–
S.L.Boock	3	6	3	17	8	5.66	–	–	1	–
B.P.Bracewell	3	6	1	4	4	0.80	–	–	1	–
J.G.Bracewell	10	14	2	227	110	18.91	1	–	7	–
M.G.Burgess	3	6	0	135	68	22.50	–	1	1	–
B.L.Cairns	6	11	1	157	32	15.70	–	–	3	–
E.J.Chatfield	4	6	2	22	10*	5.50	–	–	–	–
R.O.Collinge	1	2	0	19	19	9.50	–	–	–	–
J.V.Coney	7	12	2	371	68	37.10	–	3	9	–
B.E.Congdon	3	6	0	74	36	12.33	–	–	2	–
J.J.Crowe	5	8	0	73	23	9.12	–	–	4	–
M.D.Crowe	13	23	2	845	142	40.23	3	2	12	–
H.T.Davis	1	2	2	0	0*	–	–	–	–	–
B.A.Edgar	10	19	1	575	84	31.94	–	6	5	–
G.N.Edwards	2	4	0	35	18	8.75	–	–	4	–
S.P.Fleming	3	6	0	170	54	28.33	–	1	1	–
T.J.Franklin	4	7	1	236	101	39.33	1	1	2	–
E.J.Gray	5	7	0	129	50	18.42	–	1	2	–
M.J.Greatbatch	4	6	0	136	47	22.66	–	–	–	–
R.J.Hadlee	13	21	2	533	92*	28.05	–	5	6	–
M.N.Hart	3	5	1	99	36	24.75	–	–	1	–
B.R.Hartland	1	2	0	28	22	14.00	–	–	–	–
G.P.Howarth	7	14	2	485	123	40.41	1	2	9	–
A.H.Jones	3	5	0	143	49	28.60	–	–	1	–
G.R.Larsen	1	2	0	10	8	5.00	–	–	2	–
W.K.Lees	2	4	1	47	31*	15.66	–	–	4	–
D.K.Morrison	3	5	2	9	6	3.00	–	–	1	–
D.J.Nash	3	5	2	94	56	31.33	–	1	3	–
M.B.Owens	2	2	1	6	4	6.00	–	–	–	–
J.M.Parker	2	4	0	55	38	13.75	–	–	1	–
A.C.Parore	4	8	2	245	71	40.83	–	1	11	1
B.A.Pocock	2	2	0	12	10	6.00	–	–	1	–
M.W.Priest	1	1	0	26	26	26.00	–	–	–	–
C.Pringle	2	2	0	14	14	7.00	–	–	1	–
K.R.Rutherford	6	11	1	167	37	16.70	–	–	2	–
I.D.S.Smith	6	7	2	71	27	14.20	–	–	19	–
M.C.Snedden	4	6	2	57	21*	14.25	–	–	2	–
D.A.Stirling	2	2	1	44	26	44.00	–	–	1	–
S.A.Thomson	3	6	1	157	69	31.40	–	1	3	–
W.Watson	2	2	1	9	8*	9.00	–	–	–	–
J.G.Wright	11	21	1	714	119	35.70	1	5	3	–
B.A.Young	3	6	0	195	94	32.50	–	2	3	–

BOWLING AVERAGES

Name	Overs	Mdns	Runs	Wkts	Avge	Best	5wI	10wM
S.L.Boock	113	53	189	6	31.50	2-29	–	–
B.P.Bracewell	89.2	14	282	9	31.33	3-110	–	–
J.G.Bracewell	346.4	91	977	28	34.89	4-38	–	–
B.L.Cairns	269	75	632	20	31.60	7-74	1	1
E.J.Chatfield	174	44	513	14	36.64	5-95	1	–
R.O.Collinge	36	10	84	2	42.00	2-58	–	–
J.V.Coney	79	27	163	5	32.60	2-21	–	–
B.E.Congdon	67	22	126	0	–	–	–	–
M.D.Crowe	34	2	111	2	55.50	2-35	–	–
H.T.Davis	21	0	93	1	93.00	1-93	–	–
E.J.Gray	165	52	399	9	44.33	3-73	–	–
R.J.Hadlee	640.5	162	1603	69	23.23	6-53	6	1
M.N.Hart	147.3	60	278	4	69.50	1-50	–	–
G.P.Howarth	3	2	1	0	–	–	–	–
A.H.Jones	12	3	40	1	40.00	1-40	–	–
G.R.Larsen	44.4	11	116	2	58.00	2-116	–	–
D.K.Morrison	85.4	15	351	7	50.14	4-64	–	–
D.J.Nash	129	28	429	17	25.23	6-76	2	1
M.B.Owens	51	15	168	5	33.60	4-99	–	–
M.W.Priest	12	4	26	1	26.00	1-26	–	–
C.Pringle	78	22	201	3	67.00	1-41	–	–
K.R.Rutherford	6	0	26	0	–	–	–	–
M.C.Snedden	137	38	373	10	37.30	3-69	–	–
D.A.Stirling	44	8	181	3	60.33	2-48	–	–
S.A.Thomson	79	19	163	2	81.50	1-40	–	–
W.Watson	72.5	18	196	4	49.00	2-51	–	–

INDIA

BATTING AVERAGES – INCLUDING FIELDING

Name	Matches	Inns	NO	Runs	HS	Avge	100s	50s	Ct	St
M.Amarnath	4	7	0	213	79	30.42	–	2	3	–
M.Azharuddin	6	11	1	583	179	58.30	2	2	4	–
B.S.Bedi	3	2	0	1	1	0.50	–	–	–	–
R.M.H.Binny	3	4	0	81	40	20.25	–	–	3	–
B.S.Chandrasekhar	1	2	2	0	0*	–	–	–	–	–
C.P.S.Chauhan	4	7	0	179	80	25.57	–	2	1	–
D.R.Doshi	3	3	2	9	5*	9.00	–	–	–	–
A.D.Gaekwad	2	4	1	54	25	18.00	–	–	–	–
S.M.Gavaskar	10	16	0	791	221	49.43	1	5	8	–
K.D.Ghavri	4	6	3	43	20*	14.33	–	–	1	–
N.D.Hirwani	3	4	3	17	15*	17.00	–	–	–	–
Kapil Dev	13	20	2	638	110	35.44	1	4	3	–
S.M.H.Kirmani	3	4	1	110	58	36.66	–	1	4	3
A.R.Kumble	1	1	0	2	2	2.00	–	–	–	–
Madan Lal	4	6	0	94	26	15.66	–	–	–	–
A.Malhotra	1	2	0	5	5	2.50	–	–	2	–
Maninder Singh	3	4	1	10	6	3.33	–	–	1	–
S.V.Manjrekar	3	5	0	216	93	43.20	–	2	5	–
K.S.More	6	9	3	247	61*	41.16	–	1	24	–
S.V.Nayak	2	3	1	19	11	9.50	–	–	1	–
C.S.Pandit	1	2	0	40	23	20.00	–	–	1	–
G.A.Parkar	1	2	0	7	6	3.50	–	–	1	–
S.M.Patil	2	2	1	191	129*	191.00	1	1	–	–
M.Prabhakar	3	5	1	132	67*	33.00	–	1	–	–
B.Reddy	4	5	1	38	21	9.50	–	–	9	2
C.Sharma	2	2	0	11	9	5.50	–	–	–	–
S.K.Sharma	1	2	0	38	38	19.00	–	–	–	–
R.J.Shastri	9	16	1	503	187	33.53	2	1	6	–
N.S.Sidhu	3	5	0	56	30	11.20	–	–	–	–
K.Srikkanth	3	6	0	105	31	17.50	–	–	3	–
S.R.Tendulkar	3	5	1	245	119*	61.25	1	1	3	–
D.B.Vengsarkar	13	23	3	960	157	48.00	4	4	6	–
S.Venkataraghavan	4	5	0	36	28	7.20	–	–	1	–
G.R.Viswanath	7	12	1	530	113	48.18	1	6	8	–
A.Wasson	1	1	0	15	15	15.00	–	–	–	–
Yajurvindra Singh	1	2	1	44	43*	44.00	–	–	2	–
Yashpal Sharma	6	10	2	200	40	25.00	–	–	2	–

BOWLING AVERAGES

Name	Overs	Mdns	Runs	Wkts	Avge	Best	5wI	10wM
M.Amarnath	44.2	13	120	2	60.00	2-53	–	–
B.S.Bedi	103.3	23	249	7	35.57	2-26	–	–
R.M.H.Binny	87.2	11	251	12	20.91	5-40	1	–
B.S.Chandrasekhar	29	1	113	0	–	–	–	–
C.P.S.Chauhan	3	0	19	0	–	–	–	–
D.R.Doshi	157.1	38	455	13	35.00	6-102	1	–
A.D.Gaekwad	3	0	12	0	–	–	–	–
K.D.Ghavri	147	30	448	8	56.00	3-76	–	–
N.D.Hirwani	212	41	586	9	65.11	4-174	–	–
Kapil Dev	563.1	129	1685	43	39.18	5-125	2	–
A.R.Kumble	60	10	170	3	56.66	3-105	–	–
Madan Lal	123	35	339	9	37.66	3-18	–	–
Maninder Singh	114.1	41	187	12	15.58	4-26	–	–
S.V.Nayak	38.3	6	132	1	132.00	1-16	–	–
S.M.Patil	14	1	48	1	48.00	1-48	–	–
M.Prabhakar	155	28	554	8	69.25	4-74	–	–
C.Sharma	102.3	20	300	16	18.75	6-58	2	1
S.K.Sharma	48	5	197	3	65.66	2-75	–	–
R.J.Shastri	292.2	59	777	11	70.63	3-109	–	–
S.Venkataraghavan	115	21	345	6	57.50	3-59	–	–
A.Wasson	37	5	173	3	57.66	2-79	–	–
Yajurvindra Singh	10	2	19	0	–	–	–	–
Yashpal Sharma	3	2	1	0	–	–	–	–

PAKISTAN

BATTING AVERAGES – INCLUDING FIELDING

Name	Matches	Inns	NO	Runs	HS	Avge	100s	50s	Ct	St
Aamir Sohail	5	9	1	413	205	51.62	1	1	3	–
Abdul Qadir	7	9	1	84	20	10.50	–	–	1	–
Aqib Javed	5	4	2	5	5*	2.50	–	–	–	–
Asif Mujtaba	5	8	0	253	59	31.62	–	3	4	–
Ata-ur-Rehman	1	0	0	0	–	–	–	–	–	–
Ehteshamuddin	1	2	1	0	0*	0.00	–	–	–	–
Haroon Rashid	4	6	0	34	15	5.66	–	–	3	–
Ijaz Ahmed	4	4	0	150	69	37.50	–	2	4	–
Imran Khan	8	10	2	403	118	50.37	1	2	3	–
Inzamam-ul-Haq	4	6	1	66	26	13.20	–	–	4	–
Iqbal Qasim	3	5	1	5	5*	1.25	–	–	1	–
Javed Miandad	16	24	3	979	260	46.61	2	5	14	–
Liaqat Ali	2	4	2	16	9	8.00	–	–	–	–
Majid Khan	1	2	0	31	21	15.50	–	–	2	–
Mansoor Akhtar	8	10	0	306	75	30.60	–	3	2	–
Mohsin Kamal	4	3	2	13	10	13.00	–	–	2	–
Mohsin Khan	6	11	1	501	200	50.10	1	–	7	–
Moin Khan	4	6	1	46	15	9.20	–	–	7	–
Mudassar Nazar	11	15	1	402	124	28.71	1	2	6	–
Mushtaq Ahmed	5	6	0	35	11	5.83	–	–	1	–
Ramiz Raja	7	11	1	341	88	34.10	–	3	1	–
Rashid Latif	1	1	0	50	50	50.00	–	1	2	1
Sadiq Mohammad	3	5	0	210	97	42.00	–	2	1	–
Salim Malik	10	13	2	736	165	66.90	2	4	5	–
Salim Yousuf	5	4	1	187	91*	62.33	–	1	15	–
Sarfraz Nawaz	3	3	2	42	32*	42.00	–	–	1	–
Shoaib Mohammad	5	5	0	139	55	27.80	–	2	1	–
Sikander Bakht	5	9	1	27	7	3.37	–	–	1	–
Tahir Naqqash	2	3	0	53	39	17.66	–	–	–	–
Talat Ali	2	3	0	42	40	14.00	–	–	–	–
Tausif Ahmed	2	1	1	0	0*	–	–	–	–	–
Waqar Younis	5	6	2	51	20*	12.75	–	–	–	–
Wasim Akram	9	11	1	198	45*	19.80	–	–	4	–
Wasim Bari	6	10	3	94	24*	13.42	–	–	11	–
Wasim Raja	4	7	0	97	28	13.85	–	–	–	–
Zaheer Abbas	3	5	0	131	75	26.20	–	1	–	–

BOWLING AVERAGES

Name	Overs	Mdns	Runs	Wkts	Avge	Best	5wI	10wM
Aamir Sohail	5	2	14	0	–	–	–	–
Abdul Qadir	336.3	94	856	21	40.76	7-96	1	1

Aqib Javed	104.4	21	366	9	40.66	4-100	–	–
Asif Mujtaba	13	5	30	1	30.00	1-0	–	–
Ata-ur-Rehman	18	5	69	3	23.00	3-69	–	–
Ehteshamuddin	14	4	46	1	46.00	1-46	–	–
Imran Khan	346.3	81	845	42	20.11	7-40	4	1
Iqbal Qasim	55	15	168	4	42.00	3-101	–	–
Javed Miandad	7	2	24	1	24.00	1-14	–	–
Liaqat Ali	60	10	194	4	48.50	3-80	–	–
Mohsin Kamal	94.4	14	332	9	36.88	4-127	–	–
Mudassar Nazar	200.2	53	494	15	32.93	6-32	1	–
Mushtaq Ahmed	178.4	37	475	15	31.66	3-32	–	–
Salim Malik	1	0	5	0	–	–	–	–
Sarfraz Nawaz	63	16	129	8	16.12	5-39	1	–
Sikander Bakht	162	39	452	10	45.20	4-132	–	–
Tahir Naqqash	52	20	117	7	16.71	5-40	1	–
Tausif Ahmed	91.1	28	203	5	40.60	2-52	–	–
Waqar Younis	166	29	557	22	25.31	5-52	3	–
Wasim Akram	349.3	75	926	37	25.02	6-67	2	–
Wasim Raja	24.3	6	81	2	40.50	1-0	–	–

SRI LANKA

BATTING AVERAGES – INCLUDING FIELDING

Name	Matches	Inns	NO	Runs	HS	Avge	100s	50s	Ct	St
S.D.Anurasiri	1	2	0	17	16	8.50	–	–	–	–
A.L.F.de Mel	1	2	1	34	20*	34.00	–	–	–	–
D.S.de Silva	1	0	0	0	0	–	–	–	–	–
P.A.de Silva	3	6	0	100	42	16.66	–	–	5	–
R.L.Dias	1	2	0	70	38	35.00	–	–	2	–
A.P.Gurusinha	1	2	0	38	34	19.00	–	–	–	–
U.C.Hathurusinghe	1	2	0	91	66	45.50	–	1	–	–
S.T.Jayasuriya	1	2	0	77	66	38.50	–	1	–	–
V.B.John	1	0	0	0	0	–	–	–	–	–
D.S.B.P.Kuruppu	2	4	0	97	46	24.25	–	–	–	–
G.F.Labrooy	1	2	1	51	42	51.00	–	–	–	–
R.S.Madugalle	2	4	0	31	20	7.75	–	–	1	–
M.A.W.R. Madurasinghe	1	2	0	6	4	3.00	–	–	–	–
R.S.Mahanama	1	2	0	17	15	8.50	–	–	3	–
L.R.D.Mendis	2	4	0	282	111	70.50	1	2	1	–
C.P.H.Ramanayake	2	4	1	36	34*	12.00	–	–	1	–
A.Ranatunga	2	4	0	167	84	41.75	–	2	2	–
R.J.Ratnayake	1	2	0	69	52	34.50	–	1	1	–
J.R.Ratnayeke	2	4	3	103	59*	103.00	–	1	1	–
M.A.R. Samarasekera	1	2	0	57	57	28.50	–	1	2	–
S.A.R.Silva	2	4	1	127	102*	42.33	1	–	6	–
H.P.Tillekeratne	1	2	0	36	20	18.00	–	–	1	–
S.Wettimuny	1	2	0	203	190	101.50	1	–	–	–
K.I.W. Wijegunawardene	1	2	1	10	6*	10.00	–	–	–	–

BOWLING AVERAGES

Name	Overs	Mdns	Runs	Wkts	Avge	Best	5wI	10wM
S.D.Anurasiri	43.1	12	180	5	36.00	3-135	–	–
A.L.F.de Mel	37	10	110	4	27.50	4-110	–	–
D.S.de Silva	45	16	85	2	42.50	2-85	–	–
U.C.Hathurusinghe	17	6	40	1	40.00	1-40	–	–
S.T.Jayasuriya	1	0	1	0	–	–	–	–
V.B.John	39.1	12	98	4	24.50	4-98	–	–
G.F.Labrooy	49	7	143	4	35.75	4-119	–	–
R.S.Madugalle	3	0	4	0	–	–	–	–
M.A.W.R. Madurasinghe	16	4	41	0	–	–	–	–
C.P.H.Ramanayake	71.2	10	247	4	61.75	2-75	–	–
A.Ranatunga	15.4	8	20	2	10.00	1-6	–	–
R.J.Ratnayake	53	8	160	5	32.00	5-69	1	–
J.R.Ratnayeke	61	9	173	2	86.50	2-107	–	–
M.A.R. Samarasekera	32	5	104	3	34.66	2-38	–	–
K.I.W. Wijegunawardene	12	1	49	0	–	–	–	–

SOUTH AFRICA

BATTING AVERAGES – INCLUDING FIELDING

Name	Matches	Inns	NO	Runs	HS	Avge	100s	50s	Ct	St
W.J.Cronje	3	6	1	90	38	18.00	–	–	2	–
D.J.Cullinan	1	2	0	101	94	50.50	–	1	–	–
P.S.de Villiers	3	4	1	35	14	11.66	–	–	1	–
A.A.Donald	3	4	2	46	27	23.00	–	–	1	–
A.C.Hudson	2	4	0	30	12	7.50	–	–	2	–
G.Kirsten	3	6	0	190	72	31.66	–	2	1	–
P.N.Kirsten	3	6	1	179	104	35.80	1	–	–	–
C.R.Matthews	3	5	1	128	62*	32.00	–	1	–	–
B.M.McMillan	3	5	1	264	93	66.00	–	2	4	–
J.N.Rhodes	3	5	1	128	46	32.00	–	–	1	–
D.J.Richardson	3	5	0	138	58	27.60	–	1	7	–
K.C.Wessels	3	6	0	238	105	39.66	1	–	3	–

BOWLING AVERAGES

Name	Overs	Mdns	Runs	Wkts	Avge	Best	5wI	10wM
W.J.Cronje	37	9	94	0	–	–	–	–
P.S.de Villiers	123.3	27	388	12	32.33	4-62	–	–
A.A.Donald	89.3	15	410	12	34.16	5-74	1	–
G.Kirsten	2	1	10	0	–	–	–	–
C.R.Matthews	125.3	35	340	8	42.50	3-25	–	–
B.M.McMillan	81.2	16	267	9	29.66	3-16	–	–

Scorecards

ENGLAND v PAKISTAN

at Edgbaston on 1st, 2nd, 3rd, 5th June 1978
Toss: Pakistan
Umpires: H.D.Bird and K.E.Palmer
England won by an innings and 57 runs

PAKISTAN 1st Innings

Mudassar Nazar	c & b Botham	14
Sadiq Mohammad	c Radley b Old	23
Mohsin Khan	b Willis	35
Javed Miandad	c Taylor b Old	15
Haroon Rashid	c Roope b Willis	3
Wasim Raja	c Taylor b Old	17
Sarfraz Nawaz	not out	32
*+Wasim Bari	b Old	0
Iqbal Qasim	c Taylor b Old	0
Sikander Bakht	c Roope b Old	0
Liaqat Ali	c Brearley b Old	9
Extras (lb 3, nb 13)		16
TOTAL		164

FALL OF WICKETS – 1-20, 2-56, 3-91, 4-94, 5-103, 6-125, 7-125, 8-126, 9-126, 10-164
BOWLING – Willis 16-2-42-2, Old 22.4-6-50-7, Botham 15-4-52-1, Wood 3-2-2-0, Edmonds 4-2-2-0

ENGLAND

*J.M.Brearley	run out	38
B.Wood	lbw b Sikander Bakht	14
C.T.Radley	lbw b Sikander Bakht	106
D.I.Gower	c Miandad b Sikander Bakht	58
G.R.J.Roope	b Sikander Bakht	32
G.Miller	c Wasim Bari b Mudassar	48
I.T.Botham	c Iqbal Qasim b Liaqat Ali	100
C.M.Old	c Mudassar b Iqbal Qasim	5
P.H.Edmonds	not out	4
DID NOT BAT – +R.W.Taylor, R.G.D.Willis		
Extras (lb 26, w 5, nb 16)		47
TOTAL (for 8 wkts dec)		452

FALL OF WICKETS – 1-36, 2-101, 3-190, 4-275, 5-276, 6-399, 7-448, 8-452
BOWLING – Safraz Nawaz 6-1-12-0, Liaqat Ali 42-9-114-1, Mudassar Nazar 27-7-59-1, Iqbal Qasim 14-2-56-1, Sikander Bakht 45-13-132-4, Wasim Raja 10-1-32-0

PAKISTAN 2nd Innings

Mudassar Nazar	b Edmonds	30
Sadiq Mohammad	b Old	79
Iqbal Qasim	retired hurt	5
Mohsin Khan	c Old b Miller	38
Javed Miandad	c Brearley b Edmonds	39
Haroon Rashid	b Willis	4
Wasim Raja	b Edmonds	9
Sarfraz Nawaz	not out	6
*+Wasim Bari	c Miller b Edmonds	3
Sikander Bakht	c Roope b Miller	2
Liaqat Ali	b Willis	3
Extras (b 4, lb 4, w 1, nb 4)		13
TOTAL		231

FALL OF WICKETS – 1-94, 2-123, 3-176, 4-193, 5-214, 6-220, 7-224, 8-227, 9-231
BOWLING – Willis 23.4-3-70-2, Old 25-12-38-1, Botham 17-3-47-0, Edmonds 26-10-44-4, Miller 12-4-19-2

ENGLAND v PAKISTAN

at Lord's on 15th, 16th, 17th, 19th June 1978
Toss: England
Umpires: W.L.Budd and D.J.Constant
England won by an innings and 120 runs

ENGLAND

*J.M.Brearley	lbw b Liaqat Ali	2
G.A.Gooch	lbw b Wasim Raja	54
C.T.Radley	c Mohsin Khan b Liaqat Ali	8
D.I.Gower	b Iqbal Qasim	56
G.R.J.Roope	c Mohsin Khan b Qasim	69
G.Miller	c Javed Miandad b Qasim	0
I.T.Botham	b Liaqat Ali	108
+R.W.Taylor	c Mudassar b Sikander	10
C.M.Old	c Mohsin Khan b Sikander	0
P.H.Edmonds	not out	36
R.G.D.Willis	b Mudassar Nazar	18
Extras (lb 2, nb 1)		3
TOTAL		364

FALL OF WICKETS – 1-5, 2-19, 3-120, 4-120, 5-134, 6-252, 7-290, 8-290, 9-324, 10-364
BOWLING – Sikander Bakht 27-3-115-2, Liaqat Ali 18-1-80-3, Mudassar Nazar 4.2-0-16-1, Iqbal Qasim 30-5-101-3, Wasim Raja 12-3-49-1

PAKISTAN 1st Innings

Sadiq Mohammad	c Botham b Willis	11
Mudassar Nazar	c Edmonds b Willis	1
Mohsin Khan	c Willis b Edmonds	31
Haroon Rashid	b Old	15
Javed Miandad	c Taylor b Willis	0
Wasim Raja	b Edmonds	28
Talat Ali	c Radley b Edmonds	2
*+Wasim Bari	c Brearley b Willis	0
Iqbal Qasim	b Willis	0
Sikander Bakht	c Brearley b Edmonds	4
Liaqat Ali	not out	4
Extras (nb 9)		9
TOTAL		105

FALL OF WICKETS – 1-11, 2-22, 3-40, 4-41, 5-84, 6-96, 7-97, 8-97, 9-97, 10-105
BOWLING – Willis 13-1-47-5, Old 10-3-26-1, Botham 5-2-17-0, Edmonds 8-6-6-4

PAKISTAN 2nd Innings

Sadiq Mohammad	c Taylor b Willis	0
Mudassar Nazar	c Taylor b Botham	10
Mohsin Khan	c Roope b Willis	46
Talat Ali	c Roope b Botham	40
Haroon Rashid	b Botham	4
Javed Miandad	c Gooch b Botham	22
Wasim Raja	c & b Botham	1
*+Wasim Bari	c Taylor b Botham	2
Sikander Bakht	c Roope b Botham	1
Iqbal Qasim	b Botham	0
Liaqat Ali	not out	0
Extras (b 1, lb 3, w 5, nb 4)		13
TOTAL		139

FALL OF WICKETS – 1-1, 2-45, 3-100, 4-108, 5-114, 6-119, 7-121, 8-130, 9-130, 10-139
BOWLING – Willis 10-2-26-2, Old 15-4-36-0, Botham 20.5-8-34-8, Edmonds 12-4-21-0, Miller 9-3-9-0

ENGLAND v PAKISTAN

at Headingley on 29th, 30th June, 1st, 3rd, 4th July 1978
Toss: Pakistan
Umpires: H.D.Bird and K.E.Palmer
Match drawn

PAKISTAN

Sadiq Mohammad	c Brearley b Botham	97
Mudassar Nazar	c Botham b Old	31
Mohsin Khan	lbw b Willis	41
Talat Ali	c Gooch b Willis	0
Haroon Rashid	c Brearley b Botham	7
Javed Miandad	b Old	1
Wasim Raja	lbw b Botham	0
Sarfraz Nawaz	c Taylor b Botham	4
*+Sikander Bakht	b Old	4
Wasim Bari	not out	7
Iqbal Qasim	lbw b Old	0
Extras (lb 8, nb 1)		9
TOTAL		201

FALL OF WICKETS – 1-75, 2-147, 3-147, 4-169, 5-182, 6-183, 7-189, 8-190, 9-201, 10-201
BOWLING – Willis 26-8-48-2, Old 41.4-22-41-4, Botham 18-2-59-4, Edmonds 11-2-22-0, Miller 9-3-22-0

ENGLAND

*J.M.Brearley	c Wasim Bari b Sarfraz	0
G.A.Gooch	lbw b Sarfraz Nawaz	20
C.T.Radley	b Sikander Bakht	7
D.I.Gower	lbw b Sarfraz Nawaz	39
G.R.J.Roope	c Sadiq b Javed Miandad	11
G.Miller	not out	18
+R.W.Taylor	c Wasim Bari b Sarfraz	2
I.T.Botham	lbw b Sarfraz Nawaz	4
P.H.Edmonds	not out	1
DID NOT BAT – C.M.Old, R.G.D.Willis		
Extras (b 1, lb 5, w 1, nb 10)		17
TOTAL (for 7 wkts)		119

FALL OF WICKETS – 1-0, 2-24, 3-51, 4-77, 5-102, 6-110, 7-116
BOWLING – Safraz Nawaz 20-6-39-5, Sikander Bakht 15-4-26-1, Mudassar Nazar 5-2-12-0, Iqbal Qasim 11-8-11-0, Javed Miandad 3-0-14-1

1978

ENGLAND v NEW ZEALAND

at The Oval on 27th, 28th, 29th, 31st July, 1 August 1978
Toss: New Zealand
Umpires: D.J.Constant and B.J.Meyer
England won by 7 wickets

NEW ZEALAND 1st Innings

J.G.Wright	c Radley b Willis	62
R.W.Anderson	b Old	4
G.P.Howarth	c Edmonds b Botham	94
B.A.Edgar	c & b Miller	0
*M.G.Burgess	lbw b Willis	34
B.E.Congdon	run out	2
+G.N.Edwards	b Miller	6
R.J.Hadlee	c Brearley b Willis	5
B.L.Cairns	lbw b Willis	5
B.P.Bracewell	c Taylor b Willis	0
S.L.Boock	not out	3
Extras (b 1, lb 7, nb 11)		19
TOTAL		234

FALL OF WICKETS – 1-7, 2-130, 3-131, 4-191, 5-197, 6-207, 7-224, 8-230, 9-230, 10-234
BOWLING – Willis 20.2-9-42-5, Old 20-7-43-1, Botham 22-7-58-1, Miller 25-10-31-2, Edmonds 17-2-41-0

ENGLAND 1st Innings

*J.M.Brearley	c Edwards b Bracewell	2
G.A.Gooch	lbw b Bracewell	0
C.T.Radley	run out	49
D.I.Gower	run out	111
G.R.J.Roope	b Boock	14
G.Miller	lbw b Cairns	0
I.T.Botham	c Bracewell b Boock	22
+R.W.Taylor	c Edwards b Hadlee	8
P.H.Edmonds	lbw b Hadlee	28
C.M.Old	c Edwards b Cairns	16
R.G.D.Willis	not out	3
Extras (b 15, lb 8, nb 3)		26
TOTAL		279

FALL OF WICKETS – 1-1, 2-7, 3-123, 4-165, 5-166, 6-208, 7-212, 8-232, 9-257, 10-279
BOWLING – Hadlee 21.5-6-43-2, Bracewell 17-8-46-2, Cairns 40-16-65-2, Boock 35-18-61-2, Congdon 21-6-38-0

NEW ZEALAND 2nd Innings

J.G.Wright	lbw b Botham	25
R.W.Anderson	c Taylor b Botham	2
G.P.Howarth	b Willis	0
B.A.Edgar	b Edmonds	38
*M.G.Burgess	lbw b Botham	7
B.E.Congdon	b Edmonds	36
+G.N.Edwards	c Brearley b Edmonds	11
R.J.Hadlee	b Edmonds	7
B.L.Cairns	b Miller	27
B.P.Bracewell	b Miller	0
S.L.Boock	not out	0
Extras (b 8, lb 10, nb 11)		29
TOTAL		182

FALL OF WICKETS – 1-15, 2-19, 3-30, 4-70, 5-86, 6-105, 7-113, 8-182, 9-182, 10-182
BOWLING – Willis 13-2-39-1, Old 5-2-13-0, Botham 19-2-46-3, Miller 34-19-35-2, Edmonds 34.1-23-20-4

ENGLAND 2nd Innings

*J.M.Brearley	lbw b Boock	11
G.A.Gooch	not out	91
C.T.Radley	lbw b Bracewell	2
D.I.Gower	c Howarth b Cairns	11
G.R.J.Roope	not out	10
DID NOT BAT – G.Miller, I.T.Botham, +R.W.Taylor, P.H.Edmonds, C.M.Old, R.G.D.Willis		
Extras (b 2, lb 3, nb 8)		13
TOTAL (for 3 wkts)		138

FALL OF WICKETS – 1-26, 2-51, 3-82
BOWLING – Hadlee 11.3-3-18-0, Bracewell 13-3-26-1, Cairns 7-0-21-1, Boock 20-6-55-1, Congdon 1-0-5-0

ENGLAND v NEW ZEALAND

at Trent Bridge on 10th, 11th, 12th, 14th August 1978
Toss: England
Umpires: D.J.Constant and T.W.Spencer
England won by an innings and 119 runs

ENGLAND

G.Boycott	c & b Hadlee	131
G.A.Gooch	c Burgess b Bracewell	55
C.T.Radley	lbw b Hadlee	59
D.I.Gower	c Cairns b Boock	46
*J.M.Brearley	c Parker b Bracewell	50
P.H.Edmonds	b Cairns	6
G.Miller	c Howarth b Hadlee	4
I.T.Botham	c Hadlee b Boock	8
+R.W.Taylor	b Hadlee	22
R.G.D.Willis	not out	1
M.Hendrick	c Edwards b Bracewell	7
Extras (b 16, lb 12, w 1, nb 11)		40
TOTAL		429

FALL OF WICKETS – 1-111, 2-240, 3-301, 4-342, 5-350, 6-364, 7-374, 8-419, 9-427, 10-429
BOWLING – Hadlee 42-11-94-4, Bracewell 33.5-2-110-3, Cairns 38-7-85-1, Congdon 39-15-71-0, Boock 28-18-29-2

NEW ZEALAND 1st Innings

B.A.Edgar	c Taylor b Botham	6
R.W.Anderson	lbw b Botham	19
G.P.Howarth	not out	31
S.L.Boock	c Taylor b Willis	8
J.M.Parker	c Taylor b Hendrick	0
*M.G.Burgess	c Taylor b Botham	5
B.E.Congdon	c Hendrick b Botham	27
+G.N.Edwards	c Taylor b Botham	0
B.L.Cairns	b Edmonds	9
R.J.Hadlee	c Gooch b Botham	4
B.P.Bracewell	b Edmonds	0
Extras (lb 1, w 1, nb 9)		11
TOTAL		120

FALL OF WICKETS – 1-22, 2-27, 3-30, 4-47, 5-49, 6-99, 7-99, 8-110, 9-115, 10-120
BOWLING – Willis 12-5-22-1, Hendrick 15-9-18-1, Botham 21-9-34-6, Edmonds 15.4-5-21-2, Miller 6-1-14-0

NEW ZEALAND 2nd Innings

B.A.Edgar	c Botham b Edmonds	60
R.W.Anderson	run out	0
G.P.Howarth	c Botham b Hendrick	34
J.M.Parker	run out	38
*M.G.Burgess	c Brearley b Edmonds	7
B.E.Congdon	c Brearley b Botham	4
+G.N.Edwards	c & b Edmonds	18
B.L.Cairns	lbw b Botham	0
R.J.Hadlee	c Taylor b Botham	11
S.L.Boock	b Edmonds	2
B.P.Bracewell	not out	0
Extras (lb 6, w 1, nb 9)		16
TOTAL		190

FALL OF WICKETS – 1-5, 2-63, 3-127, 4-148, 5-152, 6-164, 7-168, 8-180, 9-190, 10-190
BOWLING – Willis 9-0-31-0, Hendrick 20-7-30-1, Botham 24-7-59-3, Edmonds 33.1-15-44-4, Miller 6-3-10-0

ENGLAND v NEW ZEALAND

at Lord's on 24th, 25th, 26th, 28th August 1978
Toss: New Zealand
Umpires: H.D.Bird and B.J.Meyer
England won by 7 wickets

NEW ZEALAND 1st Innings

J.G.Wright	c Edmonds b Botham	17
+B.A.Edgar	c Edmonds b Emburey	39
G.P.Howarth	c Taylor b Botham	123
J.M.Parker	lbw b Hendrick	14
*M.G.Burgess	lbw b Botham	68
B.E.Congdon	c Emburey b Botham	2
R.W.Anderson	b Botham	16
R.J.Hadlee	c Brearley b Botham	0
R.O.Collinge	c Emburey b Willis	19
S.L.Boock	not out	4
B.P.Bracewell	st Taylor b Emburey	4
Extras (b 4, lb 18, w 4, nb 7)		33
TOTAL		339

FALL OF WICKETS – 1-65, 2-70, 3-117, 4-247, 5-253, 6-290, 7-290, 8-321, 9-333, 10-339
BOWLING – Willis 29-9-79-1, Hendrick 28-14-39-1, Botham 38-13-101-6, Edmonds 12-3-19-0, Emburey 26.1-12-39-2, Gooch 10-0-29-0

ENGLAND 1st Innings

G.A.Gooch	c Boock b Hadlee	2
G.Boycott	c Hadlee b Bracewell	24
C.T.Radley	c Congdon b Hadlee	77
D.I.Gower	c Wright b Boock	71
*J.M.Brearley	c Edgar b Hadlee	33
I.T.Botham	c Edgar b Collinge	21
+R.W.Taylor	lbw b Hadlee	1
P.H.Edmonds	c Edgar b Hadlee	5
J.E.Emburey	b Collinge	2
M.Hendrick	b Bracewell	12
R.G.D.Willis	not out	7
Extras (b 7, lb 5, nb 22)		34
TOTAL		289

FALL OF WICKETS – 1-2, 2-66, 3-180, 4-211, 5-249, 6-255, 7-258, 8-263, 9-274, 10-289
BOWLING – Hadlee 32-9-84-5, Collinge 30-9-58-2, Bracewell 19.3-1-68-2, Boock 25-10-33-1, Congdon 6-1-12-0

NEW ZEALAND 2nd Innings

J.G.Wright	b Botham	12
+B.A.Edgar	b Botham	4
R.W.Anderson	c Taylor b Willis	1
J.M.Parker	c Taylor b Botham	3
*M.G.Burgess	c Hendrick b Botham	14
B.E.Congdon	c Taylor b Willis	3
S.L.Boock	c Radley b Willis	0
B.P.Bracewell	c Hendrick b Willis	0
G.P.Howarth	not out	14
R.J.Hadlee	run out	5
R.O.Collinge	b Botham	0
Extras (lb 3, nb 8)		11
TOTAL		67

FALL OF WICKETS – 1-10, 2-14, 3-20, 4-29, 5-33, 6-37, 7-37, 8-43, 9-57, 10-67
BOWLING – Willis 16-8-16-4, Botham 18.1-4-39-5, Emburey 3-2-1-0

ENGLAND 2nd Innings

G.A.Gooch	not out	42
G.Boycott	b Hadlee	4
C.T.Radley	b Hadlee	0
D.I.Gower	c Congdon b Bracewell	46
*J.M.Brearley	not out	8
DID NOT BAT – I.T.Botham, +R.W.Taylor, P.H.Edmonds, J.E.Emburey, M.Hendrick, R.G.D.Willis		
Extras (lb 3, w 4, nb 11)		18
TOTAL (for 3 wkts)		118

FALL OF WICKETS – 1-14, 2-14, 3-84
BOWLING – Hadlee 13.5-2-31-2, Collinge 6-1-26-0, Bracewell 6-0-32-1, Boock 5-1-11-0

1978

ENGLAND v INDIA

at Edgbaston on 12th, 13th, 14th, 16th July 1979
Toss: England
Umpires: D.J.Constant and B.J.Meyer
England won by an innings and 83 runs

ENGLAND

*J.M.Brearley	c Reddy b Kapil Dev	24
G.Boycott	lbw b Kapil Dev	155
D.W.Randall	c Reddy b Kapil Dev	15
G.A.Gooch	c Reddy b Kapil Dev	83
D.I.Gower	not out	200
I.T.Botham	b Kapil Dev	33
G.Miller	not out	63

DID NOT BAT – P.H.Edmonds, +R.W.Taylor, R.G.D.Willis, M.Hendrick

Extras (b 4, lb 27, w 11, nb 18) — 60
TOTAL (for 5 wkts dec) — 633

FALL OF WICKETS – 1-66, 2-90, 3-235, 4-426, 5-468
BOWLING – Kapil Dev 48-15-146-5, Ghavri 38-5-129-0, Amarnath 13.2-2-47-0, Chandrasekhar 29-1-113-0, Venkataraghavan 31-4-107-0, Gaekwad 3-0-12-0, Chauhan 3-0-19-0

INDIA 1st Innings

S.M.Gavaskar	run out	61
C.P.S.Chauhan	c Gooch b Botham	4
D.B.Vengsarkar	c Gooch b Edmonds	22
G.R.Viswanath	c Botham b Edmonds	78
A.D.Gaekwad	c Botham b Willis	25
M.Amarnath	b Willis	31
Kapil Dev	lbw b Botham	1
K.D.Ghavri	c Brearley b Willis	6
+B.Reddy	b Hendrick	21
*S.Venkataraghavan	c Botham b Hendrick	28
B.S.Chandrasekhar	not out	0

Extras (b 1, lb 4, w 3, nb 12) — 20
TOTAL — 297

FALL OF WICKETS – 1-15, 2-59, 3-129, 4-205, 5-209, 6-210, 7-229, 8-251, 9-294, 10-297
BOWLING – Willis 24-9-69-3, Botham 26-4-86-2, Hendrick 24.1-9-36-2, Edmonds 26-11-60-2, Boycott 5-1-8-0, Miller 11-3-18-0

INDIA 2nd Innings

S.M.Gavaskar	c Gooch b Hendrick	68
C.P.S.Chauhan	c Randall b Willis	56
D.B.Vengsarkar	c Edmonds b Hendrick	7
G.R.Viswanath	c Taylor b Botham	51
A.D.Gaekwad	c Gooch b Botham	15
M.Amarnath	lbw b Botham	10
Kapil Dev	c Hendrick b Botham	21
K.D.Ghavri	c Randall b Hendrick	4
+B.Reddy	lbw b Hendrick	0
*S.Venkataraghavan	lbw b Botham	0
B.S.Chandrasekhar	not out	0

Extras (b 7, lb 12, nb 2) — 21
TOTAL — 253

FALL OF WICKETS – 1-124, 2-136, 3-136, 4-182, 5-227, 6-240, 7-249, 8-250, 9-251, 10-253
BOWLING – Willis 14-3-45-1, Botham 29-8-70-5, Hendrick 20.4-8-45-4, Edmonds 17-6-37-0, Miller 9-1-27-0, Gooch 6-3-8-0

ENGLAND v INDIA

at Lord's on 2nd, 3rd, 4th, 6th August 1979
Toss: India
Umpires: H.D.Bird and K.E.Palmer
Match drawn

INDIA 1st Innings

S.M.Gavaskar	c Taylor b Gooch	42
C.P.S.Chauhan	c Randall b Botham	2
D.B.Vengsarkar	c Botham b Hendrick	0
G.R.Viswanath	c Brearley b Hendrick	21
A.D.Gaekwad	c Taylor b Botham	13
Yashpal Sharma	c Taylor b Botham	11
Kapil Dev	c Miller b Botham	4
K.D.Ghavri	not out	3
+B.Reddy	lbw b Botham	0
*S.Venkataraghavan	run out	0
B.S.Bedi	b Lever	0

Extras — 0
TOTAL — 96

FALL OF WICKETS – 1-12, 2-23, 3-51, 4-75, 5-79, 6-89, 7-96, 8-96, 9-96, 10-96
BOWLING – Lever 9.5-3-29-1, Bothom 19-9-35-5, Hendrick 15-7-15-2, Edmonds 2-1-1-0, Gooch 10.5-1-16-1

ENGLAND

*J.M.Brearley	c Reddy b Kapil Dev	12
G.Boycott	c Gavaskar b Ghavri	32
G.A.Gooch	b Kapil Dev	10
D.I.Gower	b Ghavri	82
D.W.Randall	run out	57
I.T.Botham	b Venkataraghavan	36
G.Miller	st Reddy b Bedi	62
P.H.Edmonds	c Reddy b Kapil Dev	20
R.W.Taylor +	c Vengsarkar b Bedi	64
J.K.Lever	not out	6

DID NOT BAT – M.Hendrick

Extras (b 11, lb 21, w 2, nb 4) — 38
TOTAL (for 9 wkts dec) — 419

FALL OF WICKETS – 1-21, 2-60, 3-71, 4-185, 5-226, 6-253, 7-291, 8-394, 9-419
BOWLING – Kapil Dev 38-11-93-3, Ghavri 31-2-122-2, Bedi 38.5-13-87-2, Venkataraghavan 22-2-79-1

INDIA 2nd Innings

S.M.Gavaskar	c Brearley b Botham	59
C.P.S.Chauhan	c Randall b Edmonds	31
D.B.Vengsarkar	c Boycott b Edmonds	103
G.R.Viswanath	c Gower b Lever	113
A.D.Gaekwad	not out	1
Yashpal Sharma	not out	5

DID NOT BAT – Kapil Dev, K.D.Ghavri, +B.Reddy, *S.Venkataraghavan, B.S.Bedi

Extras (b 2, lb 2, w 1, nb 1) — 6
TOTAL (for 4 wkts) — 318

FALL OF WICKETS – 1-79, 2-99, 3-309, 4-312
BOWLING – Lever 24-7-69-1, Botham 35-13-80-1, Hendrick 25-12-56-0, Edmonds 45-18-62-2, Gooch 2-0-8-0, Miller 17-6-37-0

ENGLAND v INDIA

at Headingley on 16th, 17th, 18th, 20th, 21st August 1979
Toss: England
Umpires: H.D.Bird and B.J.Meyer
Match drawn

ENGLAND

G.Boycott	c Viswanath b Kapil Dev	31
*J.M.Brearley	c Viswanath b Amarnath	15
G.A.Gooch	c Vengsarkar b Kapil Dev	4
D.I.Gower	lbw b Kapil Dev	0
D.W.Randall	b Ghavri	11
I.T.Botham	c Ghavri b Venkat	137
G.Miller	c Reddy b Amarnath	27
P.H.Edmonds	run out	18
+R.W.Taylor	c Chauhan b Bedi	1
R.G.D.Willis	not out	4
M.Hendrick	c sub b Bedi	0

Extras (b 4, lb 6, w 4, nb 8) — 22
TOTAL — 270

FALL OF WICKETS – 1-53, 2-57, 3-57, 4-58, 5-89, 6-176, 7-264, 8-264, 9-266, 10-270
BOWLING – Kapil Dev 27-7-84-3, Ghavri 18-4-60-1, Amarnath 20-7-53-2, Venkataraghavan 7-2-25-1, Bedi 8.5-2-26-2

INDIA

S.M.Gavaskar	b Edmonds	78
C.P.S.Chauhan	c Botham b Willis	0
M.Amarnath	c Taylor b Willis	0
G.R.Viswanath	c Brearley b Hendrick	1
Yashpal Sharma	c Botham b Miller	40
D.B.Vengsarkar	not out	65
Kapil Dev	c Gooch b Miller	3
K.D.Ghavri	not out	20

DID NOT BAT – *S.Venkataraghavan, +B.Reddy, B.S.Bedi

Extras (b 11, lb 4, w 1) — 16
TOTAL (for 6 wkts) — 223

FALL OF WICKETS – 1-1, 2-9, 3-12, 4-106, 5-156, 6-160
BOWLING – Willis 18-5-42-2, Hendrick 14-6-13-1, Botham 13-3-39-0, Edmonds 28-8-59-1, Miller 32-13-52-2, Gooch 3-1-2-0, Boycott 2-2-0-0

1979

ENGLAND v INDIA

at The Oval on 30th, 31st August, 1st, 3rd, 4th
September 1979
Toss: England
Umpires: D.J.Constant and K.E.Palmer
Match drawn

ENGLAND 1st Innings

G.Boycott	lbw b Kapil Dev	35
A.R.Butcher	c Yajurvindra b Venkat	14
G.A.Gooch	c Viswanath b Ghavri	79
D.I.Gower	lbw b Kapil Dev	0
P.Willey	c Yajurvindra b Bedi	52
I.T.Botham	st Reddy b Venkat	38
*J.M.Brearley	b Ghavri	34
+D.L.Bairstow	c Reddy b Kapil Dev	9
P.H.Edmonds	c Kapil Dev b Venkat	16
R.G.D.Willis	not out	10
M.Hendrick	c Gavaskar b Bedi	0
Extras (lb 9, w 4, nb 5)		18
TOTAL		305

FALL OF WICKETS – 1-45, 2-51, 3-51, 4-148, 5-203,
6-245, 7-272, 8-275, 9-304, 10-305
BOWLING – Kapil Dev 32-12-83-3, Ghavri 26-8-61-2,
Bedi 29.5-4-69-2, Yajurvindra 8-2-15-0,
Venkataraghavan 29-9-59-3

INDIA 1st Innings

S.M.Gavaskar	c Bairstow b Botham	13
C.P.S.Chauhan	c Botham b Willis	6
D.B.Vengsarkar	c Botham b Willis	0
G.R.Viswanath	c Brearley b Botham	62
Yashpal Sharma	lbw b Willis	27
Yajurvindra Singh	not out	43
Kapil Dev	b Hendrick	16
K.D.Ghavri	c Bairstow b Botham	7
+B.Reddy	c Bairstow b Botham	12
*S.Venkataraghavan	c & b Hendrick	2
B.S.Bedi	c Brearley b Hendrick	1
Extras (b 2, lb 3, w 5, nb 3)		13
TOTAL		202

FALL OF WICKETS – 1-9, 2-9, 3-47, 4-91, 5-130, 6-161,
7-172, 8-192, 9-200, 10-202
BOWLING – Willis 18-2-53-3, Botham 28-7-65-4,
Hendrick 22.3-7-38-3, Willey 4-1-10-0, Gooch 2-0-6-0,
Edmonds 5-1-17-0

ENGLAND 2nd Innings

G.Boycott	b Ghavri	125
A.R.Butcher	c Venkat b Ghavri	20
G.A.Gooch	lbw b Kapil Dev	31
D.I.Gower	c Reddy b Bedi	7
P.Willey	c Reddy b Ghavri	31
I.T.Botham	run out	0
*J.M.Brearley	b Venkataraghavan	11
+D.L.Bairstow	c Gavaskar b Kapil Dev	59
P.H.Edmonds	not out	27
DID NOT BAT – R.G.D.Willis and M.Hendrick		
Extras (lb 14, w 2, nb 7)		23
TOTAL (for 8 wkts dec)		334

FALL OF WICKETS – 1-43, 2-107, 3-125, 4-192, 5-194,
6-215, 7-291, 8-334
BOWLING – Kapil Dev 28.5-4-89-2, Ghavri 34-11-76-3,
Bedi 26-4-67-1, Yajurvindra 2-0-4-0,
Venkataraghavan 26-4-75-1

INDIA 2nd Innings

S.M.Gavaskar	c Gower b Botham	221
C.P.S.Chauhan	c Botham b Willis	80
D.B.Vengsarkar	c Botham b Edmonds	52
Kapil Dev	c Gooch b Willey	0
Yashpal Sharma	lbw b Botham	19
G.R.Viswanath	c Brearley b Willey	15
Yajurvindra Singh	lbw b Botham	1
*S.Venkataraghavan	run out	6
K.D.Ghavri	not out	3
+B.Reddy	not out	5
DID NOT BAT – B.S.Bedi		
Extras (b 11, lb 15, w 1)		27
TOTAL (for 8 wkts)		429

FALL OF WICKETS – 1-213, 2-366, 3-367, 4-389,
5-410, 6-411, 7-419, 8-423
BOWLING – Willis 28-4-89-1, Botham 29-5-97-3,
Hendrick 8-2-15-0, Willey 43.5-15-96-2,
Gooch 2-0-9-0, Edmonds 38-11-87-1, Butcher 2-0-9-0

1979

ENGLAND v WEST INDIES

at Trent Bridge on 5th, 6th, 7th, 9th, 10th June 1980
Toss: England
Umpires: D.J.Constant and D.O.Oslear
West Indies won by 2 wickets

ENGLAND 1st Innings

G.A.Gooch	c Murray b Roberts	17
G.Boycott	c Murray b Garner	36
C.J.Tavaré	b Garner	13
R.A.Woolmer	c Murray b Roberts	46
D.I.Gower	c Greenidge b Roberts	20
*I.T.Botham	c Richards b Garner	57
P.Willey	b Marshall	13
+A.P.E.Knott	lbw b Roberts	6
J.K.Lever	c Richards b Holding	15
R.G.D.Willis	b Roberts	8
M.Hendrick	not out	7
Extras (b 7, lb 11, w 3, nb 4)		25
TOTAL		263

FALL OF WICKETS – 1-27, 2-72, 3-74, 4-114, 5-204, 6-208, 7-228, 8-246, 9-254, 10-263
BOWLING – Roberts 25-7-72-5, Holding 23.5-7-61-1, Marshall 19-3-52-1, Richards 1-0-9-0, Garner 23-9-44-3

WEST INDIES 1st Innings

C.G.Greenidge	c Knott b Hendrick	53
D.L.Haynes	c Gower b Willis	12
I.V.A.Richards	c Knott b Willis	64
S.F.A.F.Bacchus	c Botham b Willis	30
A.I.Kallicharran	b Botham	17
+D.L.Murray	b Willis	64
*C.H.Lloyd	c Knott b Lever	9
M.D.Marshall	c Tavaré b Gooch	20
A.M.E.Roberts	lbw b Botham	21
J.Garner	c Lever b Botham	2
M.A.Holding	not out	0
Extras (b 1, lb 9, w 2, nb 4)		16
TOTAL		308

FALL OF WICKETS – 1-19, 2-107, 3-151, 4-165, 5-208, 6-227, 7-265, 8-306, 9-308, 10-308
BOWLING – Willis 20.1-5-82-4, Lever 20-2-76-1, Hendrick 19-4-69-1, Willey 5-3-4-0, Botham 20-6-50-3, Gooch 7-2-11-1

ENGLAND 2nd Innings

G.A.Gooch	run out	27
G.Boycott	b Roberts	75
C.J.Tavaré	c Richards b Garner	4
R.A.Woolmer	c Murray b Roberts	29
D.I.Gower	lbw b Garner	1
*I.T.Botham	c Richards b Roberts	4
P.Willey	b Marshall	38
+A.P.E.Knott	lbw b Marshall	7
J.K.Lever	c Murray b Garner	4
R.G.D.Willis	b Garner	9
M.Hendrick	not out	2
Extras (b 19, lb 13, w 10, nb 10)		52
TOTAL		252

FALL OF WICKETS – 1-46, 2-68, 3-174, 4-175, 5-180, 6-183, 7-218, 8-237, 9-248, 10-252
BOWLING – Roberts 24-6-57-3, Holding 26-5-65-0, Marshall 24-8-44-2, Garner 34.1-20-30-4, Greenidge 3-2-4-0

WEST INDIES 2nd Innings

C.G.Greenidge	c Knott b Willis	6
D.L.Haynes	run out	62
I.V.A.Richards	lbw b Botham	48
S.F.A.F.Bacchus	c Knott b Hendrick	19
A.I.Kallicharran	c Knott b Willis	9
*C.H.Lloyd	lbw b Willis	3
+D.L.Murray	c Hendrick b Willis	16
M.D.Marshall	b Willis	7
A.M.E.Roberts	not out	22
M.A.Holding	not out	0
DID NOT BAT – J.Garner		
Extras (lb 8, nb 9)		17
TOTAL (for 8 wkts)		209

FALL OF WICKETS – 1-11, 2-69, 3-109, 4-125, 5-129, 6-165, 7-180, 8-205
BOWLING – Willis 26-4-65-5, Lever 8-2-25-0, Hendrick 14-5-40-1, Willey 2-0-12-0, Botham 16.4-6-48-1, Gooch 2-1-2-0

ENGLAND v WEST INDIES

at Lord's on 19th, 20th, 21st, 23rd, 24th June 1980
Toss: England
Umpires: W.E.Alley and B.J.Meyer
Match drawn

ENGLAND 1st Innings

G.A.Gooch	lbw b Holding	123
G.Boycott	c Murray b Holding	8
C.J.Tavaré	c Greenidge b Holding	42
R.A.Woolmer	c Kallicharran b Garner	15
M.W.Gatting	b Holding	18
*I.T.Botham	lbw b Garner	8
D.L.Underwood	lbw b Garner	3
P.Willey	b Holding	4
+A.P.E.Knott	c Garner b Holding	9
R.G.D.Willis	b Garner	14
M.Hendrick	not out	10
Extras (b 4, lb 1, w 4, nb 6)		15
TOTAL		269

FALL OF WICKETS – 1-20, 2-165, 3-190, 4-219, 5-220, 6-231, 7-232, 8-244, 9-245, 10-269
BOWLING – Roberts 18-3-50-0, Holding 28-11-67-6, Garner 24.3-8-36-4, Croft 20-3-77-0, Richards 5-1-24-0

WEST INDIES

C.G.Greenidge	lbw b Botham	25
D.L.Haynes	lbw b Botham	184
I.V.A.Richards	c sub b Willey	145
C.E.H.Croft	run out	0
A.I.Kallicharran	c Knott b Willis	15
S.F.A.F.Bacchus	c Gooch b Willis	0
*C.H.Lloyd	b Willey	56
+D.L.Murray	c Tavare b Botham	34
A.M.E.Roberts	b Underwood	24
J.Garner	c Gooch b Willis	15
M.A.Holding	not out	0
Extras (b 1, lb 9, w 1, nb 9)		20
TOTAL		518

FALL OF WICKETS – 1-37, 2-260, 3-275, 4-326, 5-330, 6-437, 7-469, 8-486, 9-518, 10-518
BOWLING – Willis 31-12-103-3, Botham 37-7-145-3, Underwood 29.2-7-108-1, Hendrick 11-2-32-0, Gooch 7-1-26-0, Willey 25-8-73-2, Boycott 7-2-11-0

ENGLAND 2nd Innings

G.A.Gooch	b Garner	47
G.Boycott	not out	49
C.J.Tavaré	lbw b Garner	6
R.A.Woolmer	not out	19
DID NOT BAT – M.W.Gatting, *I.T.Botham, D.L.Underwood, P.Willey, +A.P.E.Knott, R.G.D.Willis, M.Hendrick		
Extras (lb 1, nb 11)		12
TOTAL (for 2 wkts)		133

FALL OF WICKETS – 1-71, 2-96
BOWLING – Roberts 13-3-24-0, Holding 15-5-51-0, Garner 15-6-21-2, Croft 8-2-24-0, Richards 1-0-1-0

ENGLAND v WEST INDIES

at Old Trafford on 10th, 11th, 12th, 14th, 15th July 1980
Toss: West Indies
Umpires: H.D.Bird and K.E.Palmer
Match drawn

ENGLAND 1st Innings

G.Boycott	c Garner b Roberts	5
G.A.Gooch	lbw b Roberts	2
B.C.Rose	b Marshall	70
W.Larkins	lbw b Garner	11
M.W.Gatting	c Richards b Marshall	33
*I.T.Botham	c Murray b Garner	8
P.Willey	b Marshall	0
+A.P.E.Knott	run out	2
J.E.Emburey	c Murray b Roberts	3
G.R.Dilley	b Garner	0
R.G.D.Willis	not out	5
Extras (lb 4, w 3, nb 4)		11
TOTAL		150

FALL OF WICKETS – 1-3, 2-18, 3-35, 4-126, 5-131, 6-132, 7-142, 8-142, 9-142, 10-150
BOWLING – Roberts 11.2-3-23-3, Holding 14-2-46-0, Garner 11-2-34-3, Marshall 12-5-36-3

WEST INDIES

C.G.Greenidge	c Larkins b Dilley	0
D.L.Haynes	c Knott b Willis	1
I.V.A.Richards	b Botham	65
S.F.A.F.Bacchus	c Botham b Dilley	0
A.I.Kallicharran	c Knott b Botham	13
*C.H.Lloyd	c Gooch b Emburey	101
+D.L.Murray	b Botham	17
M.D.Marshall	c Gooch b Dilley	18
A.M.E.Roberts	c Knott b Emburey	11
J.Garner	lbw b Emburey	0
M.A.Holding	not out	4
Extras (b 2, lb 13, w 3, nb 12)		30
TOTAL		260

FALL OF WICKETS – 1-4, 2-25, 3-25, 4-67, 5-100, 6-154, 7-209, 8-250, 9-250, 10-260
BOWLING – Willis 14-1-99-1, Dilley 28-7-47-3, Botham 20-6-64-3, Emburey 10.3-1-20-3

ENGLAND 2nd Innings

G.Boycott	lbw b Holding	86
G.A.Gooch	c Murray b Marshall	26
B.C.Rose	c Kallicharran b Holding	32
W.Larkins	c Murray b Marshall	33
M.W.Gatting	c Kallicharran b Garner	56
*I.T.Botham	lbw b Holding	35
P.Willey	not out	62
+A.P.E.Knott	c & b Garner	6
J.E.Emburey	not out	28
DID NOT BAT – G.R.Dilley and R.G.D.Willis		
Extras (b 5, lb 8, w 1, nb 13)		27
TOTAL (for 7 wkts)		391

FALL OF WICKETS – 1-32, 2-86, 3-181, 4-217, 5-290, 6-290, 7-309
BOWLING – Roberts 14-2-36-0, Holding 34-8-100-3, Garner 40-11-73-2, Marshall 35-5-116-2, Richards 16-6-31-0, Lloyd 1-0-1-0, Bacchus 1-0-3-0, Haynes 1-0-2-0, Kallicharran 1-0-2-0

1980

ENGLAND v WEST INDIES

at The Oval on 24th, 25th, 26th, 28th, 29th July 1980
Toss: England
Umpires: B.J.Meyer and D.O.Oslear
Match drawn

ENGLAND 1st Innings

G.A.Gooch	lbw b Holding	83
G.Boycott	run out	53
B.C.Rose	b Croft	50
W.Larkins	lbw b Garner	7
M.W.Gatting	b Croft	48
P.Willey	c Lloyd b Holding	34
+A.P.E.Knott	c Lloyd b Marshall	3
*I.T.Botham	lbw b Croft	9
J.E.Emburey	c Holding b Marshall	24
G.R.Dilley	b Garner	1
R.G.D.Willis	not out	1
Extras (b 7, lb 21, w 10, nb 19)		57
TOTAL		370

FALL OF WICKETS – 1-155, 2-157, 3-182, 4-269, 5-303, 6-312, 7-336, 8-343, 9-368, 10-370
BOWLING – Holding 28-5-67-2, Croft 35-9-97-3, Marshall 29.3-6-77-2, Garner 33-8-67-2, Richards 3-1-5-0

WEST INDIES

C.G.Greenidge	lbw b Willis	6
D.L.Haynes	c Gooch b Dilley	7
I.V.A.Richards	c Willey b Botham	26
S.F.A.F.Bacchus	c Knott b Emburey	61
A.I.Kallicharran	c Rose b Dilley	11
+D.L.Murray	hit wicket b Dilley	0
M.D.Marshall	c Rose b Emburey	45
J.Garner	c Gatting b Botham	46
M.A.Holding	lbw b Dilley	22
C.E.H.Croft	not out	0
*C.H.Lloyd	absent hurt	
Extras (lb 12, w 1, nb 28)		41
TOTAL		265

FALL OF WICKETS – 1-15, 2-34, 3-72, 4-99, 5-105, 6-187, 7-197, 8-261, 9-265
BOWLING – Willis 19-5-58-1, Dilley 23-6-57-4, Botham 18.2-8-47-2, Emburey 23-12-38-2, Gooch 1-0-2-0, Willey 11-5-22-0

ENGLAND 2nd Innings

G.A.Gooch	lbw b Holding	0
G.Boycott	c Murray b Croft	5
B.C.Rose	lbw b Garner	41
W.Larkins	b Holding	0
J.E.Emburey	c Bacchus b Croft	2
M.W.Gatting	c Murray b Garner	15
*I.T.Botham	c Greenidge b Garner	4
P.Willey	not out	100
+A.P.E.Knott	lbw b Holding	3
G.R.Dilley	c sub b Holding	1
R.G.D.Willis	not out	24
Extras (lb 6, w 1, nb 7)		14
TOTAL (for 9 wkts dec)		209

FALL OF WICKETS – 1-2, 2-10, 3-13, 4-18, 5-63, 6-67, 7-73, 8-84, 9-92
BOWLING – Holding 29-7-79-4, Croft 10-6-8-2, Marshall 23-7-47-0, Garner 17-5-24-3, Richards 9-3-15-0, Kallicharran 6-1-22-0

ENGLAND v WEST INDIES

at Headingley on 7th, 8th, 9th, 11th, 12th August 1980
Toss: West Indies
Umpires: W.E.Alley and K.E.Palmer
Match drawn

ENGLAND 1st Innings

G.A.Gooch	c Marshall b Garner	14
G.Boycott	c Kallicharran b Holding	4
B.C.Rose	b Croft	7
W.Larkins	c Kallicharran b Garner	9
M.W.Gatting	c Marshall b Croft	1
*I.T.Botham	c Richards b Holding	37
P.Willey	c Murray b Croft	1
+D.L.Bairstow	lbw b Marshall	40
J.E.Emburey	not out	13
C.M.Old	c Garner b Marshall	6
G.R.Dilley	b Garner	0
Extras (b 3, lb 3, w 1, nb 4)		11
TOTAL		143

FALL OF WICKETS – 1-9, 2-27, 3-28, 4-34, 5-52, 6-59, 7-89, 8-131, 9-140, 10-143
BOWLING – Holding 10-4-34-2, Croft 12-3-35-3, Garner 14-4-41-3, Marshall 11-3-22-2

WEST INDIES

C.G.Greenidge	lbw b Botham	34
D.L.Haynes	b Emburey	42
*I.V.A.Richards	b Old	31
S.F.A.F.Bacchus	c & b Dilley	11
A.I.Kallicharran	c Larkins b Dilley	37
C.L.King	c Bairstow b Gooch	12
+D.L.Murray	c Emburey b Dilley	14
M.D.Marshall	c Bairstow b Dilley	0
J.Garner	c Emburey b Gooch	0
M.A.Holding	b Old	35
C.E.H.Croft	not out	1
Extras (b 2, lb 9, w 3, nb 14)		28
TOTAL		245

FALL OF WICKETS – 1-83, 2-105, 3-133, 4-142, 5-170, 6-198, 7-198, 8-207, 9-207, 10-245
BOWLING – Dilley 23-6-79-4, Old 28.5-9-64-2, Botham 19-8-31-1, Emburey 6-0-25-1, Gooch 8-3-18-2

ENGLAND 2nd Innings

G.A.Gooch	lbw b Marshall	55
G.Boycott	c Kallicharran b Croft	47
W.Larkins	lbw b Marshall	30
M.W.Gatting	lbw b Holding	1
B.C.Rose	not out	43
*I.T.Botham	lbw b Marshall	7
P.Willey	c Murray b Holding	10
+D.L.Bairstow	not out	9
DID NOT BAT – J.E.Emburey, C.M.Old, G.R.Dilley		
Extras (b 5, lb 11, w 2, nb 7)		25
TOTAL (for 6 wkts dec)		227

FALL OF WICKETS – 1-95, 2-126, 3-129, 4-162, 5-174, 6-203
BOWLING – Holding 23-2-62-2, Croft 19-2-65-1, Garner 1-0-1-0, Marshall 19-5-42-3, King 12-3-32-0, Richards 1-1-0-0

ENGLAND v AUSTRALIA

at Lord's on 28th, 29th, 30th August, 1st, 2nd September 1980
Toss: Australia
Umpires: H.D.Bird and D.J.Constant
Match drawn

AUSTRALIA 1st Innings

G.M.Wood	st Bairstow b Emburey	112
B.M.Laird	c Bairstow b Old	24
*G.S.Chappell	c Gatting b Old	47
K.J.Hughes	c Athey b Old	117
G.N.Yallop	lbw b Hendrick	2
A.R.Border	not out	56
+R.W.Marsh	not out	16
DID NOT BAT – D.K.Lillee, A.A.Mallett, R.J.Bright, L.S.Pascoe		
Extras (b 1, lb 8, nb 2)		11
TOTAL (for 5 wkts dec)		385

FALL OF WICKETS – 1-64, 2-150, 3-260, 4-267, 5-320
BOWLING – Old 35-9-91-3, Hendrick 30-6-67-1, Botham 22-2-89-0, Emburey 38-9-104-1, Gooch 8-3-16-0, Willey 1-0-7-0

ENGLAND 1st Innings

G.A.Gooch	c Bright b Lillee	8
G.Boycott	c Marsh b Lillee	62
C.W.J.Athey	b Lillee	9
D.I.Gower	b Lillee	45
M.W.Gatting	lbw b Pascoe	12
*I.T.Botham	c Wood b Pascoe	0
P.Willey	lbw b Pascoe	5
+D.L.Bairstow	lbw b Pascoe	6
J.E.Emburey	lbw b Pascoe	3
C.M.Old	not out	24
M.Hendrick	c Border b Mallett	5
Extras (b 6, lb 8, nb 12)		26
TOTAL		205

FALL OF WICKETS – 1-10, 2-41, 3-137, 4-151, 5-158, 6-163, 7-164, 8-173, 9-200, 10-205
BOWLING – Lillee 15-4-43-4, Pascoe 18-5-59-5, Chappell 2-0-2-0, Bright 21-6-50-0, Mallett 7.2-3-25-1

AUSTRALIA 2nd Innings

G.M.Wood	lbw b Old	8
B.M.Laird	c Bairstow b Old	6
*G.S.Chappell	b Old	59
K.J.Hughes	lbw b Botham	84
A.R.Border	not out	21
DID NOT BAT – G.N.Yallop, +R.W.Marsh, D.K.Lillee, A.A.Mallett, R.J.Bright, L.S.Pascoe		
Extras (b 1, lb 8, nb 2)		11
TOTAL (for 4 wkts dec)		189

FALL OF WICKETS – 1-15, 2-28, 3-139, 4-189
BOWLING – Old 20-6-47-3, Hendrick 15-4-53-0, Botham 9.2-1-43-1, Emburey 9-2-35-0

ENGLAND 2nd Innings

G.A.Gooch	lbw b Lillee	16
G.Boycott	not out	128
C.W.J.Athey	c Laird b Pascoe	1
D.I.Gower	b Mallett	35
M.W.Gatting	not out	51
DID NOT BAT – *I.T.Botham, P.Willey, +D.L.Bairstow, J.E.Emburey, C.M.Old, M.Hendrick		
Extras (b 3, lb 2, nb 8)		13
TOTAL (for 3 wkts)		244

FALL OF WICKETS – 1-19, 2-43, 3-124
BOWLING – Lillee 19-5-53-1, Pascoe 17-1-73-1, Bright 25-9-44-0, Mallett 21-2-61-1

1980

ENGLAND v AUSTRALIA

at Trent Bridge on 18th, 19th, 20th, 21st June 1981
Toss: Australia
Umpires: W.E.Alley and D.J.Constant
Australia won by 4 wickets

ENGLAND 1st Innings

G.A.Gooch	c Wood b Lillee	10
G.Boycott	c Border b Alderman	27
R.A.Woolmer	c Wood b Lillee	0
D.I.Gower	c Yallop b Lillee	26
M.W.Gatting	lbw b Hogg	52
P.Willey	c Border b Alderman	10
*I.T.Botham	b Alderman	1
+P.R.Downton	c Yallop b Alderman	8
G.R.Dilley	b Hogg	34
R.G.D.Willis	c Marsh b Hogg	0
M.Hendrick	not out	6
Extras (lb 6, w 1, nb 4)		11
TOTAL		185

FALL OF WICKETS – 1-13, 2-13, 3-57, 4-67, 5-92, 6-96, 7-116, 8-159, 9-159, 10-185
BOWLING – Lillee 13-3-34-3, Alderman 24-7-68-4, Hogg 11.4-1-47-3, Lawson 8-3-25-0

AUSTRALIA 1st Innings

G.M.Wood	lbw b Dilley	0
J.Dyson	c Woolmer b Willis	5
G.N.Yallop	b Hendrick	13
*K.J.Hughes	lbw b Willis	7
T.M.Chappell	b Hendrick	17
A.R.Border	c & b Botham	63
+R.W.Marsh	c Boycott b Willis	19
G.F.Lawson	c Gower b Botham	14
D.K.Lillee	c Downton b Dilley	12
R.M.Hogg	c Boycott b Dilley	0
T.M.Alderman	not out	12
Extras (b 4, lb 8, w 1, nb 4)		17
TOTAL		179

FALL OF WICKETS – 1-0, 2-21, 3-21, 4-33, 5-64, 6-89, 7-110, 8-147, 9-153, 10-179
BOWLING – Dilley 20-7-38-3, Willis 30-14-47-3, Hendrick 20-7-43-2, Botham 16.5-6-34-2

ENGLAND 2nd Innings

G.A.Gooch	c Yallop b Lillee	6
G.Boycott	c Marsh b Alderman	4
R.A.Woolmer	c Marsh b Alderman	0
D.I.Gower	c sub b Lillee	28
M.W.Gatting	lbw b Alderman	15
P.Willey	lbw b Lillee	13
*I.T.Botham	c Border b Lillee	33
+P.R.Downton	lbw b Alderman	3
G.R.Dilley	c Marsh b Alderman	13
R.G.D.Willis	c Chappell b Lillee	1
M.Hendrick	not out	0
Extras (lb 8, nb 1)		9
TOTAL		125

FALL OF WICKETS – 1-12, 2-12, 3-13, 4-39, 5-61, 6-94, 7-109, 8-113, 9-125, 10-125
BOWLING – Lillee 16.4-2-46-5, Alderman 19-3-62-5, Hogg 3-1-8-0

AUSTRALIA 2nd Innings

G.M.Wood	c Woolmer b Willis	8
J.Dyson	c Downton b Dilley	38
G.N.Yallop	c Gatting b Botham	6
*K.J.Hughes	lbw b Dilley	22
T.M.Chappell	not out	20
A.R.Border	b Dilley	20
+R.W.Marsh	lbw b Dilley	0
G.F.Lawson	not out	5
DID NOT BAT – D.K.Lillee, R.M.Hogg, T.M.Alderman		
Extras (b 1, lb 6, nb 6)		13
TOTAL (for 6 wkts)		132

FALL OF WICKETS – 1-20, 2-40, 3-77, 4-80, 5-122, 6-122
BOWLING – Dilley 11.1-4-24-4, Willis 13-2-28-1, Hendrick 20-7-33-0, Botham 10-1-34-1

ENGLAND AUSTRALIA

at Lord's on 2nd, 3rd, 4th, 6th, 7th July 1981
Toss: Australia
Umpires: D.O.Oslear and K.E.Palmer
Match drawn

ENGLAND 1st Innings

G.A.Gooch	c Yallop b Lawson	44
G.Boycott	c Alderman b Lawson	17
R.A.Woolmer	c Marsh b Lawson	21
D.I.Gower	c Marsh b Lawson	27
M.W.Gatting	lbw b Bright	59
P.Willey	c Border b Alderman	82
J.E.Emburey	run out	31
*I.T.Botham	lbw b Lawson	0
+R.W.Taylor	c Hughes b Lawson	0
G.R.Dilley	not out	7
R.G.D.Willis	c Wood b Lawson	5
Extras (b 2, lb 3, w 3, nb 10)		18
TOTAL		311

FALL OF WICKETS – 1-60, 2-65, 3-134, 4-187, 5-284, 6-293, 7-293, 8-293, 9-298, 10-311
BOWLING – Lillee 35.4-7-102-0, Alderman 30.2-7-79-1, Lawson 43.1-14-81-7, Bright 15-7-31-1

AUSTRALIA 1st Innings

G.M.Wood	c Taylor b Willis	44
J.Dyson	c Gower b Botham	7
G.N.Yallop	b Dilley	1
*K.J.Hughes	c Willis b Emburey	42
T.M.Chappell	c Taylor b Dilley	2
A.R.Border	c Gatting b Botham	64
+R.W.Marsh	lbw b Dilley	47
R.J.Bright	lbw b Emburey	33
G.F.Lawson	lbw b Willis	5
D.K.Lillee	not out	40
T.M.Alderman	c Taylor b Willis	5
Extras (b 6, lb 11, w 6, nb 32)		55
TOTAL		345

FALL OF WICKETS – 1-62, 2-62, 3-69, 4-81, 5-167, 6-244, 7-257, 8-268, 9-314, 10-345
BOWLING – Willis 27.4-9-50-3, Dilley 30-8-106-3, Botham 26-8-71-2, Gooch 10-4-28-0, Emburey 25-12-35-2

ENGLAND 2nd Innings

G.A.Gooch	lbw b Lawson	20
G.Boycott	c Marsh b Lillee	60
R.A.Woolmer	lbw b Alderman	9
D.I.Gower	c Alderman b Lillee	89
M.W.Gatting	c Wood b Bright	16
*I.T.Botham	b Bright	0
P.Willey	c Chappell b Bright	12
+R.W.Taylor	b Lillee	9
G.R.Dilley	not out	27
DID NOT BAT – J.E.Emburey and R.G.D.Willis		
Extras (b 2, lb 8, nb 13)		23
TOTAL (for 8 wkts dec)		265

FALL OF WICKETS – 1-31, 2-55, 3-178, 4-217, 5-217, 6-217, 7-242, 8-265
BOWLING – Lillee 26.4-8-82-3, Alderman 17-2-42-1, Lawson 19-6-51-1, Bright 36-18-67-3

AUSTRALIA 2nd Innings

G.M.Wood	not out	62
J.Dyson	lbw b Dilley	1
G.N.Yallop	c Botham b Willis	3
*K.J.Hughes	lbw b Dilley	4
T.M.Chappell	c Taylor b Botham	5
A.R.Border	not out	12
DID NOT BAT – +R.W.Marsh, R.J.Bright, G.F.Lawson, D.K.Lillee, T.M.Alderman		
Extras (w 1, nb 2)		3
TOTAL (for 4 wkts)		90

FALL OF WICKETS – 1-2, 2-11, 3-17, 4-62
BOWLING – Willis 12-3-35-1, Dilley 7.5-1-18-2, Botham 8-3-10-1, Emburey 21-10-24-0

ENGLAND v AUSTRALIA

at Headingley on 16th, 17th, 18th, 20th, 21st July 1981
Toss: Australia
Umpires: D.G.L.Evans and B.J.Meyer
England won by 18 runs

AUSTRALIA 1st Innings

J.Dyson	b Dilley	102
G.M.Wood	lbw b Botham	34
T.M.Chappell	c Taylor b Willey	27
*K.J.Hughes	c & b Botham	89
R.J.Bright	b Dilley	7
G.N.Yallop	c Taylor b Botham	58
A.R.Border	lbw b Botham	8
+R.W.Marsh	b Botham	28
G.F.Lawson	c Taylor b Botham	13
D.K.Lillee	not out	3
T.M.Alderman	not out	0
Extras (b 4, lb 13, w 3, nb 12)		32
TOTAL (for 9 wkts dec)		401

FALL OF WICKETS – 1-55, 2-149, 3-196, 4-220, 5-332, 6-354, 7-357, 8-396, 9-401
BOWLING – Willis 30-8-72-0, Old 43-14-91-0, Dilley 27-4-78-2, Botham 39.2-11-95-6, Willey 13-2-31-1, Boycott 3-2-2-0

ENGLAND 1st Innings

G.A.Gooch	lbw b Alderman	2
G.Boycott	b Lawson	12
*J.M.Brearley	c Marsh b Alderman	10
D.I.Gower	c Marsh b Lawson	24
M.W.Gatting	lbw b Lillee	15
P.Willey	b Lawson	8
I.T.Botham	c Marsh b Lillee	50
+R.W.Taylor	c Marsh b Lillee	5
G.R.Dilley	c & b Lillee	13
C.M.Old	c Border b Alderman	0
R.G.D.Willis	not out	1
Extras (b 6, lb 11, w 6, nb 11)		34
TOTAL		174

FALL OF WICKETS – 1-12, 2-40, 3-42, 4-84, 5-87, 6-112, 7-148, 8-166, 9-167, 10-174
BOWLING – Lillee 18.5-7-49-4, Alderman 19-4-59-3, Lawson 13-3-32-3

ENGLAND 2nd Innings

G.A.Gooch	c Alderman b Lillee	0
G.Boycott	lbw b Alderman	46
*J.M.Brearley	c Alderman b Lillee	14
D.I.Gower	c Border b Alderman	9
M.W.Gatting	lbw b Alderman	1
P.Willey	c Dyson b Lillee	33
I.T.Botham	not out	149
+R.W.Taylor	c Bright b Alderman	1
G.R.Dilley	b Alderman	56
C.M.Old	b Lawson	29
R.G.D.Willis	c Border b Alderman	2
Extras (b 5, lb 3, w 3, nb 5)		16
TOTAL		356

FALL OF WICKETS – 1-0, 2-18, 3-37, 4-41, 5-105, 6-133, 7-135, 8-252, 9-319, 10-356
BOWLING – Lillee 25-6-94-3, Alderman 35.3-6-135-6, Lawson 23-4-96-1, Bright 4-0-15-0

AUSTRALIA 2nd Innings

J.Dyson	c Taylor b Willis	34
G.M.Wood	c Taylor b Botham	10
T.M.Chappell	c Taylor b Willis	8
*K.J.Hughes	c Botham b Willis	0
G.N.Yallop	c Gatting b Willis	0
A.R.Border	b Old	0
+R.W.Marsh	c Dilley b Willis	4
R.J.Bright	b Willis	19
G.F.Lawson	c Taylor b Willis	1
D.K.Lillee	c Gatting b Willis	17
T.M.Alderman	not out	0
Extras (lb 3, w 1, nb 14)		18
TOTAL		111

FALL OF WICKETS – 1-13, 2-56, 3-58, 4-58, 5-65, 6-68, 7-74, 8-75, 9-110, 10-111
BOWLING – Willis 15.1-3-43-8, Old 9-1-21-1, Dilley 2-0-11-0, Botham 7-3-14-1, Willey 3-1-4-0

1981

ENGLAND v AUSTRALIA

at Edgbaston on 30th, 31st July, 1st, 2nd August 1981
Toss: England
Umpires: H.D.Bird and D.O.Oslear
England won by 29 runs

ENGLAND 1st Innings

G.Boycott	c Marsh b Alderman	13
*J.M.Brearley	c Border b Lillee	48
D.I.Gower	c Hogg b Alderman	0
G.A.Gooch	c Marsh b Bright	21
M.W.Gatting	c Alderman b Lillee	21
P.Willey	b Bright	16
I.T.Botham	b Alderman	26
J.E.Emburey	b Hogg	3
+R.W.Taylor	b Alderman	0
C.M.Old	not out	11
R.G.D.Willis	c Marsh b Alderman	13
Extras	(b 1, lb 5, w 1, nb 10)	17
TOTAL		189

FALL OF WICKETS – 1-29, 2-29, 3-60, 4-101, 5-126, 6-145, 7-161, 8-161, 9-165, 10-189
BOWLING – Lillee 18-4-61-2, 23.1-8-42-5, Hogg 16-3-49-1, Bright 12-4-20-2

AUSTRALIA 1st Innings

G.M.Wood	run out	38
J.Dyson	b Old	1
A.R.Border	c Taylor b Old	2
R.J.Bright	lbw b Botham	27
*K.J.Hughes	lbw b Old	47
G.N.Yallop	b Emburey	30
M.F.Kent	c Willis b Emburey	46
R.W.Marsh +	b Emburey	2
D.K.Lillee	b Emburey	18
R.M.Hogg	run out	0
T.M.Alderman	not out	3
Extras	(b 4, lb 19, nb 21)	44
TOTAL		258

FALL OF WICKETS – 1-5, 2-14, 3-62, 4-115, 5-166, 6-203, 7-220, 8-253, 9-253, 10-258
BOWLING – Willis 19-3-63-0, Old 21-8-44-3, Emburey 26.5-12-43-4, Botham 20-1-64-1

ENGLAND 2nd Innings

G.Boycott	c Marsh b Bright	29
*J.M.Brearley	lbw b Lillee	13
D.I.Gower	c Border b Bright	23
G.A.Gooch	b Bright	21
M.W.Gatting	b Bright	39
P.Willey	b Bright	5
I.T.Botham	c Marsh b Lillee	3
C.M.Old	c Marsh b Alderman	23
J.E.Emburey	not out	37
+R.W.Taylor	lbw b Alderman	8
R.G.D.Willis	c Marsh b Alderman	2
Extras	(lb 6, w 1, nb 9)	16
TOTAL		219

FALL OF WICKETS – 1-18, 2-52, 3-89, 4-98, 5-110, 6-115, 7-154, 8-167, 9-217, 10-219
BOWLING – Lillee 26-9-51-2, Alderman 22-5-65-3, Hogg 10-3-19-0, Bright 34-17-68-5

AUSTRALIA 2nd Innings

G.M.Wood	lbw b Old	2
J.Dyson	lbw b Willis	13
A.R.Border	c Gatting b Emburey	40
*K.J.Hughes	c Emburey b Willis	5
G.N.Yallop	c Botham b Emburey	30
M.F.Kent	b Botham	10
+R.W.Marsh	b Botham	4
R.J.Bright	lbw b Botham	0
D.K.Lillee	c Taylor b Botham	3
R.M.Hogg	not out	0
T.M.Alderman	b Botham	0
Extras	(b 1, lb 2, nb 11)	14
TOTAL		121

FALL OF WICKETS – 1-2, 2-19, 3-29, 4-87, 5-105, 6-114, 7-114, 8-120, 9-121, 10-121
BOWLING – Willis 20-6-37-2, Old 11-4-19-1, Emburey 22-10-40-2, Botham 14-9-11-5

ENGLAND v AUSTRALIA

at Old Trafford on 13th, 14th, 15th, 16th, 17th August 1981
Toss: England
Umpires: D.J.Constant and K.E.Palmer
England won by 103 runs

ENGLAND 1st Innings

G.A.Gooch	lbw b Lillee	10
G.Boycott	c Marsh b Alderman	10
C.J.Tavare	c Alderman b Whitney	69
D.I.Gower	c Yallop b Whitney	23
*J.M.Brearley	lbw b Alderman	2
M.W.Gatting	c Border b Lillee	32
I.T.Botham	c Bright b Whitney	0
+A.P.E.Knott	c Border b Alderman	13
J.E.Emburey	c Border b Alderman	1
P.J.W.Allott	not out	52
R.G.D.Willis	c Hughes b Lillee	11
Extras	(lb 6, w 2)	8
TOTAL		231

FALL OF WICKETS – 1-19, 2-25, 3-57, 4-62, 5-109, 6-109, 7-131, 8-137, 9-175, 10-231
BOWLING – Lillee 24.1-8-55-4, Alderman 29-5-88-4, Whitney 17-3-50-2, Bright 16-6-30-0

AUSTRALIA 1st Innings

G.M.Wood	lbw b Allott	19
J.Dyson	c Botham b Willis	0
*K.J.Hughes	lbw b Willis	4
G.N.Yallop	c Botham b Willis	0
M.F.Kent	c Knott b Emburey	52
A.R.Border	c Gower b Botham	11
+R.W.Marsh	c Botham b Willis	1
R.J.Bright	c Knott b Botham	22
D.K.Lillee	c Gooch b Botham	13
M.R.Whitney	b Allott	0
T.M.Alderman	not out	2
Extras	(nb 6)	6
TOTAL		130

FALL OF WICKETS – 1-20, 2-24, 3-24, 4-24, 5-58, 6-59, 7-104, 8-125, 9-126, 10-130
BOWLING – Willis 14-0-63-4, Allott 6-1-17-2, Botham 6.2-1-28-3, Emburey 4-0-16-1

ENGLAND 2nd Innings

G.A.Gooch	b Alderman	5
G.Boycott	lbw b Alderman	37
C.J.Tavaré	c Kent b Alderman	78
D.I.Gower	c Bright b Lillee	1
M.W.Gatting	lbw b Alderman	11
*J.M.Brearley	c Marsh b Alderman	3
I.T.Botham	c Marsh b Whitney	118
+A.P.E.Knott	c Dyson b Lillee	59
J.E.Emburey	c Kent b Whitney	57
P.J.W.Allott	c Hughes b Bright	14
R.G.D.Willis	not out	5
Extras	(b 1, lb 12, nb 3)	16
TOTAL		404

FALL OF WICKETS – 1-7, 2-79, 3-80, 4-98, 5-104, 6-253, 7-282, 8-356, 9-396, 10-404
BOWLING – Lillee 46-13-137-2, Alderman 52-19-109-5, Whitney 27-6-74-2, Bright 26.4-12-68-1

AUSTRALIA 2nd Innings

G.M.Wood	c Knott b Allott	6
J.Dyson	run out	5
*K.J.Hughes	lbw b Botham	43
G.N.Yallop	b Emburey	114
A.R.Border	not out	123
M.F.Kent	c Brearley b Emburey	2
+R.W.Marsh	c Knott b Willis	47
R.J.Bright	c Knott b Willis	5
D.K.Lillee	c Botham b Allott	28
T.M.Alderman	lbw b Botham	0
M.R.Whitney	c Gatting b Willis	0
Extras	(lb 9, w 2, nb 18)	29
TOTAL		402

FALL OF WICKETS – 1-7, 2-24, 3-119, 4-198, 5-206, 6-296, 7-322, 8-373, 9-378, 10-402
BOWLING – Willis 30.5-2-96-3, Allott 17-3-71-2, Botham 36-16-86-2, Emburey 49-9-107-2, Gatting 3-1-13-0

ENGLAND v AUSTRALIA

at The Oval on 27th, 28th, 29th, 31st August, 1st September 1981
Toss: England
Umpires: H.D.Bird and B.J.Meyer
Match drawn

AUSTRALIA 1st Innings

G.M.Wood	c Brearley b Botham	66
M.F.Kent	c Gatting b Botham	54
*K.J.Hughes	hit wicket b Botham	31
G.N.Yallop	c Botham b Willis	26
A.R.Border	not out	106
D.M.Wellham	b Willis	24
+R.W.Marsh	c Botham b Willis	12
R.J.Bright	c Brearley b Botham	3
D.K.Lillee	b Willis	11
T.M.Alderman	b Botham	0
M.R.Whitney	b Botham	4
Extras	(b 4, lb 6, w 1, nb 4)	15
TOTAL		352

FALL OF WICKETS – 1-120, 2-125, 3-169, 4-199, 5-260, 6-280, 7-303, 8-319, 9-320, 10-352
BOWLING – Willis 31-6-91-4, Hendrick 31-8-63-0, Botham 47-13-125-6, Emburey 23-2-58-0

ENGLAND 1st Innings

G.Boycott	c Yallop b Lillee	137
W.Larkins	c Alderman b Lillee	34
C.J.Tavaré	c Marsh b Lillee	24
M.W.Gatting	b Lillee	53
*J.M.Brearley	c Bright b Alderman	0
P.W.G.Parker	c Kent b Alderman	0
I.T.Botham	c Yallop b Lillee	3
+A.P.E.Knott	b Lillee	36
J.E.Emburey	lbw b Lillee	0
R.G.D.Willis	b Alderman	3
M.Hendrick	not out	0
Extras	(lb 9, w 3, nb 12)	24
TOTAL		314

FALL OF WICKETS – 1-61, 2-131, 3-246, 4-248, 5-248, 6-256, 7-293, 8-293, 9-302, 10-314
BOWLING – Lillee 31.4-4-89-7, Alderman 35-4-84-3, Whitney 23-3-76-0, Bright 21-6-41-0

AUSTRALIA 2nd Innings

G.M.Wood	c Knott b Hendrick	21
M.F.Kent	c Brearley b Botham	7
*K.J.Hughes	lbw b Hendrick	6
G.N.Yallop	b Hendrick	35
A.R.Border	c Tavaré b Emburey	84
D.M.Wellham	lbw b Botham	103
+R.W.Marsh	c Gatting b Botham	52
R.J.Bright	b Botham	11
D.K.Lillee	not out	8
M.R.Whitney	c Botham b Hendrick	0
DID NOT BAT – T.M.Alderman		
Extras	(b 1, lb 8, w 1, nb 7)	17
TOTAL (for 9 wkts dec)		344

FALL OF WICKETS – 1-26, 2-36, 3-41, 4-104, 5-205, 6-271, 7-332, 8-343, 9-344
BOWLING – Willis 10-0-41-0, Hendrick 29.2-6-82-4, Botham 42-9-128-4, Emburey 23-3-76-1

ENGLAND 2nd Innings

G.Boycott	lbw b Lillee	0
W.Larkins	c Alderman b Lillee	24
C.J.Tavaré	c Kent b Whitney	8
M.W.Gatting	c Kent b Lillee	56
P.W.G.Parker	c Kent b Alderman	13
*J.M.Brearley	c Marsh b Lillee	51
I.T.Botham	lbw b Alderman	16
+A.P.E.Knott	not out	70
J.E.Emburey	not out	5
DID NOT BAT – R.G.D.Willis and M.Hendrick		
Extras	(b 2, lb 5, w 2, nb 9)	18
TOTAL (for 7 wkts)		261

FALL OF WICKETS – 1-0, 2-18, 3-88, 4-101, 5-127, 6-144, 7-237
BOWLING – Lillee 30-10-70-4, Alderman 19-6-60-2, Whitney 11-4-46-1, Bright 27-12-50-0, Yallop 8-2-17-0

1981

ENGLAND v INDIA

at Lord's on 10th, 11th, 12th, 14th, 15th June 1982
Toss: England
Umpires: D.G.L.Evans and B.J.Meyer
England won by 7 wickets

ENGLAND 1st Innings

G.Cook	lbw b Kapil Dev	4
C.J.Tavaré	c Viswanath b Kapil Dev	4
A.J.Lamb	lbw b Kapil Dev	9
D.I.Gower	c Viswanath b Kapil Dev	37
I.T.Botham	c Malhotra b Madan Lal	67
D.W.Randall	c Parkar b Kapil Dev	126
D.R.Pringle	c Gavaskar b Doshi	7
P.H.Edmonds	c Kirmani b Madan Lal	64
+R.W.Taylor	c Viswanath b Doshi	31
P.J.Allott	not out	41
*R.G.D.Willis	b Madan Lal	28
Extras (b 1, lb 5, nb 9)		15
TOTAL		433

FALL OF WICKETS –1-5, 2-18, 3-37, 4-96, 5-149, 6-166, 7-291, 8-363, 9-363, 10-433
BOWLING – Kapil Dev 43-8-125-5, Madan Lal 28.1-6-99-3, Shastri 34-10-73-0, Doshi 40-7-120-2, Yashpal Sharma 3-2-1-0

INDIA 1st Innings

*S.M.Gavaskar	b Botham	48
G.A.Parkar	lbw b Botham	6
D.B.Vengsarkar	lbw b Willis	2
G.R.Viswanath	b Botham	1
Yashpal Sharma	lbw b Pringle	4
A.Malhotra	lbw b Pringle	5
Kapil Dev	c Cook b Willis	41
R.J.Shastri	c Cook b Willis	4
+S.M.H.Kirmani	not out	6
Madan Lal	c Tavaré b Botham	6
D.R.Doshi	c Taylor b Botham	0
Extras (lb 1, nb 4)		5
TOTAL		128

FALL OF WICKETS – 1-17, 2-21, 3-22, 4-31, 5-45, 6-112, 7-116, 8-116, 9-128, 10-128
BOWLING – Botham 19.4-3-46-5, Willis 16-2-41-3, Pringle 9-4-16-2, Edmonds 2-1-5-0, Allott 4-1-15-0

INDIA 2nd Innings

*S.M.Gavaskar	c Cook b Willis	24
G.A.Parkar	b Willis	1
D.B.Vengsarkar	c Allott b Willis	157
R.J.Shastri	b Allott	23
G.R.Viswanath	c Taylor b Pringle	3
Yashpal Sharma	b Willis	37
A.Malhotra	c Taylor b Willis	0
Kapil Dev	c Cook b Botham	89
+S.M.H.Kirmani	c Gower b Willis	3
Madan Lal	lbw b Pringle	15
D.R.Doshi	not out	4
Extras (lb 2, nb 11)		13
TOTAL		369

FALL OF WICKETS – 1-6, 2-47, 3-107, 4-110, 5-252, 6-252, 7-254, 8-275, 9-341, 10-369
BOWLING – Botham 31.5-7-103-1, Willis 28-3-101-6, Pringle 19-4-58-2, Edmonds 15-6-39-0, Allott 17-3-51-1, Cook 1-0-4-0

ENGLAND 2nd Innings

G.Cook	lbw b Kapil Dev	10
C.J.Tavaré	b Kapil Dev	3
+R.W.Taylor	c Malhotra b Kapil Dev	1
A.J.Lamb	not out	37
D.I.Gower	not out	14
DID NOT BAT – I.T.Botham, D.W.Randall, D.R.Pringle, P.H.Edmonds, P.J.W.Allott, *R.G.D.Willis		
Extras (lb 2)		2
TOTAL (for 3 wkts)		67

FALL OF WICKETS – 1-11, 2-13, 3-18
BOWLING – Kapil Dev 10-1-43-3, Madan Lal 2-1-2-0, Shastri 2-0-9-0, Doshi 5-3-11-0

ENGLAND v INDIA

at Old Trafford on 24th, 25th, 26th, 27th, 28th June 1982
Toss: England
Umpires: H.D.Bird and B.J.Meyer
Match drawn

ENGLAND

G.Cook	b Doshi	66
C.J.Tavaré	b Doshi	57
A.J.Lamb	c Viswanath b Madan Lal	9
D.I.Gower	c Shastri b Madan Lal	9
I.T.Botham	b Shastri	128
D.W.Randall	c Kirmani b Doshi	0
G.Miller	c Vengsarkar b Doshi	98
D.R.Pringle	st Kirmani b Doshi	23
P.H.Edmonds	c Kirmani b Madan Lal	12
+R.W.Taylor	not out	1
*R.G.D.Willis	c Gavaskar b Doshi	6
Extras (b 2, lb 5, nb 9)		16
TOTAL		425

FALL OF WICKETS – 1-106, 2-117, 3-141, 4-161, 5-161, 6-330, 7-382, 8-413, 9-419
BOWLING – Kapil Dev 36-5-109-0, Mandan Lal 35-9-104-3, Nayak 12-1-50-0, Doshi 47.1-17-102-6, Shastri 23-8-44-1

INDIA

*S.M.Gavaskar	c Tavaré b Willis	2
R.J.Shastri	c Cook b Willis	0
D.B.Vengsarkar	c Randall b Pringle	12
G.R.Viswanath	c Taylor b Botham	54
+S.M.H.Kirmani	b Edmonds	58
Yashpal Sharma	b Edmonds	10
S.M.Patil	not out	129
Kapil Dev	c Taylor b Miller	65
Madan Lal	b Edmonds	26
S.V.Nayak	not out	2
DID NOT BAT – D.R.Doshi		
Extras (b 6, lb 2, w 3, nb 10)		21
TOTAL (for 8 wkts)		379

FALL OF WICKETS – 1-5, 2-8, 3-25, 4-112, 5-136, 6-173, 7-269, 8-366
BOWLING – Willis 17-2-94-2, Pringle 15-4-33-1, Edmonds 37-12-94-3, Botham 19-4-86-1, Miller 16-4-51-1

ENGLAND v INDIA

at The Oval on 8th, 9th, 10th, 12th, 13th July 1982
Toss: England
Umpires: H.D.Bird and A.G.T.Whitehead
Match drawn

ENGLAND 1st Innings

G.Cook	c Shastri b Patil	50
C.J.Tavaré	b Kapil Dev	39
A.J.Lamb	run out	107
D.I.Gower	c Kirmani b Shastri	47
I.T.Botham	c Viswanath b Doshi	208
D.W.Randall	st Kirmani b Shastri	95
D.R.Pringle	st Kirmani b Doshi	9
P.H.Edmonds	c sub b Doshi	14
+R.W.Taylor	lbw b Shastri	3
P.J.W.Allott	c Yashpal Sharma b Doshi	3
*R.G.D.Willis	not out	1
Extras (b 3, lb 5, nb 10)		18
TOTAL		594

FALL OF WICKETS – 1-96, 2-96, 3-185, 4-361, 5-512, 6-534, 7-562, 8-569, 9-582, 10-594
BOWLING – Kapil Dev 25-4-109-1, Madan Lal 26-8-69-0, Nayak 21-5-66-0, Patil 14-1-48-1, Doshi 46-6-175-4, Shastri 41.3-8-109-3

INDIA 1st Innings

R.J.Shastri	c Botham b Willis	66
D.B.Vengsarkar	c Edmonds b Botham	6
G.R.Viswanath	lbw b Willis	56
Yashpal Sharma	c Gower b Willis	38
S.M.Patil	c sub b Botham	62
+S.M.H.Kirmani	b Allott	43
Kapil Dev	c Allott b Edmonds	97
Madan Lal	c Taylor b Edmonds	5
S.V.Nayak	b Edmonds	11
D.R.Doshi	not out	5
*S.M.Gavaskar	absent hurt	
Extras (b 3, lb 5, nb 13)		21
TOTAL		410

FALL OF WICKETS – 1-21, 2-134, 3-135, 4-232, 5-248, 6-378, 7-394, 8-396, 9-410
BOWLING – Willis 23-4-78-3, Botham 19-2-73-2, Allott 24-4-69-1, Pringle 28-5-80-0, Edmonds 35.2-11-89-3

ENGLAND 2nd Innings

G.Cook	c Y Sharma b Kapil Dev	8
C.J.Tavaré	not out	75
A.J.Lamb	b Doshi	45
D.I.Gower	c & b Nayak	45
DID NOT BAT – I.T.Botham, D.W.Randall, D.R.Pringle, P.H.Edmonds, +R.W.Taylor, P.J.W.Allott, *R.G.D.Willis		
Extras (b 6, lb 8, nb 4)		18
TOTAL (for 3 wkts dec)		191

FALL OF WICKETS – 1-12, 2-94, 3-191
BOWLING – Kapil Dev 19-3-53-1, Madan Lal 11-6-17-0, Nayak 5.3-0-16-1, Doshi 19-5-47-1, Shastri 16-3-40-0

INDIA 2nd Innings

R.J.Shastri	c Taylor b Willis	0
S.V.Nayak	c Taylor b Pringle	6
D.B.Vengsarkar	c Taylor b Pringle	16
G.R.Viswanath	not out	75
Yashpal Sharma	not out	9
DID NOT BAT – S.M.Patil, +S.M.H.Kirmani, Kapil Dev, Madan Lal, D.R.Doshi, *S.M.Gavaskar		
Extras (lb 3, nb 2)		5
TOTAL (for 3 wkts)		111

FALL OF WICKETS – 1-0, 2-18, 3-43
BOWLING – Willis 4-0-16-1, Botham 4-0-12-0, Allott 4-1-12-0, Pringle 11-5-32-2, Edmonds 13-5-34-0

1982

ENGLAND v PAKISTAN

at Edgbaston on 29th, 30th, 31st July, 1st August 1982
Toss: England
Umpires: D.G.L.Evans and K.E.Palmer
England won by 113 runs

ENGLAND 1st Innings

D.W.Randall	b Imran Khan	17
C.J.Tavaré	c Miandad b Abdul Qadir	54
A.J.Lamb	c Wasim Bari b Sikander	6
D.I.Gower	c Wasim Bari b Imran Khan	74
I.T.Botham	b Imran Khan	2
M.W.Gatting	b Tahir Naqqash	17
G.Miller	b Imran Khan	47
I.A.Greig	c sub b Imran Khan	14
E.E.Hemmings	lbw b Imran Khan	2
+R.W.Taylor	lbw b Imran Khan	1
*R.G.D.Willis	not out	0
Extras (b 4, lb 10, w 6, nb 18)		38
TOTAL		272

FALL OF WICKETS – 1-29, 2-37, 3-164, 4-172, 5-179, 6-228, 7-263, 8-265, 9-271, 10-272
BOWLING – Imran Khan 25.3-11-52-7, Tahir Naqqash 15-4-46-1, Sikander Bakht 18-5-58-1, Mudassar Nazar 5-2-8-0, Abdul Qadir 29-7-70-1

PAKISTAN 1st Innings

Mudassar Nazar	lbw b Botham	0
Mohsin Khan	c Willis b Botham	26
Tahir Naqqash	c Taylor b Greig	12
Mansoor Akhtar	c Miller b Hemmings	58
Javed Miandad	c Willis b Hemmings	30
Zaheer Abbas	lbw b Greig	40
Wasim Raja	c Tavare b Willis	26
*Imran Khan	c Taylor b Willis	22
+Wasim Bari	not out	16
Abdul Qadir	lbw b Greig	7
Sikander Bakht	c Hemmings b Greig	1
Extras (b 5, lb 2, w 1, nb 5)		13
TOTAL		251

FALL OF WICKETS – 1-0, 2-29, 3-53, 4-110, 5-164, 6-198, 7-217, 8-227, 9-248, 10-251
BOWLING – Botham 24-1-86-2, Greig 14.2-3-53-4, Willis 15-3-42-2, Hemmings 24-5-56-2, Miller 2-1-1-0

ENGLAND 2nd Innings

D.W.Randall	b Imran Khan	105
C.J.Tavaré	c Mohsin Khan b Imran	17
A.J.Lamb	lbw b Tahir Naqqash	5
D.I.Gower	c Mudassar b Tahir Naqqash	13
M.W.Gatting	c Wasim Bari b Tahir Naqqash	5
I.T.Botham	lbw b Tahir Naqqash	0
G.Miller	b Tahir Naqqash	5
I.A.Greig	b Abdul Qadir	7
E.E.Hemmings	c Mansoor b Abdul Qadir	19
+R.W.Taylor	c Abdul Qadir b Wasim Raja	54
*R.G.D.Willis	not out	28
Extras (b 10, lb 11, w 7, nb 5)		33
TOTAL		291

FALL OF WICKETS – 1-62, 2-98, 3-127, 4-137, 5-137, 6-146, 7-170, 8-188, 9-212, 10-291
BOWLING – Imran Khan 32-5-84-2, Tahir Naqqash 18-7-40-5, Sikander Bakht 13-5-34-0, Abdul Qadir 40-10-100-2, Wasim Raja 2.3-2-0-1

PAKISTAN 2nd Innings

Mudassar Nazar	lbw b Botham	0
Mohsin Khan	lbw b Botham	35
Mansoor Akhtar	c Taylor b Botham	0
Javed Miandad	run out	10
Zaheer Abbas	c Taylor b Willis	4
Wasim Raja	c Gower b Willis	16
*Imran Khan	b Miller	65
+Wasim Bari	c Taylor b Botham	12
Tahir Naqqash	c & b Hemmings	39
Abdul Qadir	c Randall b Miller	9
Sikander Bakht	not out	1
Extras (lb 3, nb 5)		8
TOTAL		199

FALL OF WICKETS – 1-0, 2-0, 3-38, 4-54, 5-66, 6-77, 7-98, 8-151, 9-178, 10-199
BOWLING – Botham 21-7-70-4, Greig 4-1-19-0, Willis 14-2-49-2, Hemmings 10-4-27-1, Miller 7.4-1-26-2

ENGLAND v PAKISTAN

at Lord's on 12th, 13th, 14th, 15th, 16th August 1982
Toss: Pakistan
Umpires: H.D.Bird and D.J.Constant
Pakistan won by 10 wickets

PAKISTAN 1st Innings

Mohsin Khan	c Tavaré b Jackman	200
Mudassar Nazar	c Taylor b Jackman	20
Mansoor Akhtar	c Lamb b Botham	57
Javed Miandad	run out	6
Zaheer Abbas	b Jackman	75
Haroon Rashid	lbw b Botham	1
*Imran Khan	c Taylor b Botham	12
Tahir Naqqash	c Gatting b Jackman	2
+Wasim Bari	not out	24
Abdul Qadir	not out	18
DID NOT BAT – Sarfraz Nawaz		
Extras (b 3, lb 8, nb 2)		13
TOTAL (for 8 wkts dec)		428

FALL OF WICKETS – 1-53, 2-197, 3-208, 4-361, 5-364, 6-380, 7-382, 8-401
BOWLING – Botham 44-8-148-3, Jackman 36-5-110-4, Pringle 26-9-62-0, Greig 13-2-42-0, Hemmings 20-3-53-0

ENGLAND 1st Innings

D.W.Randall	b Sarfraz Nawaz	29
C.J.Tavaré	b Sarfraz Nawaz	8
A.J.Lamb	c Rashid b Tahir Naqqash	33
*D.I.Gower	c Mansoor Akhtar b Imran	29
I.T.Botham	c Mohsin Khan b Abdul Qadir	31
M.W.Gatting	not out	32
D.R.Pringle	c Rashid b Abdul Qadir	5
I.A.Greig	lbw b Abdul Qadir	3
E.E.Hemmings	b Sarfraz Nawaz	6
+R.W.Taylor	lbw b Abdul Qadir	5
R.D.Jackman	lbw b Imran Khan	0
Extras (b 11, lb 12, w 13, nb 10)		46
TOTAL		227

FALL OF WICKETS – 1-16, 2-69, 3-89, 4-157, 5-173, 6-187, 7-197, 8-217, 9-226, 10-227
BOWLING – Imran Khan 23-4-55-2, Sarfraz Nawaz 23-4-56-3, Tahir Naqqash 12-4-25-1, Abdul Qadir 24-9-39-4, Mudassar Nazar 4-1-6-0

ENGLAND 2nd Innings

D.W.Randall	b Mudassar Nazar	9
C.J.Tavaré	c Javed Miandad b Imran	82
A.J.Lamb	lbw b Mudassar Nazar	0
*D.I.Gower	c Wasim Bari b Mudassar	0
I.T.Botham	c Sarfraz b Mudassar	69
M.W.Gatting	c Wasim Bari b Mudassar	7
D.R.Pringle	c Miandad b Abdul Qadir	14
I.A.Greig	lbw b Mudassar Nazar	2
E.E.Hemmings	c Wasim Bari b Imran Khan	14
+R.W.Taylor	not out	24
R.D.Jackman	c Rashid b Abdul Qadir	17
Extras (b 10, lb 19, w 5, nb 4)		38
TOTAL		276

FALL OF WICKETS – 1-9, 2-9, 3-9, 4-121, 5-132, 6-171, 7-180, 8-224, 9-235, 10-276
BOWLING – Imran Khan 42-13-84-2, Sarfraz Nawaz 14-5-22-0, Tahir Naqqash 7-5-6-0, Abdul Qadir 37.5-15-94-2, Mudassar Nazar 19-7-32-6

PAKISTAN 2nd Innings

Mohsin Khan	not out	39
Javed Miandad	not out	26
DID NOT BAT – Mudassar Nazar, Mansoor Akhtar, Zaheer Abbas, Haroon Rashid, *Imran Khan, Tahir Naqqash, +Wasim Bari, Abdul Qadir, Sarfraz Nawaz		
Extras (b 1, lb 10, w 1)		12
TOTAL (for 0 wkts)		77

BOWLING – Botham 7-0-30-0, Jackman 4-0-22-0, Hemmings 2.1-0-13-0

ENGLAND v PAKISTAN

at Headingley on 26th, 27th, 28th, 30th, 31st August 1982
Toss: Pakistan
Umpires: D.J.Constant and B.J.Meyer
England won by 3 wickets

PAKISTAN 1st Innings

Mohsin Khan	c Taylor b Botham	10
Mudassar Nazar	b Botham	65
Mansoor Akhtar	c Gatting b Willis	0
Javed Miandad	c Fowler b Willis	54
Zaheer Abbas	c Taylor b Jackman	8
Majid Khan	lbw b Jackman	21
*Imran Khan	not out	67
+Wasim Bari	b Jackman	23
Abdul Qadir	c Willis b Botham	5
Sikander Bakht	c Tavaré b Willis	7
Ehteshamuddin	b Botham	0
Extras (b 1, lb 7, w 4, nb 3)		15
TOTAL		275

FALL OF WICKETS –1-16, 2-19, 3-119, 4-128, 5-160, 6-168, 7-207, 8-224, 9-274, 10-275
BOWLING – Willis 26-6-76-3, Botham 24.5-9-70-4, Jackman 37-14-74-3, Marks 5-0-23-0, Gatting 8-2-17-0

ENGLAND 1st Innings

C.J.Tavaré	c sub b Imran Khan	22
G.Fowler	b Ehteshamuddin	9
M.W.Gatting	lbw b Imran Khan	25
A.J.Lamb	c Mohsin Khan b Imran Khan	0
D.I.Gower	c sub b Sikander Bakht	74
I.T.Botham	c sub b Sikander Bakht	57
D.W.Randall	run out	8
V.J.Marks	b Abdul Qadir	7
+R.W.Taylor	c Javed Miandad b Imran	18
R.D.Jackman	c Mohsin Khan b Imran	11
*R.G.D.Willis	not out	1
Extras (b 4, lb 10, w 2, nb 8)		24
TOTAL		256

FALL OF WICKETS – 1-15, 2-67, 3-69, 4-77, 5-146, 6-159, 7-170, 8-209, 9-199, 10-256
BOWLING – Imran Khan 25.2-7-49-5, Ehteshamuddin 14-4-46-1, Sikander Bakht 24-5-47-2, Abdul Qadir 22-5-87-1, Mudassar Nazar 4-1-3-0

PAKISTAN 2nd Innings

Mohsin Khan	c Taylor b Willis	0
Mudassar Nazar	c Botham b Willis	0
Mansoor Akhtar	c Randall b Botham	39
Javed Miandad	c Taylor b Botham	52
Zaheer Abbas	lbw b Botham	4
Majid Khan	c Gower b Botham	10
*Imran Khan	c Randall b Botham	46
+Wasim Bari	c Taylor b Willis	7
Abdul Qadir	b Jackman	17
Sikander Bakht	c Gatting b Marks	7
Ehteshamuddin	not out	0
Extras (lb 6, w 4, nb 7)		17
TOTAL		199

FALL OF WICKETS – 1-0, 2-3, 3-81, 4-85, 5-108, 6-115, 7-128, 8-169, 9-199, 10-199
BOWLING – Willis 19-3-55-3, Botham 30-8-74-5, Jackman 28-11-41-1, Marks 2-1-8-1, Gatting 2-1-4-0

ENGLAND 2nd Innings

C.J.Tavaré	c Majid Khan b Imran Khan	33
G.Fowler	c Wasim Bari b Mudassar	86
M.W.Gatting	lbw b Imran Khan	25
A.J.Lamb	lbw b Mudassar Nazar	4
D.I.Gower	c Wasim Bari b Mudassar	7
I.T.Botham	c Majid Khan b Mudassar	4
D.W.Randall	lbw b Imran Khan	0
V.J.Marks	not out	12
+R.W.Taylor	not out	6
DID NOT BAT – R.D.Jackman and *R.G.D.Willis		
Extras (b 19, lb 16, w 1, nb 6)		42
TOTAL (for 7 wkts)		219

FALL OF WICKETS – 1-103, 2-168, 3-172, 4-187, 5-189, 6-189, 7-199
BOWLING – Imran Khan 30.2-8-66-3, Sikander Bakht 20-4-40-0, Abdul Qadir 8-2-16-0, Mudassar Nazar 22-7-55-4

1982

ENGLAND v NEW ZEALAND

at The Oval on 14th, 15th, 16th, 17th, 18th July 1983
Toss: England
Umpires: H.D.Bird and D.G.L.Evans
England won by 189 runs

ENGLAND 1st Innings

G.Fowler	lbw b Hadlee	1
C.J.Tavaré	run out	45
D.I.Gower	b Hadlee	11
A.J.Lamb	b Cairns	24
I.T.Botham	b Hadlee	15
D.W.Randall	not out	75
V.J.Marks	c Lees b Hadlee	4
P.H.Edmonds	c & b Bracewell	12
+R.W.Taylor	lbw b Hadlee	0
*R.G.D.Willis	c Crowe J.J. b Bracewell	4
N.G.Cowans	b Hadlee	3
Extras	(b 6, lb 6, nb 3)	15
TOTAL		209

FALL OF WICKETS – 1-2, 2-18, 3-67, 4-104, 5-116, 6-154, 7-184, 8-191, 9-202, 10-209
BOWLING – Hadlee 23.4-6-53-6, Chatfield 17-3-48-0, Cairns 17-3-63-1, Bracewell 8-4-16-2, Crowe M.D. 5-0-14-0

NEW ZEALAND 1st Innings

J.G.Wright	c Gower b Willis	0
B.A.Edgar	c Taylor b Willis	12
J.J.Crowe	c Randall b Willis	0
*G.P.Howarth	b Cowans	4
M.D.Crowe	b Willis	0
J.V.Coney	run out	44
R.J.Hadlee	c & b Botham	84
J.G.Bracewell	c & b Botham	7
+W.K.Lees	not out	31
B.L.Cairns	c Lamb b Botham	2
E.J.Chatfield	c Willis b Botham	0
Extras	(lb 6, nb 6)	12
TOTAL		196

FALL OF WICKETS – 1-0, 2-1, 3-10, 4-17, 5-41, 6-125, 7-149, 8-182, 9-188, 10-196
BOWLING – Willis 20-8-43-4, Cowans 19-3-60-1, Botham 16-2-62-4, Edmonds 2-0-19-0

ENGLAND 2nd Innings

G.Fowler	run out	105
C.J.Tavaré	c Howarth b Bracewell	109
D.I.Gower	c Howarth b Hadlee	25
A.J.Lamb	not out	102
I.T.Botham	run out	26
D.W.Randall	c Coney b Hadlee	3
V.J.Marks	c Crowe M.D. b Bracewell	2
P.H.Edmonds	not out	43
DID NOT BAT – +R.W.Taylor, *R.G.D.Willis, N.G.Cowans		
Extras	(b 8, lb 23)	31
TOTAL (for 6 wkts dec)		446

FALL OF WICKETS – 1-223, 2-225, 3-269, 4-322, 5-329, 6-336
BOWLING – Hadlee 37.2-7-99-2, Chatfield 35-9-85-0, Cairns 30-7-67-0, Bracewell 54-13-115-2, Crowe M.D. 3-0-9-0, Coney 27-11-39-0, Howarth 3-2-1-0

NEW ZEALAND 2nd Innings

J.G.Wright	run out	88
B.A.Edgar	c Taylor b Willis	3
J.J.Crowe	c Lamb b Willis	9
*G.P.Howarth	c Taylor b Edmonds	67
M.D.Crowe	c Taylor b Edmonds	33
J.V.Coney	lbw b Marks	2
R.J.Hadlee	c Taylor b Marks	11
+W.K.Lees	run out	8
J.G.Bracewell	c Gower b Marks	0
B.L.Cairns	c Willis b Edmonds	32
E.J.Chatfield	not out	10
Extras	(b 3, lb 1, nb 3)	7
TOTAL		270

FALL OF WICKETS – 1-10, 2-26, 3-146, 4-197, 5-202, 6-210, 7-228, 8-228, 9-228, 10-270
BOWLING – Willis 12-3-26-2, Cowans 11-2-41-0, Botham 4-0-17-0, Edmonds 40.1-16-101-3, Marks 43-20-78-3

ENGLAND v NEW ZEALAND

at Headingley on 28th, 29th, 30th July, 1st August 1983
Toss: New Zealand
Umpires: D.J.Constant and B.J.Meyer
New Zealand won by 5 wickets

ENGLAND 1st Innings

G.Fowler	c Smith b Chatfield	9
C.J.Tavaré	c Smith b Coney	69
D.I.Gower	c Coney b Cairns	9
A.J.Lamb	c Crowe M.D. b Cairns	58
I.T.Botham	c Howarth b Cairns	38
D.W.Randall	c Coney b Cairns	4
P.H.Edmonds	c Smith b Cairns	8
G.R.Dilley	b Cairns	0
+R.W.Taylor	not out	10
*R.G.D.Willis	c Crowe J.J. b Coney	9
N.G.Cowans	c Bracewell b Cairns	0
Extras	(b 4, lb 7)	11
TOTAL		225

FALL OF WICKETS – 1-18, 2-35, 3-135, 4-175, 5-185, 6-205, 7-205, 8-209, 9-225, 10-225
BOWLING – Hadlee 21-9-44-0, Chatfield 22-8-67-1, Cairns 33.2-14-74-7, Coney 12-3-21-2, Bracewell 1-0-8-0

NEW ZEALAND 1st Innings

J.G.Wright	c Willis b Cowans	93
B.A.Edgar	b Willis	84
*G.P.Howarth	run out	13
M.D.Crowe	lbw b Cowans	37
J.J.Crowe	run out	0
J.V.Coney	c Gower b Willis	19
R.J.Hadlee	b Cowans	75
J.G.Bracewell	c Dilley b Edmonds	16
+I.D.S.Smith	c Tavaré b Willis	2
B.L.Cairns	not out	24
E.J.Chatfield	lbw b Willis	0
Extras	(b 1, lb 4, w 1, nb 8)	14
TOTAL		377

FALL OF WICKETS – 1-52, 2-168, 3-169, 4-169, 5-218, 6-304, 7-348, 8-351, 9-377, 10-377
BOWLING – Willis 23.3-6-57-4, Dilley 17-4-36-0, Botham 26-9-81-0, Cowans 28-8-88-3, Edmonds 45-14-101-1

ENGLAND 2nd Innings

G.Fowler	c Smith b Chatfield	19
C.J.Tavaré	b Chatfield	23
D.I.Gower	not out	112
A.J.Lamb	b Coney	28
I.T.Botham	c Howarth b Coney	4
D.W.Randall	c Smith b Chatfield	16
P.H.Edmonds	c Smith b Chatfield	0
G.R.Dilley	c Smith b Chatfield	15
+R.W.Taylor	b Cairns	9
*R.G.D.Willis	c Coney b Cairns	4
N.G.Cowans	c Crowe M.D. b Cairns	10
Extras	(b 8, lb 3, w 1)	12
TOTAL		252

FALL OF WICKETS – 1-39, 2-44, 3-116, 4-126, 5-142, 6-142, 7-190, 8-217, 9-221, 10-252
BOWLING – Hadlee 26-9-45-0, Chatfield 29-5-95-5, Cairns 24-2-70-3, Coney 8-1-30-2

NEW ZEALAND 2nd Innings

J.G.Wright	c Randall b Willis	26
B.A.Edgar	c Edmonds b Willis	2
*G.P.Howarth	c Randall b Willis	20
M.D.Crowe	c Lamb b Willis	1
J.J.Crowe	b Willis	13
J.V.Coney	not out	10
R.J.Hadlee	not out	6
DID NOT BAT – J.G.Bracewell, +I.D.S.Smith, B.L.Cairns, E.J.Chatfield		
Extras	(b 8, lb 7, nb 10)	25
TOTAL (for 5 wkts)		103

FALL OF WICKETS – 1-11, 2-42, 3-60, 4-61, 5-83
BOWLING – Willis 14-5-35-5, Dilley 8-2-16-0, Botham 0.1-0-4-0, Cowans 5-0-23-0

ENGLAND v NEW ZEALAND

at Lord's on 11th, 12th, 13th, 15th August 1983
Toss: New Zealand
Umpires: D.J.Constant and D.G.L.Evans
England won by 127 runs

ENGLAND 1st Innings

C.J.Tavaré	b Crowe	51
C.L.Smith	lbw b Hadlee	0
D.I.Gower	lbw b Crowe	108
A.J.Lamb	c sub b Chatfield	17
M.W.Gatting	c Wright b Hadlee	81
I.T.Botham	lbw b Cairns	8
+R.W.Taylor	b Hadlee	16
N.A.Foster	c Smith b Hadlee	10
N.G.B.Cook	b Chatfield	16
*R.G.D.Willis	c Smith b Hadlee	7
N.G.Cowans	not out	1
Extras	(b 3, lb 3, w 2, nb 3)	11
TOTAL		326

FALL OF WICKETS – 1-3, 2-152, 3-175, 4-191, 5-218, 6-288, 7-290, 8-303, 9-318, 10-326
BOWLING – Hadlee 40-15-93-5, Cairns 23-8-65-1, Chatfield 36.3-8-116-2, Crowe 13-1-35-2, Coney 8-7-6-0

NEW ZEALAND 1st Innings

J.G.Wright	c Lamb b Willis	11
B.A.Edgar	c Willis b Cook	70
*G.P.Howarth	b Cook	25
M.D.Crowe	b Botham	46
J.V.Coney	b Cook	7
E.J.Gray	c Lamb b Botham	11
J.G.Bracewell	c Gower b Cook	0
R.J.Hadlee	c Botham b Cook	0
B.L.Cairns	c Lamb b Botham	5
+I.D.S.Smith	c Lamb b Botham	3
E.J.Chatfield	not out	5
Extras	(lb 5, nb 3)	8
TOTAL		191

FALL OF WICKETS – 1-18, 2-49, 3-147, 4-159, 5-176, 6-176, 7-176, 8-183, 9-184, 10-191
BOWLING – Willis 13-6-28-1, Foster 16-5-40-0, Cowans 9-1-30-0, Botham 20.4-6-50-4, Cook 26-11-35-5

ENGLAND 2nd Innings

C.J.Tavaré	c Crowe b Hadlee	16
C.L.Smith	c Coney b Hadlee	43
D.I.Gower	c Crowe b Gray	34
A.J.Lamb	c Hadlee b Gray	4
M.W.Gatting	b Gray	15
I.T.Botham	c Coney b Chatfield	61
+R.W.Taylor	c & b Coney	7
N.A.Foster	c Wright b Hadlee	3
N.G.B.Cook	c Bracewell b Chatfield	5
*R.G.D.Willis	not out	2
N.G.Cowans	c Smith b Chatfield	1
Extras	(b 5, lb 6, nb 9)	20
TOTAL		211

FALL OF WICKETS – 1-26, 2-79, 3-87, 4-119, 5-147, 6-195, 7-199, 8-208, 9-210, 10-211
BOWLING – Hadlee 26-7-42-3, Cairns 3-0-9-0, Chatfield 13.3-4-29-3, Coney 6-4-9-1, Bracewell 11-4-29-0, Gray 30-8-73-3

NEW ZEALAND 2nd Innings

J.G.Wright	c Taylor b Botham	12
B.A.Edgar	c Lamb b Cowans	27
*G.P.Howarth	c Taylor b Willis	0
M.D.Crowe	c Foster b Cowans	12
J.V.Coney	c Gatting b Foster	68
E.J.Gray	c Lamb b Cook	17
R.J.Hadlee	b Willis	30
J.G.Bracewell	lbw b Willis	4
B.L.Cairns	b Cook	16
+I.D.S.Smith	not out	17
E.J.Chatfield	c & b Cook	2
Extras	(b 3, lb 4, nb 7)	14
TOTAL		219

FALL OF WICKETS – 1-15, 2-17, 3-57, 4-61, 5-108, 6-154, 7-158, 8-190, 9-206, 10-219
BOWLING – Willis 12-5-24-3, Foster 12-0-35-1, Cowans 11-1-36-2, Botham 7-2-20-1, Cook 27.2-9-90-3

1983

ENGLAND v
NEW ZEALAND

at Trent Bridge on 25th, 26th, 27th, 28th, 29th August
1983
Toss: England
Umpires: H.D.Bird and B.J.Meyer
England won by 165 runs

ENGLAND 1st Innings

C.J.Tavare	c Cairns b Snedden	4
C.L.Smith	c Howarth b Bracewell	31
D.I.Gower	b Cairns	72
A.J.Lamb	c Howarth b Bracewell	22
M.W.Gatting	lbw b Bracewell	14
I.T.Botham	lbw b Snedden	103
D.W.Randall	c Edgar b Hadlee	83
+R.W.Taylor	b Bracewell	21
N.G.B.Cook	c Lees b Snedden	4
*R.G.D.Willis	not out	25
N.G.Cowans	c Bracewell b Cairns	7
Extras (b 11, lb 14, nb 9)		34
TOTAL		420

FALL OF WICKETS – 1-5, 2-94, 3-136, 4-156, 6-169,
6-355, 7-356, 8-379, 9-407, 10-420
BOWLING – Hadlee 30-7-98-1, Snedden 28-7-69-3,
Cairns 33.4-9-77-2, Bracewell 28-5-108-4,
Coney 2-0-10-0, Gray 3-0-24-0

NEW ZEALAND 1st Innings

T.J.Franklin	c Smith b Botham	2
B.A.Edgar	c Gatting b Cook	62
*G.P.Howarth	c & b Cook	36
J.V.Coney	c Gatting b Cook	20
E.J.Gray	run out	7
R.J.Hadlee	c Smith b Cowans	3
+W.K.Lees	lbw b Cook	1
M.D.Crowe	c & b Cook	34
M.C.Snedden	b Cowans	9
B.L.Cairns	c Gower b Cowans	26
J.G.Bracewell	not out	1
Extras (lb 5, nb 1)		6
TOTAL		207

FALL OF WICKETS – 1-4, 2-80, 3-124, 4-127, 5-131,
6-135, 7-135, 8-157, 9-201, 10-207
BOWLING – Botham 14-4-33-1, Willis 10-2-23-0,
Cowans 21-8-74-3, Cook 32-14-63-5, Gatting 5-2-8-0

ENGLAND 2nd Innings

C.J.Tavaré	c sub b Bracewell	13
C.L.Smith	c Howarth b Snedden	4
D.I.Gower	c Cairns b Bracewell	33
A.J.Lamb	not out	137
M.W.Gatting	c Lees b Cairns	11
I.T.Botham	c Edgar b Gray	27
D.W.Randall	b Hadlee	13
+R.W.Taylor	b Hadlee	0
N.G.B.Cook	c Lees b Cairns	26
*R.G.D.Willis	b Hadlee	16
N.G.Cowans	b Hadlee	0
Extras (b 6, lb 10, w 1)		17
TOTAL		297

FALL OF WICKETS – 1-5, 2-58, 3-61, 4-92, 5-149,
6-188, 7-188, 8-252, 9-297, 10-297
BOWLING – Hadlee 28-5-85-4, Snedden 8-1-40-1,
Cairns 20-9-36-2, Bracewell 21-2-88-2, Gray 15-4-31-1

NEW ZEALAND 2nd Innings

T.J.Franklin	b Willis	7
B.A.Edgar	c Gower b Cook	76
*G.P.Howarth	c Tavare b Cowans	24
M.D.Crowe	c Taylor b Cowans	0
J.V.Coney	c Taylor b Cook	68
E.J.Gray	c Gatting b Smith	3
+W.K.Lees	c Lamb b Cowans	7
R.J.Hadlee	not out	92
M.C.Snedden	c Taylor b Cook	12
B.L.Cairns	b Cook	11
J.G.Bracewell	c Taylor b Smith	28
Extras (b 2, w 1, nb 14)		17
TOTAL		345

FALL OF WICKETS – 1-18, 2-67, 3-71, 4-156, 5-161,
6-184, 7-228, 8-264, 9-290, 10-345
BOWLING – Botham 25-4-73-0, Willis 19-3-37-1,
Cowans 21-2-95-3, Cook 50-22-87-4, Gatting 2-1-5-0,
Smith 12-2-31-2

1983

ENGLAND v WEST INDIES

at Edgbaston on 14th, 15th, 16th, 18th June 1984
Toss: England
Umpires: H.D.Bird and B.J.Meyer
West Indies won by an innings and 180 runs

ENGLAND 1st Innings

G.Fowler	c Dujon b Garner	0
T.A.Lloyd	retired hurt	10
D.W.Randall	b Garner	0
*D.I.Gower	c Harper b Holding	10
A.J.Lamb	c Lloyd b Baptiste	15
I.T.Botham	c Garner b Harper	64
G.Miller	c Dujon b Garner	22
D.R.Pringle	c Dujon b Holding	4
+P.R.Downton	lbw b Garner	33
N.G.B.Cook	c Lloyd b Marshall	2
R.G.D.Willis	not out	10
Extras (b 8, lb 5, nb 8)		21
TOTAL		191

FALL OF WICKETS – 1-1, 2-5, 3-45, 4-49, 5-89, 6-103, 7-168, 8-173, 9-191
BOWLING – Marshall 14-4-37-1, Garner 14.3-2-53-4, Holding 16-4-44-2, Baptiste 11-3-28-1, Harper 4-1-8-1

WEST INDIES

C.G.Greenidge	lbw b Willis	19
D.L.Haynes	lbw b Willis	8
H.A.Gomes	c Miller b Pringle	143
I.V.A.Richards	c Randall b Cook	117
+P.J.L.Dujon	c Gower b Miller	23
*C.H.Lloyd	c Pringle b Botham	71
M.D.Marshall	lbw b Pringle	2
R.A.Harper	b Pringle	14
E.A.E.Baptiste	not out	87
M.A.Holding	c Willis b Pringle	69
J.Garner	c Lamb b Pringle	0
Extras (b 6, lb 17, w 2, nb 28)		53
TOTAL		606

FALL OF WICKETS – 1-34, 2-35, 3-241, 4-294, 5-418, 6-418, 7-421, 8-455, 9-605, 10-606
BOWLING – Willis 25-3-108-2, Botham 34-7-127-1, Pringle 31-5-108-5, Cook 38-6-127-1, Miller 15-1-83-1

ENGLAND 2nd Innings

G.Fowler	lbw b Garner	7
+P.R.Downton	c Greenidge b Harper	56
D.W.Randall	c Lloyd b Garner	1
*D.I.Gower	c Dujon b Garner	12
A.J.Lamb	c Richards b Marshall	13
I.T.Botham	lbw b Garner	38
G.Miller	c Harper b Marshall	11
D.R.Pringle	not out	46
N.G.B.Cook	run out	9
R.G.D.Willis	c Dujon b Garner	22
T.A.Lloyd	absent hurt	
Extras (b 1, lb 5, w 4, nb 10)		20
TOTAL		235

FALL OF WICKETS – 1-17, 2-21, 3-37, 4-65, 5-127, 6-138, 7-181, 8-193, 9-235
BOWLING – Marshall 23-7-65-2, Garner 23.5-7-55-5, Holding 12-3-29-0, Baptiste 5-1-18-0, Harper 13-3-48-1

ENGLAND v WEST INDIES

at Lord's on 28th, 29th, 30th June, 2nd, 3rd July 1984
Toss: West Indies
Umpires: D.G.L.Evans and B.J.Meyer
West Indies won by 9 wickets

ENGLAND 1st Innings

G.Fowler	c Harper b Baptiste	106
B.C.Broad	c Dujon b Marshall	55
*D.I.Gower	lbw b Marshall	3
A.J.Lamb	lbw b Marshall	23
M.W.Gatting	lbw b Marshall	1
I.T.Botham	c Richards b Baptiste	30
+P.R.Downton	not out	23
G.Miller	run out	0
D.R.Pringle	lbw b Garner	2
N.A.Foster	c Harper b Marshall	6
R.G.D.Willis	b Marshall	2
Extras (b 4, lb 14, w 2, nb 15)		35
TOTAL		286

FALL OF WICKETS – 1-101, 2-106, 3-183, 4-185, 5-243, 6-248, 7-251, 8-255, 9-264, 10-286
BOWLING – Garner 32-10-67-1, Small 9-0-38-0, Marshall 36.5-10-85-6, Baptiste 20-6-36-2, Harper 8-0-25-0

WEST INDIES 1st Innings

C.G.Greenidge	c Miller b Botham	1
D.L.Haynes	lbw b Botham	12
H.A.Gomes	c Gatting b Botham	10
I.V.A.Richards	lbw b Botham	72
*C.H.Lloyd	lbw b Botham	39
+P.J.L.Dujon	c Fowler b Botham	8
M.D.Marshall	c Pringle b Willis	29
E.A.E.Baptiste	c Downton b Willis	44
R.A.Harper	c Gatting b Botham	8
J.Garner	c Downton b Botham	6
M.A.Small	not out	3
Extras (lb 5, w 1, nb 7)		13
TOTAL		245

FALL OF WICKETS – 1-1, 2-18, 3-35, 4-138, 5-147, 6-173, 7-213, 8-231, 9-241, 10-245
BOWLING – Willis 19-5-48-2, Botham 27.4-6-103-8, Pringle 11-0-54-0, Foster 6-2-13-0, Miller 2-0-14-0

ENGLAND 2nd Innings

G.Fowler	lbw b Small	11
B.C.Broad	c Harper b Garner	0
*D.I.Gower	c Lloyd b Small	21
A.J.Lamb	c Dujon b Marshall	110
M.W.Gatting	lbw b Marshall	29
I.T.Botham	lbw b Garner	81
+P.R.Downton	lbw b Small	4
G.Miller	b Harper	9
D.R.Pringle	lbw b Garner	8
N.A.Foster	not out	9
DID NOT BAT – R.G.D.Willis		
Extras (b 4, lb 7, w 1, nb 6)		18
TOTAL (for 9 wkts dec)		300

FALL OF WICKETS – 1-5, 2-33, 3-36, 4-88, 5-216, 6-230, 7-273, 8-290, 9-300
BOWLING – Garner 30.3-3-91-3, Small 12-2-40-3, Marshall 22-6-85-2, Baptiste 26-8-48-0, Harper 8-1-18-1

WEST INDIES 2nd Innings

C.G.Greenidge	not out	214
D.L.Haynes	run out	17
H.A.Gomes	not out	92
DID NOT BAT – I.V.A.Richards, *C.H.Lloyd, +P.J.L.Dujon, M.D.Marshall, E.A.E.Baptiste, R.A.Harper, J.Garner, M.A.Small		
Extras (b 4, lb 4, nb 13)		21
TOTAL (for 1 wkt)		344

FALL OF WICKETS – 1-57
BOWLING – Willis 15-5-48-0, Botham 20.1-2-117-0, Pringle 8-0-44-0, Foster 12-0-69-0, Miller 11-0-45-0

ENGLAND v WEST INDIES

at Headingley on 12th, 13th, 14th, 16th July 1984
Toss: England
Umpires: D.J.Constant and D.G.L.Evans
West Indies won by 8 wickets

ENGLAND 1st Innings

G.Fowler	lbw b Garner	10
B.C.Broad	c Lloyd b Harper	32
V.P.Terry	c Harper b Holding	8
*D.I.Gower	lbw b Garner	2
A.J.Lamb	b Harper	100
I.T.Botham	c Dujon b Baptiste	45
+P.R.Downton	c Lloyd b Harper	17
D.R.Pringle	c Haynes b Holding	19
P.J.W.Allott	b Holding	3
N.G.B.Cook	b Holding	1
R.G.D.Willis	not out	4
Extras (b 4, lb 7, nb 18)		29
TOTAL		270

FALL OF WICKETS – 1-13, 2-43, 3-53, 4-87, 5-172, 6-236, 7-237, 8-244, 9-254, 10-270
BOWLING – Garner 30-11-73-2, Marshall 6-4-6-0, Holding 29.2-8-70-4, Baptiste 13-1-45-1, Harper 19-6-47-3

WEST INDIES 1st Innings

C.G.Greenidge	c Botham b Willis	10
D.L.Haynes	b Allott	18
H.A.Gomes	not out	104
I.V.A.Richards	c Pringle b Allott	15
*C.H.Lloyd	c Gower b Cook	48
+P.J.L.Dujon	lbw b Allott	26
E.A.E.Baptiste	c Broad b Allott	0
R.A.Harper	c Downton b Allott	0
M.A.Holding	c Allott b Willis	59
J.Garner	run out	0
M.D.Marshall	c Botham b Allott	4
Extras (lb 3, nb 15)		18
TOTAL		302

FALL OF WICKETS – 1-16, 2-43, 3-78, 4-148, 5-201, 6-206, 7-206, 8-288, 9-290, 10-302
BOWLING – Willis 18-1-123-2, Allott 26.5-7-61-6, Botham 7-0-45-0, Pringle 13-3-26-0, Cook 9-1-29-1

ENGLAND 2nd Innings

G.Fowler	c & b Marshall	50
B.C.Broad	c Baptiste b Marshall	2
V.P.Terry	lbw b Garner	1
*D.I.Gower	c Dujon b Harper	43
A.J.Lamb	lbw b Marshall	3
I.T.Botham	c Dujon b Garner	14
+P.R.Downton	c Dujon b Marshall	27
N.G.B.Cook	c Lloyd b Marshall	0
D.R.Pringle	lbw b Marshall	2
P.J.W.Allott	lbw b Marshall	4
R.G.D.Willis	not out	5
Extras (lb 6, nb 2)		8
TOTAL		159

FALL OF WICKETS – 1-10, 2-13, 3-104, 4-106, 5-107, 6-135, 7-138, 8-140, 9-146, 10-159
BOWLING – Garner 16-7-37-2, Marshall 26-9-53-7, Holding 7-1-31-0, Harper 16-8-30-1

WEST INDIES 2nd Innings

C.G.Greenidge	c Terry b Cook	49
D.L.Haynes	c Fowler b Cook	43
H.A.Gomes	not out	2
I.V.A.Richards	not out	22
DID NOT BAT – *C.H.Lloyd, +P.J.L.Dujon, E.A.E.Baptiste, R.A.Harper, M.A.Holding, J.Garner, M.D.Marshall		
Extras (lb 2, nb 13)		15
TOTAL (for 2 wkts)		131

FALL OF WICKETS – 1-106, 2-108
BOWLING – Willis 8-1-40-0, Allott 7-2-24-0, Pringle 8.3-2-25-0, Cook 9-2-27-2

1984

ENGLAND v WEST INDIES

at Old Trafford on 26th, 27th, 28th, 30th, 31st July 1984
Toss: West Indies
Umpires: H.D.Bird and D.O.Oslear
West Indies won by an innings and 64 runs

WEST INDIES

C.G.Greenidge	c Downton b Pocock	223
D.L.Haynes	c Cowans b Botham	2
H.A.Gomes	c Botham b Allott	30
I.V.A.Richards	c Cook b Allott	1
*C.H.Lloyd	c Downton b Allott	1
+P.J.L.Dujon	c Downton b Botham	101
W.W.Davis	b Pocock	77
E.A.E.Baptiste	b Pocock	6
R.A.Harper	not out	39
M.A.Holding	b Cook	0
J.Garner	c Terry b Pocock	7
Extras (b 4, lb 6, w 2, nb 1)		13
TOTAL		500

FALL OF WICKETS – 1-11, 2-60, 3-62, 4-70, 5-267, 6-437, 7-443, 8-470, 9-471, 10-500
BOWLING – Botham 29-5-100-2, Cowans 19-2-76-0, Allott 28-9-76-3, Cook 39-6-114-1, Pocock 45.3-14-121-4

ENGLAND 1st Innings

G.Fowler	b Baptiste	38
B.C.Broad	c Harper b Davis	42
V.P.Terry	b Garner	7
*D.I.Gower	c Dujon b Baptiste	4
A.J.Lamb	not out	100
I.T.Botham	c Garner b Baptiste	6
+P.R.Downton	c Harper b Garner	0
P.J.W.Allott	c Gomes b Davis	26
N.G.B.Cook	b Holding	13
P.I.Pocock	b Garner	0
N.G.Cowans	b Garner	0
Extras (b 5, lb 21, nb 18)		44
TOTAL		280

FALL OF WICKETS – 1-90, 2-112, 3-117, 4-138, 5-147, 6-228, 7-257, 8-278, 9-278, 10-280
BOWLING – Garner 22.2-7-51-4, Davis 20-2-71-2, Harper 23-10-33-0, Holding 21-2-50-1, Baptiste 19-8-31-3

ENGLAND 2nd Innings

G.Fowler	b Holding	0
B.C.Broad	lbw b Harper	21
+P.R.Downton	b Harper	24
*D.I.Gower	not out	57
A.J.Lamb	b Harper	9
I.T.Botham	c Haynes b Harper	1
P.J.W.Allott	b Garner	14
N.G.B.Cook	c Dujon b Garner	0
P.I.Pocock	c Garner b Harper	0
N.G.Cowans	b Harper	14
V.P.Terry	absent hurt	
Extras (b 9, lb 3, w 1, nb 3)		16
TOTAL		156

FALL OF WICKETS – 1-0, 2-39, 3-77, 4-99, 5-101, 6-125, 7-127, 8-128, 9-156
BOWLING – Garner 12-4-25-2, Davis 3-1-6-0, Harper 28.4-12-57-6, Holding 11-2-21-1, Baptiste 11-5-29-0, Richards 1-0-2-0

ENGLAND v WEST INDIES

at The Oval on 9th, 10th, 11th, 13th, 14th August 1984
Toss: West Indies
Umpires: D.J.Constant and B.J.Meyer
West Indies won by 172 runs

WEST INDIES 1st Innings

C.G.Greenidge	lbw b Botham	22
D.L.Haynes	b Allott	10
H.A.Gomes	c Botham b Ellison	18
I.V.A.Richards	c Allott b Botham	8
+P.J.L.Dujon	c Tavaré b Botham	3
*C.H.Lloyd	not out	60
M.D.Marshall	c Gower b Ellison	0
E.A.E.Baptiste	c Fowler b Allott	32
R.A.Harper	b Botham	18
M.A.Holding	lbw b Botham	0
J.Garner	c Downton b Allott	6
Extras (b 1, lb 4, w 7, nb 1)		13
TOTAL		190

FALL OF WICKETS – 1-19, 2-45, 3-64, 4-64, 5-67, 6-70, 7-124, 8-154, 9-154, 10-190
BOWLING – Agnew 12-3-46-0, Allott 17-7-25-3, Botham 23-8-72-5, Ellison 18-3-34-2

ENGLAND 1st Innings

G.Fowler	c Richards b Baptiste	31
B.C.Broad	b Garner	4
P.I.Pocock	c Greenidge b Marshall	0
C.J.Tavaré	c Dujon b Holding	16
*D.I.Gower	c Dujon b Holding	12
A.J.Lamb	lbw b Marshall	12
I.T.Botham	c Dujon b Marshall	14
+P.R.Downton	c Lloyd b Garner	16
R.M.Ellison	not out	20
P.J.W.Allott	b Marshall	16
J.P.Agnew	b Marshall	5
Extras (b 2, lb 4, nb 10)		16
TOTAL		162

FALL OF WICKETS – 1-10, 2-22, 3-45, 4-64, 5-83, 6-84, 7-116, 8-133, 9-156, 10-162
BOWLING – Garner 18-6-37-2, Marshall 17.5-5-35-5, Holding 13-2-55-2, Baptiste 12-4-19-1, Harper 1-1-0-0

WEST INDIES 2nd Innings

C.G.Greenidge	c Botham b Agnew	34
D.L.Haynes	b Botham	125
H.A.Gomes	c Tavaré b Ellison	1
I.V.A.Richards	lbw b Agnew	15
*C.H.Lloyd	c Downton b Ellison	36
+P.J.L.Dujon	c Lamb b Ellison	49
E.A.E.Baptiste	c Downton b Allott	5
M.D.Marshall	c Lamb b Botham	12
R.A.Harper	c Downton b Allott	17
M.A.Holding	lbw b Botham	30
J.Garner	not out	10
Extras (lb 12)		12
TOTAL		346

FALL OF WICKETS – 1-51, 2-52, 3-69, 4-132, 5-214, 6-237, 7-264, 8-293, 9-329, 10-346
BOWLING – Agnew 14-1-51-2, Allott 26-1-96-2, Botham 22.3-2-103-3, Ellison 26-7-60-3, Pocock 8-3-24-0

ENGLAND 2nd Innings

G.Fowler	c Richards b Marshall	7
B.C.Broad	c Greenidge b Holding	39
C.J.Tavaré	c Richards b Garner	49
*D.I.Gower	lbw b Holding	7
A.J.Lamb	c Haynes b Holding	1
I.T.Botham	c Marshall b Garner	54
+P.R.Downton	lbw b Garner	10
R.M.Ellison	c Holding b Garner	13
P.J.W.Allott	c Lloyd b Holding	4
P.I.Pocock	c & b Holding	0
J.P.Agnew	not out	2
Extras (lb 2, w 1, nb 13)		16
TOTAL		202

FALL OF WICKETS – 1-15, 2-75, 3-88, 4-90, 5-135, 6-181, 7-186, 8-200, 9-200, 10-202
BOWLING – Garner 18.4-3-51-4, Marshall 22-5-71-1, Holding 13-2-43-5, Baptiste 8-3-11-0, Harper 8-5-10-0

ENGLAND v SRI LANKA

at Lord's on 23rd, 24th, 25th, 27th, 28th August 1984
Toss: England
Umpires: H.D.Bird and D.G.L.Evans
Match drawn

SRI LANKA 1st Innings

S.Wettimuny	c Downton b Allott	190
+S.A.R.Silva	lbw b Botham	8
R.S.Madugalle	b Ellison	5
R.L.Dias	c Lamb b Pocock	32
A.Ranatunga	b Agnew	84
*L.R.D.Mendis	c Fowler b Pocock	111
P.A.de Silva	c Downton b Agnew	16
A.L.F.de Mel	not out	20
J.R.Ratnayeke	not out	5
DID NOT BAT – D.S.de Silva and V.B.John		
Extras (b 2, lb 8, w 2, nb 8)		20
TOTAL (for 7 wkts dec)		491

FALL OF WICKETS – 1-17, 2-43, 3-144, 4-292, 5-442, 6-456, 7-464
BOWLING – Agnew 32-3-123-2, Botham 29-6-114-1, Ellison 28-6-70-1, Pocock 41-17-75-2, Allott 36-7-89-1

ENGLAND

G.Fowler	c Madugalle b John	25
B.C.Broad	c Silva b de Mel	86
C.J.Tavaré	c Ranatunga b de Silva D.S.	14
*D.I.Gower	c Silva b de Mel	55
A.J.Lamb	c Dias b John	107
I.T.Botham	c sub b John	6
R.M.Ellison	c Ratnayeke b de Silva D.S.	41
+P.R.Downton	c Dias b de Mel	10
P.J.W.Allott	b de Mel	0
P.I.Pocock	c Silva b John	2
J.P.Agnew	not out	1
Extras (b 5, lb 7, w 5, nb 6)		23
TOTAL		370

FALL OF WICKETS – 1-49, 2-105, 3-190, 4-210, 5-218, 6-305, 7-354, 8-354, 9-369, 10-370
BOWLING – de Mel 37-10-110-4, John 39.1-12-98-4, Ratnayeke 22-5-50-0, de Silva D.S. 45-16-85-2, Ranatunga 1-1-0-0, Madugalle 3-0-4-0

SRI LANKA 2nd Innings

S.Wettimuny	c Gower b Botham	13
+S.A.R.Silva	not out	102
R.S.Madugalle	b Botham	3
R.L.Dias	lbw b Botham	38
A.Ranatunga	lbw b Botham	0
P.A.de Silva	c Downton b Pocock	3
*L.R.D.Mendis	c Fowler b Botham	94
A.L.F.de Mel	c Ellison b Botham	14
J.R.Ratnayeke	not out	7
DID NOT BAT – D.S.de Silva and V.B.John		
Extras (b 5, lb 4, nb 11)		20
TOTAL (for 7 wkts dec)		294

FALL OF WICKETS – 1-19, 2-29, 3-111, 4-115, 5-118, 6-256, 7-276
BOWLING – Agnew 11-3-54-0, Botham 27-6-90-6, Ellison 7-0-36-0, Pocock 29-10-78-1, Allott 1-0-2-0, Lamb 1-0-6-0, Tavaré 3-3-0-0, Fowler 1-0-8-0

1984

ENGLAND v AUSTRALIA

at Headingley on 13th, 14th, 15th, 17th, 18th June 1985
Toss: Australia
Umpires: B.J.Meyer and K.E.Palmer
England won by 5 wickets

AUSTRALIA 1st Innings
G.M.Wood	lbw b Allott	14
A.M.J.Hilditch	c Downton b Gooch	119
K.C.Wessels	c Botham b Emburey	36
*A.R.Border	c Botham b Cowans	32
D.C.Boon	lbw b Gooch	14
G.M.Ritchie	b Botham	46
+W.B.Phillips	c Gower b Emburey	30
C.J.McDermott	b Botham	18
S.P.O'Donnell	lbw b Botham	0
G.F.Lawson	c Downton b Allott	0
J.R.Thomson	not out	4
Extras (lb 13, w 4, nb 1)		18
TOTAL		331

FALL OF WICKETS – 1-23, 2-155, 3-201, 4-229, 5-229, 6-284, 7-326, 8-326, 9-327, 10-331
BOWLING – Cowans 20-4-78-1, Allott 22-3-74-2, Botham 29.1-8-86-3, Gooch 21-4-57-2, Emburey 6-1-23-2

ENGLAND 1st Innings
G.A.Gooch	lbw b McDermott	5
R.T.Robinson	c Boon b Lawson	175
*D.I.Gower	c Phillips b McDermott	17
M.W.Gatting	c Hilditch b McDermott	53
A.J.Lamb	b O'Donnell	38
I.T.Botham	b Thomson	60
P.Willey	c Hilditch b Lawson	36
+P.R.Downton	c Border b McDermott	54
J.E.Emburey	b Lawson	21
P.J.W.Allott	c Boon b Thomson	12
N.G.Cowans	not out	22
Extras (b 5, lb 16, w 5, nb 14)		40
TOTAL		533

FALL OF WICKETS – 1-14, 2-50, 3-186, 4-264, 5-344, 6-417, 7-422, 8-462, 9-484, 10-533
BOWLING – Lawson 24-4-117-3, McDermott 32-2-134-4, Thomson 34-3-166-2, O'Donnell 27-8-77-1, Border 3-0-16-0, Wessels 3-2-2-0

AUSTRALIA 2nd Innings
G.M.Wood	c Lamb b Botham	3
A.M.J.Hilditch	c Robinson b Emburey	80
K.C.Wessels	b Emburey	64
*A.R.Border	c Downton b Botham	8
D.C.Boon	b Cowans	22
G.M.Ritchie	b Emburey	1
+W.B.Phillips	c Lamb b Botham	91
S.P.O'Donnell	c Downton b Botham	24
G.F.Lawson	c Downton b Emburey	15
C.J.McDermott	c Gooch b Emburey	6
J.R.Thomson	not out	2
Extras (b 4, lb 3, w 1)		8
TOTAL		324

FALL OF WICKETS – 1-5, 2-144, 3-151, 4-159, 5-160, 6-192, 7-272, 8-307, 9-318, 10-324
BOWLING – Cowans 13-2-50-1, Allott 17-4-57-0, Botham 33-7-107-4, Gooch 9-3-21-0, Emburey 43.4-14-82-5

ENGLAND 2nd Innings
G.A.Gooch	lbw b O'Donnell	28
R.T.Robinson	b Lawson	21
*D.I.Gower	c Border b O'Donnell	5
M.W.Gatting	c Phillips b Lawson	12
A.J.Lamb	not out	31
I.T.Botham	b O'Donnell	12
P.Willey	not out	3
DID NOT BAT – +P.R.Downton, J.E.Emburey, P.J.W.Allott, N.G.Cowans		
Extras (lb 7, w 1, nb 3)		11
TOTAL (for 5 wkts)		123

FALL OF WICKETS – 1-44, 2-59, 3-71, 4-83, 5-110
BOWLING – Lawson 16-4-51-2, McDermott 4-0-20-0, Thomson 3-0-8-0, O'Donnell 15.4-5-37-3

ENGLAND v AUSTRALIA

at Lord's on 27th, 28th, 29th June, 1st, 2nd July 1985
Toss: England
Umpires: H.D.Bird and D.G.L.Evans
Australia won by 4 wickets

ENGLAND 1st Innings
G.A.Gooch	lbw b McDermott	30
R.T.Robinson	lbw b McDermott	6
*D.I.Gower	c Border b McDermott	86
M.W.Gatting	lbw b Lawson	14
A.J.Lamb	c Phillips b Lawson	47
I.T.Botham	c Ritchie b Lawson	5
+P.R.Downton	c Wessels b McDermott	21
J.E.Emburey	lbw b O'Donnell	33
P.H.Edmonds	c Border b McDermott	21
N.A.Foster	c Wessels b McDermott	3
P.J.W.Allott	not out	1
Extras (b 1, lb 4, w 1, nb 17)		23
TOTAL		290

FALL OF WICKETS – 1-26, 2-51, 3-99, 4-179, 5-184, 6-211, 7-241, 8-273, 9-283, 10-290
BOWLING – Lawson 25-2-91-3, McDermott 29.2-5-70-6, O'Donnell 22-3-82-1, Holland 23-6-42-0

AUSTRALIA 1st Innings
G.M.Wood	c Emburey b Allott	8
A.M.J.Hilditch	b Foster	14
K.C.Wessels	lbw b Botham	11
*A.R.Border	c Gooch b Botham	196
D.C.Boon	c Downton b Botham	4
G.M.Ritchie	lbw b Botham	94
+W.B.Phillips	c Edmonds b Botham	21
S.P.O'Donnell	c Lamb b Edmonds	48
G.F.Lawson	not out	5
C.J.McDermott	run out	9
R.G.Holland	b Edmonds	0
Extras (lb 10, w 1, nb 4)		15
TOTAL		425

FALL OF WICKETS – 1-11, 2-24, 3-80, 4-101, 5-317, 6-347, 7-398, 8-414, 9-425, 10-425
BOWLING – Foster 23-1-83-1, Allott 30-4-70-1, Botham 24-2-109-5, Edmonds 25.4-5-85-2, Gooch 3-1-11-0, Emburey 19-3-57-0

ENGLAND 2nd Innings
G.A.Gooch	c Phillips b McDermott	17
R.T.Robinson	b Holland	12
J.E.Emburey	b Lawson	20
P.J.W.Allott	b Lawson	0
*D.I.Gower	c Phillips b McDermott	22
M.W.Gatting	not out	75
A.J.Lamb	c Holland b Lawson	9
I.T.Botham	c Border b Holland	85
+P.R.Downton	c Boon b Holland	0
P.H.Edmonds	c Boon b Holland	1
N.A.Foster	c Border b Holland	0
Extras (b 1, lb 12, w 4, nb 3)		20
TOTAL		261

FALL OF WICKETS – 1-32, 2-34, 3-38, 4-57, 5-77, 6-98, 7-229, 8-229, 9-261, 10-261
BOWLING – Lawson 23-0-86-3, McDermott 20-2-84-2, O'Donnell 5-0-10-0, Holland 32-12-68-5

AUSTRALIA 2nd Innings
G.M.Wood	c Lamb b Botham	6
A.M.J.Hilditch	c Lamb b Botham	0
K.C.Wessels	run out	28
G.M.Ritchie	b Allott	2
*A.R.Border	not out	41
D.C.Boon	b Edmonds	1
+W.B.Phillips	c Edmonds b Emburey	29
S.P.O'Donnell	not out	9
DID NOT BAT – G.F.Lawson, C.J.McDermott, R.G.Holland		
Extras (lb 11)		11
TOTAL (for 6 wkts)		127

FALL OF WICKETS – 1-0, 2-9, 3-22, 4-63, 5-65, 6-116
BOWLING – Allott 7-4-8-1, Botham 15-0-49-2, Edmonds 16-5-35-1, Emburey 8-4-24-1

ENGLAND v AUSTRALIA

at Trent Bridge on 11th, 12th, 13th, 15th, 16th July 1985
Toss: England
Umpires: D.J.Constant and A.G.T.Whitehead
Match drawn

ENGLAND 1st Innings
G.A.Gooch	c Wessels b Lawson	70
R.T.Robinson	c Border b Lawson	38
*D.I.Gower	c Phillips b O'Donnell	166
M.W.Gatting	run out	74
A.J.Lamb	lbw b Lawson	17
I.T.Botham	c O'Donnell b McDermott	38
+P.R.Downton	c Ritchie b McDermott	0
A.Sidebottom	c O'Donnell b Lawson	2
J.E.Emburey	not out	16
P.H.Edmonds	b Holland	12
P.J.W.Allott	c Border b Lawson	7
Extras (lb 12, w 1, nb 3)		16
TOTAL		456

FALL OF WICKETS – 1-55, 2-171, 3-358, 4-365, 5-416, 6-416, 7-419, 8-419, 9-443, 10-456
BOWLING – Lawson 39.4-10-103-5, McDermott 35-3-147-2, O'Donnell 29-4-104-1, Holland 26-3-90-1

AUSTRALIA
G.M.Wood	c Robinson b Botham	172
A.M.J.Hilditch	lbw b Allott	47
R.G.Holland	lbw b Sidebottom	10
K.C.Wessels	c Downton b Emburey	33
*A.R.Border	c Botham b Edmonds	23
D.C.Boon	c & b Emburey	15
G.M.Ritchie	b Edmonds	146
+W.B.Phillips	b Emburey	2
S.P.O'Donnell	c Downton b Botham	46
G.F.Lawson	c Gooch b Botham	18
C.J.McDermott	not out	0
Extras (b 6, lb 7, w 2, nb 12)		27
TOTAL		539

FALL OF WICKETS – 1-87, 2-128, 3-205, 4-234, 5-263, 6-424, 7-437, 8-491, 9-539, 10-539
BOWLING – Botham 34.2-3-107-3, Sidebottom 18.4-3-65-1, Allott 18-4-55-1, Edmonds 66-18-155-2, Emburey 55-15-129-3, Gooch 8.2-2-13-0, Gatting 1-0-2-0

ENGLAND 2nd Innings
G.A.Gooch	c Ritchie b McDermott	48
R.T.Robinson	not out	77
*D.I.Gower	c Phillips b McDermott	17
M.W.Gatting	not out	35
DID NOT BAT – A.J.Lamb, I.T.Botham, +P.R.Downton, A.Sidebottom, J.E.Emburey, P.H.Edmonds, P.J.W.Allott		
Extras (b 1, lb 16, nb 2)		19
TOTAL (for 2 wkts)		196

FALL OF WICKETS – 1-79, 2-107
BOWLING – Lawson 13-4-32-0, McDermott 16-2-42-2, O'Donnell 10-2-26-0, Holland 28-9-69-0, Ritchie 1-0-10-0

1985

ENGLAND v AUSTRALIA

at Old Trafford on 1st, 2nd, 3rd, 5th, 6th August 1985
Toss: England
Umpires: H.D.Bird and D.R.Shepherd
Match drawn

AUSTRALIA 1st Innings

K.C.Wessels	c Botham b Emburey	34
A.M.J.Hilditch	c Gower b Edmonds	49
D.C.Boon	c Lamb b Botham	61
*A.R.Border	st Downton b Edmonds	8
G.M.Ritchie	c & b Edmonds	4
+W.B.Phillips	c Downton b Botham	36
G.R.J.Matthews	b Botham	4
S.P.O'Donnell	b Edmonds	45
G.F.Lawson	c Downton b Botham	4
C.J.McDermott	lbw b Emburey	0
R.G.Holland	not out	5
Extras (lb 3, w 1, nb 3)		7
TOTAL		257

FALL OF WICKETS – 1-71, 2-97, 3-118, 4-122, 5-193, 6-198, 7-211, 8-223, 9-224, 10-257
BOWLING – Botham 23-4-79-4, Agnew 14-0-65-0, Allott 13-1-29-0, Emburey 24-7-41-2, Edmonds 15.1-4-40-4

ENGLAND

G.A.Gooch	lbw b McDermott	74
R.T.Robinson	c Border b McDermott	10
*D.I.Gower	c Hilditch b McDermott	47
M.W.Gatting	c Phillips b McDermott	160
A.J.Lamb	run out	67
I.T.Botham	c O'Donnell b McDermott	20
+P.R.Downton	b McDermott	23
J.E.Emburey	not out	31
P.H.Edmonds	b McDermott	1
P.J.W.Allott	b McDermott	7
J.P.Agnew	not out	2
Extras (b 7, lb 16, nb 17)		40
TOTAL (for 9 wkts dec)		482

FALL OF WICKETS – 1-21, 2-142, 3-148, 4-304, 5-339, 6-430, 7-448, 8-450, 9-470
BOWLING – Lawson 37-7-114-0, McDermott 36-3-141-8, Holland 38-7-101-0, O'Donnell 21-6-82-0, Matthews 9-2-21-0

AUSTRALIA 2nd Innings

A.M.J.Hilditch	b Emburey	40
G.R.J.Matthews	c & b Edmonds	17
K.C.Wessels	c & b Emburey	50
*A.R.Border	not out	146
D.C.Boon	b Emburey	7
G.M.Ritchie	b Emburey	31
+W.B.Phillips	not out	39
DID NOT BAT – S.P.O'Donnell, G.F.Lawson, C.J.McDermott, R.G.Holland		
Extras (b 1, lb 6, nb 3)		10
TOTAL (for 5 wkts)		340

FALL OF WICKETS – 1-38, 2-85, 3-126, 4-138, 5-213
BOWLING – Botham 15-3-50-0, Agnew 9-2-34-0, Allott 6-2-4-0, Emburey 51-17-99-4, Edmonds 54-12-122-1, Gatting 4-0-14-0, Lamb 1-0-10-0

ENGLAND v AUSTRALIA

at Edgbaston on 15th, 16th, 17th, 19th, 20th August 1985
Toss: England
Umpires: D.J.Constant and D.R.Shepherd
England won by an innings and 118 runs

AUSTRALIA 1st Innings

G.M.Wood	c Edmonds b Botham	19
A.M.J.Hilditch	c Downton b Edmonds	39
K.C.Wessels	c Downton b Ellison	83
*A.R.Border	c Edmonds b Ellison	45
G.M.Ritchie	c Botham b Ellison	8
+W.B.Phillips	c Robinson b Ellison	15
S.P.O'Donnell	c Downton b Taylor	1
G.F.Lawson	run out	53
C.J.McDermott	c Gower b Ellison	35
J.R.Thomson	not out	28
R.G.Holland	c Edmonds b Ellison	0
Extras (lb 4, w 1, nb 4)		9
TOTAL		335

FALL OF WICKETS – 1-44, 2-92, 3-189, 4-191, 5-207, 6-208, 7-218, 8-276, 9-335, 10-335
BOWLING – Botham 27-1-108-1, Taylor 26-5-78-1, Ellison 31.5-9-77-6, Edmonds 20-4-47-1, Emburey 9-2-21-0

ENGLAND

G.A.Gooch	c Phillips b Thomson	19
R.T.Robinson	b Lawson	148
*D.I.Gower	c Border b Lawson	215
M.W.Gatting	not out	100
A.J.Lamb	c Wood b McDermott	46
I.T.Botham	c Thomson b McDermott	18
+P.R.Downton	not out	0
DID NOT BAT – J.E.Emburey, R.M.Ellison, P.H.Edmonds, L.B.Taylor		
Extras (b 7, lb 20, nb 22)		49
TOTAL (for 5 wkts dec)		595

FALL OF WICKETS – 1-38, 2-369, 3-463, 4-572, 5-592
BOWLING – Lawson 37-1-135-2, McDermott 31-2-155-2, Thomson 19-1-101-1, Holland 25-4-95-0, O'Donnell 16-3-69-0, Border 6-1-13-0

AUSTRALIA 2nd Innings

G.M.Wood	c Robinson b Ellison	10
A.M.J.Hilditch	c Ellison b Botham	10
K.C.Wessels	c Downton b Ellison	10
R.G.Holland	lbw b Ellison	0
*A.R.Border	b Ellison	2
G.M.Ritchie	c Lamb b Emburey	20
+W.B.Phillips	c Gower b Edmonds	59
S.P.O'Donnell	b Botham	11
G.F.Lawson	c Gower b Edmonds	3
C.J.McDermott	c Edmonds b Botham	8
J.R.Thomson	not out	4
Extras (b 1, lb 3, nb 1)		5
TOTAL		142

FALL OF WICKETS – 1-10, 2-32, 3-32, 4-35, 5-36, 6-113, 7-117, 8-120, 9-137, 10-142
BOWLING – Botham 14.1-2-52-3, Taylor 13-4-27-0, Ellison 9-3-27-4, Edmonds 15-9-13-2, Emburey 13-5-19-1

ENGLAND v AUSTRALIA

at The Oval on 29th, 30th, 31st August, 2nd, 3rd September 1985
Toss: England
Umpires: H.D.Bird and K.E.Palmer
England won by an innings and 94 runs

ENGLAND

G.A.Gooch	c & b McDermott	196
R.T.Robinson	b McDermott	3
*D.I.Gower	c Bennett b McDermott	157
M.W.Gatting	c Border b Bennett	4
J.E.Emburey	c Wellham b Lawson	9
A.J.Lamb	c McDermott b Lawson	1
I.T.Botham	c Phillips b Lawson	12
+P.R.Downton	b McDermott	16
R.M.Ellison	c Phillips b Gilbert	3
P.H.Edmonds	lbw b Lawson	12
L.B.Taylor	not out	1
Extras (b 13, lb 11, nb 26)		50
TOTAL		464

FALL OF WICKETS – 1-20, 2-371, 3-376, 4-403, 5-405, 6-418, 7-425, 8-447, 9-452, 10-464
BOWLING – Lawson 29-2-6-101-4, McDermott 31-2-108-4, Gilbert 21-2-96-1, Bennett 32-8-111-1, Border 2-0-8-0, Wessels 3-0-16-0

AUSTRALIA 1st Innings

G.M.Wood	lbw b Botham	22
A.M.J.Hilditch	c Gooch b Botham	17
K.C.Wessels	b Emburey	12
*A.R.Border	b Edmonds	38
D.M.Wellham	c Downton b Ellison	13
G.M.Ritchie	not out	64
+W.B.Phillips	b Edmonds	18
M.J.Bennett	c Robinson b Ellison	12
G.F.Lawson	c Botham b Taylor	14
C.J.McDermott	run out	25
D.R.Gilbert	b Botham	1
Extras (lb 3, w 2)		5
TOTAL		241

FALL OF WICKETS – 1-35, 2-52, 3-56, 4-101, 5-109, 6-144, 7-171, 8-192, 9-235, 10-241
BOWLING – Botham 20-3-64-3, Taylor 13-1-39-1, Ellison 18-5-35-2, Emburey 19-7-48-1, Edmonds 14-2-52-2

AUSTRALIA 2nd Innings

G.M.Wood	b Botham	6
A.M.J.Hilditch	c Gower b Taylor	9
K.C.Wessels	c Downton b Botham	7
*A.R.Border	c Botham b Ellison	58
D.M.Wellham	lbw b Ellison	5
G.M.Ritchie	c Downton b Ellison	6
+W.B.Phillips	c Downton b Botham	10
M.J.Bennett	c & b Taylor	11
G.F.Lawson	c Downton b Ellison	7
C.J.McDermott	c Botham b Ellison	2
D.R.Gilbert	not out	0
Extras (b 4, nb 4)		8
TOTAL		129

FALL OF WICKETS – 1-13, 2-16, 3-37, 4-51, 5-71, 6-96, 7-114, 8-127, 9-129, 10-129
BOWLING – Botham 17-3-44-3, Taylor 11.3-1-34-2, Ellison 17-3-46-5, Emburey 1-0-1-0

1985

ENGLAND v INDIA

at Lord's on 5th, 6th, 7th, 9th, 10th June 1986
Toss: India
Umpires: K.E.Palmer and D.R.Shepherd
India won by 5 wickets

ENGLAND 1st Innings

G.A.Gooch	b Sharma	114
R.T.Robinson	c Azharuddin b Maninder S	35
*D.I.Gower	c More b Sharma	18
M.W.Gatting	b Sharma	0
A.J.Lamb	c Srikkanth b Sharma	6
D.R.Pringle	b Binny	63
J.E.Emburey	c Amarnath b Kapil Dev	7
+P.R.Downton	lbw b Sharma	5
R.M.Ellison	c Kapil Dev b Binny	12
G.R.Dilley	c More b Binny	4
P.H.Edmonds	not out	7
Extras (lb 15, w 1, nb 7)		23
TOTAL		294

FALL OF WICKETS – 1-66, 2-92, 3-92, 4-98, 5-245, 6-264, 7-269, 8-271, 9-287, 10-294
BOWLING – Kapil Dev 31-8-67-1, Binny 18.2-4-55-3, Sharma 32-10-64-5, Maninder Singh 30-15-45-1, Amarnath 7-1-18-0, Shastri 10-3-30-0

INDIA 1st Innings

S.M.Gavaskar	c Emburey b Dilley	34
K.Srikkanth	c Gatting b Dilley	20
M.Amarnath	c Pringle b Edmonds	69
D.B.Vengsarkar	not out	126
M.Azharuddin	c & b Dilley	33
R.J.Shastri	c Edmonds b Dilley	1
R.M.H.Binny	lbw b Pringle	9
*Kapil Dev	c Lamb b Ellison	1
C.Sharma	b Pringle	2
+K.S.More	lbw b Pringle	25
Maninder Singh	c Lamb b Emburey	6
Extras (lb 5, w 1, nb 9)		15
TOTAL		341

FALL OF WICKETS – 1-31, 2-90, 3-161, 4-232, 5-238, 6-252, 7-253, 8-264, 9-303, 10-341
BOWLING – Dilley 34-7-146-4, Ellison 29-11-63-1, Emburey 27-13-28-1, Edmonds 22-7-41-1, Pringle 25-7-58-3

ENGLAND 2nd Innings

G.A.Gooch	lbw b Kapil Dev	8
R.T.Robinson	c Amarnath b Kapil Dev	11
*D.I.Gower	lbw b Kapil Dev	8
M.W.Gatting	b Sharma	40
A.J.Lamb	c More b Shastri	39
D.R.Pringle	c More b Kapil Dev	6
+P.R.Downton	c Shastri b Maninder Singh	29
R.M.Ellison	c More b Binny	19
J.E.Emburey	c & b Maninder Singh	1
G.R.Dilley	not out	2
P.H.Edmonds	c Binny b Maninder Singh	7
Extras (lb 6, w 1, nb 3)		10
TOTAL		180

FALL OF WICKETS – 1-18, 2-23, 3-35, 4-108, 5-113, 6-121, 7-164, 8-170, 9-170, 10-180
BOWLING – Kapil Dev 22-7-52-4, Binny 15-3-44-1, Sharma 17-4-48-1, Maninder Singh 20.4-12-9-3, Amarnath 2-2-0-0, Shastri 20-8-21-1

INDIA 2nd Innings

S.M.Gavaskar	c Downton b Dilley	22
K.Srikkanth	c Gooch b Dilley	0
M.Amarnath	lbw b Pringle	8
D.B.Vengsarkar	b Edmonds	33
M.Azharuddin	run out	14
R.J.Shastri	not out	20
*Kapil Dev	not out	23
DID NOT BAT – R.M.H.Binny, C.Sharma, +K.S.More, Maninder Singh		
Extras (b 1, lb 9, w 1, nb 5)		16
TOTAL (for 5 wkts)		136

FALL OF WICKETS – 1-10, 2-31, 3-76, 4-78, 5-110
BOWLING – Dilley 10-3-28-2, Ellison 6-0-17-0, Edmonds 11-2-51-1, Pringle 15-5-30-1

ENGLAND v INDIA

at Headingley on 19th, 20th, 21st, 23rd June 1986
Toss: India
Umpires: J.Birkenshaw and D.J.Constant
India won by 279 runs

INDIA 1st Innings

S.M.Gavaskar	c French b Pringle	35
K.Srikkanth	c Emburey b Pringle	31
R.J.Shastri	c Pringle b Dilley	32
D.B.Vengsarkar	c French b Lever	61
M.Azharuddin	lbw b Gooch	15
C.S.Pandit	c Emburey b Pringle	23
*Kapil Dev	lbw b Lever	0
R.M.H.Binny	c Slack b Emburey	6
Madan Lal	c Gooch b Dilley	20
+K.S.More	not out	36
Maninder Singh	c Gooch b Dilley	3
Extras (lb 5, nb 5)		10
TOTAL		272

FALL OF WICKETS – 1-64, 2-75, 3-128, 4-163, 5-203, 6-203, 7-211, 8-213, 9-267, 10-272
BOWLING – Dilley 24.2-7-54-3, Lever 30-4-102-2, Pringle 27-6-47-3, Emburey 17-4-45-1, Gooch 6-0-19-1

ENGLAND 1st Innings

G.A.Gooch	c Binny b Kapil Dev	8
W.N.Slack	b Madan Lal	0
C.L.Smith	b Madan Lal	6
A.J.Lamb	c Pandit b Binny	10
*M.W.Gatting	c More b Binny	13
C.W.J.Athey	c More b Madan Lal	32
D.R.Pringle	c Srikkanth b Binny	8
J.E.Emburey	c Kapil Dev b Binny	0
+B.N.French	b Binny	8
G.R.Dilley	b Shastri	10
J.K.Lever	not out	0
Extras (b 1, lb 2, nb 4)		7
TOTAL		102

FALL OF WICKETS – 1-4, 2-14, 3-14, 4-38, 5-41, 6-63, 7-63, 8-71, 9-100, 10-102
BOWLING – Kapil Dev 18-7-36-1, Madan Lal 11.1-3-18-3, Binny 13-1-40-5, Shastri 3-1-5-1

INDIA 2nd Innings

S.M.Gavaskar	c French b Lever	1
K.Srikkanth	b Dilley	8
R.J.Shastri	lbw b Lever	3
D.B.Vengsarkar	not out	102
M.Azharuddin	lbw b Lever	2
C.S.Pandit	b Pringle	17
+K.S.More	c Slack b Pringle	16
*Kapil Dev	c Gatting b Lever	31
Madan Lal	run out	22
R.M.H.Binny	lbw b Pringle	26
Maninder Singh	c Gatting b Pringle	1
Extras (b 4, lb 4)		8
TOTAL		237

FALL OF WICKETS – 1-9, 2-9, 3-29, 4-35, 5-70, 6-102, 7-137, 8-173, 9-233, 10-237
BOWLING – Dilley 17-2-71-1, Lever 23-5-64-4, Pringle 22.3-6-73-4, Emburey 7-3-9-0, Gooch 7-2-12-0

ENGLAND 2nd Innings

G.A.Gooch	c Srikkanth b Kapil Dev	5
W.N.Slack	c Gavaskar b Binny	19
C.L.Smith	c More b Shastri	28
A.J.Lamb	c More b Binny	10
*M.W.Gatting	not out	31
C.W.J.Athey	c More b Maninder Singh	8
J.K.Lever	c More b Maninder Singh	0
D.R.Pringle	lbw b Maninder Singh	8
J.E.Emburey	c Azharuddin b Kapil Dev	9
+B.N.French	c Vengsarkar b Maninder S	5
G.R.Dilley	run out	2
Extras (lb 9, nb 2)		11
TOTAL		128

FALL OF WICKETS – 1-12, 2-46, 3-63, 4-77, 5-90, 6-90, 7-101, 8-104, 9-109, 10-128
BOWLING – Kapil Dev 19.2-7-24-2, Madan Lal 9.4-2-30-0, Binny 8-1-18-2, Shastri 10-3-21-1, Maninder Singh 16.3-6-26-4

ENGLAND v INDIA

at Edgbaston on 3rd, 4th, 5th, 7th, 8th July 1986
Toss: England
Umpires: H.D.Bird and B.J.Meyer
Match drawn

ENGLAND 1st Innings

G.A.Gooch	c More b Kapil Dev	0
M.R.Benson	b Maninder Singh	21
C.W.J.Athey	c More b Kapil Dev	0
D.I.Gower	lbw b Sharma	49
*M.W.Gatting	not out	183
D.R.Pringle	c Amarnath b Shastri	44
J.E.Emburey	c Shastri b Maninder Singh	38
N.A.Foster	b Binny	17
P.H.Edmonds	b Sharma	18
+B.N.French	b Sharma	8
N.V.Radford	c Gavaskar b Sharma	0
Extras (lb 7, nb 5)		12
TOTAL		390

FALL OF WICKETS – 1-0, 2-0, 3-61, 4-88, 5-184, 6-278, 7-327, 8-367, 9-384, 10-390
BOWLING – Kapil Dev 31-6-89-2, Binny 17-1-53-1, Sharma 29.3-2-130-4, Maninder Singh 25-3-66-2, Shastri 14-1-45-1

INDIA 1st Innings

S.M.Gavaskar	b Pringle	29
K.Srikkanth	c Pringle b Radford	23
M.Amarnath	b Edmonds	79
D.B.Vengsarkar	c Gooch b Radford	38
M.Azharuddin	c French b Foster	64
R.J.Shastri	c Gooch b Foster	18
*Kapil Dev	c French b Foster	26
+K.S.More	c French b Emburey	48
R.M.H.Binny	c Gower b Emburey	40
C.Sharma	c Gower b Pringle	9
Maninder Singh	not out	0
Extras (b 3, lb 7, w 1, nb 5)		16
TOTAL		390

FALL OF WICKETS – 1-53, 2-58, 3-139, 4-228, 5-266, 6-275, 7-302, 8-370, 9-385, 10-390
BOWLING – Radford 35-3-131-2, Foster 41-9-93-3, Pringle 21-2-61-2, Edmonds 24-7-55-1, Emburey 18.5-7-40-2

ENGLAND 2nd Innings

G.A.Gooch	lbw b Sharma	40
M.R.Benson	b Shastri	30
C.W.J.Athey	c More b Sharma	38
D.I.Gower	c Gavaskar b Sharma	26
*M.W.Gatting	lbw b Sharma	26
D.R.Pringle	c More b Maninder Singh	7
J.E.Emburey	run out	0
N.A.Foster	b Binny	17
P.H.Edmonds	c Binny b Maninder Singh	10
+B.N.French	c More b Sharma	1
N.V.Radford	c Azharuddin b Sharma	1
Extras (b 10, lb 6, w 2, nb 11)		29
TOTAL		235

FALL OF WICKETS – 1-49, 2-102, 3-152, 4-163, 5-190, 6-190, 7-190, 8-217, 9-229, 10 235
BOWLING – Kapil Dev 7-1-38-0, Binny 16-1-41-0, Sharma 24-4-58-6, Maninder Singh 22-5-41-2, Shastri 23-8-39-1, Amarnath 2-1-2-0

INDIA 2nd Innings

S.M.Gavaskar	c French b Foster	54
K.Srikkanth	c Pringle b Edmonds	23
M.Amarnath	c French b Edmonds	16
D.B.Vengsarkar	c French b Edmonds	0
M.Azharuddin	not out	29
R.J.Shastri	c Emburey b Edmonds	0
+K.S.More	not out	31
DID NOT BAT – *Kapil Dev, R.M.H.Binny, C.Sharma, Maninder Singh		
Extras (b 1, lb 15, w 1, nb 4)		21
TOTAL (for 5 wkts)		174

FALL OF WICKETS – 1-58, 2-101, 3-101, 4-104, 5-105
BOWLING – Radford 3-0-17-0, Foster 22-9-48-1, Pringle 16-5-33-0, Edmonds 28-11-31-4, Emburey 7-1-19-0, Gatting 2-0-10-0

1986

ENGLAND v NEW ZEALAND

at Lord's on 24th, 25th, 26th, 28th, 29th July 1986
Toss: England
Umpires: H.D.Bird and A.G.T.Whitehead
Match drawn

ENGLAND 1st Innings

G.A.Gooch	c Smith b Hadlee	18
M.D.Moxon	lbw b Hadlee	74
C.W.J.Athey	c Crowe J.J. b Hadlee	44
D.I.Gower	c Crowe M.D. b Bracewell	62
*M.W.Gatting	b Hadlee	2
P.Willey	lbw b Watson	44
P.H.Edmonds	c Crowe M.D. b Hadlee	6
+B.N.French	retired hurt	0
G.R.Dilley	c Smith b Hadlee	17
N.A.Foster	b Watson	8
N.V.Radford	not out	12
Extras (b 6, lb 7, nb 7)		20
TOTAL		307

FALL OF WICKETS – 1-27, 2-102, 3-196, 4-198, 5-237, 6-258, 7-271, 8-285, 9-307
BOWLING – Hadlee 37.5-11-80-6, Watson 30-7-70-2, Crowe M.D. 8-1-38-0, Coney 4-0-12-0, Bracewell 26-8-65-1, Gray 13-9-29-0

NEW ZEALAND 1st Innings

J.G.Wright	b Dilley	0
B.A.Edgar	c Gatting b Gooch	83
K.R.Rutherford	c Gooch b Dilley	0
M.D.Crowe	c & b Edmonds	106
J.J.Crowe	c Gatting b Edmonds	18
*J.V.Coney	c Gooch b Radford	51
E.J.Gray	c Gower b Edmonds	11
R.J.Hadlee	b Edmonds	19
+I.D.S.Smith	c Edmonds b Dilley	18
J.G.Bracewell	not out	1
W.Watson	lbw b Dilley	1
Extras (b 4, lb 9, w 6, nb 15)		34
TOTAL		342

FALL OF WICKETS – 1-2, 2-5, 3-215, 4-218, 5-274, 6-292, 7-310, 8-340, 9-340, 10-342
BOWLING – Dilley 35.1-9-82-4, Foster 25-6-56-0, Radford 25-4-71-1, Edmonds 42-10-97-4, Gooch 13-6-23-1

ENGLAND 2nd Innings

G.A.Gooch	c Watson b Bracewell	183
M.D.Moxon	lbw b Hadlee	5
C.W.J.Athey	b Gray	16
D.I.Gower	b Gray	3
*M.W.Gatting	c Crowe M.D. b Gray	26
P.Willey	b Bracewell	42
P.H.Edmonds	not out	9
DID NOT BAT – +B.N.French, G.R.Dilley, N.A.Foster, N.V.Radford		
Extras (lb 6, w 1, nb 4)		11
TOTAL (for 6 wkts dec)		295

FALL OF WICKETS – 1-9, 2-68, 3-72, 4-136, 5-262, 6-295
BOWLING – Hadlee 27-3-78-1, Watson 17-2-50-0, Crowe M.D. 4-0-13-0, Bracewell 23.4-7-57-2, Gray 46-14-83-3, Rutherford 3-0-8-0

NEW ZEALAND 2nd Innings

J.G.Wright	c Gower b Dilley	0
B.A.Edgar	c Gower b Foster	0
K.R.Rutherford	not out	24
M.D.Crowe	not out	11
DID NOT BAT – J.J.Crowe, *J.V.Coney, E.J.Gray, R.J.Hadlee, +I.D.S.Smith, J.G.Bracewell, W.Watson		
Extras (lb 4, nb 2)		6
TOTAL (for 2 wkts)		41

FALL OF WICKETS – 1-0, 2-8
BOWLING – Dilley 6-3-5-1, Foster 3-1-13-1, Edmonds 5-0-18-0, Gower 1-0-1-0

ENGLAND v NEW ZEALAND

at Trent Bridge on 7th, 8th, 9th, 11th, 12th August 1986
Toss: New Zealand
Umpires: D.J.Constant and K.E.Palmer
New Zealand won by 8 wickets

ENGLAND 1st Innings

G.A.Gooch	lbw b Hadlee	18
M.D.Moxon	b Hadlee	9
C.W.J.Athey	lbw b Watson	55
D.I.Gower	lbw b Gray	71
*M.W.Gatting	b Hadlee	17
D.R.Pringle	c Watson b Stirling	21
J.E.Emburey	c Smith b Hadlee	8
P.H.Edmonds	c Smith b Hadlee	0
J.G.Thomas	b Hadlee	28
+B.N.French	c Coney b Watson	21
G.C.Small	not out	2
Extras (b 1, lb 3, nb 2)		6
TOTAL		256

FALL OF WICKETS – 1-18, 2-43, 3-126, 4-170, 5-176, 6-191, 7-191, 8-205, 9-240, 10-256
BOWLING – Hadlee 32-7-80-6, Stirling 17-3-62-1, Gray 13-4-30-1, Watson 16.5-6-51-2, Coney 7-1-18-0, Bracewell 4-1-11-0

NEW ZEALAND 1st Innings

J.G.Wright	c Athey b Small	58
B.A.Edgar	lbw b Thomas	8
J.J.Crowe	c French b Small	23
M.D.Crowe	c Edmonds b Emburey	28
*J.V.Coney	run out	24
E.J.Gray	c Athey b Edmonds	50
R.J.Hadlee	c Gooch b Thomas	68
J.G.Bracewell	c Moxon b Emburey	110
+I.D.S.Smith	lbw b Edmonds	2
D.A.Stirling	b Small	26
W.Watson	not out	8
Extras (lb 4, w 2, nb 2)		8
TOTAL		413

FALL OF WICKETS – 1-39, 2-85, 3-92, 4-142, 5-144, 6-239, 7-318, 8-326, 9-391, 10-413
BOWLING – Small 38-12-88-3, Thomas 39-5-124-2, Pringle 20-1-58-0, Edmonds 28-11-52-2, Emburey 42.5-17-87-2, Gooch 2-2-0-0

ENGLAND 2nd Innings

G.A.Gooch	c Coney b Bracewell	17
M.D.Moxon	c Smith b Hadlee	23
P.H.Edmonds	lbw b Hadlee	20
C.W.J.Athey	c Smith b Bracewell	6
D.I.Gower	c Crowe J.J. b Bracewell	26
*M.W.Gatting	c Smith b Gray	4
D.R.Pringle	c Gray b Stirling	9
J.E.Emburey	c Crowe M.D. b Hadlee	75
J.G.Thomas	c Gray b Stirling	10
+B.N.French	not out	12
G.C.Small	lbw b Hadlee	12
Extras (b 4, lb 9, w 1, nb 2)		16
TOTAL		230

FALL OF WICKETS – 1-23, 2-47, 3-63, 4-87, 5-98, 6-104, 7-178, 8-203, 9-203, 10-230
BOWLING – Hadlee 33.1-15-60-4, Stirling 18-5-48-2, Gray 24-9-55-1, Watson 9-3-25-0, Bracewell 11-5-29-3

NEW ZEALAND 2nd Innings

J.G.Wright	b Emburey	7
J.J.Crowe	lbw b Small	2
M.D.Crowe	not out	48
*J.V.Coney	not out	20
DID NOT BAT – B.A.Edgar, E.J.Gray, R.J.Hadlee, J.G.Bracewell, +I.D.S.Smith, D.A.Stirling, W.Watson		
Extras		0
TOTAL (for 2 wkts)		77

FALL OF WICKETS – 1-5, 2-19
BOWLING – Small 8-3-10-1, Thomas 4-0-16-0, Pringle 2-0-16-0, Edmonds 4-1-16-0, Emburey 6-1-15-1, Gower 0-0-4-0

ENGLAND v NEW ZEALAND

at The Oval on 21st, 22nd, 23rd, 25th, 26th August 1986
Toss: England
Umpires: H.D.Bird and D.R.Shepherd
Match drawn

NEW ZEALAND 1st Innings

J.G.Wright	b Edmonds	119
B.A.Edgar	c Gooch b Botham	1
J.J.Crowe	lbw b Botham	8
M.D.Crowe	lbw b Dilley	13
*J.V.Coney	c Gooch b Botham	38
E.J.Gray	b Dilley	30
R.J.Hadlee	c French b Edmonds	6
J.G.Bracewell	c Athey b Emburey	3
+T.E.Blain	c Gooch b Dilley	37
D.A.Stirling	not out	18
E.J.Chatfield	c French b Dilley	5
Extras (b 1, w 1, nb 7)		9
TOTAL		287

FALL OF WICKETS – 1-17, 2-31, 3-59, 4-106, 5-175, 6-192, 7-197, 8-251, 9-280, 10-287
BOWLING – Dilley 28.2-4-92-4, Small 18-5-36-0, Botham 25-4-75-3, Emburey 31-15-39-1, Edmonds 22-10-29-2, Gooch 4-1-15-0

ENGLAND 1st Innings

G.A.Gooch	c Stirling b Hadlee	32
C.W.J.Athey	lbw b Hadlee	17
D.I.Gower	b Chatfield	131
A.J.Lamb	b Chatfield	0
*M.W.Gatting	b Chatfield	121
I.T.Botham	not out	59
J.E.Emburey	not out	9
DID NOT BAT – +B.N.French, P.H.Edmonds, G.R.Dilley, G.C.Small		
Extras (lb 9, w 5, nb 5)		19
TOTAL (for 5 wkts dec)		388

FALL OF WICKETS – 1-38, 2-62, 3-62, 4-285, 5-326
BOWLING – Hadlee 23.5-6-92-2, Stirling 9-0-71-0, Chatfield 21-7-73-3, Gray 21-4-74-0, Bracewell 11-1-51-0, Coney 5-0-18-0

NEW ZEALAND 2nd Innings

J.G.Wright	not out	7
B.A.Edgar	not out	0
DID NOT BAT – J.J.Crowe, M.D.Crowe, *J.V.Coney, E.J.Gray, R.J.Hadlee, J.G.Bracewell, +T.E.Blain, D.A.Stirling, E.J.Chatfield		
Extras		0
TOTAL (for 0 wkts)		7

BOWLING – Botham 1-0-7-0

1986

ENGLAND v PAKISTAN

at Old Trafford on 4th, 5th, 6th, 8th, 9th June 1987
Toss: Pakistan
Umpires: H.D.Bird and B.J.Meyer
Match drawn

ENGLAND

C.W.J.Athey	b Wasim Akram	19
R.T.Robinson	c Yousuf b Mohsin Kamal	166
*M.W.Gatting	b Mohsin Kamal	42
N.H.Fairbrother	lbw b Mohsin Kamal	0
+B.N.French	c Imran b Wasim Akram	59
D.I.Gower	c Yousuf b Wasim Akram	22
I.T.Botham	c Wasim Akram b Tausif	48
J.E.Emburey	c Shoaib b Mohsin Kamal	19
P.A.J.DeFreitas	b Wasim Akram	11
N.A.Foster	b Tausif Ahmed	8
P.H.Edmonds	not out	23
Extras (b 9, lb 15, w 1, nb 5)		30
TOTAL		447

FALL OF WICKETS – 1-50, 2-133, 3-133, 4-246, 5-284, 6-373, 7-397, 8-413, 9-413, 10-447
BOWLING – Wasim Akram 46-11-111-4, Mohsin Kamal 39-4-127-4, Tausif Ahmed 21.4-4-52-2, Mudassar Nazar 37-8-133-0

PAKISTAN

Shoaib Mohammad	c French b Foster	0
Ramiz Raja	c Emburey b DeFreitas	15
Mansoor Akhtar	c Fairbrother b Edmonds	75
Javed Miandad	c French b Botham	21
Salim Malik	run out	6
*Imran Khan	not out	10
Mudassar Nazar	not out	0

DID NOT BAT – +Salim Yousuf, Wasim Akram, Tausif Ahmed, Mohsin Kamal

Extras (b 9, lb 2, w 1, nb 1)	13
TOTAL (for 5 wkts)	140

FALL OF WICKETS – 1-9, 2-21, 3-74, 4-100, 5-139
BOWLING – Foster 15-3-34-1, DeFreitas 12-4-36-1, Botham 14-7-29-1, Emburey 16-3-28-0, Edmonds 7-5-2-1

ENGLAND v PAKISTAN

at Lord's on 18th, 19th, 20th, 22nd, 23rd June 1987
Toss: England
Umpires: D.J.Constant and A.G.T.Whitehead
Match drawn

ENGLAND

B.C.Broad	b Mudassar Nazar	55
R.T.Robinson	c Yousuf b Mohsin Kamal	7
C.W.J.Athey	b Imran Khan	123
D.I.Gower	c Yousuf b Mudassar Nazar	8
*M.W.Gatting	run out	43
+B.N.French	b Wasim Akram	42
I.T.Botham	c Miandad b Wasim Akram	6
J.E.Emburey	run out	12
N.A.Foster	b Abdul Qadir	21
P.H.Edmonds	not out	17
G.R.Dilley	c Yousuf b Imran Khan	17
Extras (lb 12, w 1, nb 4)		17
TOTAL		368

FALL OF WICKETS – 1-29, 2-118, 3-128, 4-230, 5-272, 6-294, 7-305, 8-329, 9-340, 10-368
BOWLING – Imran Khan 34.5-7-90-2, Wasim Akram 28-1-98-2, Mohsin Kamal 9-2-42-1, Abdul Qadir 25-1-100-1, Mudassar Nazar 16-6-26-2

PAKISTAN

DID NOT BAT – Mudassar Nazar, Shoaib Mohammad, Mansoor Akhtar, Javed Miandad, Salim Malik, *Imran Khan, Ijaz Ahmed, +Salim Yousuf, Wasim Akram, Abdul Qadir, Mohsin Kamal

ENGLAND v PAKISTAN

at Headingley on 2nd, 3rd, 4th, 6th July 1987
Toss: England
Umpires: K.E.Palmer and D.R.Shepherd
Pakistan won by an innings and 18 runs

ENGLAND 1st Innings

B.C.Broad	c Yousuf b Wasim Akram	8
R.T.Robinson	lbw b Imran Khan	0
C.W.J.Athey	c Yousuf b Imran Khan	4
D.I.Gower	b Imran Khan	10
*M.W.Gatting	lbw b Wasim Akram	8
I.T.Botham	c Yousuf b Mudassar	26
D.J.Capel	c & b Mohsin Kamal	53
+C.J.Richards	lbw b Wasim Akram	6
N.A.Foster	c Malik b Mohsin Kamal	9
P.H.Edmonds	c Yousuf b Mohsin Kamal	0
G.R.Dilley	not out	1
Extras (b 1, lb 8, w 1, nb 1)		11
TOTAL		136

FALL OF WICKETS – 1-1, 2-13, 3-13, 4-31, 5-31, 6-85, 7-113, 8-133, 9-133, 10-136
BOWLING – Imran Khan 19-3-37-3, Wasim Akram 14-4-36-3, Abdul Qadir 5-0-14-0, Mudassar Nazar 14-5-18-1, Mohsin Kamal 8.4-2-22-3

PAKISTAN

Mudassar Nazar	lbw b Foster	24
Shoaib Mohammad	c Richards b Foster	16
Mansoor Akhtar	lbw b Foster	29
+Salim Yousuf	c Athey b Foster	37
Javed Miandad	c Gatting b Foster	0
Salim Malik	c Gower b Edmonds	99
*Imran Khan	c Richards b Foster	26
Ijaz Ahmed	c Athey b Foster	50
Wasim Akram	c Edmonds b Foster	43
Abdul Qadir	b Dilley	2
Mohsin Kamal	not out	3
Extras (b 5, lb 13, w 1, nb 5)		24
TOTAL		353

FALL OF WICKETS – 1-22, 2-60, 3-86, 4-86, 5-152, 6-208, 7-280, 8-318, 9-328, 10-353
BOWLING – Dilley 33-7-89-1, Foster 46.2-15-107-8, Capel 18-1-64-0, Edmonds 25-10-59-1, Gatting 9-3-16-0

ENGLAND 2nd Innings

B.C.Broad	c Yousuf b Imran Khan	4
R.T.Robinson	c Salim Malik b Imran Khan	2
C.W.J.Athey	lbw b Imran Khan	26
D.I.Gower	b Imran Khan	55
*M.W.Gatting	c Miandad b Wasim Akram	9
D.J.Capel	c Ijaz Ahmed b Imran Khan	28
+C.J.Richards	c Ijaz Ahmed b Imran Khan	2
I.T.Botham	c Mudassar b Mohsin Kamal	24
N.A.Foster	b Wasim Akram	22
P.H.Edmonds	not out	0
G.R.Dilley	b Imran Khan	0
Extras (b 5, lb 12, w 7, nb 3)		27
TOTAL		199

FALL OF WICKETS – 1-4, 2-9, 3-60, 4-94, 5-120, 6-122, 7-160, 8-197, 9-197, 10-199
BOWLING – Imran Khan 19.1-5-40-7, Wasim Akram 21-5-55-2, Abdul Qadir 27-5-60-0, Mudassar Nazar 2-0-8-0, Mohsin Kamal 9-4-19-1

1987

ENGLAND v PAKISTAN

at Edgbaston on 23rd, 24th, 25th, 27th, 28th July 1987
Toss: England
Umpires: B.J.Meyer and A.G.T.Whitehead
Match drawn

PAKISTAN 1st Innings

Mudassar Nazar	lbw b Dilley	124
Shoaib Mohammad	c Foster b Edmonds	18
Mansoor Akhtar	b Foster	26
Javed Miandad	lbw b Dilley	75
Salim Malik	c French b Dilley	24
Ijaz Ahmed	lbw b Botham	20
*Imran Khan	c Emburey b Dilley	0
+Salim Yousuf	not out	91
Wasim Akram	c Botham b Foster	26
Abdul Qadir	c Edmonds b Dilley	6
Mohsin Kamal	run out	10
Extras (b 4, lb 11, w 1, nb 3)		19
TOTAL		439

FALL OF WICKETS – 1-44, 2-83, 3-218, 4-284, 5-289, 6-289, 7-317, 8-360, 9-384, 10-439
BOWLING – Dilley 35-6-92-5, Foster 37-8-107-2, Emburey 26-7-48-0, Edmonds 24.3-12-50-1, Botham 48-13-121-1, Gatting 3-0-6-0

ENGLAND 1st Innings

B.C.Broad	c Yousuf b Imran Khan	54
R.T.Robinson	c Yousuf b Wasim Akram	80
C.W.J.Athey	b Imran Khan	0
D.I.Gower	c Yousuf b Imran Khan	61
*M.W.Gatting	c Wasim Akram b Imran	124
+B.N.French	b Imran Khan	0
I.T.Botham	c & b Wasim Akram	37
J.E.Emburey	lbw b Wasim Akram	58
N.A.Foster	run out	29
P.H.Edmonds	not out	24
G.R.Dilley	b Imran Khan	2
Extras (b 1, lb 24, w 11, nb 16)		52
TOTAL		521

FALL OF WICKETS – 1-119, 2-132, 3-157, 4-251, 5-251, 6-300, 7-443, 8-484, 9-512, 10-521
BOWLING – Imran Khan 41.5-8-129-6, Wasim Akram 43-13-83-3, Abdul Qadir 21-4-65-0, Mudassar Nazar 35-7-97-0, Mohsin Kamal 29-2-122-0

PAKISTAN 2nd Innings

Mudassar Nazar	b Dilley	10
Shoaib Mohammad	lbw b Foster	50
Mansoor Akhtar	lbw b Foster	17
Javed Miandad	c Emburey b Foster	4
Salim Malik	c & b Botham	17
Ijaz Ahmed	lbw b Botham	11
*Imran Khan	lbw b Foster	37
+Salim Yousuf	c Gatting b Edmonds	17
Wasim Akram	c Edmonds b Dilley	6
Abdul Qadir	run out	20
Mohsin Kamal	not out	0
Extras (lb 13, w 1, nb 2)		16
TOTAL		205

FALL OF WICKETS – 1-47, 2-80, 3-85, 4-104, 5-104, 6-116, 7-156, 8-165, 9-204, 10-205
BOWLING – Dilley 18-3-53-2, Foster 27-5-59-4, Emburey 4-1-3-0, Edmonds 4-1-11-1, Botham 20.3-3-66-2

ENGLAND 2nd Innings

B.C.Broad	c Mudassar Nazar b Imran	30
R.T.Robinson	c Imran b Wasim Akram	4
D.I.Gower	b Imran Khan	18
I.T.Botham	c Mohsin Kamal b Wasim	6
*M.W.Gatting	run out	8
C.W.J.Athey	not out	14
J.E.Emburey	run out	20
P.H.Edmonds	run out	0
+B.N.French	not out	1
DID NOT BAT – N.A.Foster and G.R.Dilley		
Extras (lb 7, w 1)		8
TOTAL (for 7 wkts)		109

FALL OF WICKETS – 1-37, 2-39, 3-53, 4-72, 5-73, 6-108, 7-108
BOWLING – Imran Khan 9-0-61-2, Wasim Akram 8.4-0-41-2

ENGLAND v PAKISTAN

at The Oval on 6th, 7th, 8th, 10th, 11th August 1987
Toss: Pakistan
Umpires: D.J.Constant and K.E.Palmer
Match drawn

PAKISTAN

Mudassar Nazar	c Moxon b Botham	73
Ramiz Raja	b Botham	14
Mansoor Akhtar	c French b Dilley	5
Javed Miandad	c & b Dilley	260
Salim Malik	c Gower b Botham	102
*Imran Khan	run out	118
Ijaz Ahmed	c Moxon b Dilley	69
+Salim Yousuf	c & b Dilley	42
Wasim Akram	c Botham b Dilley	5
Abdul Qadir	c Moxon b Dilley	0
Tausif Ahmed	not out	0
Extras (b 2, lb 18)		20
TOTAL		708

FALL OF WICKETS – 1-40, 2-45, 3-148, 4-382, 5-573, 6-601, 7-690, 8-707, 9-707, 10-708
BOWLING – Dilley 47.3-10-154-6, Foster 12-3-32-0, Botham 52-7-217-3, Emburey 61-10-143-0, Edmonds 32-8-97-0, Gatting 10-2-18-0, Moxon 6-2-27-0

ENGLAND 1st Innings

B.C.Broad	c Salim Yousuf b Imran	0
M.D.Moxon	c Miandad b Abdul Qadir	8
R.T.Robinson	b Abdul Qadir	30
D.I.Gower	b Tausif Ahmed	28
*M.W.Gatting	c Imran b Abdul Qadir	61
I.T.Botham	b Abdul Qadir	34
J.E.Emburey	c Salim Malik b Abdul Qadir	53
+B.N.French	c Salim Malik b Abdul Qadir	1
N.A.Foster	c Ijaz Ahmed b Tausif Ahmed	4
P.H.Edmonds	lbw b Abdul Qadir	2
G.R.Dilley	not out	0
Extras (b 4, lb 3, w 1, nb 3)		11
TOTAL		232

FALL OF WICKETS – 1-0, 2-32, 3-54, 4-78, 5-165, 6-166, 7-184, 8-198, 9-223, 10-232
BOWLING – Imran Khan 18-2-39-1, Wasim Akram 14-2-37-0, Abdul Qadir 44.4-15-96-7, Tausif Ahmed 23-9-53-2

ENGLAND 2nd Innings

B.C.Broad	c Ijaz Ahmed b Abdul Qadir	42
M.D.Moxon	c Salim Yousuf b Tausif	15
R.T.Robinson	c Wasim b Abdul Qadir	10
D.I.Gower	c Mudassar b Abdul Qadir	34
*M.W.Gatting	not out	150
I.T.Botham	not out	51
DID NOT BAT – J.E.Emburey, +B.N.French, N.A.Foster, P.H.Edmonds, G.R.Dilley		
Extras (b 4, lb 5, w 1, nb 3)		13
TOTAL (for 4 wkts)		315

FALL OF WICKETS – 1-22, 2-40, 3-89, 4-139
BOWLING – Imran Khan 26.3-8-59-0, Wasim Akram 6-3-3-0, Abdul Qadir 53-21-115-3, Tausif Ahmed 46.3-15-98-1, Mudassar Nazar 6-0-21-0, Javed Miandad 4-2-10-0

1987

ENGLAND v WEST INDIES

at Trent Bridge on 2nd, 3rd, 4th, 6th, 7th June 1988
Toss: England
Umpires: H.D.Bird and J.Birkenshaw
Match drawn

ENGLAND 1st Innings

G.A.Gooch	b Marshall	73
B.C.Broad	b Marshall	54
*M.W.Gatting	c Logie b Marshall	5
D.I.Gower	c Dujon b Ambrose	18
A.J.Lamb	lbw b Marshall	0
D.R.Pringle	b Marshall	39
+P.R.Downton	not out	16
J.E.Emburey	c Dujon b Marshall	0
P.A.J.DeFreitas	b Ambrose	3
P.W.Jarvis	b Ambrose	6
G.R.Dilley	b Ambrose	2
Extras (lb 13, w 5, nb 11)		29
TOTAL		245

FALL OF WICKETS – 1-125, 2-141, 3-161, 4-161, 5-186, 6-223, 7-223, 8-235, 9-243, 10-245
BOWLING – Marshall 30-4-69-6, Patterson 16-2-49-0, Ambrose 26-10-53-4, Walsh 20-4-39-0, Hooper 8-1-20-0, Richards 1-0-2-0

WEST INDIES

C.G.Greenidge	c Downton b Jarvis	25
D.L.Haynes	c Downton b Jarvis	60
R.B.Richardson	c Gatting b Emburey	17
*I.V.A.Richards	c Gooch b DeFreitas	80
C.L.Hooper	c Downton b DeFreitas	84
A.L.Logie	c Gooch b Pringle	20
+P.J.L.Dujon	c & b Dilley	16
M.D.Marshall	b Emburey	72
C.E.L.Ambrose	run out	43
C.A.Walsh	not out	3
DID NOT BAT – B.P.Patterson		
Extras (b 6, lb 8, nb 14)		28
TOTAL (for 9 wkts dec)		448

FALL OF WICKETS _ 1-54, 2-84, 3-159, 4-231, 5-271, 6-309, 7-334, 8-425, 9-448
BOWLING – Dilley 34-5-101-1, DeFreitas 27-5-93-2, Jarvis 18.1-1-63-2, Pringle 34-11-82-1, Emburey 16-4-95-2

ENGLAND 2nd Innings

G.A.Gooch	c Dujon b Patterson	146
B.C.Broad	c Dujon b Ambrose	16
*M.W.Gatting	b Marshall	29
D.I.Gower	not out	88
A.J.Lamb	not out	6
DID NOT BAT – D.R.Pringle, +P.R. Downton, J.E.Emburey, P.A.J.DeFreitas, P.W.Jarvis, G.R.Dilley		
Extras (lb 10, nb 6)		16
TOTAL (for 3 wkts)		301

FALL OF WICKETS – 1-39, 2-116, 3-277
BOWLING – Marshall 13-4-23-1, Patterson 24-6-69-1, Ambrose 23-4-56-1, Walsh 25-5-84-0, Hooper 14-1-33-0, Richards 9-1-26-0

ENGLAND v WEST INDIES

at Lord's on 16th, 17th, 18th, 20th, 21st June 1988
Toss: West Indies
Umpires: K.E.Palmer and D.R.Shepherd
West Indies won by 134 runs

WEST INDIES 1st Innings

C.G.Greenidge	c Downton b Dilley	22
D.L.Haynes	c Moxon b Dilley	12
R.B.Richardson	c Emburey b Dilley	5
*I.V.A.Richards	c Downton b Dilley	6
C.L.Hooper	c Downton b Small	3
A.L.Logie	c Emburey b Small	81
+P.J.L.Dujon	b Emburey	53
M.D.Marshall	c Gooch b Dilley	11
C.E.L.Ambrose	c Gower b Small	0
C.A.Walsh	not out	9
B.P.Patterson	b Small	0
Extras (lb 6, nb 1)		7
TOTAL		209

FALL OF WICKETS – 1-21, 2-40, 3-47, 4-50, 5-54, 6-184, 7-199, 8-199, 9-199, 10-209
BOWLING – Dilley 23-6-55-5, Jarvis 13-2-47-0, Small 18.5-5-64-4, Pringle 7-3-20-0, Emburey 6-2-17-1

ENGLAND 1st Innings

G.A.Gooch	b Marshall	44
B.C.Broad	lbw b Marshall	0
M.D.Moxon	c Richards b Ambrose	26
D.I.Gower	c sub b Walsh	46
A.J.Lamb	lbw b Marshall	10
D.R.Pringle	c Dujon b Walsh	1
+P.R.Downton	lbw b Marshall	11
*J.E.Emburey	b Patterson	7
G.C.Small	not out	5
P.W.Jarvis	c Haynes b Marshall	7
G.R.Dilley	b Marshall	0
Extras (lb 6, nb 2)		8
TOTAL		165

FALL OF WICKETS – 1-13, 2-58, 3-112, 4-129, 5-134, 6-140, 7-153, 8-157, 9-165, 10-165
BOWLING – Marshall 18-5-32-6, Patterson 13-3-52-1, Ambrose 12-1-39-1, Walsh 16-6-36-2

WEST INDIES 2nd Innings

C.G.Greenidge	c Emburey b Dilley	103
D.L.Haynes	c Downton b Dilley	5
R.B.Richardson	lbw b Pringle	26
*I.V.A.Richards	b Pringle	72
C.L.Hooper	c Downton b Jarvis	11
A.L.Logie	not out	95
+P.J.L.Dujon	b Jarvis	52
M.D.Marshall	b Jarvis	6
C.E.L.Ambrose	b Dilley	0
C.A.Walsh	b Dilley	0
B.P.Patterson	c Downton b Jarvis	2
Extras (lb 19, w 1, nb 5)		25
TOTAL		397

FALL OF WICKETS – 1-32, 2-115, 3-198, 4-226, 5-240, 6-371, 7-379, 8-380, 9-384, 10-397
BOWLING – Dilley 27-6-73-4, Jarvis 26-3-107-4, Small 19-1-76-0, Pringle 21-4-60-2, Emburey 15-1-62-0

ENGLAND 2nd Innings

G.A.Gooch	lbw b Marshall	16
B.C.Broad	c Dujon b Marshall	1
M.D.Moxon	run out	14
D.I.Gower	c Richardson b Patterson	1
A.J.Lamb	run out	113
D.R.Pringle	lbw b Walsh	0
+P.R.Downton	lbw b Marshall	27
*J.E.Emburey	b Ambrose	30
G.C.Small	c Richards b Marshall	7
P.W.Jarvis	not out	29
G.R.Dilley	c Richardson b Patterson	28
Extras (b 5, lb 20, w 2, nb 14)		41
TOTAL		307

FALL OF WICKETS – 1-27, 2-29, 3-31, 4-104, 5-105, 6-161, 7-212, 8-232, 9-254, 10-307
BOWLING – Marshall 25-5-60-4, Patterson 21.5-2-100-2, Ambrose 20-4-47-1, Walsh 20-1-75-1

ENGLAND v WEST INDIES

at Old Trafford on 30th June, 1st, 2nd, 4th, 5th July 1988
Toss: England
Umpires: D.J.Constant and N.T.Plews
West Indies won by an innings and 156 runs

ENGLAND 1st Innings

G.A.Gooch	c Dujon b Benjamin	27
M.D.Moxon	b Marshall	0
M.W.Gatting	lbw b Marshall	0
D.I.Gower	c Harper b Walsh	9
A.J.Lamb	c Greenidge b Ambrose	33
D.J.Capel	b Benjamin	1
+P.R.Downton	c Greenidge b Walsh	24
*J.E.Emburey	c Dujon b Walsh	1
P.A.J.DeFreitas	c Greenidge b Ambrose	15
G.R.Dilley	c Harper b Walsh	14
J.H.Childs	not out	2
Extras (lb 4, nb 5)		9
TOTAL		135

FALL OF WICKETS – 1-12, 2-14, 3-33, 4-55, 5-61, 6-94, 7-98, 8-113, 9-123, 10-135
BOWLING – Marshall 12-5-19-2, Ambrose 17-5-35-2, Walsh 18.2-4-46-4, Benjamin 13-4-31-2

WEST INDIES

C.G.Greenidge	lbw b DeFreitas	45
R.B.Richardson	b Dilley	23
C.L.Hooper	lbw b Childs	15
*I.V.A.Richards	b Capel	47
A.L.Logie	lbw b Dilley	39
+P.J.L.Dujon	c Capel b Dilley	67
R.A.Harper	b Dilley	74
M.D.Marshall	not out	43
C.E.L.Ambrose	not out	7
DID NOT BAT – W.K.M.Benjamin and C.A.Walsh		
Extras (lb 21, nb 3)		24
TOTAL (for 7 wkts dec)		384

FALL OF WICKETS – 1-35, 2-77, 3-101, 4-175, 5-187, 6-281, 7-373
BOWLING – Dilley 28.1-4-99-4, Emburey 25-7-54-0, DeFreitas 35-5-81-1, Capel 12-2-38-1, Childs 40-12-91-1

ENGLAND 2nd Innings

G.A.Gooch	lbw b Marshall	1
M.D.Moxon	c Richards b Benjamin	15
M.W.Gatting	c Richardson b Marshall	4
D.I.Gower	c Richardson b Marshall	34
A.J.Lamb	c Logie b Ambrose	9
D.J.Capel	c sub b Marshall	0
+P.R.Downton	c Harper b Marshall	6
*J.E.Emburey	c Logie b Ambrose	8
P.A.J.DeFreitas	c Harper b Marshall	0
G.R.Dilley	b Marshall	4
J.H.Childs	not out	0
Extras (b 1, lb 10, nb 1)		12
TOTAL		93

FALL OF WICKETS – 1-6, 2-22, 3-36, 4-73, 5-73, 6-73, 7-87, 8-87, 9-93, 10-93
BOWLING – Marshall 15.4-5-22-7, Ambrose 16-4-36-2, Walsh 4-1-10-0, Benjamin 4-1-6-1, Harper 2-1-4-0, Hooper 1-0-4-0

1988

ENGLAND v WEST INDIES

at Headingley on 21st, 22nd, 23rd, 25th, 26th July 1988
Toss: West Indies
Umpires: H.D.Bird and D.R.Shepherd
West Indies won by 10 wickets

ENGLAND 1st Innings

G.A.Gooch	c Dujon b Marshall	9
T.S.Curtis	lbw b Benjamin	12
C.W.J.Athey	lbw b Ambrose	16
D.I.Gower	c Dujon b Benjamin	13
A.J.Lamb	retired hurt	64
R.A.Smith	c Dujon b Ambrose	38
*C.S.Cowdrey	lbw b Marshall	0
+C.J.Richards	b Ambrose	2
D.R.Pringle	c Dujon b Marshall	0
N.A.Foster	not out	8
G.R.Dilley	c Hooper b Ambrose	8
Extras (b 1, lb 18, w 6, nb 6)		31
TOTAL		201

FALL OF WICKETS – 1-14, 2-43, 3-58, 4-80, 5-183, 6-183, 7-185, 8-185, 9-201
BOWLING – Marshall 23-8-55-3, Ambrose 25.1-8-58-4, Benjamin 9-2-27-2, Walsh 12-4-42-0

WEST INDIES 1st Innings

D.L.Haynes	lbw b Pringle	54
+P.J.L.Dujon	c Smith b Dilley	13
C.L.Hooper	lbw b Foster	19
*I.V.A.Richards	c Curtis b Foster	18
A.L.Logie	c Foster b Pringle	44
K.L.T.Arthurton	c Richards b Pringle	27
R.A.Harper	c Gower b Foster	56
M.D.Marshall	c Gooch b Pringle	3
C.E.L.Ambrose	lbw b Pringle	8
W.K.M.Benjamin	run out	9
C.A.Walsh	not out	9
Extras (lb 15)		15
TOTAL		275

FALL OF WICKETS – 1-15, 2-61, 3-97, 4-137, 5-156, 6-194, 7-210, 8-222, 9-245, 10-275
BOWLING – Dilley 20-5-59-1, Foster 32.2-6-98-3, Pringle 27-7-95-5, Cowdrey 2-0-8-0

ENGLAND 2nd Innings

G.A.Gooch	c Hooper b Walsh	50
T.S.Curtis	b Ambrose	12
C.W.J.Athey	c Dujon b Walsh	11
D.I.Gower	c Dujon b Marshall	2
R.A.Smith	lbw b Marshall	11
*C.S.Cowdrey	b Walsh	5
+C.J.Richards	b Ambrose	8
A.J.Lamb	c Dujon b Ambrose	19
D.R.Pringle	b Benjamin	3
N.A.Foster	c Hooper b Benjamin	0
G.R.Dilley	not out	2
Extras (b 3, lb 8, nb 4)		15
TOTAL		138

FALL OF WICKETS – 1-56, 2-80, 3-85, 4-85, 5-105, 6-105, 7-127, 8-132, 9-132, 10-138
BOWLING – Marshall 17-4-47-2, Ambrose 19.5-4-40-3, Benjamin 5-4-2-2, Walsh 20-9-38-3

WEST INDIES 2nd Innings

D.L.Haynes	not out	25
+P.J.L.Dujon	not out	40

DID NOT BAT – C.L.Hooper, *I.V.A.Richards, A.L.Logie, K.L.T.Arthurton, R.A.Harper, M.D.Marshall, C.E.L.Ambrose, W.K.M.Benjamin, C.A.Walsh

Extras (lb 2)		2
TOTAL (for 0 wkts)		67

BOWLING – Dilley 4-0-16-0, Foster 7-1-36-0, Cowdrey 3.3-0-13-0

ENGLAND v WEST INDIES

at The Oval on 4th, 5th, 6th, 8th August 1988
Toss: England
Umpires: H.D.Bird and K.E.Palmer
West Indies won by 8 wickets

ENGLAND 1st Innings

*G.A.Gooch	c Logie b Ambrose	9
T.S.Curtis	c Dujon b Benjamin	30
R.J.Bailey	c Dujon b Ambrose	43
R.A.Smith	c Harper b Marshall	57
M.P.Maynard	c Dujon b Ambrose	3
D.J.Capel	c Marshall b Harper	16
+C.J.Richards	c Logie b Harper	0
D.R.Pringle	c Dujon b Marshall	1
P.A.J.DeFreitas	c Haynes b Harper	18
N.A.Foster	c sub b Marshall	7
J.H.Childs	not out	0
Extras (lb 6, nb 15)		21
TOTAL		205

FALL OF WICKETS – 1-12, 2-77, 3-116, 4-121, 5-160, 6-160, 7-165, 8-196, 9-198, 10-205
BOWLING – Marshall 24.3-3-64-3, Ambrose 20-6-31-3, Walsh 10-1-21-0, Benjamin 14-2-33-1, Harper 21-7-50-3, Hooper 1-1-0-0

WEST INDIES 1st Innings

C.G.Greenidge	c DeFreitas b Foster	10
D.L.Haynes	c Richards b Foster	2
C.L.Hooper	c Gooch b Foster	11
*I.V.A.Richards	c Curtis b Foster	0
A.L.Logie	c Gooch b Foster	47
+P.J.L.Dujon	lbw b Pringle	64
R.A.Harper	run out	17
M.D.Marshall	c & b Childs	0
C.E.L.Ambrose	not out	17
W.K.M.Benjamin	b Pringle	0
C.A.Walsh	c DeFreitas b Pringle	5
Extras (lb 7, w 1, nb 2)		10
TOTAL		183

FALL OF WICKETS – 1-9, 2-16, 3-16, 4-57, 5-126, 6-155, 7-156, 8-167, 9-168, 10-183
BOWLING – Foster 16-2-64-5, DeFreitas 13-4-33-0, Pringle 17-4-45-3, Capel 7-0-21-0, Childs 6-1-13-1

ENGLAND 2nd Innings

*G.A.Gooch	c Greenidge b Ambrose	84
T.S.Curtis	lbw b Marshall	15
R.J.Bailey	b Benjamin	3
R.A.Smith	lbw b Benjamin	0
N.A.Foster	c Logie b Benjamin	34
M.P.Maynard	c & b Benjamin	10
D.J.Capel	lbw b Walsh	12
+C.J.Richards	c Dujon b Walsh	3
D.R.Pringle	b Harper	8
P.A.J.DeFreitas	c Haynes b Harper	0
J.H.Childs	not out	0
Extras (b 3, lb 15, nb 15)		33
TOTAL		202

FALL OF WICKETS – 1-50, 2-55, 3-55, 4-108, 5-125, 6-139, 7-157, 8-175, 9-177, 10-202
BOWLING – Marshall 25-6-52-1, Ambrose 24.1-10-50-1, Walsh 12-5-21-2, Benjamin 22-4-52-4, Harper 6-3-9-2

WEST INDIES 2nd Innings

C.G.Greenidge	c Richards b Childs	77
D.L.Haynes	not out	77
C.L.Hooper	b Foster	23
A.L.Logie	not out	38

DID NOT BAT – *I.V.A.Richards, +P.J.L.Dujon, R.A.Harper, M.D.Marshall, C.E.L.Ambrose, W.K.M.Benjamin, C.A.Walsh

Extras (b 2, lb 3, nb 6)		11
TOTAL (for 2 wkts)		226

FALL OF WICKETS – 1-131, 2-162
BOWLING – Foster 18-3-52-1, DeFreitas 17-2-46-0, Pringle 13-4-24-0, Capel 3-0-20-0, Childs 40-16-79-1

ENGLAND v SRI LANKA

at Lord's on 25th, 26th, 27th, 29th, 30th August 1988
Toss: England
Umpires: D.J.Constant and J.W.Holder
England won by 7 wickets

SRI LANKA 1st Innings

D.S.B.P.Kuruppu	c Gooch b Newport	46
+S.A.R.Silva	c Russell b Foster	1
M.A.R.Samarasekera	c Russell b Foster	0
P.A.de Silva	c Gooch b Newport	3
*R.S.Madugalle	lbw b Foster	3
A.Ranatunga	lbw b Newport	5
L.R.D.Mendis	c Smith b Lawrence	21
J.R.Ratnayeke	not out	59
M.A.W.R.Madurasinghe	run out	4
C.P.H.Ramanayake	lbw b Pringle	0
G.F.Labrooy	lbw b Pringle	42
Extras (b 1, lb 7, nb 2)		10
TOTAL		194

FALL OF WICKETS – 1-7, 2-44, 3-52, 4-53, 5-61, 6-63, 7-123, 8-127, 9-130, 10-194
BOWLING – Foster 21-5-51-3, Lawrence 15-4-37-1, Newport 21-4-77-3, Pringle 6.5-1-17-2, Emburey 2-1-4-0

ENGLAND 1st Innings

*G.A.Gooch	lbw b Ratnayeke	75
R.T.Robinson	c Samarasekera b Ratnayeke	19
+R.C.Russell	c Samarasekera b Labrooy	94
K.J.Barnett	c Ranatunga b Labrooy	66
A.J.Lamb	b Labrooy	63
R.A.Smith	b Ranatunga	31
D.R.Pringle	c Silva b Labrooy	14
J.E.Emburey	c de Silva b Samarasekera	0
P.J.Newport	c de Silva b Ramanayake	26
N.A.Foster	not out	14
D.V.Lawrence	c Mendis b Ramanayake	4
Extras (b 1, lb 3, w 2, nb 17)		23
TOTAL		429

FALL OF WICKETS – 1-40, 2-171, 3-233, 4-320, 5-358, 6-373, 7-378, 8-383, 9-420, 10-429
BOWLING – Ratnayeke 32-3-107-2, Labrooy 40-7-119-4, Ramanayake 27.2-3-86-2, Madurasinghe 16-4-41-0, Samarasekera 22-5-66-1, Ranatunga 6-3-6-1

SRI LANKA 2nd Innings

D.S.B.P.Kuruppu	c Barnett b Foster	25
+S.A.R.Silva	c Russell b Newport	16
M.A.R.Samarasekera	lbw b Emburey	57
P.A.de Silva	lbw b Lawrence	18
*R.S.Madugalle	b Foster	20
A.Ranatunga	b Newport	78
L.R.D.Mendis	lbw b Pringle	56
J.R.Ratnayeke	c Lamb b Lawrence	32
M.A.W.R.Madurasinghe	b Newport	2
G.F.Labrooy	not out	9
C.P.H.Ramanayake	c Gooch b Newport	2
Extras (lb 8, nb 8)		16
TOTAL		331

FALL OF WICKETS – 1-43, 2-51, 3-96, 4-145, 5-147, 6-251, 7-309, 8-311, 9-323, 10-331
BOWLING – Foster 33-10-98-2, Lawrence 21-4-74-2, Newport 26.3-7-87-4, Pringle 11-2-30-1, Emburey 18-9-34-1

ENGLAND 2nd Innings

*G.A.Gooch	c Silva b Samarasekera	36
R.T.Robinson	not out	34
K.J.Barnett	c Silva b Samarasekera	0
A.J.Lamb	c de Silva b Ranatunga	8
R.A.Smith	not out	8

DID NOT BAT – +R.C.Russell, D.R.Pringle, J.E.Emburey, P.J.Newport, N.A.Foster, D.V.Lawrence

Extras (lb 8, w 2, nb 4)		14
TOTAL (for 3 wkts)		100

FALL OF WICKETS – 1-73, 2-73, 3-82
BOWLING – Ratnayeke 7-1-16-0, Labrooy 9-0-24-0, Samarasekera 10-0-38-2, Ranatunga 8.4-4-14-1

1988

ENGLAND v AUSTRALIA

at Headingley on 8th, 9th, 10th, 12th, 13th June 1989
Toss: England
Umpires: J.W.Holder and D.R.Shepherd
Australia won by 210 runs

AUSTRALIA 1st Innings

G.R.Marsh	lbw b DeFreitas	16
M.A.Taylor	lbw b Foster	136
D.C.Boon	c Russell b Foster	9
*A.R.Border	c Foster b DeFreitas	66
D.M.Jones	c Russell b Newport	79
S.R.Waugh	not out	177
+I.A.Healy	c & b Newport	16
M.G.Hughes	c Russell b Foster	71
G.F.Lawson	not out	10

DID NOT BAT – G.D.Campbell, T.M.Alderman
Extras (lb 13, w 1, nb 7)   21
TOTAL (for 7 wkts dec)   601

FALL OF WICKETS – 1-44, 2-57, 3-174, 4-273, 5-411, 6-441, 7-588
BOWLING – DeFreitas 45.3-8-140-2, Foster 46-14-109-3, Newport 39-5-153-2, Pringle 33-5-123-0, Gooch 9-1-31-0, Barnett 6-0-32-0

ENGLAND 1st Innings

G.A.Gooch	lbw b Alderman	13
B.C.Broad	b Hughes	37
K.J.Barnett	lbw b Alderman	80
A.J.Lamb	c Boon b Alderman	125
*D.I.Gower	c Healy b Lawson	26
R.A.Smith	lbw b Alderman	66
D.R.Pringle	lbw b Campbell	6
P.J.Newport	c Boon b Lawson	36
+R.C.Russell	c Marsh b Lawson	15
P.A.J.DeFreitas	lbw b Alderman	1
N.A.Foster	not out	2

Extras (b 5, lb 7, w 1, nb 10)   23
TOTAL   430

FALL OF WICKETS – 1-35, 2-81, 3-195, 4-243, 5-323, 6-338, 7-392, 8-421, 9-424, 10-430
BOWLING – Alderman 37-7-107-5, Lawson 34.5-6-105-3, Campbell 14-0-82-1, Hughes 28-7-92-1, Waugh 6-2-27-0, Border 2-1-5-0

AUSTRALIA 2nd Innings

G.R.Marsh	c Russell b Foster	6
M.A.Taylor	c Broad b Pringle	60
D.C.Boon	lbw b DeFreitas	43
*A.R.Border	not out	60
D.M.Jones	not out	40

DID NOT BAT – S.R.Waugh, +I.A.Healy, M.G.Hughes, G.F.Lawson, G.D.Campbell, T.M.Alderman
Extras (b 2, lb 5, w 9, nb 5)   21
TOTAL (for 3 wkts dec)   230

FALL OF WICKETS – 1-14, 2-97, 3-129
BOWLING – DeFreitas 18-2-76-1, Foster 19-4-65-1, Newport 5-2-22-0, Pringle 12.5-1-60-1

ENGLAND 2nd Innings

G.A.Gooch	lbw b Hughes	68
B.C.Broad	lbw b Alderman	7
K.J.Barnett	c Taylor b Alderman	34
A.J.Lamb	c Boon b Alderman	4
*D.I.Gower	c Healy b Lawson	34
R.A.Smith	c Border b Lawson	0
D.R.Pringle	c Border b Alderman	0
P.J.Newport	c Marsh b Alderman	8
+R.C.Russell	c Healy b Hughes	2
P.A.J.DeFreitas	b Hughes	21
N.A.Foster	not out	1

Extras (b 4, lb 3, nb 5)   12
TOTAL   191

FALL OF WICKETS – 1-17, 2-67, 3-77, 4-134, 5-134, 6-153, 7-153, 8-166, 9-170, 10-191
BOWLING – Alderman 20-7-44-5, Lawson 11-2-58-2, Campbell 10-0-42-0, Hughes 9.2-0-36-3, Border 5-3-4-0

ENGLAND v AUSTRALIA

at Lord's on 22nd, 23rd, 24th, 26th, 27th June 1989
Toss: England
Umpires: H.D.Bird and N.T.Plews
Australia won by 6 wickets

ENGLAND 1st Innings

G.A.Gooch	c Healy b Waugh	60
B.C.Broad	lbw b Alderman	18
K.J.Barnett	c Boon b Hughes	14
M.W.Gatting	c Boon b Hughes	0
*D.I.Gower	b Lawson	57
R.A.Smith	c Hohns b Lawson	32
J.E.Emburey	b Alderman	0
+R.C.Russell	not out	64
N.A.Foster	c Jones b Hughes	16
P.W.Jarvis	c Marsh b Hughes	6
G.R.Dilley	c Border b Alderman	7

Extras (lb 9, nb 3)   12
TOTAL   286

FALL OF WICKETS – 1-31, 2-52, 3-58, 4-131, 5-180, 6-185, 7-191, 8-237, 9-253, 10-286
BOWLING – Alderman 20.5-4-60-3, Lawson 27-8-88-2, Hughes 23-6-71-4, Waugh 9-3-49-1, Hohns 7-3-9-0

AUSTRALIA 1st Innings

G.R.Marsh	c Russell b Dilley	3
M.A.Taylor	lbw b Foster	62
D.C.Boon	c Gooch b Dilley	94
*A.R.Border	c Smith b Emburey	35
D.M.Jones	lbw b Foster	27
S.R.Waugh	not out	152
+I.A.Healy	c Russell b Jarvis	3
M.G.Hughes	c Gooch b Foster	30
T.V.Hohns	b Emburey	21
G.F.Lawson	c Broad b Emburey	74
T.M.Alderman	lbw b Emburey	8

Extras (lb 11, nb 8)   19
TOTAL   528

FALL OF WICKETS – 1-6, 2-151, 3-192, 4-221, 5-235, 6-265, 7-331, 8-381, 9-511, 10-528
BOWLING – Dilley 34-3-141-2, Foster 45-7-129-3, Jarvis 31-3-150-1, Emburey 42-12-88-4, Gooch 6-2-9-0

ENGLAND 2nd Innings

G.A.Gooch	lbw b Alderman	0
B.C.Broad	b Lawson	20
K.J.Barnett	c Jones b Alderman	3
M.W.Gatting	lbw b Alderman	22
*D.I.Gower	c Border b Hughes	106
R.A.Smith	b Alderman	96
+R.C.Russell	c Boon b Lawson	29
J.E.Emburey	not out	36
N.A.Foster	lbw b Alderman	4
P.W.Jarvis	lbw b Alderman	5
G.R.Dilley	c Boon b Hughes	24

Extras (b 6, lb 6, nb 2)   14
TOTAL   359

FALL OF WICKETS – 1-0, 2-18, 3-28, 4-84, 5-223, 6-274, 7-300, 8-304, 9-314, 10-359
BOWLING – Alderman 38-6-128-6, Lawson 39-10-99-2, Hughes 24-8-44-2, Waugh 7-2-20-0, Hohns 13-6-33-0, Border 9-3-23-0

AUSTRALIA 2nd Innings

G.R.Marsh	b Dilley	1
M.A.Taylor	c Gooch b Foster	27
D.C.Boon	not out	58
*A.R.Border	c sub b Foster	1
D.M.Jones	c Russell b Foster	0
S.R.Waugh	not out	21

DID NOT BAT – +I.A.Healy, M.G.Hughes, T.V.Hohns, G.F.Lawson, T.M.Alderman
Extras (b 3, lb 4, nb 4)   11
TOTAL (for 4 wkts)   119

FALL OF WICKETS – 1-9, 2-51, 3-61, 4-67
BOWLING – Dilley 10-2-27-1, Foster 18-3-39-3, Jarvis 9.2-0-38-0, Emburey 3-0-8-0

ENGLAND v AUSTRALIA

at Edgbaston on 6th, 7th, 8th, 10th, 11th July 1989
Toss: Australia
Umpires: H.D.Bird and J.W.Holder
Match drawn

AUSTRALIA 1st Innings

G.R.Marsh	lbw b Botham	42
M.A.Taylor	st Russell b Emburey	43
D.C.Boon	run out	38
*A.R.Border	b Emburey	8
D.M.Jones	c sub b Fraser	157
S.R.Waugh	b Fraser	43
+I.A.Healy	b Fraser	2
M.G.Hughes	c Botham b Dilley	2
T.V.Hohns	c Gooch b Dilley	40
G.F.Lawson	b Fraser	12
T.M.Alderman	not out	0

Extras (lb 20, nb 17)   37
TOTAL   424

FALL OF WICKETS – 1-88, 2-94, 3-105, 4-201, 5-272, 6-289, 7-299, 8-391, 9-421, 10-424
BOWLING – Dilley 31-5-123-2, Jarvis 23-4-82-0, Fraser 33-8-63-4, Botham 26-5-75-1, Emburey 29-5-61-2

ENGLAND

G.A.Gooch	lbw b Lawson	8
T.S.Curtis	lbw b Hughes	41
*D.I.Gower	lbw b Alderman	8
C.J.Tavare	c Taylor b Alderman	2
K.J.Barnett	c Healy b Waugh	10
I.T.Botham	b Hughes	46
+R.C.Russell	c Taylor b Hohns	42
J.E.Emburey	c Boon b Lawson	26
A.R.C.Fraser	run out	12
P.W.Jarvis	lbw b Alderman	22
G.R.Dilley	not out	11

Extras (b 1, lb 2, nb 11)   14
TOTAL   242

FALL OF WICKETS – 1-17, 2-42, 3-47, 4-75, 5-75, 6-171, 7-171, 8-185, 9-215, 10-242
BOWLING – Alderman 26.3-6-61-3, Lawson 21-4-54-2, Hughes 22-4-68-2, Waugh 11-3-38-1, Hohns 16-8-18-1

AUSTRALIA 2nd Innings

G.R.Marsh	b Jarvis	42
M.A.Taylor	c Botham b Gooch	51
D.C.Boon	not out	22
+I.A.Healy	not out	33

DID NOT BAT – *A.R.Border, D.M.Jones, S.R.Waugh, M.G.Hughes, T.V.Hohns, G.F.Lawson, T.M.Alderman
Extras (b 4, lb 4, nb 2)   10
TOTAL (for 2 wkts)   158

FALL OF WICKETS – 1-81, 2-109
BOWLING – Dilley 10-4-27-0, Jarvis 6-1-20-1, Fraser 12-0-29-0, Emburey 20-8-37-0, Gooch 14-5-30-1, Curtis 3-0-7-0

_1989_

ENGLAND v AUSTRALIA

at Old Trafford on 27th, 28th, 29th, 31st July, 1st August 1989
Toss: England
Umpires: J.H.Hampshire and B.J.Meyer
Australia won by 9 wickets

ENGLAND 1st Innings

G.A.Gooch	b Lawson	11
T.S.Curtis	b Lawson	22
R.T.Robinson	lbw b Lawson	0
R.A.Smith	c Hohns b Hughes	143
*D.I.Gower	lbw b Hohns	35
I.T.Botham	b Hohns	0
+R.C.Russell	lbw b Lawson	1
J.E.Emburey	lbw b Hohns	5
N.A.Foster	c Border b Lawson	39
A.R.C.Fraser	lbw b Lawson	2
N.G.B.Cook	not out	0
Extras (lb 2)		2
TOTAL		260

FALL OF WICKETS – 1-23, 2-23, 3-57, 4-132, 5-140, 6-147, 7-158, 8-232, 9-252, 10-260
BOWLING – Alderman 25-13-49-0, Lawson 33-11-72-6, Hughes 17-6-55-1, Hohns 22-7-59-3, Waugh 6-1-23-0

AUSTRALIA 1st Innings

M.A.Taylor	st Russell b Emburey	85
G.R.Marsh	c Russell b Botham	47
D.C.Boon	b Fraser	12
*A.R.Border	c Russell b Foster	80
D.M.Jones	b Botham	69
S.R.Waugh	c Curtis b Fraser	92
+I.A.Healy	lbw b Foster	0
T.V.Hohns	c Gower b Cook	17
M.G.Hughes	b Cook	3
G.F.Lawson	b Fraser	17
T.M.Alderman	not out	6
Extras (b 5, lb 7, w 1, nb 6)		19
TOTAL		447

FALL OF WICKETS – 1-135, 2-143, 3-154, 4-274, 5-362, 6-362, 7-413, 8-423, 9-423, 10-447
BOWLING – Foster 34-12-74-2, Fraser 36.5-4-95-3, Emburey 45-9-118-1, Cook 28-6-85-2, Botham 24-6-63-2

ENGLAND 2nd Innings

G.A.Gooch	c Alderman b Lawson	13
T.S.Curtis	c Boon b Alderman	0
R.T.Robinson	lbw b Lawson	12
R.A.Smith	c Healy b Alderman	1
*D.I.Gower	c Marsh b Lawson	15
I.T.Botham	lbw b Alderman	4
+R.C.Russell	not out	128
J.E.Emburey	b Alderman	64
N.A.Foster	b Alderman	6
A.R.C.Fraser	c Marsh b Hohns	3
N.G.B.Cook	c Healy b Hughes	5
Extras (lb 6, w 2, nb 5)		13
TOTAL		264

FALL OF WICKETS – 1-10, 2-25, 3-27, 4-28, 5-38, 6-59, 7-201, 8-223, 9-255, 10-264
BOWLING – Alderman 27-7-66-5, Lawson 31-8-81-3, Hughes 14.4-2-45-1, Hohns 26-15-37-1, Waugh 4-0-17-0, Border 8-2-12-0

AUSTRALIA 2nd Innings

M.A.Taylor	not out	37
G.R.Marsh	c Robinson b Emburey	31
D.C.Boon	not out	10

DID NOT BAT – *A.R.Border, D.M.Jones, S.R.Waugh, +I.A.Healy, T.V.Hohns, M.G.Hughes, G.F.Lawson, T.M.Alderman

Extras (nb 3)		3
TOTAL (for 1 wkt)		81

FALL OF WICKETS – 1-62
BOWLING – Foster 5-2-5-0, Fraser 10-0-28-0, Emburey 13-3-30-1, Cook 4.5-0-18-0

ENGLAND v AUSTRALIA

at Trent Bridge on 10th, 11th, 12th, 14th August 1989
Toss: Australia
Umpires: N.T.Plews and D.R.Shepherd
Australia won by an innings and 180 runs

AUSTRALIA

G.R.Marsh	c Botham b Cook	138
M.A.Taylor	st Russell b Cook	219
D.C.Boon	st Russell b Cook	73
*A.R.Border	not out	65
D.M.Jones	c Gower b Fraser	22
S.R.Waugh	c Gower b Malcolm	0
+I.A.Healy	b Fraser	5
T.V.Hohns	not out	19

DID NOT BAT – M.G.Hughes, G.F.Lawson, T.M.Alderman

Extras (b 6, lb 23, w 3, nb 29)		61
TOTAL (for 6 wkts dec)		602

FALL OF WICKETS – 1-329, 2-430, 3-502, 4-543, 5-553, 6-560
BOWLING – Fraser 52.3-18-108-2, Malcolm 44-2-166-1, Botham 30-4-103-0, Hemmings 33-9-81-0, Cook 40-10-91-3, Atherton 7-0-24-0

ENGLAND 1st Innings

T.S.Curtis	lbw b Alderman	2
M.D.Moxon	c Waugh b Alderman	0
M.A.Atherton	lbw b Alderman	0
R.A.Smith	c Healy b Alderman	101
*D.I.Gower	c Healy b Lawson	11
+R.C.Russell	c Healy b Lawson	20
E.E.Hemmings	b Alderman	38
A.R.C.Fraser	b Hohns	29
I.T.Botham	c Waugh b Hohns	12
N.G.B.Cook	not out	2
D.E.Malcolm	c Healy b Hughes	9
Extras (lb 18, nb 13)		31
TOTAL		255

FALL OF WICKETS – 1-1, 2-1, 3-14, 4-37, 5-119, 6-172, 7-214, 8-243, 9-244, 10-255
BOWLING – Alderman 19-2-69-5, Lawson 21-5-57-2, Hohns 18-8-48-2, Hughes 7.5-0-40-1, Waugh 11-4-23-0

ENGLAND 2nd Innings

*D.I.Gower	b Lawson	5
T.S.Curtis	lbw b Alderman	6
M.A.Atherton	c & b Hohns	47
R.A.Smith	b Hughes	26
M.D.Moxon	b Alderman	18
+R.C.Russell	b Lawson	1
E.E.Hemmings	lbw b Hughes	35
A.R.C.Fraser	b Hohns	1
N.G.B.Cook	not out	7
D.E.Malcolm	b Hughes	5
I.T.Botham	absent hurt	
Extras (b 3, lb 6, w 1, nb 6)		16
TOTAL		167

FALL OF WICKETS – 1-5, 2-13, 3-67, 4-106, 5-114, 6-120, 7-134, 8-160, 9-167
BOWLING – Alderman 16-6-32-2, Lawson 15-3-51-2, Hohns 12-3-29-2, Hughes 12.3-1-46-3

ENGLAND v AUSTRALIA

at The Oval on 24th, 25th, 26th, 28th, 29th August 1989
Toss: Australia
Umpires: H.D.Bird and K.E.Palmer
Match drawn

AUSTRALIA 1st Innings

G.R.Marsh	c Igglesden b Small	17
M.A.Taylor	c Russell b Igglesden	71
D.C.Boon	c Atherton b Small	46
*A.R.Border	c Russell b Capel	76
D.M.Jones	c Gower b Small	122
S.R.Waugh	b Igglesden	14
+I.A.Healy	c Russell b Pringle	44
T.V.Hohns	c Russell b Pringle	30
M.G.Hughes	lbw b Pringle	21
G.F.Lawson	b Pringle	2
T.M.Alderman	not out	6
Extras (b 1, lb 9, nb 9)		19
TOTAL		468

FALL OF WICKETS – 1-48, 2-130, 3-149, 4-345, 5-347, 6-386, 7-409, 8-447, 9-453, 10-468
BOWLING – Small 40-8-141-3, Igglesden 24-2-91-2, Pringle 24.3-6-70-4, Capel 16-2-66-1, Cook 25-5-78-0, Atherton 1-0-10-0, Gooch 2-1-2-0

ENGLAND 1st Innings

G.A.Gooch	lbw b Alderman	0
J.P.Stephenson	c Waugh b Alderman	25
M.A.Atherton	c Healy b Hughes	12
R.A.Smith	b Lawson	11
*D.I.Gower	c Healy b Alderman	79
D.J.Capel	lbw b Alderman	4
+R.C.Russell	c Healy b Alderman	12
D.R.Pringle	c Taylor b Hohns	27
G.C.Small	c Jones b Lawson	59
N.G.B.Cook	c Jones b Lawson	31
A.P.Igglesden	not out	2
Extras (b 2, lb 7, w 1, nb 13)		23
TOTAL		285

FALL OF WICKETS – 1-1, 2-28, 3-47, 4-80, 5-84, 6-98, 7-169, 8-201, 9-274, 10-285
BOWLING – Alderman 27-7-66-5, Lawson 29.1-9-85-3, Hughes 23-3-84-1, Hohns 10-1-30-1, Waugh 3-0-11-0

AUSTRALIA 2nd Innings

G.R.Marsh	lbw b Igglesden	4
M.A.Taylor	c Russell b Small	48
D.C.Boon	run out	37
*A.R.Border	not out	51
D.M.Jones	b Capel	50
S.R.Waugh	not out	7

DID NOT BAT – +I.A.Healy, T.V.Hohns, M.G.Hughes, G.F.Lawson, T.M.Alderman

Extras (b 2, lb 7, nb 13)		22
TOTAL (for 4 wkts dec)		219

FALL OF WICKETS – 1-7, 2-100, 3-101, 4-189
BOWLING – Small 20-4-57-1, Igglesden 13-1-55-1, Pringle 16-0-53-0, Capel 8-0-35-1, Cook 6-2-10-0

ENGLAND 2nd Innings

G.A.Gooch	c & b Alderman	10
J.P.Stephenson	lbw b Alderman	11
M.A.Atherton	b Lawson	14
R.A.Smith	not out	77
*D.I.Gower	c Waugh b Lawson	7
D.J.Capel	c Taylor b Hohns	17
+R.C.Russell	not out	0

DID NOT BAT – D.R.Pringle, G.C.Small, N.G.B.Cook, A.P.Igglesden

Extras (lb 1, w 1, nb 5)		7
TOTAL (for 5 wkts)		143

FALL OF WICKETS – 1-20, 2-27, 3-51, 4-67, 5-138
BOWLING – Alderman 13-3-30-2, Lawson 15.1-2-41-2, Hughes 8-2-34-0, Hohns 10-2-37-1

1989

ENGLAND v NEW ZEALAND

at Trent Bridge on 7th, 8th, 9th, 11th, 12th June 1990
Toss: New Zealand
Umpires: H.D.Bird and J.H.Hampshire
Match drawn

NEW ZEALAND 1st Innings

T.J.Franklin	b Malcolm	33
*J.G.Wright	c Stewart b Small	8
A.H.Jones	c Stewart b Malcolm	39
M.D.Crowe	b DeFreitas	59
M.J.Greatbatch	b Hemmings	1
M.W.Priest	c Russell b DeFreitas	26
M.C.Snedden	c Gooch b DeFreitas	0
J.G.Bracewell	c Gooch b Small	28
R.J.Hadlee	b DeFreitas	0
+I.D.S.Smith	not out	2
D.K.Morrison	lbw b DeFreitas	0
Extras (b 1, lb 10, w 1)		12
TOTAL		208

FALL OF WICKETS – 1-16, 2-75, 3-110, 4-121, 5-170, 6-174, 7-191, 8-191, 9-203, 10-208
BOWLING – Small 29-9-49-2, Malcolm 19-7-48-2, Hemmings 19-6-47-1, DeFreitas 22-6-53-5

ENGLAND

*G.A.Gooch	lbw b Hadlee	0
M.A.Atherton	c Snedden b Priest	151
A.J.Stewart	c Smith b Hadlee	27
A.J.Lamb	b Hadlee	0
R.A.Smith	c Smith b Bracewell	55
N.H.Fairbrother	c Franklin b Snedden	19
+R.C.Russell	c Snedden b Morrison	28
P.A.J.DeFreitas	lbw b Bracewell	14
G.C.Small	c Crowe b Hadlee	26
E.E.Hemmings	not out	13
D.E.Malcolm	not out	4
Extras (b 2, lb 3, nb 3)		8
TOTAL (for 9 wkts dec)		345

FALL OF WICKETS – 1-0, 2-43, 3-45, 4-141, 5-168, 6-260, 7-302, 8-306, 9-340
BOWLING – Hadlee 33-6-89-4, Morrison 22-3-96-1, Snedden 36-17-54-1, Bracewell 35-8-75-2, Priest 12-4-26-1

NEW ZEALAND 2nd Innings

T.J.Franklin	not out	22
*J.G.Wright	c Russell b Small	1
A.H.Jones	c Russell b DeFreitas	13
D.K.Morrison	not out	0
DID NOT BAT – M.D.Crowe, M.J.Greatbatch, M.W.Priest, M.C.Snedden, J.G.Bracewell, R.J.Hadlee, +I.D.S.Smith		
Extras		0
TOTAL (for 2 wkts)		36

FALL OF WICKETS – 1-8, 2-36
BOWLING – Small 6-2-14-1, Malcolm 7-2-22-0, Hemmings 2-2-0-0, DeFreitas 2-2-0-1

ENGLAND v NEW ZEALAND

at Lord's on 21st, 22nd, 23rd, 25th, 26th June 1990
Toss: New Zealand
Umpires : M.J.Kitchen and D.R.Shepherd
Match drawn

ENGLAND 1st Innings

*G.A.Gooch	c & b Bracewell	85
M.A.Atherton	b Morrison	0
A.J.Stewart	lbw b Hadlee	54
A.J.Lamb	lbw b Snedden	39
R.A.Smith	c Bracewell b Morrison	64
N.H.Fairbrother	c Morrison b Bracewell	2
+R.C.Russell	b Hadlee	13
P.A.J.DeFreitas	c Franklin b Morrison	38
G.C.Small	b Morrison	3
E.E.Hemmings	b Hadlee	0
D.E.Malcolm	not out	0
Extras (lb 13, w 1, nb 22)		36
TOTAL		334

FALL OF WICKETS – 1-3, 2-151, 3-178, 4-216, 5-226, 6-255, 7-319, 8-322, 9-332, 10-334
BOWLING – Hadlee 29-5-113-3, Morrison 18.4-4-64-4, Snedden 21-4-72-1, Bracewell 21-3-72-2

NEW ZEALAND

T.J.Franklin	c Russell b Malcolm	101
*J.G.Wright	c Stewart b Small	98
A.H.Jones	c Stewart b Malcolm	49
M.D.Crowe	c Russell b Hemmings	1
M.J.Greatbatch	b Malcolm	47
K.R.Rutherford	c Fairbrother b Malcolm	0
R.J.Hadlee	b Hemmings	86
J.G.Bracewell	run out	4
+I.D.S.Smith	c Small b Malcolm	27
M.C.Snedden	not out	13
D.K.Morrison	not out	2
Extras (b 12, lb 15, w 2, nb 5)		34
TOTAL (for 9 wkts dec)		462

FALL OF WICKETS – 1-185, 2-278, 3-281, 4-284, 5-285, 6-408, 7-415, 8-425, 9-448
BOWLING – Malcolm 43-14-94-5, Small 35-4-127-1, DeFreitas 35.4-1-122-0, Hemmings 30-13-67-2, Gooch 13-7-25-0, Atherton 1-1-0-0

ENGLAND 2nd Innings

*G.A.Gooch	b Hadlee	37
M.A.Atherton	c Bracewell b Jones	54
A.J.Stewart	c sub b Bracewell	42
A.J.Lamb	not out	84
R.A.Smith	hit wicket b Bracewell	0
N.H.Fairbrother	not out	33
DID NOT BAT – +R.C.Russell, P.A.J.DeFreitas, G.C.Small, E.E.Hemmings, D.E.Malcolm		
Extras (b 8, lb 8, nb 6)		22
TOTAL (for 4 wkts dec)		272

FALL OF WICKETS – 1-68, 2-135, 3-171, 4-175
BOWLING – Hadlee 13-2-32-1, Morrison 16-0-81-0, Bracewell 34-13-85-2, Jones 12-3-40-1, Rutherford 3-0-18-0

ENGLAND v NEW ZEALAND

at Edgbaston on 5th, 6th, 7th, 9th, 10th July 1990
Toss: New Zealand
Umpires: J.W.Holder and B.J.Meyer
England won by 114 runs

ENGLAND 1st Innings

*G.A.Gooch	c Hadlee b Morrison	154
M.A.Atherton	lbw b Snedden	82
A.J.Stewart	c Parore b Morrison	9
A.J.Lamb	c Parore b Hadlee	2
R.A.Smith	c Jones b Bracewell	19
N.H.Fairbrother	lbw b Snedden	2
+R.C.Russell	b Snedden	43
C.C.Lewis	c Rutherford b Bracewell	32
Go.C.Small	not out	44
E.E.Hemmings	c Parore b Hadlee	20
D.E.Malcolm	b Hadlee	0
Extras (b 4, lb 15, nb 9)		28
TOTAL		435

FALL OF WICKETS – 1-170, 2-193, 3-198, 4-245, 5-254, 6-316, 7-351, 8-381, 9-435, 10-435
BOWLING – Hadlee 37.5-8-97-3, Morrison 26-7-81-2, Snedden 35-9-106-3, Bracewell 42-12-130-2, Crowe 1-0-2-0

NEW ZEALAND 1st Innings

T.J.Franklin	c Smith b Hemmings	66
*J.G.Wright	c Russell b Malcolm	24
A.H.Jones	c Russell b Malcolm	2
M.D.Crowe	lbw b Lewis	11
M.J.Greatbatch	b Malcolm	45
K.R.Rutherford	c Stewart b Hemmings	29
R.J.Hadlee	c Atherton b Hemmings	8
J.G.Bracewell	b Hemmings	25
+A.C.Parore	not out	12
M.C.Snedden	lbw b Hemmings	2
D.K.Morrison	b Hemmings	1
Extras (b 9, lb 11, w 2, nb 2)		24
TOTAL		249

FALL OF WICKETS – 1-45, 2-67, 3-90, 4-161, 5-163, 6-185, 7-223, 8-230, 9-243, 10-249
BOWLING – Small 18-7-44-0, Malcolm 25-7-59-3, Lewis 19-5-51-1, Hemmings 27.3-10-58-6, Atherton 9-5-17-0

ENGLAND 2nd Innings

*G.A.Gooch	b Snedden	30
M.A.Atherton	c Rutherford b Bracewell	70
A.J.Stewart	lbw b Bracewell	15
A.J.Lamb	st Parore b Bracewell	4
R.A.Smith	c & b Hadlee	14
N.H.Fairbrother	lbw b Bracewell	3
+R.C.Russell	c sub b Hadlee	0
C.C.Lewis	c Parore b Hadlee	1
G.C.Small	not out	11
E.E.Hemmings	b Hadlee	0
D.E.Malcolm	b Hadlee	0
Extras (lb 6, nb 4)		10
TOTAL		158

FALL OF WICKETS – 1-50, 2-87, 3-99, 4-129, 5-136, 6-141, 7-146, 8-157, 9-158, 10-158
BOWLING – Hadlee 21-3-53-5, Morrison 3-1-29-0, Snedden 9-0-32-1, Bracewell 16-5-38-4

NEW ZEALAND 2nd Innings

T.J.Franklin	lbw b Malcolm	5
*J.G.Wright	c Smith b Lewis	46
A.H.Jones	c Gooch b Small	40
M.D.Crowe	lbw b Malcolm	25
M.J.Greatbatch	c Atherton b Hemmings	22
K.R.Rutherford	c Lamb b Lewis	18
R.J.Hadlee	b Malcolm	13
+A.C.Parore	c Lamb b Lewis	20
J.G.Bracewell	c Atherton b Malcolm	0
M.C.Snedden	not out	21
D.K.Morrison	b Malcolm	6
Extras (lb 9, w 1, nb 4)		14
TOTAL		230

FALL OF WICKETS – 1-25, 2-85, 3-111, 4-125, 5-155, 6-163, 7-180, 8-180, 9-203, 10-230
BOWLING – Small 16-5-56-1, Malcolm 24.4-8-46-5, Lewis 22-3-76-3, Hemmings 29-13-43-1

1990

ENGLAND v INDIA

at Lord's on 26th, 27th, 28th, 30th, 31st July 1990
Toss: India
Umpires: H.D.Bird and N.T.Plews
England won by 247 runs

ENGLAND 1st Innings

*G.A.Gooch	b Prabhakar	333
M.A.Atherton	b Kapil Dev	8
D.I.Gower	c Manjrekar b Hirwani	40
A.J.Lamb	c Manjrekar b Sharma	139
R.A.Smith	not out	100
J.E.Morris	not out	4
DID NOT BAT – +R.C.Russell, C.C.Lewis,		
E.E.Hemmings, A.R.C.Fraser, D.E.Malcolm		
Extras (b 2, lb 21, w 2, nb 4)		29
TOTAL (for 4 wkts dec)		653

FALL OF WICKETS – 1-14, 2-141, 3-449, 4-641
BOWLING – Kapil Dev 34-5-120-1,
Prabhakar 43-6-187-1, Sharma 33-5-122-1,
Shastri 22-0-99-0, Hirwani 30-1-102-1

INDIA 1st Innings

R.J.Shastri	c Gooch b Hemmings	100
N.S.Sidhu	c Morris b Fraser	30
S.V.Manjrekar	c Russell b Gooch	18
D.B.Vengsarkar	c Russell b Fraser	52
*M.Azharuddin	b Hemmings	121
S.R.Tendulkar	b Lewis	10
M.Prabhakar	c Lewis b Malcolm	25
Kapil Dev	not out	77
+K.S.More	c Morris b Fraser	8
S.K.Sharma	c Russell b Fraser	0
N.D.Hirwani	lbw b Fraser	0
Extras (lb 1, w 4, nb 8)		13
TOTAL		454

FALL OF WICKETS – 1-63, 2-102, 3-191, 4-241, 5-288,
6-348, 7-393, 8-430, 9-430, 10-454
BOWLING – Malcolm 25-1-106-1, Fraser 39.1-9-104-5,
Lewis 24-3-108-1, Gooch 6-3-26-1,
Hemmings 20-3-109-2

ENGLAND 2nd Innings

*G.A.Gooch	c Azharuddin b Sharma	123
M.A.Atherton	c Vengsarkar b Sharma	72
D.I.Gower	not out	32
A.J.Lamb	c Tendulkar b Hirwani	19
R.A.Smith	b Prabhakar	15
DID NOT BAT – J.E.Morris, +R.C.Russell,		
C.C.Lewis, E.E.Hemmings, A.R.C.Fraser,		
D.E.Malcolm		
Extras (lb 11)		11
TOTAL (for 4 wkts dec)		272

FALL OF WICKETS – 1-204, 2-207, 3-250, 4-272
BOWLING – Kapil Dev 10-0-53-0,
Prabhakar 11.2-2-45-1, Sharma 15-0-75-2,
Shastri 7-0-38-0, Hirwani 11-0-50-1

INDIA 2nd Innings

R.J.Shastri	c Russell b Malcolm	12
N.S.Sidhu	c Morris b Fraser	1
S.V.Manjrekar	c Russell b Malcolm	33
D.B.Vengsarkar	c Russell b Hemmings	35
*M.Azharuddin	c Atherton b Lewis	37
S.R.Tendulkar	c Gooch b Fraser	27
M.Prabhakar	lbw b Lewis	8
Kapil Dev	c Lewis b Hemmings	7
+K.S.More	lbw b Fraser	16
S.K.Sharma	run out	38
N.D.Hirwani	not out	0
Extras (b 3, lb 1, nb 6)		10
TOTAL		224

FALL OF WICKETS – 1-9, 2-23, 3-63, 4-114, 5-127,
6-140, 7-158, 8-181, 9-206, 10-224
BOWLING – Malcolm 10-0-65-2, Fraser 22-7-39-3,
Lewis 8-1-26-2, Hemmings 21-2-79-2,
Atherton 1-0-11-0

ENGLAND v INDIA

at Old Trafford on 9th, 10th, 11th, 13th, 14th August 1990
Toss: England
Umpires: J.H.Hampshire and J.W.Holder
Match drawn

ENGLAND 1st Innings

*G.A.Gooch	c More b Prabhakar	116
M.A.Atherton	c More b Hirwani	131
D.I.Gower	c Tendulkar b Kapil Dev	38
A.J.Lamb	c Manjrekar b Kumble	38
+R.C.Russell	c More b Hirwani	8
R.A.Smith	not out	121
J.E.Morris	b Kumble	13
C.C.Lewis	b Hirwani	3
E.E.Hemmings	lbw b Hirwani	19
A.R.C.Fraser	c Tendulkar b Kumble	1
D.E.Malcolm	b Shastri	13
Extras (b 2, lb 9, w 1, nb 6)		18
TOTAL		519

FALL OF WICKETS – 1-225, 2-292, 3-312, 4-324,
5-366, 6-392, 7-404, 8-434, 9-459, 10-519
BOWLING – Kapil Dev 13-2-67-1,
Prabhakar 25-2-112-1, Kumble 43-7-105-3,
Hirwani 62-10-174-4, Shastri 17.5-2-50-1

INDIA 1st Innings

R.J.Shastri	c Gooch b Fraser	25
N.S.Sidhu	c Gooch b Fraser	13
S.V.Manjrekar	c Smith b Hemmings	93
D.B.Vengsarkar	c Russell b Fraser	6
*M.Azharuddin	c Atherton b Fraser	179
S.R.Tendulkar	c Lewis b Hemmings	68
M.Prabhakar	c Russell b Malcolm	4
Kapil Dev	lbw b Lewis	0
+K.S.More	b Fraser	6
A.R.Kumble	run out	2
N.D.Hirwani	not out	15
Extras (b 5, lb 4, nb 12)		21
TOTAL		432

FALL OF WICKETS – 1-26, 2-48, 3-57, 4-246, 5-358,
6-364, 7-365, 8-396, 9-401, 10-432
BOWLING – Malcolm 26-3-96-1, Fraser 35-5-124-5,
Hemmings 29.2-8-74-2, Lewis 13-1-61-1,
Atherton 16-3-68-0

ENGLAND 2nd Innings

*G.A.Gooch	c More b Prabhakar	7
M.A.Atherton	lbw b Kapil Dev	74
D.I.Gower	b Hirwani	16
A.J.Lamb	b Kapil Dev	109
R.A.Smith	not out	61
J.E.Morris	retired hurt	15
+R.C.Russell	not out	16
DID NOT BAT – C.C.Lewis, E.E.Hemmings,		
A.R.C.Fraser, D.E.Malcolm		
Extras (lb 15, nb 7)		22
TOTAL (for 4 wkts dec)		320

FALL OF WICKETS – 1-15, 2-46, 3-180, 4-248
BOWLING – Kapil Dev 22-4-69-2,
Prabhakar 18-1-80-1, Kumble 17-3-65-0,
Hirwani 15-0-52-1, Shastri 9-0-39-0

INDIA 2nd Innings

R.J.Shastri	b Malcolm	12
N.S.Sidhu	c sub b Fraser	0
S.V.Manjrekar	c sub b Hemmings	50
D.B.Vengsarkar	b Lewis	32
*M.Azharuddin	c Lewis b Hemmings	11
S.R.Tendulkar	not out	119
Kapil Dev	b Hemmings	26
M.Prabhakar	not out	67
DID NOT BAT – +K.S.More, A.R.Kumble,		
N.D.Hirwani		
Extras (b 17, lb 3, nb 6)		26
TOTAL (for 6 wkts)		343

FALL OF WICKETS – 1-4, 2-35, 3-109, 4-109, 5-127,
6-183
BOWLING – Malcolm 14-5-59-1, Fraser 21-3-81-1,
Hemmings 31-10-75-3, Lewis 20-3-86-1,
Atherton 4-0-22-0

ENGLAND v INDIA

at The Oval on 23rd, 24th, 25th, 27th, 28th August 1990
Toss: India
Umpires: N.T.Plews and D.R.Shepherd
Match drawn

INDIA

R.J.Shastri	c Lamb b Malcolm	187
N.S.Sidhu	c Russell b Fraser	12
S.V.Manjrekar	c Russell b Malcolm	22
D.B.Vengsarkar	c & b Atherton	33
*M.Azharuddin	c Russell b Williams	78
M.Prabhakar	lbw b Fraser	28
S.R.Tendulkar	c Lamb b Williams	21
Kapil Dev	st Russell b Hemmings	110
+K.S.More	not out	61
A.Wasson	b Hemmings	15
N.D.Hirwani	not out	2
Extras (b 7, lb 8, w 6, nb 16)		37
TOTAL (for 9 wkts dec)		606

FALL OF WICKETS – 1-16, 2-61, 3-150, 4-289, 5-335,
6-368, 7-478, 8-552, 9-576
BOWLING – Malcolm 35-7-110-2, Fraser 42-17-112-2,
Williams 41-5-148-2, Gooch 12-1-44-0,
Hemmings 36-3-117-2, Atherton 7-0-60-1

ENGLAND 1st Innings

*G.A.Gooch	c Shastri b Hirwani	85
M.A.Atherton	c More b Prabhakar	7
N.F.Williams	lbw b Prabhakar	38
D.I.Gower	lbw b Wasson	8
J.E.Morris	c More b Wasson	7
A.J.Lamb	b Kapil Dev	7
R.A.Smith	c Manjrekar b Shastri	57
+R.C.Russell	run out	35
E.E.Hemmings	c Vengsarkar b Prabhakar	51
A.R.C.Fraser	c More b Prabhakar	0
D.E.Malcolm	not out	15
Extras (b 8, lb 9, w 4, nb 9)		30
TOTAL		340

FALL OF WICKETS – 1-18, 2-92, 3-111, 4-120, 5-139,
6-231, 7-233, 8-295, 9-299, 10-340
BOWLING – Kapil Dev 25-7-70-1,
Prabhakar 32.4-9-74-4, Wasson 19-3-79-2,
Hirwani 35-12-71-1, Shastri 12-2-29-1

ENGLAND 2nd Innings

*G.A.Gooch	c Manjrekar b Hirwani	88
M.A.Atherton	lbw b Kapil Dev	86
D.I.Gower	not out	157
J.E.Morris	c More b Wasson	32
A.J.Lamb	c Shastri b Kapil Dev	52
R.A.Smith	not out	7
DID NOT BAT – N.F.Williams, +R.C.Russell,		
E.E.Hemmings, A.R.C.Fraser, D.E.Malcolm		
Extras (b 16, lb 22, w 5, nb 12)		55
TOTAL (for 4 wkts dec)		477

FALL OF WICKETS – 1-176, 2-251, 3-334, 4-463
BOWLING – Kapil Dev 24-5-66-2,
Prabhakar 25-8-56-0, Wasson 18-2-94-1,
Hirwani 59-18-137-1, Shastri 28-2-86-0

1990

ENGLAND v WEST INDIES

at Headingley on 6th, 7th, 8th, 9th, 10th June 1991
Toss: West Indies
Umpires: H.D.Bird and D.R.Shepherd
England won by 115 runs

ENGLAND 1st Innings

*G.A.Gooch	c Dujon b Marshall	34
M.A.Atherton	b Patterson	2
G.A.Hick	c Dujon b Walsh	6
A.J.Lamb	c Hooper b Marshall	11
M.R.Ramprakash	c Hooper b Marshall	27
R.A.Smith	run out	54
+R.C.Russell	lbw b Patterson	5
D.R.Pringle	c Logie b Patterson	16
P.A.J.DeFreitas	c Simmons b Ambrose	15
S.L.Watkin	b Ambrose	2
D.E.Malcolm	not out	5
Extras (lb 5, w 2, nb 14)		21
TOTAL		198

FALL OF WICKETS – 1-13, 2-45, 3-45, 4-64, 5-129, 6-149, 7-154, 8-177, 9-181, 10-198
BOWLING – Ambrose 26-8-49-2, Patterson 26.2-8-67-3, Walsh 14-7-31-1, Marshall 13-4-46-3

WEST INDIES 1st Innings

P.V.Simmons	c Ramprakash b DeFreitas	38
D.L.Haynes	c Russell b Watkin	7
R.B.Richardson	run out	29
C.L.Hooper	run out	0
*I.V.A.Richards	c Lamb b Pringle	73
A.L.Logie	c Lamb b DeFreitas	6
+P.J.L.Dujon	c Ramprakash b Watkin	6
M.D.Marshall	c Hick b Pringle	0
C.E.L.Ambrose	c Hick b DeFreitas	0
C.A.Walsh	c Gooch b DeFreitas	3
B.P.Patterson	not out	5
Extras (lb 1, nb 5)		6
TOTAL		173

FALL OF WICKETS – 1-36, 2-54, 3-58, 4-102, 5-139, 6-156, 7-160, 8-165, 9-167, 10-173
BOWLING – Malcolm 14-0-69-0, DeFreitas 17.1-5-34-4, Watkin 14-2-55-2, Pringle 9-3-14-2

ENGLAND 2nd Innings

*G.A.Gooch	not out	154
M.A.Atherton	c Dujon b Ambrose	6
G.A.Hick	b Ambrose	6
A.J.Lamb	c Hooper b Ambrose	0
M.R.Ramprakash	c Dujon b Ambrose	27
R.A.Smith	lbw b Ambrose	0
+R.C.Russell	c Dujon b Ambrose	4
D.R.Pringle	c Dujon b Marshall	27
P.A.J.DeFreitas	lbw b Walsh	3
S.L.Watkin	c Hooper b Marshall	0
D.E.Malcolm	b Marshall	4
Extras (b 4, lb 9, w 1, nb 7)		21
TOTAL		252

FALL OF WICKETS – 1-22, 2-38, 3-38, 4-116, 5-116, 6-124, 7-222, 8-236, 9-238, 10-252
BOWLING – Ambrose 28-6-52-6, Patterson 15-1-52-0, Walsh 30-5-61-1, Marshall 34-4-58-3, Hooper 4-1-11-0, Richards 4-1-5-0

WEST INDIES 2nd Innings

P.V.Simmons	b DeFreitas	0
D.L.Haynes	c Smith b Pringle	19
R.B.Richardson	c Lamb b DeFreitas	68
C.L.Hooper	c Lamb b Watkin	5
*I.V.A.Richards	c Gooch b Watkin	3
A.L.Logie	c Gooch b Watkin	3
+P.J.L.Dujon	lbw b DeFreitas	33
M.D.Marshall	lbw b Pringle	1
C.E.L.Ambrose	c Pringle b DeFreitas	14
C.A.Walsh	c Atherton b Malcolm	9
B.P.Patterson	not out	0
Extras (lb 1, nb 6)		7
TOTAL		162

FALL OF WICKETS – 1-0, 2-61, 3-77, 4-85, 5-88, 6-136, 7-137, 8-139, 9-162, 10-162
BOWLING – Malcolm 6.4-0-26-1, DeFreitas 21-4-59-4, Watkin 7-0-38-3, Pringle 22-6-38-2

ENGLAND v WEST INDIES

at Lord's on 20th, 21st, 22nd, 23rd, 24th June 1991
Toss: West Indies
Umpires: B.J.Meyer and K.E.Palmer
Match drawn

WEST INDIES 1st Innings

P.V.Simmons	c Lamb b Hick	33
D.L.Haynes	c Russell b Pringle	60
R.B.Richardson	c DeFreitas b Hick	57
C.L.Hooper	c Lamb b Pringle	111
*I.V.A.Richards	lbw b DeFreitas	63
A.L.Logie	b DeFreitas	5
+P.J.L.Dujon	c Lamb b Pringle	20
M.D.Marshall	lbw b Pringle	25
C.E.L.Ambrose	c & b Malcolm	5
C.A.Walsh	c Atherton b Pringle	10
I.B.A.Allen	not out	1
Extras (b 3, lb 7, nb 19)		29
TOTAL		419

FALL OF WICKETS – 1-90, 2-102, 3-198, 4-322, 5-332, 6-366, 7-382, 8-402, 9-410, 10-419
BOWLING – DeFreitas 31-6-93-2, Malcolm 19-3-76-1, Watkin 15-2-60-0, Pringle 35.1-6-100-5, Hick 18-4-77-2, Gooch 2-0-3-0

ENGLAND

*G.A.Gooch	b Walsh	37
M.A.Atherton	b Ambrose	5
G.A.Hick	c Richardson b Ambrose	0
A.J.Lamb	c Haynes b Marshall	1
M.R.Ramprakash	c Richards b Allen	24
R.A.Smith	not out	148
+R.C.Russell	c Dujon b Hooper	46
D.R.Pringle	c Simmons b Allen	35
P.A.J.DeFreitas	c Dujon b Marshall	29
S.L.Watkin	b Ambrose	6
D.E.Malcolm	b Ambrose	0
Extras (lb 1, nb 22)		23
TOTAL		354

FALL OF WICKETS – 1-5, 2-6, 3-16, 4-60, 5-84, 6-180, 7-269, 8-316, 9-353, 10-354
BOWLING – Ambrose 34-10-87-4, Marshall 30-4-78-2, Walsh 26-4-90-1, Allen 23-2-88-2, Hooper 5-2-10-1

WEST INDIES 2nd Innings

P.V.Simmons	lbw b DeFreitas	2
D.L.Haynes	not out	4
R.B.Richardson	c Hick b Malcolm	1
C.L.Hooper	not out	1
DID NOT BAT – *I.V.A.Richards, A.L.Logie, +P.J.L.Dujon, M.D.Marshall, C.E.L.Ambrose, C.A.Walsh, I.B.A.Allen		
Extras (lb 2, nb 2)		4
TOTAL (for 2 wkts)		12

FALL OF WICKETS – 1-9, 2-10
BOWLING – DeFreitas 3-2-1-1, Malcolm 2.5-0-9-1

ENGLAND v WEST INDIES

at Trent Bridge on 4th, 5th, 6th, 8th, 9th July 1991
Toss: England
Umpires: J.H.Hampshire and M.J.Kitchen
West Indies won by 9 wickets

ENGLAND 1st Innings

*G.A.Gooch	lbw b Marshall	68
M.A.Atherton	lbw b Ambrose	32
G.A.Hick	c Dujon b Ambrose	43
A.J.Lamb	lbw b Ambrose	13
M.R.Ramprakash	b Ambrose	13
R.A.Smith	not out	64
+R.C.Russell	c Logie b Allen	3
D.R.Pringle	c sub b Allen	0
P.A.J.DeFreitas	b Walsh	8
R.K.Illingworth	c Hooper b Ambrose	13
D.V.Lawrence	c Allen b Marshall	4
Extras (lb 17, w 1, nb 21)		39
TOTAL		300

FALL OF WICKETS – 1-108, 2-113, 3-138, 4-186, 5-192, 6-212, 7-217, 8-228, 9-270, 10-300
BOWLING – Ambrose 34-7-74-5, Marshall 21.5-6-54-2, Walsh 24-4-75-1, Allen 17-0-69-2, Hooper 6-4-10-0, Richards 1-0-1-0

WEST INDIES 1st Innings

P.V.Simmons	b Illingworth	12
D.L.Haynes	c Smith b Lawrence	18
R.B.Richardson	b Lawrence	43
C.L.Hooper	c Russell b DeFreitas	11
*I.V.A.Richards	b Illingworth	80
A.L.Logie	c Ramprakash b DeFreitas	78
+P.J.L.Dujon	c Hick b Pringle	19
M.D.Marshall	c Illingworth b DeFreitas	67
C.E.L.Ambrose	b Illingworth	17
C.A.Walsh	lbw b Pringle	12
I.B.A.Allen	not out	4
Extras (b 2, lb 13, w 1, nb 20)		36
TOTAL		397

FALL OF WICKETS – 1-32, 2-32, 3-45, 4-118, 5-239, 6-272, 7-324, 8-358, 9-392, 10-397
BOWLING – DeFreitas 31.1-9-67-3, Lawrence 24-2-116-2, Illingworth 33-8-110-3, Pringle 25-6-71-2, Hick 5-0-18-0

ENGLAND 2nd Innings

*G.A.Gooch	b Ambrose	13
M.A.Atherton	b Marshall	4
G.A.Hick	c Dujon b Ambrose	0
A.J.Lamb	lbw b Marshall	29
M.R.Ramprakash	c Dujon b Ambrose	21
R.A.Smith	c Richards b Walsh	15
+R.C.Russell	b Walsh	3
D.R.Pringle	c Simmons b Walsh	3
P.A.J.DeFreitas	not out	55
R.K.Illingworth	c Simmons b Walsh	13
D.V.Lawrence	c Hooper b Allen	34
Extras (lb 14, w 3, nb 4)		21
TOTAL		211

FALL OF WICKETS – 1-4, 2-8, 3-25, 4-67, 5-100, 6-106, 7-106, 8-115, 9-153, 10-211
BOWLING – Ambrose 27-7-61-3, Marshall 21-6-49-2, Walsh 24-7-64-4, Allen 7-2-23-1

WEST INDIES 2nd Innings

P.V.Simmons	c Russell b Lawrence	1
D.L.Haynes	not out	57
R.B.Richardson	not out	52
DID NOT BAT – C.L.Hooper, *I.V.A.Richards, A.L.Logie, +P.J.L.Dujon, M.D.Marshall, C.E.L.Ambrose, C.A.Walsh, I.B.A.Allen		
Extras (nb 5)		5
TOTAL (for 1 wkt)		115

FALL OF WICKETS – 1-1
BOWLING – DeFreitas 11-3-29-0, Lawrence 12.2-0-61-1, Illingworth 2-0-5-0, Pringle 7-2-20-0

1991

ENGLAND v WEST INDIES

at Edgbaston on 25th, 26th, 27th, 28th July 1991
Toss: West Indies
Umpires : B.Dudleston and D.R.Shepherd
West Indies won by 7 wickets

ENGLAND 1st Innings

*G.A.Gooch	b Marshall	45
H.Morris	c Dujon b Patterson	3
M.A.Atherton	lbw b Walsh	16
G.A.Hick	c Richards b Ambrose	19
A.J.Lamb	lbw b Marshall	9
M.R.Ramprakash	c Logie b Walsh	29
+R.C.Russell	c Richardson b Ambrose	12
D.R.Pringle	b Ambrose	2
P.A.J.DeFreitas	c Richardson b Marshall	10
C.C.Lewis	lbw b Marshall	13
R.K.Illingworth	not out	0
Extras (b 4, lb 3, nb 23)		30
TOTAL		188

FALL OF WICKETS – 1-6, 2-53, 3-88, 4-108, 5-129, 6-159, 7-163, 8-163, 9-184, 10-188
BOWLING – Ambrose 23-6-64-3, Patterson 11-2-39-1, Walsh 21-6-43-2, Marshall 12.4-1-33-4, Hooper 3-2-2-0

WEST INDIES 1st Innings

P.V.Simmons	c Hick b Lewis	28
D.L.Haynes	c Russell b DeFreitas	32
R.B.Richardson	lbw b Lewis	104
C.L.Hooper	b Illingworth	31
*I.V.A.Richards	c Lewis b Pringle	22
A.L.Logie	c Atherton b Lewis	28
+P.J.L.Dujon	lbw b DeFreitas	6
M.D.Marshall	not out	6
C.E.L.Ambrose	c Hick b Lewis	1
C.A.Walsh	c & b Lewis	18
B.P.Patterson	b Lewis	3
Extras (lb 7, nb 6)		13
TOTAL		292

FALL OF WICKETS – 1-52, 2-93, 3-148, 4-194, 5-257, 6-258, 7-266, 8-267, 9-285, 10-292
BOWLING – DeFreitas 25.3-9-40-2, Lewis 35-10-111-6, Pringle 23-9-48-1, Illingworth 17-2-75-1, Gooch 6-1-11-0, Hick 1-1-0-0

ENGLAND 2nd Innings

*G.A.Gooch	b Patterson	40
H.Morris	lbw b Patterson	1
M.A.Atherton	c Hooper b Patterson	1
G.A.Hick	b Ambrose	1
A.J.Lamb	c Dujon b Walsh	25
M.R.Ramprakash	c Dujon b Marshall	25
+R.C.Russell	c Dujon b Patterson	0
D.R.Pringle	c Logie b Marshall	45
P.A.J.DeFreitas	b Patterson	7
C.C.Lewis	c sub b Ambrose	65
R.K.Illingworth	not out	5
Extras (b 5, lb 21, nb 14)		40
TOTAL		255

FALL OF WICKETS – 1-2, 2-4, 3-5, 4-71, 5-94, 6-96, 7-127, 8-144, 9-236, 10-255
BOWLING – Ambrose 33-16-42-2, Patterson 31-6-81-5, Walsh 7-1-20-1, Marshall 19.4-3-53-2, Hooper 12-3-26-0, Simmons 3-0-7-0

WEST INDIES 2nd Innings

P.V.Simmons	lbw b DeFreitas	16
D.L.Haynes	c Hick b DeFreitas	8
R.B.Richardson	c Hick b DeFreitas	0
C.L.Hooper	not out	55
*I.V.A.Richards	not out	73
DID NOT BAT – A.L.Logie, +P.J.L.Dujon, M.D.Marshall, C.E.L.Ambrose, C.A.Walsh, B.P.Patterson		
Extras (lb 4, nb 1)		5
TOTAL (for 3 wkts)		157

FALL OF WICKETS – 1-23, 2-23, 3-24
BOWLING – DeFreitas 13-2-54-3, Lewis 16-7-45-0, Pringle 7-1-31-0, Illingworth 4.4-0-23-0

ENGLAND v WEST INDIES

at The Oval on 8th, 9th, 10th, 11th, 12th August 1991
Toss: England
Umpires: J.W.Holder and M.J.Kitchen
England won by 5 wickets

ENGLAND 1st Innings

*G.A.Gooch	lbw b Ambrose	60
H.Morris	c Lambert b Ambrose	44
M.A.Atherton	c Hooper b Walsh	0
R.A.Smith	lbw b Marshall	109
M.R.Ramprakash	c Lambert b Hooper	25
+A.J.Stewart	c Richardson b Patterson	31
I.T.Botham	hit wicket b Ambrose	31
C.C.Lewis	not out	47
P.A.J.DeFreitas	c Dujon b Walsh	7
D.V.Lawrence	c Richards b Walsh	9
P.C.R.Tufnell	c Haynes b Patterson	2
Extras (b 8, lb 10, w 1, nb 35)		54
TOTAL		419

FALL OF WICKETS – 1-112, 2-114, 3-120, 4-188, 5-263, 6-336, 7-351, 8-386, 9-411, 10-419
BOWLING – Ambrose 36-8-83-3, Patterson 25.1-3-87-2, Walsh 32-5-91-3, Marshall 24-5-62-1, Hooper 34-1-78-1

WEST INDIES 1st Innings

P.V.Simmons	lbw b Lawrence	15
D.L.Haynes	not out	75
R.B.Richardson	c Stewart b Botham	20
C.L.Hooper	c Stewart b DeFreitas	3
C.B.Lambert	c Ramprakash b Tufnell	39
+P.J.L.Dujon	lbw b Lawrence	0
M.D.Marshall	c Botham b Tufnell	0
*I.V.A.Richards	c Stewart b Tufnell	2
C.E.L.Ambrose	c Botham b Tufnell	0
C.A.Walsh	c Gooch b Tufnell	0
B.P.Patterson	c Botham b Tufnell	2
Extras (lb 9, nb 11)		20
TOTAL		176

FALL OF WICKETS – 1-52, 2-95, 3-98, 4-158, 5-160, 6-161, 7-172, 8-172, 9-172, 10-176
BOWLING – DeFreitas 13-6-38-1, Lawrence 16-1-67-2, Tufnell 14.3-3-25-6, Botham 11-4-27-1, Lewis 3-1-10-0

WEST INDIES 2nd Innings

P.V.Simmons	c Lewis b Botham	36
D.L.Haynes	lbw b Lawrence	43
C.B.Lambert	lbw b Botham	14
R.B.Richardson	c Gooch b Lawrence	121
C.L.Hooper	c Gooch b Tufnell	54
*I.V.A.Richards	c Morris b Lawrence	60
+P.J.L.Dujon	c Stewart b Lawrence	5
M.D.Marshall	b DeFreitas	17
C.E.L.Ambrose	lbw b DeFreitas	0
C.A.Walsh	lbw b Lawrence	14
B.P.Patterson	not out	1
Extras (b 7, lb 5, w 2, nb 6)		20
TOTAL		385

FALL OF WICKETS – 1-53, 2-71, 3-125, 4-208, 5-305, 6-311, 7-356, 8-356, 9-378, 10-385
BOWLING – DeFreitas 20-9-42-2, Lawrence 25.5-5-4-106-5, Tufnell 46-6-150-1, Botham 16-4-40-2, Lewis 25-12-35-0

ENGLAND 2nd Innings

*G.A.Gooch	lbw b Marshall	29
H.Morris	c Dujon b Patterson	2
M.A.Atherton	c Hooper b Patterson	13
R.A.Smith	c Patterson b Walsh	26
M.R.Ramprakash	lbw b Lambert	19
+A.J.Stewart	not out	38
I.T.Botham	not out	4
DID NOT BAT – C.C.Lewis, P.A.J.DeFreitas, D.V.Lawrence, P.C.R.Tufnell		
Extras (b 4, w 1, nb 10)		15
TOTAL (for 5 wkts)		146

FALL OF WICKETS – 1-3, 2-40, 3-80, 4-80, 5-142
BOWLING – Ambrose 8-0-48-0, Patterson 9-0-63-2, Walsh 9-3-18-1, Marshall 5-3-9-1, Lambert 0.4-0-4-1

ENGLAND v SRI LANKA

at Lord's on 22nd, 23rd, 24th, 26th, 27th August 1991
Toss: England
Umpires: H.D.Bird and J.H.Hampshire
England won by 137 runs

ENGLAND 1st Innings

*G.A.Gooch	c & b Ramanayake	38
H.Morris	lbw b Ratnayake	42
A.J.Stewart	not out	113
R.A.Smith	c Tillekeratne b Ratnayake	4
M.R.Ramprakash	c Mahanama b Hathurusinghe	0
I.T.Botham	c Mahanama b Ramanayake	22
C.C.Lewis	c de Silva b Anurasiri	11
+R.C.Russell	b Anurasiri	17
P.A.J.DeFreitas	b Ratnayake	1
D.V.Lawrence	c & b Ratnayake	3
P.C.R.Tufnell	lbw b Ratnayake	0
Extras (b 9, lb 8, nb 14)		31
TOTAL		282

FALL OF WICKETS – 1-70, 2-114, 3-119, 4-120, 5-160, 6-183, 7-246, 8-258, 9-276, 10-282
BOWLING – Ratnayake 27-4-69-5, Ramanayake 24-5-75-2, Wijegunawardene 10-1-36-0, Hathurusinghe 17-6-40-1, Anurasiri 17-4-45-2

SRI LANKA 1st Innings

D.S.B.P.Kuruppu	b DeFreitas	5
U.C.Hathurusinghe	c Tufnell b DeFreitas	66
A.P.Gurusinha	lbw b DeFreitas	4
*P.A.de Silva	c Lewis b DeFreitas	42
R.S.Mahanama	c Russell b Botham	2
S.T.Jayasuriya	c Smith b DeFreitas	11
+H.P.Tillekeratne	c Morris b Lawrence	20
R.J.Ratnayake	b DeFreitas	52
C.P.H.Ramanayake	lbw b DeFreitas	0
K.I.W.Wijegunawardene	not out	6
S.D.Anurasiri	b Lawrence	1
Extras (lb 15)		15
TOTAL		224

FALL OF WICKETS – 1-12, 2-22, 3-75, 4-86, 5-105, 6-139, 7-213, 8-213, 9-220, 10-224
BOWLING – DeFreitas 26-8-70-7, Lawrence 15.1-3-61-2, Lewis 10-5-29-0, Botham 10-3-26-1, Tufnell 7-2-23-0

ENGLAND 2nd Innings

*G.A.Gooch	b Anurasiri	174
H.Morris	c Mahanama b Anurasiri	23
A.J.Stewart	c de Silva b Anurasiri	43
R.A.Smith	not out	63
+R.C.Russell	not out	12
DID NOT BAT – M.R.Ramprakash, I.T.Botham, C.C.Lewis, P.A.J.DeFreitas, D.V.Lawrence, P.C.R.Tufnell		
Extras (b 15, lb 23, w 1, nb 10)		49
TOTAL (for 3 wkts dec)		364

FALL OF WICKETS – 1-78, 2-217, 3-322
BOWLING – Ratnayake 26-4-91-0, Ramanayake 20-2-86-0, Wijegunawardene 2-0-13-0, Anurasiri 26.1-8-135-3, Jayasuriya 1-0-1-0

SRI LANKA 2nd Innings

D.S.B.P.Kuruppu	lbw b Lewis	21
U.C.Hathurusinghe	c Morris b Tufnell	25
A.P.Gurusinha	b Tufnell	34
*P.A.de Silva	c Russell b Lawrence	18
R.S.Mahanama	c Botham b Tufnell	15
S.T.Jayasuriya	c Russell b Lewis	66
+H.P.Tillekeratne	b Tufnell	16
R.J.Ratnayake	c sub b Lawrence	17
C.P.H.Ramanayake	not out	34
K.I.W.Wijegunawardene	c Botham b DeFreitas	4
S.D.Anurasiri	lbw b Tufnell	16
Extras (b 1, lb 16, nb 2)		19
TOTAL		285

FALL OF WICKETS – 1-50, 2-50, 3-111, 4-119, 5-159, 6-212, 7-212, 8-241, 9-253, 10-285
BOWLING – DeFreitas 22-8-45-1, Lawrence 23-7-83-2, Lewis 18-4-31-2, Botham 6-2-15-0, Tufnell 34.3-14-94-5

1991

ENGLAND v PAKISTAN

at Edgbaston on 4th, 5th, 6th, 7th, 8th June 1992
Toss: England
Umpires: M.J.Kitchen and B.J.Meyer
Match drawn

PAKISTAN

Aamir Sohail	c Stewart b DeFreitas	18
Ramiz Raja	lbw b DeFreitas	47
Asif Mujtaba	c Russell b DeFreitas	29
*Javed Miandad	not out	153
Salim Malik	lbw b DeFreitas	165
Inzamam-ul-Haq	not out	8

DID NOT BAT – +Moin Khan, Mushtaq Ahmed, Waqar Younis, Aqib Javed, Ata-ur-Rehman
Extras (b 2, lb 5, nb 19)   26
TOTAL (for 4 wkts dec)   446

FALL OF WICKETS – 1-33, 2-96, 3-110, 4-432
BOWLING – DeFreitas 33-6-121-4, Lewis 33-3-116-0, Pringle 28-2-92-0, Botham 19-6-52-0, Hick 13-1-46-0, Gooch 10-5-9-0, Ramprakash 1-0-3-0

ENGLAND

*G.A.Gooch	c Mujtaba b Aqib Javed	8
A.J.Stewart	c Salim b Ata-ur-Rehman	190
G.A.Hick	c Miandad b Waqar Younis	51
R.A.Smith	lbw b Mushtaq Ahmed	127
M.R.Ramprakash	c Moin b Ata-ur-Rehman	0
A.J.Lamb	c Miandad b Ata-ur-Rehman	12
C.C.Lewis	b Mushtaq Ahmed	24
+R.C.Russell	not out	29
D.R.Pringle	not out	0

DID NOT BAT – I.T.Botham, P.A.J.DeFreitas
Extras (b 5, lb 5, w 1, nb 7)   18
TOTAL (for 7 wkts dec)   459

FALL OF WICKETS – 1-28, 2-121, 3-348, 4-348, 5-378, 6-415, 7-446
BOWLING – Waqar Younis 24-2-96-1, Aqib Javed 16-3-86-1, Mushtaq Ahmed 50-8-156-2, Ata-ur-Rehman 18-5-69-3, Asif Mujtaba 8-1-29-0, Aamir Sohail 2-0-8-0, Salim Malik 1-0-5-0

ENGLAND v PAKISTAN

at Lord's on 18th, 19th, 20th, 21st June 1992
Toss: England
Umpires: B.Dudleston and J.H.Hampshire
Pakistan won by 2 wickets

ENGLAND 1st Innings

*G.A.Gooch	b Wasim Akram	69
A.J.Stewart	c Miandad b Asif Mujtaba	74
G.A.Hick	c Miandad b Waqar Younis	13
R.A.Smith	c sub b Wasim Akram	9
A.J.Lamb	b Waqar Younis	30
I.T.Botham	b Waqar Younis	2
C.C.Lewis	lbw b Waqar Younis	2
+R.C.Russell	not out	22
P.A.J.DeFreitas	c Inzamam-ul-Haq b Waqar	3
I.D.K.Salisbury	hit wicket b Mushtaq Ahmed	4
D.E.Malcolm	lbw b Mushtaq Ahmed	0

Extras (b 6, lb 12, nb 9)   27
TOTAL   255

FALL OF WICKETS – 1-123, 2-153, 3-172, 4-197, 5-213, 6-221, 7-232, 8-242, 9-247, 10-255
BOWLING – Wasim Akram 19-5-49-2, Aqib Javed 14-3-40-0, Waqar Younis 21-4-91-5, Mushtaq Ahmed 19.1-5-57-2, Asif Mujtaba 3-3-0-1

PAKISTAN 1st Innings

Aamir Sohail	c Russell b DeFreitas	73
Ramiz Raja	b Lewis	24
Asif Mujtaba	c Smith b Malcolm	59
*Javed Miandad	c Botham b Salisbury	9
Salim Malik	c Smith b Malcolm	55
Inzamam-ul-Haq	c & b Malcolm	0
Wasim Akram	b Salisbury	24
+Moin Khan	c Botham b DeFreitas	12
Mushtaq Ahmed	c Russell b DeFreitas	4
Waqar Younis	b Malcolm	14
Aqib Javed	not out	5

Extras (b 4, lb 3, nb 7)   14
TOTAL   293

FALL OF WICKETS – 1-43, 2-123, 3-143, 4-228, 5-228, 6-235, 7-263, 8-271, 9-276, 10-293
BOWLING – DeFreitas 26-8-58-3, Malcolm 15.5-1-70-4, Lewis 29-7-76-1, Salisbury 23-3-73-2, Botham 5-2-9-0

ENGLAND 2nd Innings

*G.A.Gooch	lbw b Aqib Javed	13
A.J.Stewart	not out	69
I.D.K.Salisbury	lbw b Wasim Akram	12
G.A.Hick	c Moin Khan b Mushtaq	11
R.A.Smith	b Mushtaq Ahmed	8
A.J.Lamb	lbw b Mushtaq Ahmed	12
I.T.Botham	lbw b Waqar Younis	6
C.C.Lewis	b Waqar Younis	15
+R.C.Russell	b Wasim Akram	1
P.A.J.DeFreitas	c Inzamam-ul-Haq b Wasim	0
D.E.Malcolm	b Wasim Akram	0

Extras (b 5, lb 8, nb 15)   28
TOTAL   175

FALL OF WICKETS – 1-40, 2-73, 3-108, 4-120, 5-137, 6-148, 7-174, 8-175, 9-175, 10-175
BOWLING – Wasim Akram 17.4-2-66-4, Aqib Javed 12-3-23-1, Waqar Younis 13-3-40-2, Mushtaq Ahmed 9-1-32-3, Asif Mujtaba 1-0-1-0

PAKISTAN 2nd Innings

Aamir Sohail	b Salisbury	39
Ramiz Raja	c Hick b Lewis	0
Asif Mujtaba	c Russell b Lewis	0
*Javed Miandad	c Russell b Lewis	0
Salim Malik	c Lewis b Salisbury	12
Inzamam-ul-Haq	run out	8
Wasim Akram	not out	45
+Moin Khan	c Smith b Salisbury	3
Mushtaq Ahmed	c Hick b Malcolm	5
Waqar Younis	not out	20

DID NOT BAT – Aqib Javed
Extras (b 2, lb 5, w 1, nb 1)   9
TOTAL (for 8 wkts)   141

FALL OF WICKETS – 1-6, 2-10, 3-18, 4-41, 5-62, 6-68, 7-81, 8-95
BOWLING – Malcolm 15-2-42-1, Lewis 16-3-43-3, Salisbury 14.1-0-49-3

ENGLAND v PAKISTAN

at Old Trafford on 2nd, 3rd, 4th, 6th, 7th July 1992
Toss: Pakistan
Umpires: R.Palmer and D.R.Shepherd
Match drawn

PAKISTAN 1st Innings

Aamir Sohail	b Lewis	205
Ramiz Raja	c Russell b Malcolm	54
Asif Mujtaba	c Atherton b Lewis	57
*Javed Miandad	c Hick b Munton	88
+Moin Khan	c Gower b Malcolm	15
Salim Malik	b Gooch	34
Inzamam-ul-Haq	c Gooch b Malcolm	26
Wasim Akram	st Russell b Gooch	0
Waqar Younis	not out	2
Mushtaq Ahmed	c Lewis b Gooch	6

DID NOT BAT – Aqib Javed
Extras (b 9, lb 4, w 2, nb 3)   18
TOTAL (for 9 wkts dec)   505

FALL OF WICKETS – 1-115, 2-241, 3-378, 4-428, 5-432, 6-492, 7-497, 8-497, 9-505
BOWLING – Malcolm 31-3-117-3, Lewis 24-5-90-2, Munton 30-6-112-1, Salisbury 20-0-117-0, Gooch 18-2-39-3, Hick 3-0-17-0

ENGLAND

*G.A.Gooch	c Moin Khan b Waqar	78
A.J.Stewart	c Inzamam-ul-Haq b Wasim	15
M.A.Atherton	c Moin Khan b Wasim	0
R.A.Smith	lbw b Aqib Javed	11
D.I.Gower	c Moin Khan b Wasim	73
G.A.Hick	b Aqib Javed	22
C.C.Lewis	c Moin Khan b Wasim	55
+R.C.Russell	c Aamir Sohail b Aqib Javed	4
I.D.K.Salisbury	c Aamir Sohail b Wasim	50
T.A.Munton	not out	25
D.E.Malcolm	b Aqib Javed	4

Extras (b 8, lb 8, w 2, nb 35)   53
TOTAL   390

FALL OF WICKETS – 1-41, 2-42, 3-93, 4-186, 5-200, 6-252, 7-256, 8-315, 9-379, 10-390
BOWLING – Wasim Akram 36-4-128-5, Waqar Younis 32-6-96-1, Aqib Javed 21.4-1-100-4, Asif Mujtaba 1-1-0-0, Mushtaq Ahmed 10-1-50-0

PAKISTAN 2nd Innings

Aamir Sohail	c Smith b Lewis	1
Ramiz Raja	c Hick b Lewis	88
Asif Mujtaba	c Atherton b Lewis	40
*Javed Miandad	not out	45
Salim Malik	b Gooch	16
Wasim Akram	c Atherton b Gooch	13
+Moin Khan	not out	11

DID NOT BAT – Inzamam-ul-Haq, Waqar Younis, Mushtaq Ahmed, Aqib Javed
Extras (b 8, lb 5, w 5, nb 7)   25
TOTAL (for 5 wkts dec)   239

FALL OF WICKETS – 1-1, 2-143, 3-148, 4-195, 5-217
BOWLING – Malcolm 12-2-57-0, Lewis 17-5-46-3, Munton 17-6-26-0, Salisbury 13-0-67-0, Gooch 16-5-30-2, Hick 2-2-0-0

1992

ENGLAND v PAKISTAN

at Headingley on 23rd, 24th, 25th, 26th July 1992
Toss: Pakistan
Umpires: M.J.Kitchen and K.E.Palmer
England won by 6 wickets

PAKISTAN 1st Innings

Aamir Sohail	c Atherton b Mallender	23
Ramiz Raja	b Pringle	17
Asif Mujtaba	b Mallender	7
*Javed Miandad	c Smith b Pringle	6
Salim Malik	not out	82
Inzamam-ul-Haq	c Hick b Munton	5
Wasim Akram	run out	12
+Moin Khan	c Hick b Lewis	2
Waqar Younis	c Hick b Mallender	6
Mushtaq Ahmed	b Lewis	11
Aqib Javed	c Hick b Munton	0
Extras (b 1, lb 2, w 7, nb 16)		26
TOTAL		197

FALL OF WICKETS – 1-37, 2-54, 3-60, 4-68, 5-80, 6-111, 7-117, 8-128, 9-192, 10-197
BOWLING – Lewis 23-6-48-2, Mallender 23-7-72-3, Pringle 17-6-41-2, Munton 10.3-3-22-2, Gooch 6-3-11-0

ENGLAND 1st Innings

*G.A.Gooch	b Mushtaq Ahmed	135
M.A.Atherton	b Wasim Akram	76
R.A.Smith	c Miandad b Aqib	42
+A.J.Stewart	lbw b Waqar Younis	8
D.I.Gower	not out	18
M.R.Ramprakash	lbw b Mushtaq Ahmed	0
G.A.Hick	b Waqar Younis	1
C.C.Lewis	lbw b Waqar Younis	0
D.R.Pringle	b Waqar Younis	0
N.A.Mallender	b Waqar Younis	1
T.A.Munton	c Inzamam-ul-Haq b Mushtaq	0
Extras (b 1, lb 14, w 1, nb 23)		39
TOTAL		320

FALL OF WICKETS – 1-168, 2-270, 3-292, 4-298, 5-298, 6-303, 7-305, 8-305, 9-313, 10-320
BOWLING – Wasim Akram 36-12-80-1, Aqib Javed 16-3-48-1, Waqar 30-3-117-5, Mushtaq Ahmed 29.5-6-60-3, Aamir Sohail 2-2-0-0

PAKISTAN 2nd Innings

Aamir Sohail	c Stewart b Mallender	1
Ramiz Raja	c Atherton b Munton	63
Asif Mujtaba	c Hick b Mallender	11
*Javed Miandad	c Stewart b Mallender	4
Salim Malik	not out	84
Inzamam-ul-Haq	c Smith b Pringle	19
Wasim Akram	c Ramprakash b Pringle	17
+Moin Khan	c Hick b Mallender	3
Mushtaq Ahmed	lbw b Pringle	0
Waqar Younis	b Mallender	3
Aqib Javed	run out	0
Extras (b 4, lb 1, w 2, nb 9)		16
TOTAL		221

FALL OF WICKETS – 1-11, 2-53, 3-64, 4-96, 5-147, 6-177, 7-205, 8-206, 9-213, 10-221
BOWLING – Lewis 16-3-55-0, Mallender 23-7-50-5, Pringle 19-2-66-3, Munton 10-0-40-1, Gooch 1-0-5-0

ENGLAND 2nd Innings

*G.A.Gooch	c Asif Mujtaba b Mushtaq	37
M.A.Atherton	lbw b Waqar Younis	5
R.A.Smith	c sub b Waqar Younis	0
D.I.Gower	not out	31
+A.J.Stewart	c Moin Khan b Mushtaq	2
M.R.Ramprakash	not out	12
DID NOT BAT – G.A.Hick, C.C.Lewis, D.R.Pringle, N.A.Mallender, T.A.Munton		
Extras (b 5, lb 3, nb 4)		12
TOTAL (for 4 wkts)		99

FALL OF WICKETS – 1-27, 2-27, 3-61, 4-65
BOWLING – Wasim Akram 17-4-36-0, Waqar Younis 12-2-28-2, Mushtaq Ahmed 13.4-3-27-2

ENGLAND v PAKISTAN

at The Oval on 6th, 7th, 8th, 9th August 1992
Toss: England
Umpires: H.D.Bird and D.R.Shepherd
Pakistan won by 10 wickets

ENGLAND 1st Innings

*G.A.Gooch	c Asif Mujtaba b Aqib	20
+A.J.Stewart	c Ramiz Raja b Wasim	31
M.A.Atherton	c Rashid Latif b Waqar	60
R.A.Smith	b Mushtaq Ahmed	33
D.I.Gower	b Aqib Javed	27
M.R.Ramprakash	lbw b Wasim Akram	2
C.C.Lewis	lbw b Wasim Akram	4
D.R.Pringle	b Wasim Akram	1
N.A.Mallender	b Wasim Akram	4
P.C.R.Tufnell	not out	0
D.E.Malcolm	b Wasim Akram	2
Extras (b 4, lb 8, w 1, nb 10)		23
TOTAL		207

FALL OF WICKETS – 1-39, 2-57, 3-138, 4-182, 5-190, 6-196, 7-199, 8-203, 9-205, 10-207
BOWLING – Wasim Akram 22.1-3-67-6, Waqar Younis 16-4-37-1, Aqib Javed 16-6-44-2, Mushtaq Ahmed 24-7-47-1

PAKISTAN 1st Innings

Aamir Sohail	c Stewart b Malcolm	49
Ramiz Raja	b Malcolm	19
Shoaib Mohammad	c & b Tufnell	55
*Javed Miandad	c & b Lewis	59
Salim Malik	b Malcolm	40
Asif Mujtaba	run out	50
Wasim Akram	c Stewart b Malcolm	7
+Rashid Latif	c Smith b Malcolm	50
Waqar Younis	c Gooch b Malcolm	6
Mushtaq Ahmed	c Lewis b Mallender	9
Aqib Javed	not out	0
Extras (b 2, lb 6, w 4, nb 24)		36
TOTAL		380

FALL OF WICKETS – 1-64, 2-86, 3-197, 4-214, 5-278, 6-292, 7-332, 8-342, 9-359, 10-380
BOWLING – Mallender 28.5-6-93-2, Malcolm 29.6-9-94-5, Lewis 30-8-70-1, Tufnell 34-9-87-1, Pringle 6-0-28-0

ENGLAND 2nd Innings

*G.A.Gooch	c Aamir Sohail b Waqar	24
+A.J.Stewart	lbw b Waqar	8
M.A.Atherton	c Rashid Latif b Waqar	4
R.A.Smith	not out	84
D.I.Gower	b Waqar Younis	1
M.R.Ramprakash	c Asif Mujtaba b Mushtaq	17
C.C.Lewis	st Rashid Latif b Mushtaq	14
D.R.Pringle	b Wasim Akram	1
N.A.Mallender	c Mushtaq b Wasim Akram	3
P.C.R.Tufnell	b Wasim Akram	0
D.E.Malcolm	b Waqar Younis	0
Extras (b 1, lb 8, nb 9)		18
TOTAL		174

FALL OF WICKETS – 1-29, 2-47, 3-55, 4-59, 5-92, 6-153, 7-159, 8-173, 9-173, 10-174
BOWLING – Wasim Akram 21-6-36-3, Waqar Younis 18-5-52-5, Aqib Javed 9-2-25-0, Mushtaq Ahmed 23-6-46-2, Aamir Sohail 1-0-6-0

PAKISTAN 2nd Innings

Aamir Sohail	not out	4
Ramiz Raja	not out	0
DID NOT BAT – Shoaib Mohammad, *Javed Miandad, Salim Malik, Asif Mujtaba, Wasim Akram, +Rashid Latif, Waqar Younis, Mushtaq Ahmed, Aqib Javed		
Extras (w 1)		1
TOTAL (for 0 wkts)		5

BOWLING – Ramprakash 0.1-0-5-0

1992

ENGLAND v AUSTRALIA

at Old Trafford on 3rd, 4th, 5th, 6th, 7th June 1993
Toss: England
Umpires: H.D.Bird and K.E.Palmer
Australia won by 179 runs

AUSTRALIA 1st Innings

M.A.Taylor	c & b Such	124
M.J.Slater	c Stewart b DeFreitas	58
D.C.Boon	c Lewis b Such	21
M.E.Waugh	c & b Tufnell	6
*A.R.Border	st Stewart b Such	17
S.R.Waugh	b Such	3
+I.A.Healy	c Such b Tufnell	12
B.P.Julian	c Gatting b Such	0
M.G.Hughes	c DeFreitas b Such	2
S.K.Warne	not out	15
C.J.McDermott	run out	8
Extras (b 8, lb 8, nb 7)		23
TOTAL		289

FALL OF WICKETS – 1-128, 2-183, 3-221, 4-225,
5-232, 6-260, 7-264, 8-266, 9-267, 10-289
BOWLING – Caddick 15-4-38-0, DeFreitas 23-8-46-1,
Lewis 13-2-44-0, Such 33.3-9-67-6, Tufnell 28-5-78-2

ENGLAND 1st Innings

*G.A.Gooch	c Julian b Warne	65
M.A.Atherton	c Healy b Hughes	19
M.W.Gatting	b Warne	4
R.A.Smith	c Taylor b Warne	4
G.A.Hick	c Border b Hughes	34
+A.J.Stewart	b Julian	27
C.C.Lewis	c Boon b Hughes	9
P.A.J.DeFreitas	lbw b Julian	5
A.R.Caddick	c Healy b Warne	7
P.M.Such	not out	14
P.C.R.Tufnell	c Healy b Hughes	1
Extras (b 6, lb 10, nb 5)		21
TOTAL		210

FALL OF WICKETS – 1-71, 2-80, 3-84, 4-123, 5-148,
6-168, 7-178, 8-183, 9-203, 10-210
BOWLING – McDermott 18-2-50-0,
Hughes 20.5-5-59-4, Julian 11-2-30-2,
Warne 24-10-51-4, Border 1-0-4-0

AUSTRALIA 2nd Innings

M.A.Taylor	lbw b Such	9
M.J.Slater	c Caddick b Such	27
D.C.Boon	c Gatting b DeFreitas	93
M.E.Waugh	b Tufnell	64
*A.R.Border	c & b Caddick	31
S.R.Waugh	not out	78
+I.A.Healy	not out	102
DID NOT BAT – B.P.Julian, M.G.Hughes,		
S.K.Warne, C.J.McDermott		
Extras (b 6, lb 14, w 8)		28
TOTAL (for 5 wkts dec)		432

FALL OF WICKETS – 1-23, 2-46, 3-155, 4-234, 5-252
BOWLING – Caddick 20-3-79-1, DeFreitas 24-1-80-1,
Lewis 9-0-43-0, Such 31-6-78-2, Tufnell 37-4-112-1,
Hick 9-1-20-0

ENGLAND 2nd Innings

*G.A.Gooch	handled the ball	133
M.A.Atherton	c Taylor b Warne	25
M.W.Gatting	b Hughes	23
R.A.Smith	b Warne	18
G.A.Hick	c Healy b Hughes	22
+A.J.Stewart	c Healy b Warne	11
C.C.Lewis	c Taylor b Warne	43
P.A.J.DeFreitas	lbw b Julian	7
A.R.Caddick	c Warne b Hughes	25
P.M.Such	c Border b Hughes	9
P.C.R.Tufnell	not out	0
Extras (lb 11, w 1, nb 4)		16
TOTAL		332

FALL OF WICKETS – 1-73, 2-133, 3-171, 4-223, 5-230,
6-238, 7-260, 8-299, 9-331, 10-332
BOWLING – McDermott 30-9-76-0,
Hughes 27.2-4-92-4, Julian 14-1-67-1,
Warne 49-26-86-4

ENGLAND v AUSTRALIA

at Lord's on 17th, 18th, 19th, 20th, 21st June 1993
Toss: Australia
Umpires: M.J.Kitchen and D.R.Shepherd
Australia won by an innings and 62 runs

AUSTRALIA

M.A.Taylor	st Stewart b Tufnell	111
M.J.Slater	c sub b Lewis	152
D.C.Boon	not out	164
M.E.Waugh	b Tufnell	99
*A.R.Border	b Lewis	77
S.R.Waugh	not out	13
DID NOT BAT – +I.A.Healy, M.G.Hughes,		
S.K.Warne, T.B.A.May, C.J.McDermott		
Extras (lb 1, w 1, nb 14)		16
TOTAL (for 4 wkts dec)		632

FALL OF WICKETS – 1-260, 2-277, 3-452, 4-491
BOWLING – Caddick 38-5-120-0, Foster 30-4-94-0,
Such 36-6-90-0, Tufnell 39-3-129-2, Lewis 36-5-151-2,
Gooch 9-1-26-0, Hick 8-3-21-0

ENGLAND 1st Innings

*G.A.Gooch	c May b Hughes	12
M.A.Atherton	b Warne	80
M.W.Gatting	b May	5
R.A.Smith	st Healy b May	22
G.A.Hick	c Healy b Hughes	20
+A.J.Stewart	lbw b Hughes	3
C.C.Lewis	lbw b Warne	0
N.A.Foster	c Border b Warne	16
A.R.Caddick	c Healy b Hughes	21
P.M.Such	c Taylor b Warne	7
P.C.R.Tufnell	not out	2
Extras (lb 8, nb 9)		17
TOTAL		205

FALL OF WICKETS – 1-33, 2-50, 3-84, 4-123, 5-131,
6-132, 7-167, 8-174, 9-189, 10-205
BOWLING – Hughes 20-5-52-4, Waugh M.E. 6-1-16-0,
Waugh S.R. 4-1-5-0, May 31-12-64-2,
Warne 35-12-57-4, Border 3-1-3-0

ENGLAND 2nd Innings

*G.A.Gooch	c Healy b Warne	29
M.A.Atherton	run out	99
M.W.Gatting	lbw b Warne	59
R.A.Smith	c sub b May	5
G.A.Hick	c Taylor b May	64
+A.J.Stewart	lbw b May	62
C.C.Lewis	st Healy b May	0
N.A.Foster	c Waugh M.E. b Border	20
A.R.Caddick	not out	0
P.M.Such	b Warne	4
P.C.R.Tufnell	b Warne	0
Extras (b 10, lb 13)		23
TOTAL		365

FALL OF WICKETS – 1-71, 2-175, 3-180, 4-244, 5-304,
6-312, 7-361, 8-361, 9-365, 10-365
BOWLING – Hughes 31-9-75-0,
Waugh M.E. 17-4-55-0, Waugh S.R. 2-0-13-0,
May 51-23-81-4, Warne 48.5-17-102-4,
Border 16-9-16-1

ENGLAND v AUSTRALIA

at Trent Bridge on 1st, 2nd, 3rd, 5th, 6th July 1993
Toss: England
Umpires: B.J.Meyer and R.Palmer
Match drawn

ENGLAND 1st Innings

M.N.Lathwell	c Healy b Hughes	20
M.A.Atherton	c Boon b Warne	11
R.A.Smith	c & b Julian	86
+A.J.Stewart	c Waugh M.E. b Warne	25
*G.A.Gooch	c Border b Hughes	38
G.P.Thorpe	c Waugh S.R. b Hughes	6
N.Hussain	c Boon b Warne	71
A.R.Caddick	lbw b Hughes	15
M.J.McCague	c Waugh M.E. b Hughes	9
M.C.Ilott	c Taylor b May	6
P.M.Such	not out	0
Extras (b 5, lb 23, w 4, nb 2)		34
TOTAL		321

FALL OF WICKETS – 1-28, 2-63, 3-153, 4-159, 5-174,
6-220, 7-290, 8-304, 9-321, 10-321
BOWLING – Hughes 31-7-92-5, Julian 24-3-84-1,
Warne 40-17-74-3, May 14.4-7-31-1,
Waugh S.R. 8-4-12-0, Waugh M.E. 1-1-0-0

AUSTRALIA 1st Innings

M.J.Slater	lbw b Caddick	40
M.A.Taylor	c Stewart b McCague	28
D.C.Boon	b McCague	101
M.E.Waugh	c McCague b Such	70
S.R.Waugh	c Stewart b McCague	13
+I.A.Healy	c Thorpe b Ilott	9
B.P.Julian	c Stewart b Ilott	5
*A.R.Border	c Smith b Such	38
M.G.Hughes	b Ilott	17
S.K.Warne	not out	35
T.B.A.May	lbw b McCague	1
Extras (b 4, lb 8, w 4)		16
TOTAL		373

FALL OF WICKETS – 1-55, 2-74, 3-197, 4-239, 5-250,
6-262, 7-284, 8-311, 9-356, 10-373
BOWLING – McCague 32.3-5-121-4, Ilott 34-8-108-3,
Such 20-7-51-2, Caddick 22-5-81-1

ENGLAND 2nd Innings

M.N.Lathwell	lbw b Warne	33
M.A.Atherton	c Healy b Hughes	9
R.A.Smith	c Healy b Warne	50
+A.J.Stewart	lbw b Hughes	6
*G.A.Gooch	c Taylor b Warne	120
A.R.Caddick	c Boon b Julian	12
G.P.Thorpe	not out	114
N.Hussain	not out	47
DID NOT BAT – M.J.McCague, M.C.Ilott,		
P.M.Such		
Extras (b 11, lb 11, nb 9)		31
TOTAL (for 6 wkts dec)		422

FALL OF WICKETS – 1-11, 2-100, 3-109, 4-117, 5-159,
6-309
BOWLING – Hughes 22-8-41-2, Julian 33-10-110-1,
Warne 50-21-108-3, May 38-6-112-0,
Waugh S.R. 1-0-3-0, Waugh M.E. 6-3-15-0,
Border 5-0-11-0

AUSTRALIA 2nd Innings

M.J.Slater	b Such	26
M.A.Taylor	c Atherton b Such	28
D.C.Boon	c Stewart b Caddick	18
M.E.Waugh	b Caddick	1
*A.R.Border	c Thorpe b Caddick	2
S.R.Waugh	not out	47
+I.A.Healy	lbw b Ilott	5
B.P.Julian	not out	56
DID NOT BAT – M.G.Hughes, S.K.Warne,		
T.B.A.May		
Extras (b 5, lb 5, w 4, nb 5)		19
TOTAL (for 6 wkts)		202

FALL OF WICKETS – 1-46, 2-74, 3-75, 4-81, 5-93,
6-115
BOWLING – McCague 19-6-58-0, Ilott 18-5-44-1,
Such 23-6-58-2, Caddick 16-6-32-3

1993

ENGLAND v AUSTRALIA

at Headingley on 22nd, 23rd, 24th, 25th, 26th July 1993
Toss: Australia
Umpires: H.D.Bird and N.T.Plews
Australia won by an innings and 148 runs

AUSTRALIA

M.J.Slater	b Ilott	67
M.A.Taylor	lbw b Bicknell	27
D.C.Boon	lbw b Ilott	107
M.E.Waugh	b Ilott	52
*A.R.Border	not out	200
S.R.Waugh	not out	157
DID NOT BAT – +I.A.Healy, M.G.Hughes,		
P.R.Reiffel, S.K.Warne, T.B.A.May		
Extras (b 8, lb 22, w 4, nb 9)		43
TOTAL (for 4 wkts dec)		653

FALL OF WICKETS – 1-86, 2-110, 3-216, 4-321
BOWLING – McCague 28-2-115-0, Ilott 51-11-161-3,
Caddick 42-5-138-0, Bicknell 50-8-155-1,
Gooch 16-5-40-0, Thorpe 6-1-14-0

ENGLAND 1st Innings

M.N.Lathwell	c Healy b Hughes	0
M.A.Atherton	b Reiffel	55
R.A.Smith	c & b May	23
+A.J.Stewart	c Slater b Reiffel	5
*G.A.Gooch	lbw b Reiffel	59
G.P.Thorpe	c Healy b Reiffel	0
N.Hussain	b Reiffel	15
A.R.Caddick	c Waugh M.E. b Hughes	9
M.P.Bicknell	c Border b Hughes	12
M.J.McCague	c Taylor b Warne	0
M.C.Ilott	not out	0
Extras (b 2, lb 3, nb 17)		22
TOTAL		200

FALL OF WICKETS – 1-0, 2-43, 3-50, 4-158, 5-158,
6-169, 7-184, 8-195, 9-200, 10-200
BOWLING – Hughes 15.5-3-47-3, Reiffel 26-6-65-5,
May 15-3-33-1, Warne 23-9-43-1, Waugh M.E. 3-0-7-0

ENGLAND 2nd Innings

M.N.Lathwell	b May	25
M.A.Atherton	st Healy b May	63
R.A.Smith	lbw b Reiffel	35
+A.J.Stewart	c Waugh M.E. b Reiffel	78
*G.A.Gooch	st Healy b May	26
G.P.Thorpe	c Taylor b Reiffel	13
N.Hussain	not out	18
A.R.Caddick	lbw b Hughes	12
M.P.Bicknell	lbw b Hughes	0
M.J.McCague	b Hughes	11
M.C.Ilott	c Border b May	4
Extras (b 5, lb 3, w 1, nb 11)		20
TOTAL		305

FALL OF WICKETS – 1-60, 2-131, 3-149, 4-202, 5-256,
6-263, 7-279, 8-279, 9-295, 10-305
BOWLING – Hughes 30-10-79-3, Reiffel 28-8-87-3,
May 27-6-65-4, Warne 40-16-63-0,
Waugh M.E. 2-1-3-0

ENGLAND v AUSTRALIA

at Edgbaston on 5th, 6th, 7th, 8th, 9th August 1993
Toss: England
Umpires: J.H.Hampshire and D.R.Shepherd
Australia won by 8 wickets

ENGLAND 1st Innings

G.A.Gooch	c Taylor b Reiffel	8
*M.A.Atherton	b Reiffel	72
R.A.Smith	b Waugh M.E.	21
M.P.Maynard	c Waugh S.R. b May	0
+A.J.Stewart	c & b Warne	45
G.P.Thorpe	c Healy b May	37
N.Hussain	b Reiffel	3
J.E.Emburey	not out	55
M.P.Bicknell	c Waugh M.E. b Reiffel	14
P.M.Such	b Reiffel	1
M.C.Ilott	c Healy b Reiffel	3
Extras (b 4, lb 6, nb 7)		17
TOTAL		276

FALL OF WICKETS – 1-17, 2-71, 3-76, 4-156, 5-156,
6-160, 7-215, 8-262, 9-264, 10-276
BOWLING – Hughes 19-4-53-0, Reiffel 22.5-3-71-6,
Waugh M.E. 15-5-43-1, Waugh S.R. 5-2-4-0,
May 19-9-32-2, Warne 21-7-63-1

AUSTRALIA 1st Innings

M.A.Taylor	run out	19
M.J.Slater	c Smith b Such	22
D.C.Boon	lbw b Emburey	0
M.E.Waugh	c Thorpe b Ilott	137
*A.R.Border	c Hussain b Such	3
S.R.Waugh	c Stewart b Bicknell	59
+I.A.Healy	c Stewart b Bicknell	80
M.G.Hughes	b Bicknell	38
P.R.Reiffel	b Such	20
S.K.Warne	c Stewart b Emburey	10
T.B.A.May	not out	3
Extras (b 7, lb 8, nb 2)		17
TOTAL		408

FALL OF WICKETS – 1-34, 2-39, 3-69, 4-80, 5-233,
6-263, 7-370, 8-379, 9-398, 10-408
BOWLING – Bicknell 34-9-99-3, Ilott 24-4-85-1,
Such 52.5-18-90-3, Emburey 39-9-119-2

ENGLAND 2nd Innings

G.A.Gooch	b Warne	48
*M.A.Atherton	c Border b Warne	28
R.A.Smith	lbw b Warne	19
M.P.Maynard	c Healy b May	10
+A.J.Stewart	lbw b Warne	5
G.P.Thorpe	st Healy b Warne	60
N.Hussain	c Waugh S.R. b May	0
J.E.Emburey	c Healy b May	37
M.P.Bicknell	c Waugh S.R. b May	0
P.M.Such	not out	7
M.C.Ilott	b May	15
Extras (b 11, lb 9, nb 2)		22
TOTAL		251

FALL OF WICKETS – 1-60, 2-104, 3-115, 4-115, 5-124,
6-125, 7-229, 8-229, 9-229, 10-251
BOWLING – Hughes 18-7-24-0, Reiffel 11-2-30-0,
Waugh M.E. 5-2-5-0, May 48.2-15-89-5,
Warne 49-23-82-5, Border 2-1-1-0

AUSTRALIA 2nd Innings

M.J.Slater	c Thorpe b Emburey	8
M.A.Taylor	c Thorpe b Such	4
D.C.Boon	not out	38
M.E.Waugh	not out	62
DID NOT BAT – *A.R.Border, S.R.Waugh,		
+I.A.Healy, M.G.Hughes, P.R.Reiffel, S.K.Warne,		
T.B.A.May		
Extras (b 3, lb 5)		8
TOTAL (for 2 wkts)		120

FALL OF WICKETS – 1-12, 2-12
BOWLING – Bicknell 3-0-9-0, Ilott 2-0-14-0,
Such 20.3-4-58-1, Emburey 18-4-31-1

ENGLAND v AUSTRALIA

at The Oval on 19th, 20th, 21st, 22nd, 23rd August 1993
Toss: England
Umpires: M.J.Kitchen and B.J.Meyer
England won by 161 runs

ENGLAND 1st Innings

G.A.Gooch	c Border b Waugh S.R.	56
*M.A.Atherton	lbw b Waugh S.R.	50
G.A.Hick	c Warne b May	80
M.P.Maynard	b Warne	20
N.Hussain	c Taylor b Warne	30
+A.J.Stewart	c Healy b Hughes	76
M.R.Ramprakash	c Healy b Hughes	6
A.R.C.Fraser	b Reiffel	28
S.L.Watkin	c Waugh S.R. b Reiffel	13
P.M.Such	c Waugh M.E. b Hughes	4
D.E.Malcolm	not out	0
Extras (lb 7, w 1, nb 9)		17
TOTAL		380

FALL OF WICKETS – 1-88, 2-143, 3-177, 4-231, 5-253,
6-272, 7-339, 8-363, 9-374, 10-380
BOWLING – Hughes 30-7-121-3, Reiffel 28.5-4-88-2,
Waugh S.R. 12-2-45-2, Warne 20-5-70-2,
Waugh M.E. 1-0-17-0, May 10-3-32-1

AUSTRALIA 1st Innings

M.A.Taylor	c Hussain b Malcolm	70
M.J.Slater	c Gooch b Malcolm	4
D.C.Boon	c Gooch b Malcolm	13
M.E.Waugh	c Stewart b Fraser	10
*A.R.Border	c Stewart b Fraser	48
S.R.Waugh	b Fraser	20
+I.A.Healy	not out	83
M.G.Hughes	c Ramprakash b Watkin	7
P.R.Reiffel	c Maynard b Watkin	0
S.K.Warne	c Stewart b Fraser	16
T.B.A.May	c Stewart b Fraser	15
Extras (b 5, lb 6, w 2, nb 4)		17
TOTAL		303

FALL OF WICKETS – 1-9, 2-30, 3-53, 4-132, 5-164,
6-181, 7-196, 8-196, 9-248, 10-303
BOWLING – Malcolm 26-5-86-3, Watkin 28-4-87-2,
Fraser 26.4-4-87-5, Such 14-4-32-0

ENGLAND 2nd Innings

G.A.Gooch	c Healy b Warne	79
*M.A.Atherton	c Warne b Reiffel	42
G.A.Hick	c Boon b May	36
M.P.Maynard	c Reiffel b Hughes	9
N.Hussain	c Waugh M.E. b Hughes	0
+A.J.Stewart	c Waugh M.E. b Reiffel	35
M.R.Ramprakash	c Slater b Hughes	64
A.R.C.Fraser	c Healy b Reiffel	13
S.L.Watkin	lbw b Warne	4
P.M.Such	lbw b Warne	10
D.E.Malcolm	not out	0
Extras (b 5, lb 12, w 1, nb 3)		21
TOTAL		313

FALL OF WICKETS – 1-77, 2-157, 3-180, 4-180, 5-186,
6-254, 7-276, 8-283, 9-313, 10-313
BOWLING – Hughes 31.2-9-110-3, Reiffel 24-8-55-3,
Warne 40-15-78-3, May 24-6-53-1

AUSTRALIA 2nd Innings

M.J.Slater	c Stewart b Watkin	12
M.A.Taylor	b Watkin	8
D.C.Boon	lbw b Watkin	0
M.E.Waugh	c Ramprakash b Malcolm	49
*A.R.Border	c Stewart b Malcolm	17
S.R.Waugh	lbw b Malcolm	26
+I.A.Healy	c Maynard b Watkin	5
M.G.Hughes	c Watkin b Fraser	12
P.R.Reiffel	c & b Fraser	42
S.K.Warne	lbw b Fraser	37
T.B.A.May	not out	4
Extras (b 2, lb 6, w 2, nb 7)		17
TOTAL		229

FALL OF WICKETS – 1-23, 2-23, 3-30, 4-92, 5-95,
6-106, 7-142, 8-143, 9-217, 10-229
BOWLING – Malcolm 20-3-84-3, Watkin 25-9-65-4,
Fraser 19.1-5-44-3, Such 9-4-17-0, Hick 8-3-11-0

1993

ENGLAND v NEW ZEALAND

at Trent Bridge on 2nd, 3rd, 4th, 5th, 6th June 1994
Toss: New Zealand
Umpires: H.D.Bird and S.A.Bucknor
England won by an innings and 90 runs

NEW ZEALAND 1st Innings

B.A.Young	c Hick b DeFreitas	15
B.R.Hartland	c Hick b DeFreitas	6
*K.R.Rutherford	lbw b DeFreitas	25
M.D.Crowe	c Rhodes b White	16
S.P.Fleming	c White b DeFreitas	54
S.A.Thomson	c Hick b Fraser	14
+A.C.Parore	c Rhodes b Malcolm	38
G.R.Larsen	c Fraser b Such	8
M.N.Hart	c Hick b Fraser	36
D.J.Nash	c Rhodes b Malcolm	19
H.T.Davis	not out	0
Extras (lb 6, nb 14)		20
TOTAL		251

FALL OF WICKETS – 1-13, 2-37, 3-66, 4-78, 5-108,
6-168, 7-188, 8-194, 9-249, 10-251
BOWLING – Malcolm 17.4-5-45-2, Fraser 21-10-40-2,
DeFreitas 23-4-94-4, Such 19-7-28-1, White 13-3-38-1

ENGLAND

*M.A.Atherton	c Parore b Larsen	101
A.J.Stewart	c Larsen b Davis	8
G.A.Gooch	c Crowe b Thomson	210
G.A.Hick	b Nash	18
R.A.Smith	run out	78
C.White	c Larsen b Hart	19
+S.J.Rhodes	c Thomson b Nash	49
P.A.J.DeFreitas	not out	51
A.R.C.Fraser	c Fleming b Larsen	8
DID NOT BAT – P.M.Such, D.E.Malcolm		
Extras (lb 9, w 6, nb 10)		25
TOTAL (for 8 wkts dec)		567

FALL OF WICKETS – 1-16, 2-279, 3-314, 4-375, 5-414,
6-482, 7-528, 8-567
BOWLING – Davis 21-0-93-1, Nash 36-5-153-2,
Larsen 44.4-11-116-2, Hart 35-7-123-1,
Thomson 38-6-73-1

NEW ZEALAND 2nd Innings

B.R.Hartland	lbw b DeFreitas	22
B.A.Young	c Rhodes b Fraser	53
*K.R.Rutherford	c Atherton b Such	14
M.D.Crowe	lbw b DeFreitas	28
S.P.Fleming	c White b Hick	11
S.A.Thomson	c White b Such	6
+A.C.Parore	c Rhodes b DeFreitas	42
G.R.Larsen	c Stewart b DeFreitas	2
M.N.Hart	lbw b Fraser	22
D.J.Nash	c Rhodes b DeFreitas	5
H.T.Davis	not out	0
Extras (lb 1, nb 20)		21
TOTAL		226

FALL OF WICKETS – 1-59, 2-95, 3-95, 4-122, 5-141,
6-141, 7-147, 8-201, 9-224, 10-226
BOWLING – Malcolm 10-2-39-0, Fraser 23-8-53-2,
DeFreitas 22.3-4-71-5, Such 34-12-50-2,
White 3-3-0-0, Hick 14-6-12-1

ENGLAND v NEW ZEALAND

at Lord's on 16th, 17th, 18th, 19th, 20th June 1994
Toss: New Zealand
Umpires: S.A.Bucknor and N.T.Plews
Match drawn

NEW ZEALAND 1st Innings

B.A.Young	lbw b Fraser	0
B.A.Pocock	c Smith b Such	10
*K.R.Rutherford	c Stewart b DeFreitas	37
M.D.Crowe	c Smith b DeFreitas	142
S.P.Fleming	lbw b Fraser	41
S.A.Thomson	run out	69
+A.C.Parore	c Rhodes b Taylor	40
M.N.Hart	b Such	25
D.J.Nash	b White	56
C.Pringle	c Hick b DeFreitas	14
M.B.Owens	not out	2
Extras (b 3, lb 15, w 1, nb 21)		40
TOTAL		476

FALL OF WICKETS – 1-0, 2-39, 3-67, 4-138, 5-318,
6-350, 7-391, 8-397, 9-434, 10-476
BOWLING – Fraser 36-9-102-2, DeFreitas 35-8-102-3,
Taylor 20-4-64-1, Such 30-8-84-2, White 21.1-4-84-1,
Gooch 5-1-13-0, Hick 2-0-9-0

ENGLAND 1st Innings

*M.A.Atherton	lbw b Hart	28
A.J.Stewart	c Parore b Nash	45
G.A.Gooch	lbw b Nash	13
R.A.Smith	c & b Nash	6
G.A.Hick	c Young b Pringle	58
C.White	run out	51
+S.J.Rhodes	not out	32
P.A.J.DeFreitas	c Parore b Thomson	11
A.R.C.Fraser	c & b Nash	10
J.P.Taylor	c Parore b Nash	0
P.M.Such	c Parore b Nash	4
Extras (b 4, lb 12, nb 7)		23
TOTAL		281

FALL OF WICKETS – 1-65, 2-95, 3-95, 4-101, 5-193,
6-225, 7-241, 8-265, 9-271, 10-281
BOWLING – Owens 7-0-34-0, Nash 25-6-76-6,
Pringle 23-5-65-1, Hart 44-21-50-1,
Thomson 22-8-40-1

NEW ZEALAND 2nd Innings

B.A.Pocock	lbw b DeFreitas	2
B.A.Young	c Hick b Such	94
*K.R.Rutherford	lbw b DeFreitas	0
M.D.Crowe	b DeFreitas	9
S.P.Fleming	lbw b Taylor	39
S.A.Thomson	not out	38
+A.C.Parore	not out	15
DID NOT BAT – M.N.Hart, D.J.Nash, C.Pringle, M.B.Owens		
Extras (lb 4, nb 10)		14
TOTAL (for 5 wkts dec)		211

FALL OF WICKETS – 1-9, 2-9, 3-29, 4-144, 5-170
BOWLING – Fraser 15-0-50-0, DeFreitas 16-0-63-3,
Taylor 6-2-18-1, Such 25-5-55-1, White 4-1-21-0,
Hick 2-2-0-0

ENGLAND 2nd Innings

*M.A.Atherton	c Young b Nash	33
A.J.Stewart	c Crowe b Nash	119
G.A.Gooch	lbw b Nash	0
R.A.Smith	c Parore b Nash	23
G.A.Hick	lbw b Pringle	37
C.White	c Thomson b Nash	9
+S.J.Rhodes	not out	24
P.A.J.DeFreitas	lbw b Owens	3
A.R.C.Fraser	lbw b Hart	2
J.P.Taylor	not out	0
DID NOT BAT – P.M.Such		
Extras (b 2, lb 1, nb 1)		4
TOTAL (for 8 wkts)		254

FALL OF WICKETS – 1-60, 2-60, 3-136, 4-210, 5-217,
6-240, 7-244, 8-250
BOWLING – Owens 10-3-35-1, Nash 29-8-93-5,
Pringle 16-5-41-1, Hart 41-23-55-1,
Thomson 12-4-27-0

ENGLAND v NEW ZEALAND

at Old Trafford on 30th June, 1st, 2nd, 4th, 5th July 1994
Toss: England
Umpires: S.B.Lambson and D.R.Shepherd
Match drawn

ENGLAND

*M.A.Atherton	lbw b Nash	111
A.J.Stewart	c Pringle b Nash	24
G.A.Gooch	c Young b Nash	0
R.A.Smith	b Owens	13
G.A.Hick	c Nash b Owens	20
C.White	c Hart b Owens	42
+S.J.Rhodes	c Parore b Nash	12
P.A.J.DeFreitas	b Owens	69
D.Gough	c sub b Pringle	65
A.R.C.Fraser	c Thomson b Hart	10
P.M.Such	not out	5
Extras (lb 8, w 1, nb 2)		11
TOTAL		382

FALL OF WICKETS – 1-37, 2-37, 3-68, 4-104, 5-203,
6-224, 7-235, 8-365, 9-372, 10-382
BOWLING – Nash 39-9-107-4, Owens 34-12-99-4,
Pringle 39-12-95-1, Hart 27.3-9-50-1,
Thomson 7-1-23-0

NEW ZEALAND 1st Innings

B.A.Young	c Rhodes b DeFreitas	25
M.J.Greatbatch	c Hick b Gough	0
*K.R.Rutherford	c Gooch b DeFreitas	7
S.P.Fleming	c Rhodes b Gough	14
M.D.Crowe	c Gooch b White	70
M.N.Hart	c Atherton b Gough	0
S.A.Thomson	c Rhodes b DeFreitas	9
+A.C.Parore	c Rhodes b White	7
D.J.Nash	not out	8
C.Pringle	b White	0
M.B.Owens	c Stewart b Gough	4
Extras (nb 7)		7
TOTAL		151

FALL OF WICKETS – 1-2, 2-12, 3-47, 4-82, 5-93, 6-113,
7-125, 8-140, 9-140, 10-151
BOWLING – Fraser 12-3-17-0, Gough 16.3-2-47-4,
DeFreitas 17-2-61-3, Such 5-2-8-0, White 7-1-18-3

NEW ZEALAND 2nd Innings

B.A.Young	lbw b DeFreitas	8
M.J.Greatbatch	c DeFreitas b White	21
*K.R.Rutherford	c Rhodes b Gough	13
S.P.Fleming	c Hick b Fraser	11
M.D.Crowe	c Hick b DeFreitas	115
S.A.Thomson	c Smith b Gough	21
+A.C.Parore	c Gooch b DeFreitas	71
M.N.Hart	not out	16
D.J.Nash	not out	6
DID NOT BAT – C.Pringle, M.B.Owens		
Extras (b 8, lb 13, nb 5)		26
TOTAL (for 7 wkts)		308

FALL OF WICKETS – 1-8, 2-34, 3-48, 4-73, 5-132,
6-273, 7-287
BOWLING – Fraser 19-7-34-1, Gough 31.2-5-105-2,
DeFreitas 30-6-60-3, Such 10-2-39-0, White 14-3-36-1,
Gooch 2-0-13-0

1994

ENGLAND v SOUTH AFRICA

at Lord's on 21st, 22nd, 23rd, 24th July 1994
Toss: South Africa
Umpires: H.D.Bird and S.G.Randell
South Africa won by 356 runs

SOUTH AFRICA 1st Innings

A.C.Hudson	c Gooch b Gough	6
G.Kirsten	c DeFreitas b Hick	72
W.J.Cronje	c Crawley b Fraser	7
*K.C.Wessels	c Rhodes b Gough	105
P.N.Kirsten	c Rhodes b Gough	8
J.N.Rhodes	b White	32
B.M.McMillan	c Rhodes b Fraser	29
+D.J.Richardson	lbw b Gough	26
C.R.Matthews	b White	41
P.S.de Villiers	c Rhodes b Fraser	8
A.A.Donald	not out	5
Extras (lb 9, nb 9)		18
TOTAL		357

FALL OF WICKETS – 1-18, 2-35, 3-141, 4-164, 5-239, 6-241, 7-281, 8-334, 9-348, 10-357
BOWLING – DeFreitas 18-5-67-0, Gough 28-6-76-4, Salisbury 25-2-68-0, Fraser 24.5-7-72-3, Hick 10-5-22-1, White 13-2-43-2

ENGLAND 1st Innings

*M.A.Atherton	c Wessels b Donald	20
A.J.Stewart	b Donald	12
J.P.Crawley	c Hudson b de Villiers	9
G.A.Hick	c Richardson b de Villiers	38
G.A.Gooch	lbw b de Villiers	20
C.White	c Richardson b Donald	10
+S.J.Rhodes	b McMillan	15
I.D.K.Salisbury	not out	6
P.A.J.DeFreitas	c Wessels b Donald	20
D.Gough	c & b Donald	12
A.R.C.Fraser	run out	3
Extras (b 2, lb 5, nb 8)		15
TOTAL		180

FALL OF WICKETS – 1-19, 2-41, 3-68, 4-107, 5-119, 6-136, 7-141, 8-161, 9-176, 10-180
BOWLING – Donald 19.3-5-74-5, de Villiers 16-5-28-3, Matthews 16-6-46-0, McMillan 10-1-25-1

SOUTH AFRICA 2nd Innings

G.Kirsten	st Rhodes b Hick	44
A.C.Hudson	lbw b Fraser	3
W.J.Cronje	c Fraser b Gough	32
*K.C.Wessels	c Crawley b Salisbury	28
P.N.Kirsten	b Gough	42
J.N.Rhodes	b Gough	32
B.M.McMillan	not out	39
+D.J.Richardson	c Rhodes b Fraser	3
C.R.Matthews	b Gough	25
DID NOT BAT – P.S.de Villiers, A.A.Donald		
Extras (b 8, lb 10, nb 12)		30
TOTAL (for 8 wkts dec)		278

FALL OF WICKETS – 1-14, 2-73, 3-101, 4-141, 5-208, 6-209, 7-220, 8-278
BOWLING – DeFreitas 14-3-43-0, Gough 19.3-5-46-4, Salisbury 19-4-53-1, Fraser 23-5-62-2, Hick 24-14-38-1, White 3-0-18-0

ENGLAND 2nd Innings

*M.A.Atherton	c McMillan b de Villiers	8
A.J.Stewart	c Richardson b Matthews	27
J.P.Crawley	c Hudson b McMillan	7
G.A.Hick	lbw b McMillan	11
G.A.Gooch	lbw b Donald	28
C.White	c Wessels b Matthews	0
+S.J.Rhodes	not out	14
P.A.J.DeFreitas	c Kirsten G. b Matthews	1
D.Gough	retired hurt	0
I.D.K.Salisbury	lbw b Donald	0
A.R.C.Fraser	lbw b McMillan	1
Extras (b 1, lb 1)		2
TOTAL		99

FALL OF WICKETS – 1-16, 2-29, 3-45, 4-74, 5-74, 6-82, 7-85, 8-88, 9-99
BOWLING – Donald 12-5-29-2, de Villiers 12-4-26-1, Matthews 14-6-25-3, McMillan 6.5-2-16-3, Cronje 1-0-1-0

ENGLAND v SOUTH AFRICA

at Headingley on 4th, 5th, 6th, 7th, 8th August 1994
Toss: England
Umpires : R.S.Dunne and D.R.Shepherd
Match drawn

ENGLAND 1st Innings

G.A.Gooch	c McMillan b de Villiers	23
*M.A.Atherton	c & b McMillan	99
G.A.Hick	c McMillan b de Villiers	25
G.P.Thorpe	c Rhodes b McMillan	72
A.J.Stewart	b McMillan	89
J.P.Crawley	lbw b Matthews	38
+S.J.Rhodes	not out	65
P.A.J.DeFreitas	b Donald	15
D.Gough	run out	27
A.R.C.Fraser	c Cronje b de Villiers	6
DID NOT BAT – P.C.R.Tufnell		
Extras (b 1, lb 5, nb 12)		18
TOTAL (for 9 wkts dec)		477

FALL OF WICKETS – 1-34, 2-84, 3-226, 4-235, 5-350, 6-367, 7-394, 8-447, 9-477
BOWLING – Donald 39-9-135-1, de Villiers 39.3-12-108-3, Matthews 39-7-97-1, McMillan 37-12-93-3, Cronje 16-3-38-0

SOUTH AFRICA 1st Innings

A.C.Hudson	c Atherton b Gough	9
G.Kirsten	c Rhodes b DeFreitas	7
+D.J.Richardson	b Fraser	48
W.J.Cronje	b DeFreitas	0
*K.C.Wessels	c Crawley b Fraser	25
P.N.Kirsten	c Stewart b DeFreitas	104
J.N.Rhodes	c Rhodes b Gough	46
B.M.McMillan	b Tufnell	78
C.R.Matthews	not out	62
P.S.de Villiers	st Rhodes b Tufnell	13
A.A.Donald	c Crawley b DeFreitas	27
Extras (b 8, lb 7, nb 13)		28
TOTAL		447

FALL OF WICKETS – 1-13, 2-31, 3-31, 4-91, 5-105, 6-199, 7-314, 8-391, 9-410, 10-447
BOWLING – Gough 37-3-153-2, DeFreitas 29.1-6-89-4, Fraser 31-5-92-2, Tufnell 32-13-81-2, Gooch 3-0-9-0, Hick 1-0-8-0

ENGLAND 2nd Innings

G.A.Gooch	c Richardson b Matthews	27
*M.A.Atherton	c sub b de Villiers	17
G.A.Hick	lbw b McMillan	110
G.P.Thorpe	run out	73
A.J.Stewart	not out	36
J.P.Crawley	c Cronje b McMillan	0
DID NOT BAT – +S.J.Rhodes, P.A.J.DeFreitas, D.Gough, A.R.C.Fraser, P.C.R.Tufnell		
Extras (lb 1, nb 3)		4
TOTAL (for 5 wkts dec)		267

FALL OF WICKETS – 1-39, 2-57, 3-190, 4-267, 5-267
BOWLING – de Villiers 25-3-98-1, Matthews 24-8-53-1, McMillan 15.3-0-66-2, Cronje 12-3-39-0, Kirsten G. 2-1-10-0

SOUTH AFRICA 2nd Innings

A.C.Hudson	c & b Tufnell	12
G.Kirsten	c Rhodes b DeFreitas	65
W.J.Cronje	not out	13
*K.C.Wessels	b Tufnell	7
P.N.Kirsten	not out	8
DID NOT BAT – +D.J.Richardson, J.N.Rhodes, B.M.McMillan, C.R.Matthews, P.S.de Villiers, A.A.Donald		
Extras (b 2, lb 2, nb 7)		11
TOTAL (for 3 wkts)		116

FALL OF WICKETS – 1-43, 2-93, 3-104
BOWLING – Gough 10-5-15-0, DeFreitas 14-3-41-1, Fraser 7-2-19-0, Tufnell 23-8-31-2, Hick 6-3-6-0

ENGLAND v SOUTH AFRICA

at The Oval on 18th, 19th, 20th, 21st August 1994
Toss: South Africa
Umpires: R.S.Dunne and K.E.Palmer
England won by 8 wickets

SOUTH AFRICA 1st Innings

G.Kirsten	c Rhodes b DeFreitas	2
P.N.Kirsten	b Malcolm	16
W.J.Cronje	lbw b Benjamin	38
*K.C.Wessels	lbw b Benjamin	45
D.J.Cullinan	c Rhodes b DeFreitas	7
J.N.Rhodes	retired hurt	8
B.M.McMillan	c Hick b DeFreitas	93
+D.J.Richardson	c Rhodes b Benjamin	58
C.R.Matthews	c Hick b Benjamin	0
P.S.de Villiers	c Stewart b DeFreitas	14
A.A.Donald	not out	14
Extras (b 8, lb 10, w 1, nb 18)		37
TOTAL		332

FALL OF WICKETS – 1-2, 2-43, 3-73, 4-85, 5-136, 6-260, 7-266, 8-301, 9-332
BOWLING – DeFreitas 26.2-5-93-4, Malcolm 25-5-81-1, Gough 19-1-85-0, Benjamin 17-2-42-4, Hick 5-1-13-0

ENGLAND 1st Innings

G.A.Gooch	c Richardson b Donald	8
*M.A.Atherton	lbw b de Villiers	0
G.A.Hick	b Donald	39
G.P.Thorpe	b Matthews	79
A.J.Stewart	b de Villiers	62
J.P.Crawley	c Richardson b Donald	5
+S.J.Rhodes	lbw b de Villiers	11
P.A.J.DeFreitas	run out	37
D.Gough	not out	42
J.E.Benjamin	lbw b Donald	0
D.E.Malcolm	c sub b Matthews	4
Extras (b 1, w 1, nb 15)		17
TOTAL		304

FALL OF WICKETS – 1-1, 2-33, 3-93, 4-145, 5-165, 6-219, 7-222, 8-292, 9-293, 10-304
BOWLING – Donald 17-2-76-3, de Villiers 19-3-62-4, Matthews 21-4-82-2, McMillan 12-1-67-0, Cronje 8-3-16-0

SOUTH AFRICA 2nd Innings

P.N.Kirsten	c DeFreitas b Malcolm	1
G.Kirsten	c & b Malcolm	0
W.J.Cronje	b Malcolm	0
*K.C.Wessels	c Rhodes b Malcolm	28
D.J.Cullinan	c Thorpe b Gough	94
B.M.McMillan	c Thorpe b Malcolm	25
+D.J.Richardson	lbw b Malcolm	3
C.R.Matthews	c Rhodes b Malcolm	0
J.N.Rhodes	c Rhodes b Malcolm	10
P.S.de Villiers	not out	0
A.A.Donald	b Malcolm	0
Extras (lb 5, nb 9)		14
TOTAL		175

FALL OF WICKETS – 1-0, 2-1, 3-1, 4-73, 5-137, 6-143, 7-143, 8-175, 9-175, 10-175
BOWLING – DeFreitas 12-3-25-0, Malcolm 16.3-2-57-9, Gough 9-1-39-1, Benjamin 11-1-38-0, Hick 2-0-11-0

ENGLAND 2nd Innings

G.A.Gooch	b Matthews	33
*M.A.Atherton	c Richardson b Donald	63
G.A.Hick	not out	81
G.P.Thorpe	not out	15
DID NOT BAT – A.J.Stewart, J.P.Crawley, +S.J.Rhodes, P.A.J.DeFreitas, D.Gough, J.E.Benjamin, D.E.Malcolm		
Extras (lb 6, nb 7)		13
TOTAL (for 2 wkts)		205

FALL OF WICKETS – 1-56, 2-180
BOWLING – Donald 12-1-96-1, de Villiers 12-0-66-0, Matthews 11.3-4-37-1

1994

ENGLAND v WEST INDIES

at Headingley on 8th, 9th, 10th, 11th June 1995
Toss : West Indies
Umpires : H.D.Bird and S.Venkataraghavan
West Indies won by 9 wickets

ENGLAND 1st Innings

R.A.Smith	c Richardson b Benjamin	16
*M.A.Atherton	c Murray b Bishop	81
G.A.Hick	c Campbell b Benjamin	18
G.P.Thorpe	lbw b Bishop	20
+A.J.Stewart	c Hooper b Bishop	2
M.R.Ramprakash	c Campbell b Bishop	4
P.A.J.DeFreitas	c Murray b Benjamin	23
D.Gough	c Ambrose b Bishop	0
P.J.Martin	c Murray b Ambrose	2
R.K.Illingworth	not out	17
D.E.Malcolm	b Benjamin	0
Extras (b 1, nb 15)		16
TOTAL		199

FALL OF WICKETS – 1-52, 2-91, 3-142, 4-148, 5-153, 6-154, 7-154, 8-157, 9-199, 10-199
BOWLING – Ambrose 17-4-56-1, Walsh 13-2-50-0, Bishop 16-2-32-5, Benjamin 13.5-2-60-4

WEST INDIES 1st Innings

C.L.Hooper	c Thorpe b Malcolm	0
S.L.Campbell	run out	69
B.C.Lara	c Hick b Illingworth	53
J.C.Adams	c Martin b Hick	58
K.L.T.Arthurton	c Stewart b DeFreitas	42
*R.B.Richardson	lbw b Hick	0
+J.R.Murray	c Illingworth b DeFreitas	20
I.R.Bishop	run out	5
C.E.L.Ambrose	c Gough b Malcolm	15
C.A.Walsh	c Stewart b Gough	4
K.C.G.Benjamin	not out	0
Extras (b 4, lb 11, nb 1)		16
TOTAL		282

FALL OF WICKETS – 1-0, 2-95, 3-141, 4-216, 5-219, 6-243, 7-254, 8-254, 9-275, 10-282
BOWLING – Malcolm 7.3-0-48-2, Gough 5-1-24-1, DeFreitas 23-3-82-2, Martin 27-9-48-1, Illingworth 24-9-50-1, Hick 4-0-15-1

ENGLAND 2nd Innings

R.A.Smith	c Arthurton b Ambrose	6
*M.A.Atherton	c Murray b Walsh	17
G.A.Hick	c Walsh b Bishop	27
G.P.Thorpe	c Campbell b Walsh	61
+A.J.Stewart	c Murray b Benjamin	4
M.R.Ramprakash	b Walsh	18
P.A.J.DeFreitas	c sub b Walsh	1
D.Gough	c sub b Ambrose	29
P.J.Martin	c Lara b Bishop	19
R.K.Illingworth	not out	10
D.E.Malcolm	b Ambrose	5
Extras (b 1, lb 3, nb 7)		11
TOTAL		208

FALL OF WICKETS – 1-6, 2-55, 3-55, 4-82, 5-130, 6-136, 7-152, 8-193, 9-193, 10-208
BOWLING – Ambrose 20.2-6-44-3, Walsh 22-4-60-4, Bishop 19-3-81-2, Benjamin 6-1-19-1

WEST INDIES 2nd Innings

C.L.Hooper	not out	73
S.L.Campbell	c Atherton b Martin	2
B.C.Lara	not out	48

DID NOT BAT – J.C.Adams, K.L.T.Arthurton, *R.B.Richardson, +J.R.Murray, I.R.Bishop, C.E.L.Ambrose, C.A.Walsh, K.C.G.Benjamin
Extras (b 1, lb 3, nb 2) 6
TOTAL (for 1 wkt) 129

FALL OF WICKETS – 1-11
BOWLING – Malcolm 4-0-12-0, DeFreitas 4-0-33-0, Martin 8-2-49-1, Illingworth 3-0-31-0

ENGLAND v WEST INDIES

at Lord's on 22nd, 23rd, 24th, 25th, 26th June 1995
Toss : England
Umpires : D.R.Shepherd and S.Venkataraghavan
England won by 72 runs

ENGLAND 1st Innings

*M.A.Atherton	b Ambrose	21
+A.J.Stewart	c Arthurton b Gibson	34
G.A.Hick	c Lara b Bishop	13
G.P.Thorpe	c Lara b Ambrose	52
R.A.Smith	b Hooper	61
M.R.Ramprakash	c Campbell b Hooper	0
D.G.Cork	b Walsh	30
D.Gough	c Campbell b Gibson	11
P.J.Martin	b Walsh	29
R.K.Illingworth	not out	16
A.R.C.Fraser	lbw b Walsh	1
Extras (b 1, lb 10, nb 4)		15
TOTAL		283

FALL OF WICKETS – 1-29, 2-70, 3-74, 4-185, 5-187, 6-191, 7-205, 8-255, 9-281, 10-283
BOWLING – Ambrose 26-6-72-2, Walsh 22.4-6-50-3, Gibson 20-2-81-2, Bishop 17-4-33-1, Hooper 14-3-36-2

WEST INDIES 1st Innings

S.L.Campbell	c Stewart b Gough	5
C.L.Hooper	b Martin	40
B.C.Lara	lbw b Fraser	6
J.C.Adams	lbw b Fraser	54
*R.B.Richardson	c Stewart b Fraser	49
K.L.T.Arthurton	c Gough b Fraser	75
+J.R.Murray	c & b Martin	16
O.D.Gibson	lbw b Gough	29
I.R.Bishop	b Cork	8
C.E.L.Ambrose	c Ramprakash b Fraser	12
C.A.Walsh	not out	11
Extras (b 8, lb 11)		19
TOTAL		324

FALL OF WICKETS – 1-6, 2-23, 3-88, 4-166, 5-169, 6-197, 7-246, 8-272, 9-305, 10-324
BOWLING – Gough 27-2-84-2, Fraser 33-13-66-5, Cork 22-4-72-1, Martin 23-5-65-2, Illingworth 7-2-18-0

ENGLAND 2nd Innings

*M.A.Atherton	c Murray b Walsh	9
+A.J.Stewart	c Murray b Walsh	36
G.A.Hick	b Bishop	67
G.P.Thorpe	c Richardson b Ambrose	42
R.A.Smith	lbw b Ambrose	90
M.R.Ramprakash	c sub b Bishop	0
D.G.Cork	c Murray b Bishop	23
D.Gough	b Ambrose	20
P.J.Martin	c Arthurton b Ambrose	1
R.K.Illingworth	lbw b Walsh	4
A.R.C.Fraser	not out	2
Extras (b 6, lb 27, w 2, nb 7)		42
TOTAL		336

FALL OF WICKETS – 1-32, 2-51, 3-150, 4-155, 5-240, 6-290, 7-320, 8-329, 9-334, 10-336
BOWLING – Ambrose 24-5-70-4, Walsh 28.1-1-91-3, Gibson 14-1-51-0, Bishop 22-5-56-3, Hooper 9-1-31-0, Adams 2-0-4-0

WEST INDIES 2nd Innings

C.L.Hooper	c Martin b Gough	14
S.L.Campbell	c Stewart b Cork	93
B.C.Lara	c Stewart b Gough	54
J.C.Adams	c Hick b Cork	13
*R.B.Richardson	lbw b Cork	0
K.L.T.Arthurton	c sub b Cork	0
+J.R.Murray	c sub b Gough	9
O.D.Gibson	lbw b Cork	14
I.R.Bishop	not out	10
C.E.L.Ambrose	c Illingworth b Cork	11
C.A.Walsh	c Stewart b Cork	0
Extras (lb 5)		5
TOTAL		223

FALL OF WICKETS – 1-15, 2-99, 3-124, 4-130, 5-138, 6-177, 7-198, 8-201, 9-223, 10-223
BOWLING – Gough 20-0-79-3, Fraser 25-9-57-0, Cork 19.3-5-43-7, Martin 7-0-30-0, Illingworth 7-4-9-0

ENGLAND v WEST INDIES

at Edgbaston on 6th, 7th, 8th July 1995
Toss : England
Umpires : M.J.Kitchen and I.D.Robinson
West Indies won by an innings and 64 runs

ENGLAND 1st Innings

*M.A.Atherton	c Murray b Ambrose	0
+A.J.Stewart	lbw b Benjamin	37
G.A.Hick	c Richardson b Walsh	3
G.P.Thorpe	c Campbell b Ambrose	30
R.A.Smith	c Arthurton b Bishop	46
J.E.R.Gallian	b Benjamin	7
D.G.Cork	lbw b Walsh	4
D.Gough	c Arthurton b Bishop	1
P.J.Martin	c sub b Walsh	1
R.K.Illingworth	b Bishop	0
A.R.C.Fraser	not out	0
Extras (lb 4, w 4, nb 10)		18
TOTAL		147

FALL OF WICKETS – 1-4, 2-9, 3-53, 4-84, 5-100, 6-109, 7-124, 8-141, 9-147, 10-147
BOWLING – Ambrose 7.5-1-26-2, Walsh 17.1-4-54-3, Bishop 6.2-0-18-3, Benjamin 13-4-45-2

WEST INDIES

C.L.Hooper	c Stewart b Cork	40
S.L.Campbell	b Cork	79
B.C.Lara	lbw b Cork	21
J.C.Adams	lbw b Cork	10
*R.B.Richardson	b Fraser	69
K.L.T.Arthurton	lbw b Fraser	8
+J.R.Murray	c Stewart b Martin	26
I.R.Bishop	c Martin b Illingworth	16
K.C.G.Benjamin	run out	11
C.A.Walsh	run out	0
C.E.L.Ambrose	not out	4
Extras (b 5, lb 5, nb 6)		16
TOTAL		300

FALL OF WICKETS – 1-73, 2-105, 3-141, 4-156, 5-171, 6-198, 7-260, 8-292, 9-292, 10-300
BOWLING – Fraser 31-7-93-2, Gough 18-3-68-0, Cork 22-5-69-4, Martin 19-5-49-1, Illingworth 8-4-11-1

ENGLAND 2nd Innings

*M.A.Atherton	b Walsh	4
R.A.Smith	b Bishop	41
G.A.Hick	c Hooper b Bishop	3
G.P.Thorpe	c Murray b Bishop	0
D.G.Cork	c sub b Walsh	16
P.J.Martin	lbw b Walsh	0
J.E.R.Gallian	c Murray b Walsh	0
D.Gough	c Campbell b Walsh	12
R.K.Illingworth	c Hooper b Bishop	0
A.R.C.Fraser	not out	1
+A.J.Stewart	absent hurt	
Extras (nb 12)		12
TOTAL		89

FALL OF WICKETS – 1-17, 2-20, 3-26, 4-61, 5-62, 6-63, 7-88, 8-88, 9-89
BOWLING – Walsh 15-2-45-5, Bishop 13-3-29-4, Benjamin 2-0-15-0

1995

ENGLAND v
WEST INDIES

at Old Trafford on 27th, 28th, 29th, 30th July 1995
Toss : West Indies
Umpires : H.D.Bird and C.J.Mitchley
England won by 6 wickets

WEST INDIES 1st Innings

C.L.Hooper	c Crawley b Cork	16
S.L.Campbell	c Russell b Fraser	10
B.C.Lara	lbw b Cork	87
J.C.Adams	c Knight b Fraser	24
*R.B.Richardson	c Thorpe b Fraser	2
K.L.T.Arthurton	c Cork b Watkinson	17
+J.R.Murray	c Emburey b Watkinson	13
I.R.Bishop	c Russell b Cork	9
C.E.L.Ambrose	not out	7
K.C.G.Benjamin	b Cork	14
C.A.Walsh	c Knight b Fraser	11
Extras (lb 1,nb 5)		6
TOTAL		216

FALL OF WICKETS – 1-21, 2-35, 3-86, 4-94, 5-150,
6-166, 7-184, 8-185, 9-205, 10-216
BOWLING – Fraser 16.2-5-45-4, Cork 20-1-86-4,
White 5-0-23-0, Emburey 10-2-33-0,
Watkinson 9-2-28-2

ENGLAND 1st Innings

N.V.Knight	b Walsh	17
*M.A.Atherton	c Murray b Ambrose	47
J.P.Crawley	b Walsh	8
G.P.Thorpe	c Murray b Bishop	94
R.A.Smith	c sub b Ambrose	44
C.White	c Murray b Benjamin	23
+R.C.Russell	run out	35
M.Watkinson	c sub b Walsh	37
D.G.Cork	not out	56
J.E.Emburey	b Bishop	8
A.R.C.Fraser	c Adams b Walsh	4
Extras (b 18,lb 11,w 1,nb 34)		64
TOTAL		437

FALL OF WICKETS – 1-45, 2-65, 3-122, 4-226, 5-264,
6-293, 7-337, 8-378, 9-418, 10-437
BOWLING – Ambrose 24-2-91-2, Walsh 38-5-92-4,
Bishop 29-3-103-2, Benjamin 28-4-83-1,
Adams 8-1-21-0, Arthurton 9-2-18-0

WEST INDIES 2nd Innings

S.L.Campbell	c Russell b Watkinson	44
K.L.T.Arthurton	run out	17
B.C.Lara	c Knight b Fraser	145
J.C.Adams	c & b Watkinson	1
*R.B.Richardson	b Cork	22
+J.R.Murray	lbw b Cork	0
C.L.Hooper	lbw b Cork	0
I.R.Bishop	c Crawley b Watkinson	9
K.C.G.Benjamin	c Knight b Fraser	15
C.E.L.Ambrose	not out	23
C.A.Walsh	b Cork	16
Extras (b 5,lb 9,nb 8)		22
TOTAL		314

FALL OF WICKETS – 1-36, 2-93, 3-97, 4-161, 5-161,
6-161, 7-191, 8-234, 9-283, 10-314
BOWLING – Fraser 19-5-53-2, Cork 23.5-2-111-4,
White 6-0-23-0, Emburey 20-5-49-0,
Watkinson 23-4-64-3

ENGLAND 2nd Innings

N.V.Knight	c sub b Bishop	13
*M.A.Atherton	run out	22
J.P.Crawley	not out	15
G.P.Thorpe	c Ambrose b Benjamin	0
R.A.Smith	retired hurt	1
C.White	c sub b Benjamin	1
+R.C.Russell	not out	31

DID NOT BAT – M.Watkinson, D.G.Cork,
J.E.Emburey, A.R.C.Fraser

Extras (lb 2,w 1,nb 8)		11
TOTAL (for 4 wkts)		94

FALL OF WICKETS – 1-39, 2-41, 3-45, 4-48
BOWLING – Ambrose 5-1-16-0, Walsh 5-0-17-0,
Bishop 12-6-18-1, Benjamin 9-1-29-2, Adams 2-0-7-0,
Arthurton 2.5-1-5-0

1995

Cornhill's Top Twenty

To be a Test-playing all-rounder, the prime essential is that a player has to warrant his place as a batsman and (in most cases) as a bowler. That is why Ian Botham was such a key player for England. If he had not been able to bowl, he would have been in the team as a batsman; had he not been a batsman of prodigious talent, he would have been chosen for his bowling. And his catching was something special, too! Hence the anguished search for a replacement at No. 6. The nearest England have come to finding Botham's successor until now has been Alec Stewart. As a batsman he is out of the top drawer, and he is a competent wicketkeeper, if not quite in the Evans-Knott-Taylor class. However you look at it, with the current crop of players Stewart is clearly the one who should (bruised and broken fingers always permitting) keep and bat at six; the concept is not flawed – only the execution of it, with Alec not scoring so freely in the middle order. May England, however, have found a player who, with proper care and attention, can both bowl and ultimately bat at six in either Darren Gough or Dominic Cork? Both their Test careers are in their infancy and questions are already being asked about Gough. Has the early adulation perhaps had an adverse affect on him? The emergence of Cork this summer after a successful graduation through the 'A' side has been most welcome. He is as determined as Gough, if without his bounce, and is certainly a better batsman than Gough. Both will have to improve their batting significantly to warrant regular selection at six, but if one of them can do it, and force himself permanently into both Cornhill's Top Twenty lists, we will certainly be saluting a player for himself rather than as 'a new Botham'.

BATTING AVERAGES (Qualifying requirements : 6 completed innings)

NAME	MATCHES	INNS	NO	RUNS	HS	AVGE	100s	50s
G.Boycott	18	32	2	1487	155	49.56	5	5
R.A.Smith	36	66	11	2716	148*	49.38	7	17
G.P.Thorpe	9	18	2	768	114*	48.00	1	7
G.A.Gooch	72	127	3	5880	333	47.41	15	26
A.J.Stewart	25	43	4	1682	190	43.12	3	8
R.T.Robinson	14	23	2	900	175	42.85	3	2
D.I.Gower	65	113	9	4454	215	42.82	10	19
M.W.Gatting	39	71	8	2453	183*	38.93	6	12
C.T.Radley	6	8	0	308	106	38.50	1	2
M.A.Atherton	32	59	0	2266	151	38.40	4	17
A.J.Lamb	43	76	8	2550	139	37.50	11	6
I.T.Botham	57	87	4	2944	208	35.46	8	13
D.W.Randall	13	20	1	667	126	35.10	2	4
C.J.Tavare	17	31	1	1049	109	34.96	1	8
G.Miller	12	15	2	414	98	31.84	–	3
P.Willey	13	24	3	654	100*	31.14	1	3
N.Hussain	4	8	2	184	71	30.66	–	1
G.Fowler	9	17	0	514	106	30.23	2	2
G.A.Hick	20	34	1	997	110	30.21	1	6
R.C.Russell	22	34	8	775	128*	29.80	1	2

BOWLING AVERAGES (Qualifying requirements : 10 wickets taken)

NAME	OVERS	MDNS	RUNS	WKTS	AVGE	BEST	5wI	10wM
D.G.Cork	107.2	17	381	20	19.05	7-43	1	–
R.M.Ellison	189.5	47	465	24	19.37	6-77	2	1
N.A.Mallender	74.5	20	215	10	21.50	5-50	1	–
C.M.Old	307.1	107	624	27	23.11	7-50	1	–
R.G.D.Willis	1023.2	233	3025	129	23.44	8-43	6	–
G.R.Dilley	706.3	148	2097	78	26.88	6-154	3	–
S.L.Watkin	89	17	305	11	27.72	4-65	–	–
I.T.Botham	1967.3	459	6024	216	27.88	8-34	15	2
A.R.C.Fraser	685.3	175	1769	60	29.48	5-66	4	–
P.A.J.DeFreitas	851	185	2481	84	29.53	7-70	3	–
N.G.B.Cook	334.1	94	854	27	31.62	5-35	2	–
D.E.Malcolm	544.4	95	1883	59	31.91	9-57	4	1
P.H.Edmonds	1027.5	347	2203	68	32.39	4-6	–	–
M.Hendrick	381.4	130	787	24	32.79	4-45	–	–
P.J.W.Allott	326.5	68	905	26	34.80	6-61	1	–
D.R.Pringle	749.2	164	2142	61	35.11	5-95	3	–
N.A.Foster	621.4	140	1703	48	35.47	8-107	2	–
D.V.Lawrence	152.2	25	605	17	35.58	5-106	1	–
D.Gough	240.2	34	821	23	35.69	4-46	–	–
P.M.Such	362.5	100	805	22	36.59	6-67	1	–